CRUCIFIXION—RESURRECTION

Crucifixion—Resurrection

The Pattern of the Theology and Ethics of the New Testament

Edwyn Clement Hoskyns, Bart, D.D.
&
Francis Noel Davey, D.D.

Edited with a
Biographical Introduction
by
Gordon S. Wakefield

LONDON
SPCK

First published 1981
SPCK
Holy Trinity Church
Marylebone Road
London NW1 4DU

Printed in Great Britain by
Willmer Brothers Limited
Rock Ferry, Merseyside

ISBN   0   281   03705   1

Contents

Contents

Illustrations

Acknowledgements

To Canon Charles Smyth, whose friendship and encouragement for more than twenty years have been a great gift to me; to Professor Donald Mackinnon, for his great interest and knowledge of the period, generously shared; to the Venerable J. O. Cobham, whose papers I have kept too long; to the late Sir Kenneth Pickthorn and Lady Pickthorn; to Professor C. K. Barrett, Sir John Dykes Bower, Mr J. P. T. Bury, Sir Desmond Lee, Sir Humphrey Mynors, and, as so often, Dr Gordon Rupp; to Bishop John Ramsbotham and Bishop Edward Roberts. The Revd Richard E. Parsons, a research student, has discussed his work on Hoskyns with me, lent me his review-cuttings, and an unpublished paper on Hoskyns and Kittel, and helped with the bibliography and the proofs.

For information about Noel Davey, I am particularly indebted to the Revd Peter Davey, his son; Dr Valentine McMaster Davey, his brother; and to Mr John Padfield, formerly of SPCK; Miss Ann B. Leech of Manchester, and Mr Harry P. Williams of Wrexham.

Bishop Michael Ramsey has not only read the typescript, but saved me from error at one point, and most graciously contributed a foreword.

My greatest thanks, however, must be reserved for three whose help in their different ways has been unique. Noel Davey himself gave me friendship, papers, books and much conversation. I wish that the result could match his scholarship, and approximate in some measure to his own devotion to Hoskyns and kindness to me. Christopher Evans has advised on the main work, read it and analysed it, and provided reminiscences, advice, the insights of his erudition and acute mind, and the joy of his company and correspondence. I cannot expect him to regard the work as wholly satisfying, but he understands the difficulties. And Mary, Lady Hoskyns, has supplied an immense amount of biographical material through conversation, notes, letters, and unpublished manuscripts. Her graciousness has been unfailing, her patience monumental, and her example of Christian faith a strengthening of my own.   G.S.W.

Foreword

I am honoured at having a tiny share in this book which happily contains the memoir of a most lovable man who died more than forty years ago, and a work on which, with his collaborator, he was engaged before his death. I believe that amidst some inevitable comment that the man and the work are 'dated', readers will find that both the man and the work speak to these times.

Hoskyns had a remarkable influence, and I was one of those who as a young student came under his spell. Though I never became an uncritical devotee, I learned from him, more vividly than from anyone else, that the study of the New Testament is an exciting adventure, and while it calls for a rigorous critical discipline it is not made less scientific if the student brings to it his own experience of faith.

In the 1920s the Form Criticism of the Gospels had scarcely appeared on the English academic scene, but the work of literary criticism with the analysis of sources and their editing was taken very seriously. Hoskyns insisted upon the most painstaking critical study. It was exciting to follow him as in his lectures he traced the religious experience of the early church, the relation of the experience to the events from which it sprang, and the interpretation of both events and experience in theological terms. Then, if the student happily thought that he was beginning to 'arrive', Hoskyns would disconcertingly show that there was no stage of contented arrival but an inexhaustible mystery to be explored.

Of Hoskyns's earlier writings it was the essay on 'The Christ of the Synoptic Gospels' in *Essays Catholic and Critical* (1926) which influenced me most, for there, in relation to the literary criticism which dominated the scene, he seemed to show convincingly the continuity between the historical Jesus and the Christ of apostolic faith. At the end of the day the posthumous commentary on *The Fourth Gospel*, although it has been followed by a whole era of valuable commentaries, still shows things found nowhere else, including the use of patristic exegesis. But *The Riddle of the New*

Testament (1931) is nearer to the Hoskyns whom I remember as a teacher. Its faults were evident, an over-pressing of conclusions and a neglect of the pre-literary phase of the traditions. But its influence long continued, as the many reprints and translations into other languages prove, and it showed that no phase of the apostolic age is really intelligible apart from the centrality of the death and resurrection of the Messiah. It is thus the progenitor of the work now being published.

The memoir by Gordon Wakefield gives some lovely glimpses of Hoskyns's restless intellect, width of human interests, and Christian integrity. Much of his work was done without collaboration, but he found in Noel Davey first one on whom he could try out ideas, and subsequently one who himself provided both many ideas and, in the case of the *Riddle*, the writing itself. So far from being only the anvil Davey was himself a large part of the hammer. Noel Davey was my own contemporary, and a loved friend from undergraduate days. He had an almost quixotic perfectionism, a lovely wit, and a deep devotion to the Church. That *Crucifixion–Resurrection* was not published several decades ago was due, I think, partly to Davey's perfectionism, partly to the wound caused to his sensitive nature by a feeling of exclusion from academic work in Cambridge, and partly by his immersion in the tasks of S.P.C.K., tasks which became very creative in his hands. It is hard to measure the difference between what is called the climate of Hoskyns's time and the climate of today, but with a sense of history we can remember that not seldom a person and a work belonging to the early years of a century have carried a message into the century's later years. It is in the light of this that the memoir and the work are now being published.

+ MICHAEL RAMSEY

Editorial Preface

The chapters which follow have a long history. *The Riddle of the New Testament* was published in 1931 and, soon afterwards, Sir Edwyn Hoskyns turned his mind to a sequel. *The Riddle* was an examination of the New Testament as history, but the history posed theological questions. Noel Davey described the project thus :

> In this sequel—intended, like the *Riddle*, for general readers—we would seek to analyse the New Testament as theology, and to find what meaning those who wrote it, and those they wrote about, attached to their theologizing. Our object would not be to ask what significance or validity these ideas might have for men in the modern world, or to attempt to translate them into contemporary categories—that might be the subject of a third book. It would simply be to try to understand the minds of the New Testament writers regarding their calling, their faith, their life in the Church, the world they lived in. The book was to be called *Crucifixion–Resurrection* because the key, for those who wrote the New Testament, seemed to lie in these inextricably related concepts.
>
> Hoskyns drew up a list of chapter headings and, following the procedure used in writing the *Riddle*, I began the preliminary drafting. Progress was neither easy nor rapid. Hoskyns, who had a far clearer picture of what must be done than I, was at work on his translation of Barth's *Epistle to the Romans,* which was published in 1933. Subsequently he devoted his vacations to revising his manuscript of *The Fourth Gospel.* But *Crucifixion–Resurrection* was never far from his mind, and he continually noted anything he thought relevant. From the autumn of 1935 we were able to work more closely together. By that time I had a certain amount in draft, and Hoskyns turned seriously to the task and produced (in retrospect it seems with remarkable speed) what are now printed as Chapters 2, 3, 6, 7, 8, and 9. My drafting had served its purpose, as traces of it show.

But, once the ink began to flow through his pen, Hoskyns was carried along on his argument and developed it in a shape very different from that of the first synopsis. After his sudden death, in May 1937, I found a later synopsis, which he must have drawn up while writing. But even this synopsis differs in certain respects from the ordering of the chapters as he finished them.

I found myself left, then, with several completed chapters, of very great interest but by themselves hardly publishable. In addition, there were a few paragraphs written by Hoskyns which we had tentatively agreed, and two chapters and a proposed transition written by myself, which Hoskyns had seen and commented on more kindly, I think, than they deserved, for these I have jettisoned entirely. For what it was worth, my own approach to New Testament Theology and Ethics has been more influenced by the planning of this book than by any other factor. Yet I was conscious that I had been lagging far behind my co-author, and that I needed time for reading and thinking and, if possible, more experience of teaching theology, before I could attempt to complete it. My first duty must be to get *The Fourth Gospel* published. But soon after that was done (1940) all long-term planning disappeared under the stress of war, and before the war was over I found myself directed (in an ecclesiastical way) into work of the kind that is never finished and has no benefit of long vacation. It was, I am afraid, far longer than it should have been before it dawned on me that, if *Crucifixion—Resurrection* was ever to be published, it must be completed in essentially the wrong way—in the few minutes that can be snatched at the end of a working-day, and by using any occasional courses or lectures I might be asked, and find time, to give, as means of working up my material.

It was not until he gave a course of lectures in 1959 that Davey returned seriously to work on this material. He did not have much time during the years of reorganization at S.P.C.K., and in the end deferred the completion of the work until his retirement in 1971. But this, alas! was to be brief. He had done little, if anything, on the script when he died in March 1973.

Among his remains were all Hoskyns's notes on the subject, including some vivid postcards and portions of letters, some

xiv

synopses and drafts, a few lectures of his own, and the first thirteen chapters of this book.

It is particularly frustrating that the work of the two authors breaks off where it does, for although the chapter on the resurrection narratives ends positively enough, and I myself have no quarrel with it, such a cautious and rather sceptical assessment of the Easter stories clearly presupposes that a long literary road has still to be travelled. Yet no third author can finish the journey.

It would be possible for someone else to write a book of his own based on this material. The *Editorial Epilogue* may provide some clues as to how I would have done that myself. But this would not be Hoskyns/Davey. It would lack those features for which their disciples and those most eager for their distinctive interpretations would look. They formed a theological and literary partnership like no other, and it would be as impertinent as misguided to substitute for their last legacy a work which, however indebted to their understanding, might be such as they would in parts have disowned.

I confess that the 'organization' of this work bewilders me. Davey discloses above that Hoskyns seems to have changed his mind about the scheme more than once. Sometimes the chapters seem to be dealing with biblical theology at large rather than with the specific subject of New Testament Theology and Ethics, and I cannot see how the unwritten chapters could have proceeded without much repetition and overlapping, since the treatment of the themes in the earlier sections seems so often to presuppose the totality crucifixion–resurrection, although the significance of the resurrection for the New Testament writers is not considered until Chapter 13. Davey's notes propose that the discussion of the parables be deferred until the 'post-resurrection' restatement of the earlier themes. But he deals finely with miracles in the chapter on 'The Poor—and the Poverty of Jesus'; yet Hoskyns's fragments urge that parables and miracles belong together.

In the event, all one can do is to present what Davey left, with a few indications as to how it might have proceeded to its end. I have done this by appending to the resurrection chapter (see p. 293) an Easter sermon of Hoskyns', which Davey himself preached almost forty years later, on what was to be the last Easter Day of his own life. He called it 'a simple whoop of triumph'. Then I have added an edited version of some lectures of Davey's which were a preparation for the fuller and more technical treatment of what Hoskyns calls 'the ultimate problems of human life in the light of the revelation of the power of the living God'. These are—history, time, knowledge, and personality, usually reckoned to be the preserves of the philosophers, among whom Hoskyns and Davey are not to be counted. They include some recapitulation and even now have traces of the lecture style. I have then attempted a summing up by way of epilogue, which also touches on some of the themes otherwise passed by.

Mountains of New Testament scholarship and years of history stand between us and Hoskyns, while Davey's own writing takes account of little after C. H. Dodd. But it would be distracting to interpolate a dialogue with more recent writers by way of notes to the text, even if I had professional mastery of the literature. Some of the issues have been raised in the preceding biographical study, while the epilogue refers to current debates on the resurrection, though not, needless to say, exhaustively.

Crucifixion–Resurrection stands then as a work conceived in the 1930s by a theologian who taught amid the contentions of liberals and Barthians, as Hitler's war loomed, when the pacifist controversy pierced to the marrow, and Reinhold Niebuhr's prophetic voice was beginning to sound against false simplicities. But because Hoskyns was wrestling with the same biblical texts as we are, and immersed in the problems of the same humanity, it is more than probable that something in these pages will speak to our world too. Perhaps the fundamental insights could prove the catalyst for the simmering cauldron of our theological discontents.

GORDON S. WAKEFIELD

Biographical Introduction

Francis Noel Davey

His Life to 1942

Students of the New Testament in the middle decades of this century were very much aware of a literary partnership which produced two notable and not uncontroversial books bearing the imprint of Faber and Faber, publishers of T. S. Eliot, W. H. Auden, and other cultural representatives. The books were *The Riddle of the New Testament* (1931) and *The Fourth Gospel* (1940); the authors, Edwyn Clement Hoskyns and Francis Noel Davey. The volume now presented is a long-delayed sequel to *The Riddle,* which Hoskyns began before his death in 1937 and Davey's retirement was too short for him to finish.

Francis Noel Davey was the junior partner, a pupil of Hoskyns at Corpus Christi, Cambridge, who entered the college in 1925, a little older than the average freshman. He was born on Christmas Day 1904—hence the second baptismal name by which he was always known.

His father was Edward Octavius Davey, artist in water-colours and oils, his mother a Scotswoman. Noel was born at South Norwood, but in 1909 the family moved to Tower House, Great Dunmow, Essex, where Edward Davey concentrated on landscapes. It was a bucolic existence amid the poultry and domestic animals, but with vivid nightly conversations on all manner of subjects, especially historical and artistic, and a large share in village pageants for which Edward Davey designed costumes.

Noel began his formal education with other children in a friend's house. He was musical, and played the piano with great facility from the age of six. He had a quick, darting mind, wide in its interests and infectiously enthusiastic about all of them. Early in the war he went to a preparatory school at Littlehampton, and thereafter to Brighton College, towards which his loyalty was mingled with the sense that over-emphasis on games may have insufficiently nurtured academic ability. He left in 1922 without a scholarship

3

and with no prospect of a career. It was a bleak and anxious time, but he managed to obtain a post at a private school in Ealing. Here he made friends with a group of Anglo-Catholics and resolved to seek ordination.

But how? His family were low to middle Church and did not relish ritualism, but they were not opposed to his vocation. The chief problem was financial. The war had adversely affected his father's income and a rich uncle in India was in a temporary state of near bankruptcy through German inflation and a slump in tea.

When at home, Noel Davey was in the habit of cycling to Sung Mass at Thaxted, six miles from Dunmow, of whose resplendent perpendicular church the doughty and aesthetic Conrad Noel was vicar. One Sunday he was late, so he decided to stop for Service half-way, at Great Easton, where the incumbent was an equally remarkable man of similar churchmanship and politics, Percy Widdrington. It so happened that the organist had not arrived that day through illness, and the Rector seized on Davey as he entered the porch and asked him if he could play, which he did. Afterwards he was invited to the rectory and thus began a great friendship. One result of it was Davey's association with the 'Christendom Group' of Anglo-Catholic sociologists of which Widdrington was the pioneer;[1] another was that, many years later, Davey became Widdrington's son-in-law.

Widdrington encouraged Davey's priestly vocation and suggested that he might seek admission to the Community of the Resurrection at Mirfield. Davey was much drawn to the religious life, but his family was opposed. And so it was through a very different intervention that he came to go to Corpus.

A relative by marriage was the Rev Jonathan Howell, a fiery Welshman who had been vicar of All Saints, Derby, but was by this time retired and helping-out in the country. He was an extreme evangelical, but, impressed by the young man's ardour, decided to help him all he could. He was an old Corpus man, and remembered the college in the 1880s as a centre of evangelicalism to which a Catholic might go and be purged of his excesses. So he did all he could to help, used his influence at Corpus and raised money, chiefly

---

[1] See Maurice B. Reckitt, *P. E. T. Widdrington, A Study in Vocation and Versatility* (London 1961), and E. R. Norman, *Church and Society in England 1770–1970* (Oxford 1976), pp. 319ff, 365–6, 398.

by enlisting the aid of the uncle in India, whose fortunes were by now recovering. Thus not without irony did Davey enter the college where Hoskyns was Dean of Chapel and his Anglo-Catholicism would be not so much undermined as given a new foundation. He took a second in modern and medieval languages in 1927 and a first in Part I of the theological tripos in 1929. In 1928 he became a foundation scholar. By 1931 he had collaborated with Hoskyns in *The Riddle of the New Testament*.

Hoskyns did not find writing easy. He began by lighting a cigarette and would think about the first sentence as he puffed away. Once the words came, he would stub out the cigarette into a large ash-tray and write the sentence down. Then he would take another cigarette and the process would be repeated, and so on until by the end of the morning the ash-tray was full of half-smoked cigarettes. By the time Davey got his first, Hoskyns had published many reviews, some articles, the chapter in *Essays Catholic and Critical*, the section on the Johannine Epistles in Gore, Goudge, and Guillaume, *A New Commentary on Holy Scripture*, a few lectures and pamphlets, while 'Jesus the Messiah' for *Mysterium Christi* was on the way. But would he have produced a book without Davey?

The younger man—be it noted but twenty-six years of age, and little more than five years away from being an usher without prospects at Ealing—was far more than amanuensis. He wrote *The Riddle of the New Testament*.[1] He would read each chapter in draft to Sir Edwyn—once at least in the company of Lady Hoskyns —and then revise it in the light of the former's criticisms which would sometimes be radical.

The Riddle is a most vivid and exciting piece of theological literature. It has gone through innumerable editions, has been translated into eighteen languages, and was almost unique among English New Testament studies in being translated into German in 1936. It is open to much criticism. It is too fluent and self-assured, and some of its assertions have not withstood more recent scholarship. But its main thesis—in brief, that the Jesus of history and the Christ of faith cannot completely be disentangled—has

---

[1] I owe this to Noel Davey himself, as does W. G. Kümmel the account in *The New Testament: The History of the Investigation of Some of its Problems*. (SCM, second impression, 1978), p. 460, n. 498.

been vindicated. It reaches the right conclusion though it does not do justice to the complexity of the evidence and has something of the nature of an 'inspired guess'.[1]

Gordon Selwyn called for a fuller treatment of the philosophic and theological implications of *The Riddle*,[2] but during the years from 1931 Hoskyns was chiefly absorbed in the *Römerbrief* and *The Fourth Gospel*, on which he had been engaged since 1923, when Methuen invited him to write the Westminster Commentary on the latter book. In the end, this was left to Davey to finish and see through the press. But Hoskyns's mind was also busy with plans for *Crucifixion–Resurrection* in answer to Selwyn's request and his own conviction. He intended that this should be composed in the same way as *The Riddle*, and that Davey should do the actual writing. Every now and then, he would send Davey letters or post-cards as some idea flashed into his mind, or some new publication demanded notice. In October 1936, for instance, he became excited by A. E. Housman's *Last Poems*, and felt that they made it imperative to deal with the New Testament ethics of agriculture, soldiering and games. 'Housman sets the problem of faith before us Cambridge people in its most acute biblical and non-biblical form.' Davey was somewhat mystified. Nevertheless he preserved and arranged all such fragments.

In 1929 Davey left Cambridge and worked on *The Riddle* as Gladstone student at St Deiniol's Library, Hawarden, the residential foundation based on Gladstone's own legacy. The following year he became a curate at the Church of St John Chrysostom, Victoria Park, Manchester.

His sermons are still remembered by elderly parishioners 'for maturity and glimpses of scholarship', while C. H. Dodd, then Rylands Professor of Biblical Criticism and Exegesis at Manchester University, would sometimes, although a Congregationalist, go to St Chrysostom's to hear him. He was especially good with children,

---

[1] Cf. C. F. D. Moule: 'Revised Reviews IV – Sir Edwyn Hoskyns and Noel Davey: The Riddle of the New Testament' (*Theology* Vol. LXIV, No. 490, April 1961), pp. 144ff. This article maintains that the Suffering Servant motif in Christ's ministry is overemphasized and that there is something repellent in the way in which Jesus is presented as modelling himself so self-consciously on OT types. For another critique see W. G. Kümmel, op. cit., pp. 400–04. But Kümmel concludes his survey with *The Riddle* and, like Moule, regards it as a most impressive and important work.

[2] *Theology*, Vol. XXIII, October 1931, pp. 229ff.

re-formed the Catechism class, which was a hundred strong when he left, organized outings, conveyed his enthusiasm for cricket and castles, and added much to the art and music of the liturgy. He was somewhat awesome and monkish, his tall figure often clad in a priest's cloak. He was revered as well as loved and the people believed him destined for outstanding service.

In 1932 he returned to St Deiniol's as sub-warden, but his energies were not confined to scholarship. He resumed as Scout-master of the Ewloe troop, which he revived and increased by winning over a disruptive gang from a housing estate, for whom he bought uniforms. The dozen or so boys were expected to repay him at twopence or threepence a week, but it is doubtful if he broke even. In 1930 the Ewloe troop won the Mostyn shield. Davey believed in tough scouting, and preferred camps in remote places where sanitary provisions had to be dug out. More than one of the boys' mothers has paid him over the years the simple tribute which would probably have pleased him most: 'He was a gentleman.'

Noel Davey was the sub-warden of St Deiniol's referred to in a sermon of Austin Farrer's preached in Keble College Chapel in 1967:

> When the Archbishop of Canterbury (Michael Ramsey) was a young and mischievous man, he and I went into the Chapel at Hawarden Library. I remarked that the crucifix was missing from the altar. 'Yes,' said Michael Ramsey, 'the sub-warden has taken it away. He thinks it more significant to have *nothing* there. He has been reading some German theologians, and has come to the conclusion that *blank nothing* is the truest symbol of the crucifixion.[1]

Austin Farrer made good use of the story to show the futility of abandoning all visible and sacramental expressions of the gospel, but he reacted too heavily to a comment made half-teasingly. The cross had been moved to be cleaned or repaired. Davey had no intention of not replacing it, but he had, in its absence, reflected aloud to Ramsey that perhaps 'nothing' was the best symbol of the event which shook the earth and veiled the sun. It was a thought

[1] Austin Farrer, 'The Transforming Will' in *The End of Man* (London 1973), pp. 103–4.

very much in the spirit of Hoskyns. And the Marcan Passion might be adduced in his support.

In 1935 Davey became vicar of St Benet's, Cambridge, the Corpus living in the shadow of the college, with its Saxon tower. He transformed the interior, cleaning the roof and bringing back some of the ancient gilt and colour. Not a little of the work was done by himself, though friends helped, and Desmond Lee, who has no head for heights, still remembers a brief, unhappy time on the scaffolding. Here again, C. H. Dodd, by then Norris-Hulse Professor at Cambridge, sometimes came to listen to his sermons.

In 1937 Davey was elected into a Fellowship at Corpus and became Theological Lecturer in succession to Hoskyns. The donnish life delighted him, and he mastered learned articles over lone lunches and installed a grand piano and the harpsichord he had possessed in Manchester, in his sitting-room.

He was a superb supervisor in the Cambridge sense, better as a tutor than as a lecturer and better with the more able than with the mediocre. He did not think it his task simply to purvey information about the New Testament, so much as to share his conviction that its study was, in the words of Kingsley Barrett, one of his pupils, 'the most responsible and rewarding that any scholar could undertake'.[1]

During these years he was often asked to write and to review. He contributed a piece on 'The Early Church and Messianic History' to a course of lectures on early Church history given by a galaxy of scholars and published in 1938. But his most interesting and important essay at this time is his chapter in Maurice Reckitt's wartime symposium, *Prospect for Christendom*. This emanated from the 'Christendom Group'. Davey's subject is 'The Hope of Christendom Authentic'. It shows how busy his mind was with the themes of *Crucifixion–Resurrection* :

> If God has affirmed, in Christ, the pattern and rhythm of his creation, it is only through the Cross. Christians may have to cease to call men 'father', and they may have to forsake their families and their wives, to disown their community with their neighbours and to suffer, as Christians, at the tribunal of the State, if the will of God is to triumph over the false definitions

[1] C. K. Barrett, *The Gospel of John and Judaism*. (SPCK 1975), ix.

and perversions of men; they may even have to bear the accusation of enmity of the human race.[1]

But this is never God's last word. Hence the importance of the New Testament letters. 'The gospel is the most realistic of all philosophies, because it defines men as they are, transient and particular beings in a particular and transient environment, and bids them work out their salvation in fear and trembling, by reason of the exceeding great glory already encompassing them.'[2]

On 8 March, 1942, Davey preached the University Sermon. His Mother had died that morning. His wife received the news first and wondered if she should tell him before he had to preach on so testing an occasion. After some hesitation, she decided she had no alternative, and so it was in the shock and sorrow of bereavement that he ascended the pulpit of Great St Mary's. The sermon, which is reproduced below, represents the quintessence of Hoskyns's teaching from the mind and voice of his most devoted disciple (pp. 16ff).

It had a mixed reception. Some hailed it as prophetic, others found it obscure; and he himself confessed that he had far more material than he was able to use, and that the sermon was too long and ill-proportioned. It seemed to Charles Raven, the Regius Professor of Divinity, to smack too much of the biblical positivism which had, in his view, blighted all hope of the unitive theology to which his own work was dedicated. At any rate, Davey's university lectureship was not renewed, and later that same year he became rector of Coddenham in Suffolk.

Noel Davey at SPCK[3]

Dr W. K. Lowther Clarke, then Editorial Secretary of S.P.C.K., wrote in August 1943 to Davey inquiring 'Is it any use suggesting your name as a possible successor to me?' Davey showed no great eagerness for the post: he would not allow the Committee to consider him as having applied; he would, if offered the position, give the offer due consideration. A family letter, written before he was

---

[1] Maurice B. Reckitt, ed., *Prospect for Christendom*. (Faber and Faber 1945), p. 22.
[2] Ibid. p. 23.
[3] Contributed by Robin Brookes.

interviewed, expressed his feelings at the time. 'Four activities always seem to carry me away with them, as though they were what I ought to be about: (1) lecturing on the New Testament, (2) supervising theological students, (3) preaching to ordinary people, (4) trying to help people pastorally. The question is, how far would S.P.C.K. call for these ministrations?' He accepted as the will of God the Divinity Faculty's judgement on his lecturing at Cambridge, and was prepared to believe that his future might lie in the country, to help and perhaps lead the Church to a better discharging of its pastoral duties there. His Bishop, Dr Richard Brook of St Edmundsbury and Ipswich, had expressed on those lines the case for his remaining in Suffolk. William Temple, who as Archbishop of Canterbury was President of S.P.C.K., wrote to Davey in support of the Standing Committee's invitation, but was anxious that he should not feel under any pressure to accept. In reply, Davey expressed himself as follows:

> If it is true that I would perhaps be able to nurse young authors and to co-ordinate and direct the output of religious and theological literature, it would, I suppose, call for the use of the gifts I seem to have, and ought to further the objects I have most at heart. I would love the technical business of producing accurate and attractive books, and be greatly interested in the artistic and musical side of the work. I would also enjoy collaborating with members of other denominations.

He accepted, and worked with Lowther Clarke in the latter half of 1944, succeeding him in January 1945 as Editorial Secretary. He correctly forecast the way in which his gifts would be employed in the ensuing decade. The authors whom he saw into print with their first books include such as C. K. Barrett, a former pupil, then a Methodist minister in Darlington; W. D. Davies, a Congregational minister in Cambridgeshire; W. Flemington of Wesley House, Cambridge; S. G. F. Brandon, whose *Fall of Jerusalem and the Christian Church* was written while he was a Chaplain in the Services; Ulrich Simon, a refugee from Nazi Germany who had spent much of the war as a curate in Slough. He delighted, as he had predicted, in the making of books. He was at his happiest when engrossed in work which required typographical ingenuity and an artistic sense, for example, the popular reports of the Lambeth

Conferences. Often hypercritical where his own writing was concerned, he was supremely confident in reshaping the work of others. The official Lambeth Reports owed not a little to his editing. On his Literature Advisory Group, he brought together many of the Church's keenest intellects: A. R. Vidler, E. L. Mascall, Charles Smyth, Ian Ramsey, Kenneth Ross, Dennis Nineham, all friends and near contemporaries, made a sparkling constellation.

Davey gave much time to the development of films, filmstrips, and audio-visual aids, and wrote many of the scripts himself. In the early 1960s, he supplied theological direction for the presentation of the New English Bible New Testament on records, providing, in the words of Andrew Cruickshank, one of the distinguished actors who took part, a bridge between the producer and actors and the translators.

In the middle 1950s, S.P.C.K. introduced a new constitution with the object of bringing together the three activities of publishing, bookselling, and 'the appeal' which financed the Society's overseas literature work. These had been respectively in the province of the Editorial, Financial, and General Secretaries. Briefly as Editorial and General Secretary, and then for fifteen years as Director, Davey took responsibility for all the Society's activities. A purely administrative role would not have suited him; he identified with publishing too much to release many of the strings; his brain was fertile as ever, but he was able less often than in the past to develop an idea into an actual manuscript, and the new responsibilities certainly put paid to his chances of major theological writing on his own account. But great achievements could be set against this. He gained recognition throughout the Anglican Communion of 'literature . . . as an important instrument of the Church in fulfilling its mission' (*Lambeth Conference, 1958,* Resolution 71), and when Bishop Stephen Bayne, a friend of many years, came to London as the first Anglican Executive Officer, it was under Davey's direction that the document *Literature for the Anglican Communion* was produced, which charted the course for a five-year programme of development. These were the years in which Davey began to travel widely overseas, becoming a respected figure throughout the Anglican Communion. When Anglicanism defined the principle of Mutual Responsibility and Interdependence, at Toronto in 1963, he saw to it that the implications for publishing and bookselling were not overlooked. He hoped that Anglican publishers in Britain, the U.S.A., Canada, and Australia first of all, and subsequently in developing areas, would work ever more closely with the exchange of information, co-editions, and shared distribution facilities. This last dream was largely unfulfilled. He would have needed to recruit to his staff an experienced publisher of steady judgement whose abilities and interests complemented his own. As it was, the idea had scarcely been canvassed before the Governing Body began to question S.P.C.K's entire publishing role, amid the proliferation of religious publishing, much of it of a radical kind, in the mid-1960s.

The Society's bookselling prospered in this period. Here Davey did not need to exercise a day-to-day control, but the staffing of the bookshops brought to him many problems of a personal kind, over which he would agonize until, and sometimes after, others forced his hand.

The success of S.P.C.K. in establishing itself as publisher to the Anglican Communion had a less desirable corollary at home, where a younger generation saw it as standing for an Anglican position of a safe, traditionalist kind. Davey protested at the unfairness of the suggestion that the Society's history tied it to the Anglicanism of yesterday; in fact it had fully kept pace with the Church's growing ecumenical awareness. Indeed, it was about this time that he called together the heads of the main Society-based publishing houses and invited them to consider a consortium for such of their activities as could be handled jointly. There now began a period of close co-operation with the official Methodist publisher, Epworth Press, which could easily have become a union had the Churches moved into 'stage one' of Anglican-Methodist unity.

The mid-1960s also saw the release in the Church of England of the flood of liturgical change. Before the advent of the Liturgical Commission, Davey had been, in virtue of his office, one of the Archbishops' advisers on liturgical matters. He now made sure that S.P.C.K. gave absolute priority to the publishing of Alternative Services. He was himself largely responsible for the design of the printed text of Series 2 Communion, and he took the step of inviting the Queen's Printer and the University Presses to share in publication of the authorized services. He believed it would help the new services if they appeared under the same imprints as the old, and if the Presses had an interest in their success.

Throughout his years at S.P.C.K., Davey carried with him something of the ethos of the older universities. Those appointed to his staff, often young graduates, found themselves informally in the role of pupils. His occasional exasperation he reserved for their seniors. To the young he was a looming presence, kindly but quizzical, sometimes richly humorous, often baffling, sometimes giving them a glimpsed perception that the work in which they were engaged was part of something larger, in which the truths of the Fourth Gospel and the European cultural tradition were somehow at one. An annual ceremony was the checking of the Lectionary proofs. This began with a solemn declaration of the date of Easter. There followed an oral reconstruction of the lectionary, often at breakneck speed, from source material. Whatever the nature of his daily post, anything to do with the lectionary—or Kalendar, as he preferred to call it—unfailingly absorbed his attention.

The year 1956 saw the transfer of the S.P.C.K. office from Northumberland Avenue to Holy Trinity Church in Marylebone Road. It was one of the first churches to be adapted for office use, and in Davey's time it clearly remained a church, in which he and other priests in the staff said the Office and daily celebrated the Eucharist. For much of the time there were daily intercessions for the work of the Society and a public lunch-hour service on Wednesdays.

As he had accepted the life of a country priest in Suffolk, so he accepted S.P.C.K. as the main setting of his priesthood. Here, as there, it was not his way to seek another sphere. Perhaps, in the early years, he half expected to be called to a theological college, where his personal gifts as a teacher could flower again; instead, he was a midwife to the printed word and to every kind of audio-visual communication. His theology served to centre the whole enterprise on the theme of crucifixion-resurrection. But he also exercised a parish ministry in the London churches of St Mary's, Primrose Hill, and St Cyprian's, Clarence Gate, being in virtual charge of the former during a long interregnum. His chaplaincy, from 1958, to St Luke's Nursing Home for the Clergy, close to the Society's new office, was a privilege which he greatly prized.

In the 1960s some of his friends hoped that he might be given the opportunity to become dean of one of the great cathedrals, a position which he would have held with distinction, but it was not to be. As Director of S.P.C.K. he held a position virtually unique in the Anglican world, and he remained at the helm while the Society was obtaining a Royal Charter, and retired at the end of 1970 aged 66. During the following two years, it was not so much academic theology as the prospect for the church in the countryside that claimed his attention. *Rural Ministry,* a report which he had edited from the findings of two groups of Suffolk clergy and laity, was published in the week of his death.

Davey married Grizelle Margaret Widdrington on 26 September, 1939, and had three sons and two daughters. He entered into family life with the total dedication and delight of his previous donnish existence. He used his camping skills and convictions on family holidays, and imparted his enthusiasms. Christmas, his own birthday too, was marked by special customs and rituals—presents delayed until after the Services, which began with Midnight Mass, a light lunch, and then a grand climax in the evening family feast.

He lived under the perpetual influence of Hoskyns and with an obligation to finish Hoskyns's work. Even when at S.P.C.K., he used sometimes to dream that Hoskyns was rebuking him for wrong editorial decisions over *The Fourth Gospel.* Criticism hurt him more even than it does most of us. With children, and with people he knew and trusted, he was always at ease. In 1947 he wrote *The Good Shepherd and His Flock,* a book of Sunday School lessons, which, with a rare sensitiveness to children's understanding and interests, inculcate theology and churchmanship at a far higher standard than most such efforts.

Through all the years he was not only a mine of erudition but quicksilver itself. Every rift was loaded with ore—one never had lunch with him, or any lengthy conversation, without emerging better informed and with something perhaps of the exhilaration which Hoskyns himself conveyed. Once he decided with Dom Gregory Dix that Cranmer's 'Prayer of Humble Access' must have been composed in a summer's afternoon of inspiration and has been some embarrassment ever since; once he wondered what a Liturgy devised solely from the Fourth Gospel might be like. He was planning a small volume to be called *A Short Collection of Longer*

Acts of Prayer taken from classical writers, with some modern contributions and some from his own hand. A cyclostyled draft is extant, but nothing more.

His achievements were honoured by the award of the C.B.E., and by the Lambeth Doctorate of Divinity from Michael Ramsey. But beyond all his gifts, his learning, his association with Hoskyns, his teaching, his work at S.P.C.K., his profound theology, is the simple fact that those who knew him best loved him most.

University Sermon

Preached in Great St Mary's Church on Sunday, 8 March 1942
by the Reverend F. N. Davey, M.A. Fellow of Corpus Christi College

I am Alpha and Omega, the first and the last,
the beginning and the end.   (Rev. 22.13)

Our experience in time forces upon us very urgent questions. We are acutely conscious that the present is slipping away from us and the future pressing down upon us, and that we are incapable of detaching our world, our environment, ourselves, not only from origins inalterably past, but also from consequences inevitably to come. By no energy, and by no passivity, of thought or action, can we escape from the succession 'Begun, continued, ended.' For us the only significant object of study and experience is change. These facts compel us to ask: Has the continuing succession which we experience an unbegun beginning and an unending end? Is there a changelessness that eludes our temporal analysis? And, if so, how is the succession we know as history related to the unknowable, changeless beginning and ending? Not at all? Or in such a way that our hopes and fears for the future of our present interests bear true witness that what we call the present has a final, though now hidden, significance?

Suspended between before and after, which we readily project to starting-point and terminus; bitterly conscious of the restless, ruthless flux that makes us yearn for free finality, some of us bend the tyrannous idiom of time to our groping speech about God. Plato makes use of an Orphic saying which describes God as holding in his hand the beginning, the end, and the midst of all that is (*Laws*, iv. 7). 'Thus saith the Lord,' cries the Second Isaiah, 'I am the first and I am the last' (Isa. 44.6)—'declaring the end from the beginning, and from ancient times things that are not yet' (46.10). Such pronouncements, sometimes vague, often unreal, always concluding from the known to the unknown, were common in later Greek and

16

Jewish writings. When, therefore, the author of the Revelation hears God declare (Rev. 21.6), 'I am the Alpha and the Omega, the beginning and the end,' he tells us only what we might have read, in very similar words, in the books of others besides the Platonists. But here, at the end of his vision, these words are uttered, not by the invisible, incomprehensible God, but by Christ, the living one, who was dead and is alive for evermore. He, that same Jesus whom men once saw and touched, whom men once condemned and executed, is the Alpha and the Omega, the first and the last, the beginning and the end. This we read not in the philosophies of men. This we could not conclude from any universalization of our experience or projection of our desire. For this is the scandal of the Gospel: the paradox flung at us as God's truth by the apostles of the Word made flesh: the folly that provoked the Jews to violence and the Greeks to scorn. Jesus Christ, that elusive, ill-remembered figure of a few short months, denied by men, forsaken by God—the same yesterday, and to-day, and for ever (Heb. 13.8): not only the author and perfecter of our faith (Heb. 12.2), but the firstborn of creation by whom all things were created, and the firstborn from the dead, through whom and to whom all things in heaven and earth are consummated (Col. 1.15–20).

Created, I have said, and consummated. These words signify more than bare temporal concepts. Christ, the beginning and the end, is no remote starter and judge in the race of time. Nor yet is he the mere elemental principle from which and into which—picture it how you like, as linear, cyclic, or expanding process—the experienced universe issues and resolves. Far more intimate and far more ultimate, is Christ's relation to everything in our world. St Augustine tells us that he is the Beginning, 'because he speaks to us, teaching us what we are, restoring us whence we are': he is, that is to say, 'our beginning' (*Conf.* 11.8). 'And he is our end (again I quote Augustine), not as one that consumes, but as one that consummates: the end therefore of our purpose, because, however much we attempt, in him we are made perfect, and by him are made perfect, and this is our perfection, that unto him we come home' (*Enarr, in Ps.* 56.2). St Clement of Alexandria expounds Christ as the Alpha and Omega of whom alone the end becomes beginning and ends again at the beginning without any break, only in order to show the cosmic scope of the promises embracing those that

17

accept Jesus: 'Wherefore to believe in him and by him,' he says, 'is to become a unit, indissolubly united in him; and to disbelieve is to be separated, disjoined, divided' (*Stromateis*, 4.25). Response to Jesus now: present submission to his love: is the way to far more than what we call in our jargon 'an integrated personality', to far more than the myths, ancient and modern, of virtuous manhood or mature citizenship of the universe. Response to Jesus now is the way to that embodiment into the new creation of God which is his final perfecting purpose for all that he has made. The end of the Gospel is infinite, its power absolute, its scope universal; yet it is wholly contained, wholly achieved, made wholly and immediately accessible to us now, in Jesus.

How mean, by contrast, is the subject of human expectation; how feeble its ground; how dark its end. We have hopes or fears for our affairs, our friends, ourselves. We base them on luck or the course of things. We expect a happy ending or a dire fate, or something duller and more respectable in between. About the subject of our hope we may perhaps be fairly certain: we think we know what we are, even if we define ourselves in terms of 'unyielding despair', or try to bale out of ourselves into some Lippmannesque apathy. But of the ground of our hopes—what will bring us fruition; or of their end—what constitutes fruition; all our science gives us but a meagre glimpse.

The Christian is in wholly different case. For him, too, hope has its subject, ground, and end. But the order is reversed. The end of Christian hope is the supreme certainty that at once illuminates its ground and defines its subject. For this reason I propose to speak; first of the End of the Christian hope, *what we are to hope for*; secondly of the Ground of the Christian hope, *why we are to hope*; and thirdly of the Subject of the Christian hope, *what we are to have hope about*. We shall then be in a position to enquire, fourthly, in what sense we are to look for the realization of the Christian hope in this present plane of experience, and, lastly, in what sense we are to suppose time and space to be finally related to God.

First, the End of the Christian hope. What is certain is not some egocentric awareness of self and circumstance—*cogito ergo sum*! The axe is laid at the root of all that. It is precisely that the affirming word of God has thrown into question. The supreme certainty is GOD ALL IN ALL (1 Cor. 15.28): Christ consummating all things

18

by ordering them in his own perfect subjection to the Father. This is the sovereign truth of the Gospel, its light, its power, its joy. But it is—the glory of God. For this reason it confounds human conception. You and I can picture it only by relating it to ourselves, by describing what it means to us, or may make of us. But to relate it to ourselves is to become occupied with ourselves—that is the mark of our sin—and away goes the God-centred Gospel! But now, look at that life in the flesh which was perfectly accomplished on the Cross. Here, in this frame of clay, Jesus glorified the Father (John 17.4). His Father's will was his will, his Father's work his work, his Father's joy his joy. No word or deed of his, then, is adequately explained as his: all from God and to God. This we apprehend but darkly, and only when God's new Genesis shows us the light of his glory in the face of Jesus Christ (2 Cor. 4.6). For so entirely selfless was Christ's glorying of the Father in time and space, that to our human eyes it seems utterly inglorious—unless we romanticize it! Yet the inglorious event *was* the glory of Jesus (John 13.31), *was* the glory which he had with the Father before the world was (John 17.5), *was* the eternal, selfless rejoicing of the Son in the glory of the Father. This glorying of the Father by the Son; this persistent, single attitude of love which we dimly descry as eternally revealing and eternally reflecting back the Godhead, has no need of the created universe, or to be demonstrated in flesh and blood. It is perfect, complete, from eternity to eternity, in God's essential being. Creation cannot change, or defraud, or add to, the glory of Jesus—cannot comprehend it even, since, as we know it, creation is so centred upon itself that it cannot receive him whose centre, whose all in all, is God. When he came in the flesh, we thrust him out from among us. Yet already, in his life and his death, he has conquered the self-centredness of the creature, overcome it, caught it up to himself and glorified it with his own glory, demonstrating the miraculous possibility of its entire and selfless subjection to his glorying of the Father. More than this. There were men who saw his flesh and beheld his glory (John 1.14): to whom he gave the glory given him by the Father (John 17.22), so that he was glorified, not only in his own flesh, but also in them (John 17.10): men whom God called through the word of Christ, justified by the work of Christ, glorified with the worth of Christ (Rom. 8.30). The end

19

of the Christian hope is therefore Christ in us the hope of glory (Col. 1.27).

Secondly, the Ground of the Christian hope. I turn from the word of the Gospel to the power of the kingdom (1 Cor. 4.20); from the glorious truth of Christ which our temporal and self-centred state cannot comprehend, to the glorifying grace of Christ which comprehends the temporal in eternity and restates the self-centred in terms of God.

Everywhere we are embraced by God's vehement love in Christ. This is his persistent attitude towards us; in creating us, in providing for us, in lavishing his spirit upon us. From his love we can never escape. But we can, and will, fail to perceive his love and so respond to it, if we do not fix our eyes upon its only perfect concrete expression, the life and death and resurrection of Jesus.

But what does Christ's resurrection mean? We apprehend it most easily as the end of a chronological sequence: the manifestation in time and space of God's glorious reversal of a shameful historical situation. We picture Jesus suffering, dying, then raised to un-ending life. No doubt the apostles were led to apprehend the glory of Jesus through the chronological sequence of their experience. No doubt for our temporal minds, like theirs, apprehension of his glory comes first through the contrast between present and future. But to the apostles the resurrection of which they had concrete assurance was an eternal, non-chronological *truth and act*, cutting right across time and space. The glory they then apprehended drove them back to the life and death of Jesus. This was not merely because they could no longer understand any part of his inglorious life and death except as the manifestation of the glory of God; and not merely because they could not even then apprehend God's glory in itself, apart from Christ's actual historical flesh. They were driven back to the life and death of Jesus because they understood the intersection of the eternal and the temporal in his flesh neither as the prolonga-tion of the one plane into the other, nor yet as the congruous juxta-position of the two planes, but as God's free and dynamic raising up into his eternity of an actual life and death. A life and death, be it added, which expressly repudiated its temporal context as an end in itself, and depended, completely, humbly, and unpretentiously, upon God.

So complex was this perception, that every metaphor they put to it—chronological, eschatological, sacrificial, dialectical—broke on their lips. Yet so simple was it, that they perceived the whole truth of God about Jesus, themselves, their calling, the universe, uniquely achieved and declared in his crucifixion and resurrection from the dead. I would ask you then, while considering the ground of our hope, to remember that any mention of the historical living and dying of Jesus is inevitably a declaration of the historical manifestation of his risen glory; and that any reference to the self-oblation of Jesus in the flesh is inevitably a description of the power of the living God raising him from the dead.

Consider now the life God has given us. Work, thought, friendship, prayer—are not such activities as these the most satisfying we know? Yet, are they wholly satisfying? Do we either perform them as we would, or receive from them what their opportunity seemed to promise? No doubt the sin in us may explain the constant snatching of the cup from our lips, the continual withdrawing of our goal beyond our horizon. Yet, Jesus worked, taught, loved, prayed—and was judged to have done all things well, to have taught with authority, to have loved to the utmost, to have prayed with godly fear. Why then did his work appear to achieve nothing, his teaching seem fruitless, his friends fail, his prayer go unheeded? Face that squarely, and what a fool's paradise seems our self-sufficient world! But the life of Jesus was no fool's paradise. The cross did not stultify; but, rather, glorified it. The movement to death which it characterized as absolute human insufficiency was chosen by God as the sole apt context for his glory. He whose working was God's work, whose teaching was God's wisdom, whose loving was God's love, whose prayer was God's good pleasure, consummated creation, not by any visible achievement such as our secure self-sufficiency can measure or strain after, but in sheer creaturely obedience to God, and stark unself-centred dependence upon him.

The cross so willingly embraced by Jesus is now defined as the visible manifestation of the aggressive love of God for man, and as the responsive love of the perfect man for God. Are you aware of its attack, and its appeal? Do you know the essential vanity of life in this world? Are you oppressed with the unusual burden of law and conscience? Have you penetrated to the sad limit of even the dearest relationships? Is the holy of holies for you not light but darkness? Somewhere—somewhere in your experience—there is the cankerous warning: Here nothing permanent in itself! Here no achievement of self-gotten excellence! Here no intrinsically satisfying intimacy! Here no inherently consoling intercourse with God! It is the pressure of God's love that forces you to scepticism. It is the pressure of God's love that exposes your 'important' business as an aimless whirl; your cultivation of 'deep' friendships as a superficial pastime; your philosophic, aesthetic, scientific, or mystical 'objectivity' as a subjective hoax! It is the pressure of God's love that renders utterly elusive and illusory the very idea of you! It is God that has subjected the creation to vanity; that has shut up all things under sin; that has enbondaged us and slays us! Yes, but follow the harsh metaphors through—in hope (Rom. 8.20)! for the sake of his promise (Gal. 3.22)! to make us his own sons (Gal. 4.3–6)! to give us eternal life (2 Cor. 3.6)! For precisely where we, as natural men, encounter failure, frustration, and death, God, the triumphant and victorious lover, offers us himself (Rom. 7.7–25; 8.31–39)! And precisely where Christ as perfect man offers himself to God, he offers on our behalf that complete detachment from creatures (Matt. 6.19–23), that perfection like God's (Matt. 5.48), that renunciation of natural ties (Luke 14.26, etc.), that surrender of life itself (Mark 8.35, etc.), which he has demanded of us, in language far harsher than St Paul's, as the only sufficient response to the love of God.

So the words of Jesus, his work, and above all the dark agony of his supreme hour, light up our world. The Spirit of Christ is shown converging upon us in every part of our experience in order to save us from our own lie. While we reject him, we are indeed subject to wrath, folly, enmity, death, which strip away the smooth illusions of our egotism, leaving our world a *Waste Land*. But when we look at Christ and hear him; when we accept the crucifying-resurrecting love of God; then the waste land bursts into flower, mediates Christ's glory, furnishes the sole basis of our glorying, and constitutes the powerful instrument of our glorification. Then, and then only, do we apprehend possibilities entirely new—a use of creatures that leaves God room to use them; a knowledge of God that consists in being known; a love of the neighbour created by God's death for him; the Abba Father voiced by the Spirit of Christ. Then and then only do we know that whether we heed

Christ or not; whether we reject the truth or glimpse it darkly by faith, nothing can separate us, or any man, or any part of creation, from the ground of the Christian hope, which is the Cross and the Resurrection. Ceaselessly and universally the Spirit of God and of Christ toils to shape all things to their beginning and to clothe them with their end—with their beginning and end which have been propounded and accomplished once for all in the flesh of Jesus and in his resurrection from the dead.

Thirdly, as with the end and the ground of the Christian hope, so with its Subject. That too is defined for us in Jesus. Nothing created is outside the scope of Christian hope: only what will not be conformed to Christ sets itself outside. I must, therefore, have no hope for myself apart from Christ: every hope for myself remade by Christ.

But how can I picture 'myself remade by Christ'? This is not the 'I' I now know, but an 'I' purged of self-centredness, filled up with God; created, not out of the 'I' which I breathe out at my last gasp, but out of every moment of my earthly existence; and not only out of the spiritual part of me; but out of the whole me, and my use of my body, and my use of my mind, and my use of creatures, and my relations with my fellows, and my response to Jesus. All this given me by God to surrender to his re-creating power. Written over it the hope of incorporation into the glorious Body of Christ. Shall I then regard the Christian hope as the guarantee that this little 'I' I now cleave to so fondly will be perpetuated for ever? Shall I carica- ture the Christian hope as the mere assurance of my individual immortality? Or again, shall I picture the glory of Christ in me as a reward or a consolation such as I can now imagine or experience? All that I now experience as self and as conducing to the well-being of self must die: all that I have hope for is what God can accept in Christ transformed to be the means of Christ's glorying of him in me raised from the dead.

But not only is this 'I' I now know in the natural order the subject of the Christian hope, but every other category which we now experience. Christ is the end of the two made one in marriage, of the family knit together by ties of blood, of the community, small or large, woven together by mutual dependence. As with the indi- vidual entity, so with these corporate entities. Redeemed by Christ, they are consummated in his glory. Indeed, though individuality is

the most obvious category of our experience, the dependent, corporate relationships that throw individuality into question are the
better parables of the Kingdom of God. It is not the individual by
himself, but the world-wide fellowship, the local community, the
household, even the married couple, that are dignified in the New
Testament as opportunities for the temporal apprehension of the
glorious communion of the saints in Christ. The subject of the
Christian hope is the creation as a whole and in every significant
part, in so far as the parts and the whole are enabled by the truth
and grace of Christ to perform their natural function.

Fourthly, what is our hope in this world? Simply this, that Jesus
Christ cannot be kept out of it. He is raised up here, wherever
God's will is done; wherever God and the neighbour, his chief
emissary, reign in the place usurped in our unredeemed lives by
self. The love created by Christ, and nothing else, bestrides without
discontinuity the gulf we call death (1 Cor. 13.8–10). The final,
glorious subjection of the creation to God is concretely anticipated
wherever, by his grace, men and women order their lives upon the
assumption that the Christian hope is true. Our hope is therefore,
and most emphatically, neither a retreat from the world nor a
retreat from time and space. Each situation in which we find ourselves offers the possibility of an approximation to the pattern of
Christ's life and death; and we rejoice in hope (Rom. 5.2–5)
because we know that such approximations have their place in the
ultimate conformity to Christ established beyond death. This means
that Christ's perfect dependence upon God, and his perfect need
of his fellows, must be the goal, not of individual piety only, but of
every category of our life. Here is a demand to follow Christ with
our entire energy, reason, and will, as absolute for social as for
individual action.

Consequently, the Christian hope may be said to be realized here
on earth only where, in patience, seeking for glory and honour and
incorruption, men do what God has set them here to do, knowing
that apart from him they can do no good thing. It differs then,
absolutely, from the hopes of unredeemed men. Our generation,
trying desperately to emancipate itself from the bondage of hopes
and fears created by moods of optimism and pessimism, has been
paralysed and stultified, not only by the 'fear' engendered by a
'scientific' anticipation of the horrors of human war, but also, and

even more disastrously, by the 'hope' engendered by a 'scientific' anticipation of the glorious achievements of human peace. The mind of Christ frees us from all such bondage, crude and sophisticated. For we have his assurance that, however unbridled be the power of evil in this present world, the concrete situation before us holds the possibility of a real, actual, recognizable achievement of the grace of God, as we offer it, and our whole interest in it, to God, in faith and obedience. And every such achievement, in all its relativity, is an element in the final triumph of God that lies beyond history.

Lastly, GOD ALL IN ALL has already crowned creation with the glory of his Son—to reveal the Godhead, to reflect him back—not only in the obedient flesh of Christ, but everywhere where Christ's obedience lays hold on men's lives. Our present situation, where this truth is obscured and where we are stretched in a tension between faith and sight, must therefore seem intolerable, even though we know that tribulation creating patience is the sole ground of our hope (Rom. 5.3–5). Our citizenship is in heaven (Phil. 3.20). We must therefore long to depart from the flesh and be with Christ (Phil. 1.23). We cannot now judge (1 Cor. 4.5) even our own obedience to God. We know only that we are known (1 Cor. 13.12), that our sufficiency is of God (2 Cor. 3.5), that apart from God's grace we fall (1 Cor. 10.12), that everywhere, and above all where least we look for it, the fleshy principle of self works to beguile us once again and turn our love of God to lust. We are bound to say in shame: How Christ's knowledge of God's eternally triumphant glory would glorify us and fill us—were we not so choked and smirched with ourselves that there is no room in us for God alone! We are bound to cry out in faith: How Christ's knowledge of God's eternally triumphant glory *will* glorify and fill us, when this pettiness shall have been scoured away, and we behold him (John 17.24), who is the brightness of the Father's glory (Heb. 1.2), face to face (1 Cor. 13.12). For when we see him as he is, we shall be like him (1 John 3.2), entirely concerned with and centred upon the Godhead. But this 'when,' so future to us, is in Christ an ever present fact! No more self-interest, then, no more self-gratification, no more self-love. Only Jesus, beginning us having made an end of us, the Word uttering to us and in us the eternal Amen which is

God's final affirmation of his creation as utterly good (2 Cor. 1.20), in which time and space are rolled up and transcended in the one perfect, and acceptable moment of the Son's loving response to the love of the Father.

Edwyn Clement Hoskyns

9 August 1884 to 28 June 1937

When I went up to Cambridge in 1946, Sir Edwyn Hoskyns had been dead for just over nine years. His name was not a household word in the Divinity School, though the Regius Professor, Charles Raven, would refer to him with misgivings in his introductory lectures, and Lady Margaret's Professor, the Hebraist, F. S. Marsh, would shake his head in affectionate bewilderment over 'Clement' and his tendency to discern the numinous in hard places and textual lacunae. Some of us heard Gordon Rupp speak of him with admiration and commend the *Cambridge Sermons,* while Charles Smyth returned from St Margaret's, Westminster, to preach a University Sermon in a course on 'The Cambridge Tradition in Theology'. His subject was 'The Cambridge Puritans' but, determined that a prophet should not be without honour even in his own country, he prefaced it with a reference to the Cambridge biblical scholars, 'Westcott, Hort, and *Hoskyns*', displacing Lightfoot from the triad.[1] And as frequenters of C. H. Dodd's course on St John, we would consult, on his advice, if not buy, the second edition of Hoskyns's commentary, *The Fourth Gospel.*

We knew that Hoskyns had been revered by a group of disciples in the 1920s and 30s, that he had been a 'biblical theologian', whatever that meant, and had attracted opposition as well as applause. In 1953, dining in the train between London and Manchester, I fell into conversation with an old Corpus, Cambridge, man, who had just kissed hands on appointment as Ambassador to Paraguay. As an undergraduate, he had found Hoskyns's sermons hard to fathom, and he asked me to explain just where his importance lay. I tried to do so, and doubtless but darkened his understanding further.

For my own part, I used *The Fourth Gospel* regularly, but it was when my responsibilities at the Epworth Press brought me into

[1] *The Cambridge Review,* 1 February 1947.

association with Noel Davey, General Secretary and then Director of S.P.C.K., that I began more seriously to try to assess Hoskyns's work. This became imperative when I was writing the life of Robert Newton Flew, some of whose pupils were among Hoskyns's devotees, and who reviewed *Cambridge Sermons* for the final number of T. S. Eliot's literary review, *The Criterion*. Davey talked very freely, and when *Robert Newton Flew* was published in 1971, encouraged me to contemplate a biographical study of Hoskyns. He asked me to delay until he had finished *Crucifixion–Resurrection* because he felt that Hoskyns's work was incomplete without it. But within six months of that conversation, Davey had died, and so the 'life' appears, briefer than first planned, and bound up with an all-too-inadequate memoir of Davey himself, and with the *magnum opus* resembling a cathedral with the tower half-built and a brick wall instead of an apse and east window.

Background and Birth

Who was he, this clerical baronet, whom the uninitiated, dazzled by the 'Sir' and not noticing the 'Reverend', are apt to think was a layman?

He was the product of a fascinating ancestry on both sides. The Hoskyns are a Herefordshire family of Welsh extraction, whose tombs, from the seventeenth century, are in the church at Abbey Dore. They emerge in the reign of James I in the person of John Hoskyns of Winchester and New College, Serjeant at-law, friend of Ben Jonson, and one of the poets who frequented the Mermaid Tavern. But the Serjeant was no prisoner of the taproom though his nose was large. He helped Jonson to clean up his plays, and wrote between 1598 and 1603 a set of *Direccons for Speech and Style,* part of which Jonson plagiarized in his *Timber: or, Discoveries: Made Upon Men and Matter.* He was an energetic member of Parliament for the City of Hereford from 1604 to 1629, respectful of the royal prerogative, but jealous also of the rights of Parliament. In 1614 he was committed to the Tower for a full year, after an intemperate speech in which he charged the Scots with riotous disloyalty comparable to the thirteenth-century uprising at the Sicilian Vespers. This was not likely to please their compatriot

King. 'In the matter of religion,' says John Hoskyns's biographer, 'he was anti-papist but conservative.'[1] He was very much a Church of England man, opposed to recusants and Romish infiltrators, yet all for a celibate clergy, at least in cathedrals and colleges.

The Serjeant's first wife was Benedicta, or Bennet, Bourne, widow of a fellow-templar. Their only son was christened Benedict, or Bennet, an early instance of the way in which the family, throughout the centuries, bestowed upon the children the names of parents and of the families into which they married. It was Benedict, also a lawyer, who bought the baronetcy from Charles II in 1676. The arms consist of a chevron between three lions rampant, surmounted by a crowned lion with flames of fire issuing from his mouth. The motto is 'Bind the tongue, or the tongue will bind thee'.

Bennet's son John, the second baronet, was the second President of the Royal Society in 1682, succeeding in that office Sir Christopher Wren. He had thirteen children by Agnes Hungerford of Down Ampney. His eldest son died childless, so the title passed to the second son, named Hungerford after his mother, the first of four baronets so called. He had fought in Marlborough's armies and was twice married; first to Maria, or Mary, daughter of Lord Chandos of Canons Park, Edgware (with its links with Handel and the Chandos anthems), with whom the Leighs were connected. And so the names of Leigh and Chandos were added to the Hoskyns lineage.

As with most titled families, the tradition was for the elder sons to seek a career in politics or the army, while the younger took holy orders. But in the nineteenth and twentieth centuries, death strangely threw the succession awry. The ninth baronet was a third son and a clergyman, the Reverend Canon Sir John Leigh Hoskyns. He had been at Rugby under Arnold and that incalculable influence remained. He was Rector of Aston Tyrrold in Berkshire for sixty-six years and died in 1911. Of his sons, John died unmarried, Chandos, John's twin, the tenth baronet, who died in 1914, had three daughters, while Leigh, the next brother, lost his only son in the war. At his demise the next in succession was the fourth son, Edwyn, then Bishop of Southwell and aged seventy-three.

Edwyn was a representative of the new episcopate which had

[1] Osborn, Louise Brown, *The Life, Letters and Writings of John Hoskyns 1566–1638.* Yale University Press 1937.

resulted from the Oxford movement. He had arrived at Southwell in 1904, after an education which began in the benign and dedicated family life of Aston Tyrrold parsonage with its country pursuits and gentlemanly kindness to the 'lower orders', and continued at Haileybury and Jesus College, Cambridge, where, in 1873, he became a rowing blue. From a boy he felt called to the priesthood and 'directed all his cares and studies this way'. His first curacy was at Welwyn in Hertfordshire, where he seems to have learned, or first displayed, a talent for organization, which reached its apotheosis at Southwell, and which Randall Davidson, the Archbishop of Canterbury, acclaimed at his death. From Welwyn, Edwyn Hoskyns proceeded to St Clement's, Notting Hill, and St Dunstan's, Stepney.

To both he brought order, and to St Dunstan's, in particular, the colour and comeliness of Tractarian worship. He was not an extreme Anglo-Catholic, like some of the slum priests. He was always doubtful about reservation of the sacrament and cringed when someone lamented the lack of it by saying 'They have taken away my Lord'. But he loved the Holy Eucharist. And his warm personality translated the incarnational theology of the *Lux Mundi* school into daily life. 'He made of every meal a kind of party.'[1]

He used the position which the Church still had in society to further its teachings and to maintain the home as its nursery. For him the unit of Church and nation alike was the family, and the parish priest, in those days when the vaster population was immobile, must minister 'from generation to generation', to quote the title of a paper which he read to the Evangelistic Committee of the East London Church Fund in 1890. The revivalist evangelical's was not the way he counselled; rather the long patient ministry of edification, care for people at the nuptial altar and through all the changing scenes of family life.

In Stepney he had an action brought against him by Mrs Annie Besant, the secularist, whose candidature as one of the representatives for Stepney on the London School Board he vehemently opposed. She claimed that Hoskyns had libelled her by using in a handbill a quotation from another free-thinker, which implied that she was permissive in matters of sexual morality. The jury disagreed among themselves, but Hoskyns's costs were paid by a public

[1] There is a memoir by Selwyn, E. G., *Sir Edwyn Hoskyns Bishop of Southwell (1904–1925)*. SPCK 1926.

subscription, which was large enough to build St Faith's Church, Stepney, as well. And before he left the East End, Mrs Besant had recanted the views which so alarmed him.

He went next to the large Lancashire town of Bolton, with its new Victorian Gothic church. Here he made his mark as a preacher, forthright and powerful, prophetic in his denunciation of social ills, persuasive in his pleas for personal holiness. He had a manly presence and a fine voice. After five years, he moved to Burnley, to which a suffragan bishopric, then of the Manchester diocese, was attached.

In 1904 he was one of the leaders of a Mission of Help to South Africa in the wake of the Boer War and, at greater remove, the rending controversies surrounding Bishop Colenso. He was saddened and disturbed by the socially inferior position of the blacks and incipient apartheid, and gave some offence by his unequivocal statements.

While he was in South Africa he was appointed to the see of Southwell, a place of which he confessed he had never heard until the approach from Downing Street. It was a large, ungainly, unnatural diocese consisting of the counties of Nottingham and Derby. It had been put together by relieving Lincoln and Lichfield of a county each and contained more than 500 parishes extending from the borders of Lincolnshire to those of Cheshire. But Hoskyns never allowed himself to be a remote administrator. Efficient he was, but he travelled his diocese relentlessly, visiting his parishes, schools, and clergy. Though he acquired an early motor car, he was very often sleeping away from home as he went the diocesan rounds —Ashbourne, Wirksworth, Buxton, Repton, Worksop, Mansfield, the suburbs of Sheffield, and many a village and mining town. The well-being and financial security of his clergy concerned him, and he wished to be accessible to ordained and lay alike, their Father in God.[1]

Bishop Hoskyns promoted the Church's mission to miners in the expanding Nottinghamshire coalfield, he loved children, and although his principles would not allow him to countenance intercommunion, he maintained as good relations with Swanwick, conference centre of the Student Movement and of the new

[1] This is brought out in the MS of a sermon his son preached in Chesterfield Parish Church at the inauguration of the Diocese of Derby 1927. See below p. 58f.

phenomenon of ecumenism, as with the more congenial Society of the Sacred Mission at Kelham.

In 1908, due to the impression he had made four years earlier, he was asked to become Archbishop of Cape Town. He refused—though the offer at once humbled and attracted him—because he could not 'throw over' Southwell.

Before the 1914 war and its interruption of plans, Hoskyns had determined that his diocese must be divided, and he worked indefatigably for this, but he did not live to see the creation of the diocese of Derby in 1927. He would also have liked some share in the revision of the Prayer Book, ill-fated as that proved to be; this too was denied him. Fatal cancer of the throat was diagnosed in the autumn of 1925 and on 2 October a London specialist gave him two months to live.

He had time to prepare for the end. His vivid sermons on Bible characters were compared to those of his great contemporary, Alexander Whyte of Free St George's, Edinburgh. He would certainly have won the approval of that Catholic Puritan in the way in which, in Samuel Rutherford's phrase, he 'forefancied his death-bed'. He had books ready, Walter Hilton's *Scale of Perfection* and *The Priest's Book of Devotion*. He said the offices, received the sacrament, and engaged in meditation. One Saturday evening he was brought soup for supper, but he had been asleep and when he woke thought it was Sunday morning and so declined it in order to receive communion fasting. The following Tuesday night, he asked for his pectoral cross and ring, which had been beside the bed, to be put on. He spent his waking hours with the cross in his hands as he murmured 'Jesu mercy!' and the Sanctus. About eight o'clock next morning, he gently died. It was 2 December, two months to the day from the consultant's prognosis.

This was Edwyn Clement Hoskyns's ancestry on his father's side, thoroughly English and Anglican in culture, though with a touch of the Welsh marches, culminating in a good bishop, doughty but with a charm to which all testified, his establishment Christianity quickened by a serious and Catholic strain of spirituality, typical of the Tractarians, but with its roots in the contemporaries of the Serjeant: Andrewes, Donne, and Herbert. His mother was very different, though English enough.

While he was Vicar of St Clement's, Notting Hill, Edwyn

Hoskyns married a petite and vivacious girl, who came riding to him on horseback from Kensington Square. She was Mary Constance Maude Benson, known in the family, after the custom of those days, as May. One of her brothers, 'Con', had been in the Cambridge boat with Hoskyns.

Her family originated in Cumberland. John Benson of Stang End married in 1570 a niece of Edwin Sandys, Elizabeth I's near Puritan Archbishop of York. By the beginning of the nineteenth century the Bensons were in Liverpool and in trade, and subsequently they moved to London. But May's father, Robert Benson, of Craven Hill Gardens, who died in 1875, became bankrupt. Fortunately May was looked after by the Croppers of Liverpool, and money settled on her escaped the debacle. She always seemed to have a comfortable £800 a year of her own. Her brother Robert (Robin), however, with whom she lived in Kensington Square, had to begin business all over again, which he did with great success as a financier. His former firm is now part of the house of Kleinwort Benson.

Prosperity turned him into a collector and patron of the arts. He filled his house with Italian paintings, Dynasty china, and Persian carpets, and was made a trustee of the National Gallery. He introduced Brahms to London artistic circles, and when Wagner's *Tristan and Isolde* was first performed at Covent Garden, a stool belonging to May was among the properties.

The friends of the Bensons were the intellectual *avant-garde* of the day—Burne-Jones, Andrew Lang, the young Kipling, Hubert Parry—and May was on the edge of literary and musical culture, though she herself had not received an education adequate for such company, and confined herself to painting in water-colours, needlework, and household management.

With the inconsistency inseparable from all our lives, the Bensons were socialists of the school of William Morris. This writer, artist, designer, and poet, who declined the laureateship on the death of Tennyson, was no Marxist, but a passionate opponent of the nineteenth-century economic system, which he wished to see replaced by a return to the art and craft guilds of the middle ages. Thirty years later, the Christian Socialism of Conrad Noel at Thaxted owed something to his influence. It is easy to dismiss Morris as a naive romantic, challenging the machine age with handlooms, trying to turn its trade unions into troupes of country dancers, waving tapestries at its banknotes; but he had profound and provocative ideas about the integration of art and life, and he wished to redeem Victorian squalor and poverty by bringing beauty everywhere and evoking the hidden artist in each human soul.

It was this inspiration, as well as the link with one of her brothers, which brought Miss Benson to Notting Hill. At that time the district was 'a veritable no-man's-land. The school caretaker lived in a caravan; a gipsy encampment was in the Mission Room, of which the floor had been torn up by the people and used as firewood; the principal occupations of the inhabitants were laundry-work and professional begging; the drunkenness, especially among women, was appalling.'[1] One of Hoskyns's answers was to found a 'Lily Club' for laundry girls. With this Miss Benson came to help, and remained as mistress of the vicarage.

It was an interesting union of two different strands of English life, the somewhat muscular High Church clergyman with his landed political forebears, Tory though with a social conscience, and the slim young woman of the salons with her socialist and suffragist principles.

She was no pseudo-intellectual slut, but skilled in the good ordering of the household. Wherever they went, she made a home of attractiveness and comfort, and her taste in furniture and wall-papers doubtless owed a good deal to William Morris. She would not, however, live in a palace when the time came, and the Bishop's residence at Southwell has been known as 'Bishop's Manor' ever since. But romantic excitement may sometimes have been stronger than her practical sense, as we infer from the letter her husband wrote in explanation of his refusal of the archbishopric of Cape Town:

> Darling,
>
> You are very good and I know that you would be quite calm whatever happened, as long as you had not to look after your luggage and buy your ticket. At the same time I do not think that you realize the great discomforts which are experienced in colonial life. That you would appreciate the gorgeous scenery,

[1] Selwyn, E. G., op. cit., p. 8.

the mountains, sea and flowers, I believe, but we are both too old.

Though she painted, May did not cook. She was 'progressive' about her children's early education and would study the newest theories and methods and buy the latest gadgets, with the result that Clement learned arithmetic from bean bags, and never achieved any grasp of mathematics, while of the two girls, Phyllis and Evelyn, the latter could not read when she was seven. The girls were not sent to school but taught by inadequate governesses. And in spite of her lovingness, it was father, not mother, who knew if the children were ill.

When she married, May was innocent about child-birth and babies. She was soon pregnant, but when her time was well advanced, her husband took her punting from Oxford to London. She had to leave the river in a hurry and was soon delivered of a boy. He appeared on 9 August 1884, 'with the parish nurse and the parish bag'. He was named Edwyn, after his father, and Clement after the patron saint of the church at Notting Hill—the apostolic father, Clement of Rome.

Education

Perhaps it was due to his mother's educational eccentricities, but Clement was what we call, sometimes in hope rather than experience, a 'late-developer'. When his father was at Stepney and he less than ten years old, Winnington-Ingram, then at Oxford House, Bethnal Green, and before long to be Bishop of London, would play pitch and toss with him. The future Bishop's rule was 'Heads I win, tails you lose'. But Clement never saw through the cheating and was always puzzled as to why he lost. The innocence was commendable; the intelligence hardly astute.

Once away from his mother, his education was conventional for his class. His prep. school was Rottingdean, where he was nicknamed 'Puggy' because he was stockily pugnacious. Here the academic pulse was taken and reported every month, and the comments show alarming fluctuations between the 'grand little trier' and the untidy, casual teenager, careless in behaviour and lacking

35

in application. He went on to Haileybury in 1897. Here his musical talent gained awards. At fourteen and fifteen, he seems to have been considered young for his years, rather mercurial, occasionally petulant, and finding it difficult to believe that he was often wrong. His 'scholarship' is deemed poor to the last, but 'sometimes there is a solid and thoughtful meaning behind his apparently wild answers'. He had 'vivacity of mind', though a poor verbal memory, and was prone to be inaccurate. He liked to be in the library surrounded by books, but did not know how to use them.

He followed his father again to Jesus, Cambridge. Here he lived a full life, belonged to the Hawks Club and was a good oarsman, though not a blue. He did not disgrace himself academically with a second in History, but at this stage there was nothing to show that he would ever make any contribution to theology or scholarship in any form. He seemed destined to be a good parish priest; charming, devoted, human.

But the Dean of Jesus, F. J. Foakes-Jackson, later to be a Professor at Union Theological Seminary, New York, seems to have been more discerning. Foakes-Jackson, an eminent hellenist and church historian, was a sensitive, pastoral Dean, and he may have recognized that although Hoskyns was no great classicist or systematic theologian in the making, he was eager, impressionable, and capable of getting beneath the surface of historical questions. At any rate he sent him to Germany for a year from 1906.

This was decisive in Hoskyns's formation; as decisive as Charles Raven's refusal to go to Germany a year or two later may have been for him.[1] Hoskyns's father gave him £100, and he departed, first for a month to an Englishman who taught German by a crash course—no English allowed either in conversation or by letter. After this, he went to Berlin and sat under Harnack, the great liberal theologian, against whose standpoint he came to join the reaction. More importantly, he entered the orbit of Albert Schweitzer, and also of Adolf Schlatter, a fairly conservative critic,

---

[1] Cf. Raven, C. E., *A Wanderer's Way.* (London 1928), pp. 78f. quoted in Dillistone, F. W., *Charles Raven.* (Hodder and Stoughton 1975), pp. 59f. '. . . I was unwilling to do so, partly from fear of strange places and a foreign tongue, partly because I was getting bored with academic life and found the prospect of a further period as a student distasteful, and partly because desiring to be in a position to marry it was unsafe to count solely upon a fellowship.'

whose concern was with the theology of the New Testament. But more significant at this time than individual influences was Hoskyns's entry into the world of German theology, which, even when Harnack was in the ascendant—indeed not least then, had a passion and urgency lacking in Cambridge. This made its impact on the rather slow, some thought rather stupid, young man, and called out the intensity of his own nature. Though he was not uncritical, particularly of the separation of theology from the religion and life of the German churches, his experience sounded depths of his being which Anglicanism had not touched. In his spare time in Germany he sang *lieder* under the tutelage of a Fraulein Schmidt, and rowed on the Spree.

Priesthood and War Service

Back home, Hoskyns spent a year at Wells Theological College, and then, in 1908, went to serve his title at St Ignatius, Sunderland, a mining parish founded in the expansion under Bishop Lightfoot. He had been offered a curacy at St Mary Redcliffe, Bristol, nursery of bishops. But he had no such ambitions. He had seen enough of his father's life.

In Sunderland he spent much of his time at the daughter church of St Polycarp. There are octogenarians who remember him yet. He liked preaching at this stage, and helped to produce the Parish Cantata. After Evensong, on most Sundays, he would bicycle to Seaham, where Alec Ramsbotham, married to a great friend of his sister, Evelyn, was Vicar. Ramsbotham was an authority on church music, particularly of the Tudor period. Hoskyns and he would sing Schubert, Schumann, and the rest until midnight, when, fortified by tea, they would turn to plainsong, at which point the infant John Ramsbotham, Hoskyns's godson, future pupil, and in later life Bishop of Jarrow and Wakefield, would wake up. He also travelled to Germany to give two lectures in the University of Tübingen— one on the Oxford Movement, the other on the Jesuit Modernist, George Tyrrell.

In 1912 Hoskyns became Warden of Stephenson Hall, a hostel for Church of England men at Sheffield University. This may well have been on the recommendation of Foakes-Jackson. But the onset of war saw him volunteer for chaplaincy service. He became chaplain to a battalion of the Manchester Regiment in 1915, and served in the Middle East, India, and on the Somme; by the end of the war he was Senior Chaplain of the Sixth Division.

His letters survive. They are full of alert, intelligent, and intellectual comment. In Egypt he learned Arabic and observed the Copts and the Muslims at close quarters. He is critical of Anglo-Catholicism because it has not seen further than Rome and is so bedazzled and hypnotized by that relationship that it neglects the Catholicism both of the Orthodox tradition and of the Celtic Church which Rome suppressed. He is grateful to have had F. C. Burkitt's lectures on Eastern Christianity, and Anglo-Catholics in their lust for authority should learn that the better understanding is not with magisterial Rome but with the East, which 'has unconsciously been trying to say—that authority is in the traditional life handed down and expressed in its worship, government, creeds, discipline, etc. and that there is no such thing as external authority'. He doubts whether Muslims should be proselytized; certainly not by pietistic evangelicals whose individualistic doctrine of the atonement is unrelated to the Church and the communal life; rather should Christians seek the purification of Islam.

He admires Rome greatly, of course, and at their best the Roman priests offer men in desperate need the gospel of forgiveness and a moral theology which Anglicans lack. Above all, they have the Mass as central to worship and to life, whereas non-Roman Christians of the West are apt to regard this as a private solemnity for the particularly pious. They crowd Evensong, with its dangers of sentimentality, not the altar, which makes the absolute demands while giving the final succour.

Hoskyns has some interesting comments on liturgical reform, which anticipate what has taken place over weary decades since. He wants the aretalogy, the recital of what God has done, not only to include the Old and New Testaments but more recent events, though unadorned by romantic imagination or the pseudo-miraculous. There are glimpses of the Hoskyns of the future—a dislike of the superficial, the easy brilliance of a William Temple, the flat if vivid Christian humanism of Donald Hankey, which misses the meaning of the Church and the holy tradition, the officer cult of respectability and the school code. 'I long to sacrifice

38

an ox, and sprinkle its blood over the battalion, especially over the C.O.'

He was hopeful for the Church in the main, though he foresaw a desperate fight with obscurantism after the war; and the colonels, God-fearing and C. of E., were a menace to the future of Church and nation alike, charming, devoted, monogamous, but authoritarian, incapable of discussion with subordinates, treating their men as they do their horses, with extreme care but not as articulate human beings. 'They are the men who have built up our Empire, but unless we can change them, they will be the men who will make the word Empire unintelligible to the masses. . . . If we hold them up as pillars of the Church we shall fail, because we shall be backing up just that element in the nation which is doomed to complete impotence or worse.'

Hoskyns seems to have been beloved by all ranks. The Vicar of Dunmow in Essex, father of Francis House (later Head of Religious Broadcasting and Archdeacon of Macclesfield), incumbent of the very parish where the schoolboy Noel Davey was then residing, told of a visit to the Dunmow Clerical Society by a Congregational minister who described his service with a Lancashire regiment.

> One chaplain, he said, was simply worshipped by every man from the C.O. to the humblest private. He was always cheerful even in the most depressing conditions, and every one knew that he had again and again done brave things which in any other regiment would have brought him any number of medals. Besides all this, he was a true man of God. I asked for his name and found it was Hoskyns.

Hoskyns had written that honours were the invention of the devil, mostly given to the Staff and calculated to create the greatest possible amount of bad feeling between them and the men at the front. But on 1 August 1918 he was himself awarded the Military Cross:

> Under heavy shell fire he personally placed wounded in a safe place and was solely responsible for preventing them falling into the hands of the enemy. He remained with them until all had been evacuated, being slightly wounded himself. Next day he

shewed conspicuous courage in tending wounded in an exposed position under heavy shell and machine gun fire for nine hours without a break.

Before that, he had marched with the C.O. at the head of the battalion as they went early in an April morning to relieve a division in the front line. 'One of the company commanders came up to me and said—"Padre, we could not go into battle without you." It is little things like those which make life worth living.'

His own wound was slight, nothing more than a finger graze, and he emerged from the war as fit as he had entered it. Yet there may have been hidden strains which delayed their full manifestation for a score of years, and helped to bring about his untimely death.

He obtained his demobilization in February 1919 to take up the teaching of theology and a Fellowship at Corpus Christi College, Cambridge.

Corpus and His Fulfilment

The College of Corpus Christi and the Blessed Virgin Mary at Cambridge had sunk into academic decline during the long Mastership of the Conservative Evangelical, Edward Henry Perowne, from 1879 to 1906. Between dons and undergraduates there was a great gulf fixed, and the former showed little interest in the lives and academic progress of their juniors. Of natural science, there was virtually none. On Dr Perowne's death a vigorous new Master was elected, Robert Thomas Caldwell, the first layman to hold the office. His policy might be epitomized as 'new blood and new learning'. Within months, a young scientist from King's, Will Spens, had been made a Director of Natural Science, and in 1910, G. G. G. Butler, later Sir Geoffrey, and a nephew of Montagu Butler, the Master of Trinity, was brought from his uncle's college to develop historical studies. Other new Fellows included E. G. Selwyn, a classicist from King's, later first editor of *Theology* (1920–33), author of the Macmillan Commentary on 1 Peter (1946) and Dean of Winchester, whose first wife was Clement Hoskyns's sister, Phyllis, and K. W. M. Pickthorn, later Sir Kenneth, a historian of Trinity, who became one of the University representatives in

Parliament and member for the Carlton division of Nottingham-shire when University seats were abolished.

Men like this gave the college a new stamp, and under the Masterships of Caldwell's successor, Dr E. C. Pearce (1914–27), afterwards first Bishop of Derby, and Will Spens himself (1927–52), the Corpus Combination Room formed a distinctive com-munity, High Church and High Tory. As a pupil of Charles Smyth's wrote:

> Corpus Christi—C.C.C.
> Tory Anglicans are we.[1]

But this was somewhat exaggerated and resented when used as a taunt by Oxford men such as Isaiah Berlin. There was certainly no political test. Yet there was a deliberate reaction against the more resplendent King's, with its Bloomsbury links and its supercilious rationalism, personified by so engaging a character as Goldsworthy Lowes Dickinson, prophet of the League of Nations, whom both his biographer (E. M. Forster) and his bedder considered the best person they had known, but who was agnostic and not incapable of discrimination against Christians and churchmen. 'It was a recog-nized thing that no Kingsman who was prominently identified with the Cambridge University Church Society stood much chance of a fellowship at his own college: that is why Will Spens and Gordon Selwyn crossed the road to Corpus, and Stephen Gaselee (after-wards Librarian of the Foreign Office) became a Fellow of Magdalene.'[2]

Into this company Clement Hoskyns was elected while absent on chaplaincy service in 1916, and appointed College Lecturer in Divinity. It was a surprising choice, when the aim was to increase the academic standards of Corpus, for a second-class historian with no degree in theology at all was preferred to a technically equipped and able scholar such as, for instance, B. T. D. Smith. The Fellows were hesitant, but Will Spens overruled them—'We must have him.' Perhaps Gordon Selwyn, who was Spens's brother-in-law as well as Hoskyns's, had some share in it. But Foakes-Jackson, who by this time to Hoskyns's great sorrow and disappointment had

---

[1] Charles Smyth, 'A Page from the Past' (*Theology*, LXXVI, No. 642, December 1973), p. 647.
[2] Ibid., p. 648.

gone to be a Professor at Union Theological Seminary, New York, may have been directly or indirectly involved.

It had fallen to 'Foakey' as he was called, to preach the very first University Sermon in Cambridge after the outbreak of war, on the first Sunday of the Michaelmas term, 8 October 1914. He was fearful lest those obscurantists, whom Hoskyns too regarded as a danger, might blame German theology for the war. 'This will serve as a sufficient pretext for a reaction against all modernism in religious thought and for the discouragement of the application of the methods of scholarship to Christian problems . . . Unintelligent traditionalism will be followed by a wave of scepticism more fatal than anything in the past to Christian life and belief . . .'[1]

The preacher then went on to offer a critique of German church life as a warning to his own countrymen. German Christianity, he said, had little corporate existence, no collective voice; it was built on the personality of Luther and the ruins of the Reformation. At this point, in the version published in *The Cambridge Review*, there is a footnote which refers to a communication from the Reverend Clement Hoskyns, who told the preacher, 'I once read a paper on the Oxford Movement to the German pastors who were working in England. At the end, the leader of them (a pupil of Harnack's) said, "We have no Church, our Church is only a temporary erection based on the ruins of the Reformation and founded on the personality of Luther".'

It seems clear that much of Foakes-Jackson's sermon derived from what Hoskyns had reported of religion in Germany. His next point, for instance, laments the divorce between religion and speculative theology. Academic freedom had been purchased at this price. Schweitzer was an exception, but then he was Alsatian rather than German, and so nearer to the French.

And, lastly, German theology had minimized the figure of Jesus. God was much invoked in Imperial pronouncements; the name of Christ was conspicuously absent.

Will Spens and Geoffrey Butler from Corpus listened to this sermon with great approval. But as this final point was developed, the plea for Catholic Christology and the unequivocal declaration of the impotence of a Christianity without Christ was blurred in

[1] See *The Cambridge Review*, 14 October, 1914, pp. 16ff.

their ears by a somewhat liberal Protestant proclamation of God as Father of all men and a pious hope for post-war reconciliation in scholarship and the Church, which was a trifle inclined to sentimentality. This they dismissed as unadulterated 'Foakey'. What they had not forgotten nearly two years later was the contribution of Clement Hoskyns.

The story of his election to Corpus is an illustration of how sometimes a haphazard method of hunches and personal recommendation bordering on nepotism secures better results than the most scrupulous processes of appointment after advertising, short-listing, and interviews. Hoskyns was an infectious teacher and the Corpus results in theology were the envy of his classicist and historian colleagues. He was marvellously able to inspire men whose performance had hitherto been unremarkable, and they often achieved a higher class when they turned from one of the other disciplines to theology.

Not that he allowed them too much excitement at first! For him, there were no short cuts, and in the authentic Cambridge manner he discouraged speculative and creative flights until the feet were firmly grounded in the basic technicalities. When Edward Roberts, one day to be Bishop of Malmesbury and then of Ely, read his first essay to him on the synoptic problem, Hoskyns said, very gently, 'But Roberts, I asked you to state not solve the problem'.

He soon made 'The Theology and Ethics of the New Testament' his special subject. In those days, the Faculty of Divinity did not appoint lecturers. A Fellow of a College who wished to lecture would advertise his course in the University *Reporter*, and Deans of colleges and directors of studies would send along a few undergraduates to investigate the quality. If the course seemed useful, more would attend and the lecturer, who was paid by numbers, would become established.

Hoskyns had an enthusiastic lecture style. He was not witty, nor did he have a bank of jokes to be cashed annually at the same points of exposition; but he was possessed by his themes. And he incorporated new material each year in the light of his continuing research. It was said that his lectures were like sermons and his sermons lectures. Corpus Chapel restrained him more than the Divinity School. His vitality and excitement were in contrast to many of the other lecturers in the Faculty, impeccable, erudite, dry as dust. The young Kingsley Barrett, from a non-Wesleyan Methodist background, felt that this New Testament theologian was proclaiming the evangelical faith in which he had been brought up; the last year of Hoskyns's lectures, with death in the wings, fired his resolve to be a New Testament scholar. On the other hand, there were less devoted hearers, who would while away the hours by counting the number of times he used his favourite clichés.[1]

Hoskyns entered fully into college life and was never content merely to be 'the parson about the place'. He showed tremendous interest in the Boat Club and the Amalgamated Clubs, of which he was the treasurer, and proposed the alliance with Corpus Christi College, Oxford, which was concluded in 1926 and was the first of its kind, whereby the high table of each was opened to the other. He was given to hospitality. When he became President of the college, an old office equivalent to Vice-Master which had been revived in 1913, he exulted in preparations for the Feast. More important, he instituted a breakfast after the Sunday morning Eucharist to which members of the college were invited in small groups in turn. He felt it essential that he should know the undergraduates.

Hoskyns succeeded Geoffrey Butler as President on the latter's death. He had already followed him as Librarian. He soon had cards printed giving his name—by now Sir Edwyn Hoskyns, Bart —and his new dignity, and gained thereby immediate entrance to university and monastic libraries on the continent. He took particular interest in the great collection of manuscripts which Archbishop Matthew Parker had entrusted to Corpus, and, as *The Times* obituary put it, 'continued Butler's work of making it understood and accessible'. Two of the *Cambridge Sermons* are about the significance of the Reformation archbishop and his manuscripts at a time (1932) when Hoskyns felt that England was in danger of losing its nerve.

Music remained a great interest. He helped to appoint Boris Ord as Organ Scholar in 1919, and John Dykes Bower, later organist of St Paul's Cathedral, to succeed him, when he removed to King's. With Boris Ord he founded the Bene't Music Club, which met in

[1] Vidler, A. R., *20th Century Defenders of the Faith*. (SCM 1965), p. 91.

his rooms every Sunday evening of full term. Sir John Dykes Bower
writes:

> These weekly concerts, which were delightful social as well as
> musical occasions, were arranged by the Organ Scholar. From
> time to time the Organ Scholar found it difficult to make up a
> complete programme. Thereupon Clement would immediately
> come to the rescue by calling on his remarkable repertoire of
> *Lieder* by Schubert, Schumann, Brahms, and Wolf. I remember,
> as no doubt do other Corpus Organ Scholars, accompanying him
> in the whole of Schubert's *Die Schöne Mullerin* cycle and many
> numbers from *Die Winterreise,* all of which, of course, he sang
> in German. He did not have an outstanding voice, but he always
> sang with complete assurance: at the rare moment of un-
> certainty, the accompanist would hear a whispered exhortation
> —'Back me up, back me up!'. This exhortation would generally
> indicate the coming of a note slightly above his higher range, and
> at the moment of its approach he would almost instinctively rise
> up on his toes!

He established between Corpus and the Diocese of Winchester the
Wolvesey exhibitions, which began in 1925. Gordon Selwyn was
by now Rector of Havant en route to the Winchester Deanery, and
doubtless he had a share in the negotiations. The exhibitioners had
to be ordinands and were expected to obtain at least a second class
in the tripos. But if, while at Cambridge, an exhibitioner lost his
faith or his vocation, the college pledged itself to continue the
scholarship, though naturally the diocese contracted out.

Hoskyns was Senior Proctor of the University in 1921, and the
office had important personal consequences. During this academic
year a 'Grace' which would have enabled members of the women's
colleges, Newnham and Girton, to receive degrees was rejected.
A student mob 'celebrated' this by marching on Newnham and
breaking down its memorial gates. The Proctors were kept busy,
and the dons of Newnham also, and oral tradition has it that it
was in the course of this 'incident' that Hoskyns encountered a
young Research Fellow, Mary Trym Budden. She had recently
become an Anglo-Catholic, made her first confession, and experienced contrition and penitential joy. They had in fact met the
previous summer and were 'walking out' by the time of the demon-

stration. Indeed Hoskyns's proctorial negotiations with the Principal of Newnham interrupted the courtship. They were married in Little St Mary's, Cambridge, on 27 July 1922. The Master of Corpus, Dr Pearce, then Vice-Chancellor, officiated. Boris Ord played the organ. The Bishops of Southwell and Lichfield were present, and Gordon Selwyn celebrated a nuptial Mass.

In many ways his young wife's gifts complemented his; she a mathematician, he comparatively innumerate; she representing the new age of professional and academic womanhood, he from a more traditionalist background; she, like his mother in this if not in other ways, a suffragist and politically to the left, he a Tory. It was after he had proposed marriage that he told her, somewhat fearfully, of his likely succession to the title. She had never imagined herself allied to such dignity, but undeterred she gave him a secure home and bore him four sons and a daughter in the fourteen years and eleven months of their life together.

The Development of His Theology

Will Spens was not only a natural scientist but a lay theologian. Scottish Episcopalian by nurture and a strong churchman, he was well aware, as a rigorous and honest scientist, that the application of scientific method to the problems of Christianity made a naive faith impossible. It was not simply that the creation stories in Genesis could not be taken as scientific accounts : the historic basis of Christianity itself was called into question. Classic Christianity claims that Jesus was conceived by a virgin without male intervention, that he worked wonders in defiance of what the myths or models of the scientists have called 'the laws of nature', and that he was 'raised from the dead' so that the tomb in which he had been buried was found empty. But all this rests on documents which are somewhat fragmentary and confused, which were compiled some little time after the events, and which have little or no outside support apart from the continuing faith of the Christian community of those who, in each following age, have handed on belief in Jesus or been newly converted to it through their own experience.

Spens was impressed by the Roman Catholic modernists, who had been so harshly condemned by the encyclical *Pascendi Gregis* in 1907 and dispersed by the resulting heresy-hunt. He wanted a theology which would reconcile Catholic truth and scientific enquiry and provide for intellectual and spiritual freedom within the security of the Christian tradition. In 1915 he published a course of lectures on *Belief and Practice* (second edition 1917). This is a remarkable book, in some ways prophetic both of future ecumenism and of synodical government in the Church of England. Spens seeks to place the warrant for Catholic faith neither in Scripture nor in the oracular pronouncements of a supposedly infallible *magisterium*, but in continuing religious experience. He regards this as scientific. 'The theories of science have their significance in large measure, and have their primary authority, in the fact that they express, relate, and enable us to predict available experience.'[1] Thus 'if theological thought is to possess any high degree of authority, not only must such thought be closely related to experience, but the consensus of opinion must be a free consensus'.[2]

On 21 June 1917, Hoskyns wrote to his family from the mud and blood of the French battlefields:

> I am reading Spens's book very carefully, it is really quite first rate, but of course needs a great deal more working out; that will be our task after the war. It is a difficult book, and will require a great deal of simplifying and expanding, but it is a book which ought to guide men who have to administer dioceses, because it does open up a point of view which covers most of the questions under discussion, it makes freedom possible within the catholic tradition; personally I can see no other way out.

Doubtless this was his temper when he went to Corpus a year and a half later. He was a liberal Catholic, convinced of the necessity of the Church and the tradition and the centrality of the Eucharist, but suspicious of the Romeward and authoritarian tendencies of much Anglo-Catholicism, fearful of a drift into bigoted obscurantism, persuaded of a task of doctrinal restatement. He had written from Egypt in 1915, voicing sentiments which may be paralleled in much recent theological discussion:

> I cannot help thinking that it is along the lines of Dostoevsky's

[1] Spens, Will, *Belief and Practice,* 2nd edition. (Longmans 1917), p. 23.
[2] Ibid., p. 78.

Idiot that we may get nearer to a solution of the identification of Jesus with the Logos—Word—or Christ—which is the central fact of Christianity, and we may perhaps find a different method of interpreting the Incarnation, not so much in terms of 'coming down' and 'going up' but that when fundamental human nature is revealed it is in fact the Nature of God. Jesus being the revelation of fundamental human nature is also the revelation of the Nature of God; in this way we may escape from the blind alley into which the doctrine of the two natures has led us, and it may help us to grasp the fact which Catholic Christianity has up till now expressed in the only terms possible, namely the descent of the divine person from heaven and his ascent to heaven, having in that descent and ascent taken to himself human nature. Lake has grasped the Logos or the Christ but he funks the Incarnation and therefore has not explained what he sets out to explain; but Lake is on the right road in protesting against the popular deification of a man, into which popular protestantism has drifted.[1]

Two years later, he writes from France that he has just finished Paul Bourget's novel *Lazarine*. 'Certainly the French Catholic modernist has a very firm grip on the meaning of Christianity.' English religious fiction is shallow in comparison, either with no knowledge of irreligion or no understanding of the Church.

I am coming to feel that the real point we have to deal with is—are we to regard the person of Jesus Christ as an isolated person or not? and then if not isolated in what sense can we share his nature and person? If he is to be isolated, Christianity seems to be left high and dry, and its doctrines entirely out of touch with us. If we bring him into touch with us we run the risk of losing the revelation of Christianity; that is I believe the real point we have to tackle. I have enjoyed Bourget because rooted in the life of the Church and yet perfectly in touch with the life of the French, he brings the two together. . . . I find myself getting

[1] The reference is to Kirsopp Lake (1872–1946), New Testament scholar and church historian, who might have been at Trinity, Cambridge, from 1913 had not Geoffrey Butler's uncle regarded him as dangerously unorthodox. Instead he went to America. It is not clear to which of his writings Hoskyns refers. By 1916 he had published *The Historical Evidence for the Resurrection* (1907) and *The Earlier Epistles of St Paul* (1911). Later he collaborated with Foakes-Jackson in *The Beginnings of Christianity* (1920–33).

Sir Edwyn Hoskyns as an army chaplain during the First World War

Noel Davey as a young man at Cambridge.

nearer to our religion, when reading the very modern novels of Bourget and Dostoevsky than by any other means. . . .

Now the Hoskyns of his wartime letters was not precisely the Hoskyns who thrilled the devotees of his lecture room in the last decade of his life. Nor indeed was the Hoskyns who began at Corpus. J. O. Cobham first attended his lectures on 'The Theology and Ethics of the New Testament' in 1921–2, and Hoskyns declared the aim of the study to be:

1. to describe the varieties of primitive Christian theology;
2. to describe the experience that lay behind these theologies and held them together;
3. to account for the development of theology in the New Testament;
4. to discover the original starting point of the Christian religion.

By the time Christopher Evans was listening to him in 1931–2, he was defining his subject in two rather turgid sentences, product doubtless of much wrestling:

> The study of the theology of the New Testament is concerned with the analysis and description of that energetic and specific faith in God which controlled Christian believers in the first century A.D., in so far as the books of the New Testament bear witness to that faith.

And:

> The study of the ethics of the New Testament is concerned with the analysis and description of the actual behaviour of those men and women whose thought and actions were, during the first century A.D., controlled by specifically Christian faith in God, and of the nature of the forces which directed their concrete behaviour, in so far as the books of the New Testament bear witness to such behaviour and such forces.[1]

'Experience' has been dropped; 'faith' comes in. He had become less tentative, more convinced; a stronger critic of what to him was bogus and delusory; more ardent in his proclamation that we live

[1] Evans, C. F., *Explorations in Theology* 2 (1977), p. 101.

on a veritable tight-rope and can walk by faith alone; more hectic in his contentions, more numinous in his effect.

What accounted for the change?

He had always been impressionable and sensitive, eager to grasp and discuss ideas, not tossed by every wind of doctrine nor put off course by each book he read or theologian he encountered, but deeply responsive to the needs of his time as he saw them, while apt to mistrust easy solutions and not inclined to jump on bandwagons however glorious the goal to which they crowdedly careered.

He remained constant in his alertness and exuberance, which increased rather than diminished as he grew into his work. Pedestrian dogmatism and bitterness of soul were alike alien to him. He was temperamentally allergic to pietism of all kinds and to the churchiness of Anglo-Catholics—he could never learn the 'Anglo-Catholic walk' in church at Sunderland—and he charged them with lack of 'moral dignity'. In Egypt he got on splendidly with a Norfolk doctor: 'He is a very unchurchy person . . . and we have great talks on theology and I always find myself with him versus Hargreaves, the Church Missionary Society doctor', who was more interested in prayer meetings than in doing his own work. Years later, he developed nausea while conducting a retreat at Kelham and got through on brandy and water. When, in 1930, year of a Lambeth Conference, he led a retreat at Cuddesdon attended by many visiting bishops, he chose no 'mystical' or devotional theme or 'fragments of a modified scholastic philosophy', but John 13, which he interpreted in terms of 'surrender'. He asked the Principal, Eric Graham, to find someone else to hear confessions. 'Oh, but the confessions of priests are so interesting' rejoined Graham. But Hoskyns was adamant. Not that he was by any means opposed to the practice of confession, but if the retreatants talked to *him,* he wanted it to be about the Scripture and the gospel, not a grubbing around in their own souls.

Very near to the end of his life, when his excitability was perhaps tending to imbalance, he took Noel Davey and Christopher Evans for an afternoon walk in the Cambridge streets. He was keen to show them a saddler's shop in Pembroke Street, shades of the landed gentleman, and then they went into Little St Mary's, the Anglo-Catholic church in which he had been married and where he sometimes officiated. It was then even more heavy with incense than now, and the nave and sanctuary were less austere with more statues and images. A woman was kneeling at prayer and Davey instinctively lowered his voice. Hoskyns cried out, 'Are you afraid of the prayers of a pietist?' And remarking on the absence of any lectern with the open Bible on it, he exclaimed, 'You see, it might be a temple of Serapis!'

There is no doubt that the sentiments of Karl Barth's *Römerbrief* would always have found approving echo: 'Religion is not a thing to be desired and extolled; it is a misfortune which takes fatal hold upon some men and by then is passed on to others.'[1] Adolf Schlatter, another influence, attacked the notion that the New Testament contains not theology but religion. For him, theology deals with our relation to God, which moves us *totally*. Religion is intellectual. 'Because, through God's relationship with us, knowledge of God comes to relate us to him, the New Testament is consciously and irreconcilably opposed to every form of thought which is only meant to produce a religious concept'.[2] These sentiments were heightened with the years, but would always have been *sympathique*. And Hoskyns was always, in one sense, a humanist. He loved life to the full and believed that the Crucified, through his resurrection, gives us back the whole world, which sin, not God, has taken away. He read *The Farmer and Stockbreeder* as well as the Bible. He was disturbed by conscience-ridden priests and others who could not simply accept good things when they came.

He was always convinced of the importance of scholarship, and he revelled in combination room discussions, for, as J. O. Cobham has said, 'he assumed that the scholar in every field, history, classics, medicine, law, science would encounter the same problems of our human condition as he himself found in the New Testament.'

He was a staunch opponent of Fundamentalism. As a protest against the reinterpretation of Christian faith in terms of the latest intellectual fashion, or as a criticism of the 'intolerable dogmatism' of some biblical critics, it had point. In a sermon preached in Corpus Chapel in the Michaelmas term of 1928, he used the musical analogy to illustrate the correct meaning of 'fundamental':

---

[1] Barth, Karl, *Epistle to the Romans* tr. E. C. Hoskyns. (OUP 1933), p. 258.
[2] Schlatter, A., *The Theology of the New Testament* and *Dogmatics* tr. Robert Morgan in *The Nature of New Testament Theology*. (SCM Press 1973), p. 162.

Musically it is applied to the lowest note of a chord and denotes that upon which a chord depends. Or it means a note or tone which contains within it a whole series of harmonies. The fundamental bass, for example, generates a chord or harmony. The fundamental tone generates harmonies. Music as we know it consists in bringing out into the open the whole wealth of harmony and the delicacy of the harmonics contained in the fundamental bass.

By analogy therefore, Fundamentalism is the claim that the biblical language does contain within it the truth of religion, and if we steadily refuse to blaze forth that language, we shall inevitably miss the truths which it generates, and which it enables us to hear.

In this sense the word fundamental does but describe the prime activity of the Church. But unfortunately the Fundamentalists mean much more than this. They assert that the Bible is the ultimate foundation, and they refuse to allow any serious attempt to bring out the harmonics secreted in the Bible. There is therefore no place left either for biblical criticism, or for theology, or for philosophy, or for the possibility that other fields of study can throw any light on the importance of the biblical material. This is something very different from returning to the importance of the Bible. It is returning to the crudest possible theory of verbal inspiration. And its results are disastrous. First it leads to an almost complete disappearance of that charity to all men which is the test of all true religion, and in particular of the Christian religion. Secondly, it is productive of that pride which makes men almost unteachable. Thirdly, it seems to end in actual misunderstanding of the Bible itself. The third effect is perhaps the most serious because the lack of charity and the pride which Fundamentalism seems to engender are in a large measure the result of this subtle biblical misunderstanding.[1]

Hoskyns was also unwavering in his belief in the necessity of the Church. At Corpus, immediately after the war, he and the Master, E. C. Pearce, and Will Spens reordered the chapel life to make what was, in effect, the 'Parish Communion' at 8.30 a.m. the main service of Sunday. The rite was 1662 and there were no vestments.

---

[1] Hoskyns, E. C., *We are the Pharisees.* (SPCK 1960), pp. 66–7.

which would have 'split the college from top to bottom'. Nor was there a sermon. Hoskyns saw the Church as the community of believers gathered round the altar of the Lord and this was the focus of the whole of Christian life. Later on, from a different standpoint, he was still convinced, indeed more than ever, that Christianity was churchmanship.

In a sermon preached in the Easter term of 1928, he said :

Can you see that the word Church is a more real word than the word Christian? A Christian means a man who exhibits the spirit and follows the precepts and example of Christ. 'To be a Christian', said Dean Farrar, 'is to act as Christ acted'. Can you or I dare to arrogate to ourselves such a title? Or can we even accept its application to ourselves without indignant repudiation? How rarely the word Christian occurs in the New Testament compared with the word Church! And this is significant. The word Church, as we have seen, suggests the people of Israel, sinful, disobedient, thoroughly unsatisfactory, and yet possessing the revealed Law of God, chosen by God to proclaim not their goodness or their righteousness but His power and His mercy. So it is with the Church. We dare not claim anything for ourselves. We, as those outside, are under the judgement of God. But as men of His *Ecclesia,* we possess the word and wisdom of God; we share in the worship of God in spirit and in truth. We are, or should be, witnesses to the truth, with no real power of confidence in our power to explain or interpret according to the wisdom of men, with no desire to set ourselves up as models of righteousness, but confident that the revelation of God, I will not say *stands* in the Bible, in the sacraments, in the creeds and in the Christ, but occurs, acts, is energetic and effective through them.[1]

Liberal Protestantism had little allure for Hoskyns. He had parted from Harnack in the course of studies carried on at Wells and Sheffield after his return from Germany. He could not sympathize with liberal Protestants' nervousness about the logical extension of the higher critical method into 'form criticism', and their easy certainties that they had the key to final Christian understanding through the reconstruction of the Jesus of history by the selection

[1] Hoskyns, E. C., *Cambridge Sermons*, 1970 edn. (SPCK), p. 77.

of those features in the Gospels most congenial to the enlightened twentieth-century mind. Hoskyns felt it impossible to discover— certainly in the most primitive Christian writings—a Jesus intelligible and inoffensive to the cultured, tolerant Englishman of Oxbridge, the Jesus of such noble and moving hymns as 'O Thou great Friend to all the sons of men', or 'O Son of Man, our Hero, strong and tender', proclaiming God's Fatherhood and human brotherhood, a Christ, above all, gentle and pacifist. Schweitzer had shown that the original Jesus was apocalyptic and strange, and so had the Roman Catholic modernists. Hoskyns was, as he confessed in a letter to Alec Vidler, part of a somewhat uneasy exchange, held for a time by Loisy and saved from the more depressing consequences of the liberal-radical criticism of the New Testament by the latter's faith in the Church as 'an altogether bigger thing than the particular beliefs and practices of primitive Christianity'.[1] In 1926, he wrote in his contribution to *Essays Catholic and Critical,* that the modernists :

> ... maintained that Catholicism is the result of a development in which the Gospel of Jesus formed but one element. The dogmas of the Church and its sacrificial sacramentalism are pagan in origin; and for that reason can be shown to correspond to demands essentially human. Catholicism is a synthesis between the Gospel of Jesus and popular pagan religion; and because it is a synthesis, Catholicism can claim to be the universal religion.[2]

But that essay on 'The Christ of the Synoptic Gospels' showed the weakness of both Protestant and Catholic liberalism when confronted with what the Gospels actually say. It was not so earth-shattering and influential as Roger Lloyd's lyrical account of it in his rather selective and complacent *The Church of England 1900– 1965* would assert. Lloyd indeed presents it as Hoskyns's major contribution, which it most certainly was not.[3] But it was important in its time, and in its conclusions :

---

[1] See Vidler, Alec, *A Variety of Catholic Modernists.* (Cambridge 1970), pp. 188ff.

[2] *Essays Catholic and Critical* by members of the Anglican Communion, ed. Edward Gordon Selwyn. (SPCK 1926), pp. 158–9.

[3] Roger Lloyd's book, a revised and continued edition of a work in two volumes brought out by Longmans in 1946 and 1950, was published by SCM Press in 1965. It has all the virtues of Canon Lloyd's easy style, but it has some astonishing omissions – no reference at all, for instance, to Charles Raven.

The contrast is not between the Jesus of history and the Christ of faith, but between the Christ humiliated and the Christ returning in glory. . . . The contrast is not between a reformed and unreformed Judaism, but between Judaism and the new supernatural order by which it is at once destroyed and fulfilled : not between the disciples of a Jewish prophet and the members of an ecclesiastically ordered sacramental *cultus,* but between the disciples of Jesus, who, though translated into the sovereignty of God, are as yet ignorant both of his claims and of the significance of their own conversion, and the same disciples initiated into the mystery of his person and of his life and death, leading the mission to the world, the patriarchs of the new Israel of God. The contrast is not between an ethical teaching and a dreamy eschatology, or between a generous humanitarianism and an emotional religious experience stimulated by mythological beliefs, but between a supernatural order characterized by a radical moral purification involving persistent moral conflict and the endurance of persecution, and a supernatural order in which there is no place either for moral conflict or for persecution.[1]

This reconstruction, so different from that of the liberals, frees the historian from assuming that some 'foreign' influence diverted the channels of Christianity between the crucifixion and the letters of St Paul. There is a spontaneous development, so Hoskyns claims, between all the New Testament writings and the literature of the Catholic Church of the second century, and 'there seems no reason to doubt that the characteristic features of Catholic piety have their origin in the Lord's own interpretation of His own Person and of the significance of His disciples for the world.'[2] This is very much the thesis of Hoskyns's 'Congress' pamphlet, *Christ and Catholicism,* three years earlier, as to some extent it is of *The Riddle of the New Testament* (1931).

In all this we may trace some development, but no fundamental change. He was throughout an un-churchy churchman, a believer in critical method and intellectual freedom, and convinced that 'liberal' solutions were too tidy and selective and did not sufficiently reckon with those elements of the authentic tradition which were

[1] Hoskyns in *Essays Catholic and Critical,* pp. 176–7.
[2] Ibid., p. 178.

both a stumbling-block to the modern mind and the proof that Catholicism was no false path but followed in one straight line from the synoptic Gospels to the apostolic Fathers.

But we have to reckon with four great influences during the period 1919 to 1937.

1. *His Continuing Associations with German Scholarship*

In 1923, Hoskyns preached three sermons on 'The Idea of the Holy' at the time when Rudolf Otto's great book was first appearing in English. He encouraged J. O. Cobham to go to Marburg to sit under Otto, Friedrich Heiler, Rudolf Bultmann, Paul Tillich, and others. By 1930 he was *au fait* with form criticism. *The Fourth Gospel* shows a mastery of continental scholarship, and his copy of Adolf Schlatter's *Der Evangelist Johannes* (1930) was tattered with constant use. But the two most significant influences were undoubtedly Gerhard Kittel and Karl Barth.

Gerhard Kittel was the son of a famous Old Testament scholar and was born at Breslau in 1888. He became a Professor at Tübingen in 1929, but Hoskyns probably first encountered him through a book published three years earlier, *Die Probleme des Palästinischen Spätjudentums und das Urchristentum.* They met as a result of the Stockholm Conference at two conferences of British and German theologians convened by G. K. A. Bell and Adolf Deissmann in 1928 and 1929 at Canterbury and Wartburg respectively. The resulting volume was *Mysterium Christi* (1930), to which Kittel contributed his famous paper on 'The Jesus of History', which first gave wide provenance to the phrase 'the scandal of particularity'; and Hoskyns wrote on 'Jesus the Messiah'. Gordon Selwyn in a letter to Lady Hoskyns in 1951 regards this as possibly his best piece of work, 'so clear and decisive'. In it he refers to Kittel's 1926 book, which to Hoskyns convincingly established 'the messianic background of the intensity of the moral teaching of Jesus'. Hoskyns is clearly moving towards the conviction that the biblical revelation, however unsophisticated, should control the work both of the Christian dogmatist and the Christian philosopher, neither of whom must obscure 'the particularity of the Old Testament' or refuse to recognize that 'in the end' this is only intelligible in the light of its narrowed fulfilment in Jesus the Messiah, and of its expanded fulfilment in the Church.[1]

After the Wartburg Conference, Hoskyns, at Kittel's invitation, gave a lecture at Tübingen on the Church of England, which was attended by both Protestants and Roman Catholics. He stayed in the Kittel household, and Frau Kittel helped him with his German. But the chief importance of Hoskyns's association with Kittel was in their common study of the words of the Bible. Kittel was the editor of the *Theologisches Wörterbuch zum Neuen Testament,* which Hoskyns introduced to English readers by an article in *Theology* in 1933. But he may have anticipated this by his own studies, to which Kittel later bore testimony. In 1932–3, Hoskyns preached a course at Corpus on *The Vocabulary of the New Testament: The Language of the Church,* but the most quoted sentence of his on the subject comes from one of his sermons on *Sin* preached *five years* earlier:

> Can we rescue a word, and discover a universe? Can we study a language, and awake to the Truth? Can we bury ourselves in a lexicon, and arise in the presence of God?[2]

The fashion started by Hoskyns and Kittel of investigating the development of language through theological influences has now passed, killed off by Dr Austin Farrer, Professor James Barr, and others, as well as by the exaggerations and fancifulness of its practitioners. But it is interesting that these studies were contemporaneous with the beginnings of linguistic philosophy, and that in 1976, Professor Raymond Williams provided *Keywords : A Vocabulary of Culture and Society,* which for complexity makes Hoskyns's Corpus sermons, about which some of his hearers grumbled, almost like Sunday School lessons, and yet which illumines brilliantly the whole of our common life. Hoskyns saw words as forged in living experience and capable of change under the power of spiritual influences. To study them was to learn not only of history and culture but of faith and, possibly, to 'arise in the presence of God'.

[1] Bell, G. K. A., and Deissman, Adolf, ed., *Mysterium Christi.* (Longmans 1930), p. 89.
[2] Cambridge Sermons, p. 70.

Hoskyns never met Karl Barth, but he probably read the second edition of the commentary on *Romans* published in 1921. On 24 March 1924 he wrote to J. O. Cobham:

> I find Barth, from a scholarly point of view, a dangerous book: it is passionately written, contains very good stuff, but too desperately German, and apt to lead to sentimentalism which is what he himself does not intend; but preserve us from his disciples! On the other hand, he raises the right questions and I can well understand Bultmann's general but qualified approval.

He was to quote Bultmann far more in his lectures. In January 1928 he reviewed *Karl Barth's 'Kritische Theologie'* by Dr Th. L. Haitjema translated into German from the Dutch by Peter Schumacher, for *The Journal of Theological Studies.*[1] The review is expository both of Barth and the Roman Catholic lay theologian Jacques Maritain, who was moving along similar lines, but 'there emerges an uncomfortable suspicion that whereas Maritain might understand Barth, Barth has as yet shown no glimmering of a perception of the significance of that Catholicism by which men like Maritain are moved and redeemed'.

In his exposition, Hoskyns writes: 'The assumption which underlies everything that Barth writes is that God is God and men are men, and that the line which separates the two can be crossed neither by human thought, nor by human experience. . . . The problem is therefore not what Barth thinks about God but what God thinks about Barth. . . . Not what Barth thinks about Jesus Christ but what Christ thinks about him and how the Word of God judges him.' Those lucid expository sentences do not disclose Hoskyns's own hand, but about the time he was composing the review, he preached a sermon in Chesterfield Parish Church, on the foundation of the diocese of Derby. We have already referred to this. Hoskyns had a dual interest in that the new diocese had been carved out of his father's Southwell, and its first bishop was the Master of Corpus, Dr E. C. Pearce. He pays tribute to both men, and goes on: 'But it is not to the honouring of men, of human personalities that I would direct your attention primarily this evening. . . .'

[1] *The Journal of Theological Studies*, Vol. XXIX, No. 114, p. 202.

The Church exists in the world only to bear witness to the power of God, to His sovereign, regal power and holiness, to His miraculous power and glory, and just in so far as the Church bears her witness, you and I are brought under the judgement of God, stript and naked of all pride in human achievement and human intellect, sinners, miserable sinners. It is not what we think about God that matters but what he thinks about us; it is not what we think about Christ and the Church and the scriptures which is of any great value, but how we are judged by the word of God and his Son, Jesus Christ.

The language is almost identical to that of the review in which Hoskyns is expounding Barth objectively and going on to show his limitations. In the sermon, he makes such language his own, as he continued to do for the rest of his life.

The process was aided by his translation of Barth's *Römerbrief* into English, which was published in 1933. This was a remarkable achievement, which involved immense labour, meticulous care, and an ability to enter into the author's mind, which is a rare gift even among scholars. Seldom can a theologian have been so well served in his translator.

Hoskyns often expressed his reservations about Barth. He did not relish the forthcoming *Church Dogmatics,* which he anticipated wearily as 'one more system'. He once said to Charles Smyth, 'Barth is quite right about man, but quite wrong about God!' He told Noel Davey that he was unhappy about the Barthian division between creation and the knowledge of God. 'A Letter from England' written in 1936 for the *Festschrift* for Barth's fiftieth birthday is brief and notable for its omissions.[1] But it applauds Barth's definition of theology as *ministerium verbi divini,* it welcomes him as an ally in the fight against the characteristic English substitution of piety for theology and for the paradoxical truth, of which Hoskyns's unpublished papers are full, that the relevance of the Bible and of the Christian faith lies not in their compatibility with our civilized and rationalistic notions, but in their strangeness.

In this sense, Hoskyns often spoke in Barthian tones. And those students who wrote on his blackboard an advertisement slogan of

[1] Reprinted in *Cambridge Sermons,* pp. 218ff.

the day and then significantly altered it were not misrepresenting him:

Barth, I take it!

2. *The Politics of the Right*

Hoskyns was inevitably Tory in politics as he was Anglican in religion, but the years spent in the Corpus combination room, as well as the suspicions of populist movements and idealisms which his theology engendered, were inclined to confirm and strengthen his political attitudes.

At Suez in 1916 the Lancashires held a debate on the motion, 'That the experience of the present war would make warfare between civilized states impossible in the future'. The proposer was a young socialist, who had, none the less, enlisted:

> He made me realize the idealism of some of these younger Socialists as never before. The other speakers all emphasized the teaching of history and the fact of human nature, and he asserted that human nature and history could be changed, and must be changed, after the war. It struck me as he was speaking that he had got hold of the fundamental truth of Christianity . . . History will prove him wrong as it proved the early Christians wrong, but it is men like that who make other men better men. What a problem eschatology is! and yet without the belief that something tremendous is about to happen we are degraded to mere common sense which will not move a flea . . . I could not help pointing out the parallel between that attitude and the attitude of the early Christians.

In Cambridge twenty years later, Hoskyns would not have written like that, possibly because such idealism had possessed the minds of so many and Hoskyns saw its dangers in the world of *realpolitik*. One night in a discussion at King's, the Provost, J. T. (later Sir John) Sheppard, in an emotional outburst described the young people of the 1930s being led like sheep to the edge of a precipice. 'What would you do?' he asked rhetorically. And after a silence Hoskyns, embarrassed, said, 'Push them over'.

He told that to Noel Davey on his return, with some self-reproach, and it doubtless kept him awake all night—'I have said a terrible thing'—but it illustrates the change.

In his letters from France he describes war as diabolical, 'there is no redeeming feature about it', though that was from the midst of especial devastation and atrocity. Later, he confesses that were it not for the killed he could enjoy battle. He certainly did not return as those whom Bernard Shaw cruelly called the 'shell-shocked chaplains', Studdert-Kennedy and Dick Sheppard. In his Armistice Day sermons he included some protest against the way in which Remembrance was observed in the late 1920s.

It appears as though we have permitted sorrow for the dead to absorb our observance. But rejoicing ought to be our chief note of the day, gratitude for a victory by which our country was freed from the human threat and the human tyranny. On the other hand, our horror ought to penetrate far deeper, till we recognize in war not a thing isolated and peculiar but one of the many signs that we all form part of a world enslaved and in active revolution against the holiness of God. The mere interruption of a comfortable security, or supposed security, seems hardly worthy of a mournful celebration.[1]

Those words are true to the Bible and to Christian faith, but they would have seemed unfeeling at a cenotaph, with many who still mourned with bitter personal grief the young men who had marched out to die. In 1934 Hoskyns preached more fully on the theme. 'The commemoration of Armistice Day requires a gospel to make sense of it,'[2] he said, and one must admire his effort to turn people's minds away from the shallow and sentimental, represented by such hymns as 'O valiant hearts' with their almost blasphemous talk of 'our lesser Calvaries'.

In 1932–3 he preached on the soldiers in the gospel story. Jesus never condemns the profession of the fighting man, never adduces against him the commandment 'Thou shalt do no murder'. The soldier is the parable of destruction, of God's wrath against evil. 'Death and suffering are never regarded in the Bible merely with horror, certainly not as the most terrible things in human life. No New Testament writer can adopt the attitude of modern writers to death or to suffering. Their horror is reserved for sin, not death; for rebellion against God, not for suffering. They long less for

---

[1] Ibid., p. 46.
[2] Ibid., pp. 164–9.

freedom from death and pain than for freedom from sin. And more than that, there can be no ultimate freedom from sin until sin is destroyed.' There is no idealizing of war, or of the military profession. 'War is a far more terrible thing to the Christian than it is to the ordinary pacifist; for it is the place where human pride receives its most obvious blow, and where sin becomes most clearly evident.'[1] Hard sayings indeed, which few would understand, the many being impaled between the exhilaration, callousness, and coarseness of the aggressive instinct, and the waste and horror of it all.

Corpus Toryism received its definitive expression in a booklet by Kenneth Pickthorn which was not published until 1944, in a series of *Signposts on Post-War Problems* issued under Conservative Party auspices.[2] This was not the political solution which was going to prevail in the aftermath of Second War hostilities, but some of its sentiments are still part of Conservative philosophy and have been revived in the 1970s. 'The conservative habit of mind' says the author 'conduces to a belief in original sin and therefore to tolerance, moderation, and a reality of consent.' 'Politics is the art of directing public force.' It has a limited objective, is not omnicompetent or capable of providing panaceas. Man is not simply a political animal and there is a 'transcending He' who 'escapes material constraints and baffles all human calculation', 'a religious not a political entity'. 'The oldest and most common form of materialism is the attempt to set up the Kingdom of God by force.' Virtue cannot be compelled—'least of all by making other men pay taxes'.

Hoskyns would have agreed, and on similar theological grounds, taking a totally different view from Anglo-Catholics such as his contemporary, Conrad Noel, and those who in the Eastern tradition base a whole spirituality on Deification—the belief that we are called to be partakers of the divine nature and must not set any limits to what God's grace can do in souls and in society. For Hoskyns, the tension between our sinful state and the perfection for which we are destined can never be resolved in this life. We must at once be in the world, conditioned by its relativities and

---

[1] *We are the Pharisees*, pp. 29–30.
[2] Pickthorn, Kenneth, *Principles or Prejudices*. Signpost Booklets on Post-War Problems, 1944.

sinfulness, and yet over against it. But the final solution does not lie 'just round the corner' and it is cruel to talk as though it did, for then we shall not be prepared for calamity if it comes, and we may be deceived into thinking that 'some imposed, false *cosmo-politan doctrinaire propaganda dogmatism'* is the gospel. And that way lies a retribution which our children may suffer more than we. (Hoskyns probably felt that nations pursuing their own self-interest, restrained by the balance of power and terror, holding also certain principles of Christian civilization, would guarantee peace and justice more effectively than a world organization with its tendency to humbug and hypocrisy. He could not share Goldsworthy Lowes Dickinson's faith in the League of Nations.)

We must also reckon with a historian's vocation to criticize received opinions and popular views. Thus at the height of the depression, with dole-queues ever-lengthening and poverty represented in most compassionate minds by slum-dwellers and hunger-marchers, Hoskyns asked his hearers to think also of the frustrated politician, and the Tory land-owner, 'struggling to keep together the heritage he has received from his father' for the good not only of his family but of the village; of the French statesman wanting to protect his country; of War Office officials militarily vigilant in a pacifist age. He snipes at Galsworthy and other popular novelists and by implication defends 'men of property'. 'The poor are not a fixed easily recognizable quantity of men and women'.[1]

But we must not think that Hoskyns's sympathies for youthful or any other idealism had totally dried up over the Corpus years. There is a very remarkable sermon of 1933, in the 'Vocabulary' course, on 'Quench not the Spirit', which includes these words as exegesis:

> Do not understand the Gospel in such a manner as to paralyse human romance or to crush human exaltation of spirit, or to damp down the desire for reformation, or to stifle the expression of human affection. Are not these movements of the spirits of men, even when they are altogether undisciplined, parables, witnesses, signposts by which we are led to conceive of the workings

[1] *Cambridge Sermons*, p. 135. Sir Desmond Lee has suggested that among present-day scholars, E. R. Norman, Reith Lecturer 1978, author of *Church and Society 1770 to 1970*, (OUP 1976), has something of Hoskyns's 'intellectual bite'.

and operations of the Holy Spirit of God? And if our spirits are thus related to the Spirit of God, do they not become more than parables and signposts and tokens and witnesses? Do they not become, in this relativity, genuinely and essentially related to God, manifestations of His Glory?[1]

Christians move along a path 'narrow and sharp as the edge of a razor' between idolatry—worship of some ideology or movement —and 'detachment and cynical aloofness'. He ends, 'We may perhaps have been wise for Christ's sake, but have we ever been fools for Christ's sake? Or, for that matter, have we ever been fools for the sake of any other proper or improper cause whatever?'

Did Hoskyns think back then to 'the hut in the desert, one little lamp, about 150 men, and in the middle . . . the young socialist trying to convince older and rougher men that human nature could be changed and appealing to them to change it'?

There is a rather distressing uncertainty over Hoskyns's attitude to the rise of National Socialism in Germany. His friend, Gerhard Kittel, joined the Nazi party in 1933, and, at first at any rate, Hoskyns was inclined to give Hitler the benefit of the doubt. The movement seemed to promise moral reformation over against liberal permissiveness and socialist millenarianism. He hoped too that it might lead to the reconciliation of Catholics and Protestants in Germany, which his letters after the Armistice, reporting his conversations with pastors and priests, show to have been much in his concern. And his theology prevented him from believing that Christianity could flourish only under a certain type of political system or from confusing social democracy with the Kingdom of God.

In 1933, Kittel gave a public lecture in Tübingen entitled *Die Judenfrage*. This, while eschewing Nazi myths of race and blood, and not descending to the most vulgar abuse and hatred, blamed the decadence of Germany on the assimilated and secularized Jew and advocated a form of apartheid and a separate Jewish Christian Church. This caused great distress among Kittel's admirers and aggrieved letters from, among others, Karl Barth in Basel and Herbert Loewe, Reader in Rabbinics at Cambridge. Hoskyns, however, seems to have had some arrangement with Fabers, through

---

[1] Ibid., p. 149.

T. S. Eliot, to publish an English version. One of his pupils, Richard Gutteridge, translated it with a friend, Robert Smith, but Kittel does not seem to have been willing to allow its distribution in England. He told Gutteridge, coldly, when the latter was about to leave Tübingen, 'I have nothing to give to Sir Edwyn.' Perhaps he was smarting from the sorrowful anger of such as Loewe. But Gutteridge did publish an article in *Theology* in 1933, which while not blind to the excesses and dangers of the Hitler regime, was not unhopeful because of those theologians like Kittel who were at the centre of the German-Christian movement and might help to give it 'a firm grounding in the word of God and the spirit of the Reformation'. Hoskyns had been through this piece sentence by sentence with Gutteridge and thoroughly approved of it.

As for Kittel, he and Hoskyns remained friends. Hoskyns persuaded the University of Cambridge to invite him to give two lectures on the compiling of the *Wörterbuch,* which were delivered on 20 and 21 October 1937 under the title *Lexicographa Sacra,* with Kittel wearing his Nazi membership badge, to the disgust of many. But, by then, Hoskyns was dead.

There is no evidence that he was ever awakened to the enormities of National Socialism, but we must remember that he died more than two years before the Second World War, and four or five before 'the final solution'. Anti-semitism, supported by the repeated scriptural attacks on the People of Israel for their obduracy and by early Christian hostility to 'the Jews' for their share in Christ's death and opposition to the infant Church, was much more prevalent among conservatives and catholics—witness Chesterton and Belloc —than it is now comfortable to recall. Neither do all liberals have a clean record here, and it is ironic that the 'German Christians' numbered many of those whose theological position Hoskyns most deplored, whereas Barth was the inspiration of resistance. But the loyalties of friendship are surely a dominant factor. Kittel was 'a gentle and warm-hearted person'. Arnold Erhardt, himself a refugee, once told Gordon Rupp that Kittel had helped many of the Nazis' Jewish victims, and he retained throughout the friendship of George Bell. When a delegation of British churchmen paid a first post-war visit to Tübingen, in 1945, and the commander of the French zone asked Bell, 'Have you any friends here?', Bell blushed and said, 'Yes, one, and you have put him in prison', meaning Kittel. Hoskyns, for his part, had a genius for friendship, and although it is sad that his support of Kittel caused coldness between him and Martin Buber, among others, the advantages and agonies of hindsight must not allow us wholly to condemn him for misjudgements not unconnected with one of his strongest and most engaging virtues.[1]

3. *Archbishop Parker and the Homilies*

It seems undoubtedly the case that Hoskyns became more of a Prayer Book man during the years of his work in Cambridge. The Parker manuscripts and his duty as Dean to instruct the college in the doctrines of the Church of England thrust him into the six-teenth century and this coincided with his development as a biblical theologian. He preached four sermons on Archbishop Parker in 1925, three on the Thirty-Nine Articles in 1929, a year's course on the Prayer Book in 1931–2, and the published sermons on the Parker manuscripts and the Homilies in 1934 and 1934–5. Included in the Prayer Book series are addresses on 'The Saints', The Psalter, The Litany, The Holy Communion, and 'The Prayer Book Non-Revolutionary'.

This gave him, what is rare in an Anglo-Catholic, an under-standing of the English Reformers, and he did not try to pretend that they were really not true Protestants at all. When he comes to

---

[1] For the whole subject see James Bentley, 'British Theologians and the Third Reich' printed in *The Listener* as 'The Most Irresistible Temptation', 16 November 1978; Robert P. Eriksen, 'Theologian in the Third Reich': The Case of Gerhard Kittel' (*Journal of Contemporary Theology*, July 1977), p. 595–62; Richard Gutteridge, *Open Thy Mouth for the Dumb! The German Evangelical Church and the Jews, 1879–1950.* I am also indebted to an unpublished paper by the Revd Richard E. Parsons on 'Hoskyns and Kittel'. Parsons and Bentley both reject as inaccurate a remark I made in *Robert Newton Flew* (1971), p. 84 and repeated in 'Hoskyns and Raven: The Theological Issue', (*Theology*, LXXVIII, November 1975), p. 574, that once Hoskyns knew of the nature of *Die Judenfrage* he 'was so shocked by its contents that he immediately saw the Nazi regime for what it was, renounced his interest in the book and drew away from his friend' (Kittel). They are right and supported by Gutteridge. Yet what I wrote in 1971 was approved by Noel Davey and by Donald MacKinnon. Three points must not be lost sight of: (i) Gutteridge testifies that Kittel was 'a gentle and warm-hearted person' (op. cit., p. 145, n. 67) and he was doubtless a loyal and valued friend. (ii) Bentley's assertion that 'Scholars, such as Sir Edwyn Hoskyns, seem to have gone out of their way to call attention to the anti-Jewish statements in the NT' cannot be substantiated in Hoskyns's case. He gave them no racist connotation, but used them against Christians – *We* are the Pharisees. (iii) There is no doubt as to where Hoskyns would have stood in 1939.

Cranmer's Communion Service, he does not repeat easy jibes about 'the mutilation of the canon'; he appreciates that this magnificent rite has a shape and a theology of its own. The 'ancient structure of the Church's worship is broken again and again to make room for the deep-seated cry for forgiveness', but this is not neurotic mor· bidity. It is a profound understanding of the human condition, as true of us as of our forefathers, and unless we grasp it we shall be corrupted by pride, which will destroy all our life and loves. And it is the presupposition of the gospel. 'While we were yet sinners Christ died for us.'

In the end Hoskyns's theology was completely Catholic and completely Protestant too. Properly understood, the two words are almost synonymous.

4. *The Bible*

Throughout all this period, Hoskyns lived in the Scriptures. They were his professional preoccupation; their exegesis was his constant labour; their gospel of divine action turned him from all classic philosophies of being. And the Bible did not cast a miasma of pietism over his pleasures and friendships, for it is the book of human life, of eating and drinking, marrying and giving in marriage, war and peace, birth, death, love, hate, the stars in their courses, and the cattle on a thousand hills. But he dare not make it his bedside book, else he would not sleep for the excitement of it. Then he turned to the Odes of Horace and medieval Latin lyrics, to Johnson, Fielding, and Sterne.

He found the clue to the interpretation of Scripture in its unity. First, the unity of the two Testaments. His essay in *Mysterium Christi* is headed by a quotation from Migne's *Patrologia Latina* in which Physiologus declares that 'the well-instructed Christian man must trust in the two Testaments as the ibex relies upon the strength of his two horns'. And *The Riddle of the New Testament* is constantly seeking for the explanation of Christ's works and sayings by reference back to the Hebrew scriptures.

There is an internal unity in the New Testament itself. In his letters from the front, Hoskyns toys with the idea of beginning the interpretation of the whole from 1 John. Christopher Evans has said that in moments of enthusiasm Hoskyns would even maintain that the whole of the gospel was to be found in 2 Peter and Jude.[1] Would he have found it also in The Revelation of St John on which he was to have written the Moffatt New Testament Commentary? But there is a numinous passage in which he proclaims the one great unifying theme of all the Scriptures:

> The Bible is held together by one great theme and its authors are moving along one line. The Bible writers are pushed on and on until they stand at the place where human achievement, human civilization, is seen to be less secure than it appears to be. The Bible writers are pushed on and on until human works, even good works, are seen to fail to attain their goal, until they are clearly seen to be, in fact, human. The writers of the books of the Bible have discovered that they are poor, that they have no secure place upon which they can stand. They have discovered that they are men and not God. They stand where the Tower of Babel falls; they have seen the Christ crucified; and they know that the road of progress is a barred road, that the line of development is a broken line. The Bible word for this barred road, for this broken line, for this scarlet thread that runs through human life is, of course, sin.
>
> The Bible writers are therefore moving along a precipice, along the same precipice over which you and I fall when we become cynical and sceptical, when we say that there is no truth, no righteousness, no peace, no ultimate life. But at the point where we stagger and fall, prophets and apostles and evangelists lift up their voices and sing Alleluia, the Lord be praised! At the time when everything looks black, when the Temple lies in ruins and the Christ is crucified, their faith bursts out, at the point where all are known to be poor and sinners and mortal, they cry, Forgiveness, resurrection, life—God.[2]

Yet 'the Bible is our protection against all attempts to simplify the Christian religion.'[3] It comes to us from an alien culture and in strange tongues. It is not intended to make faith easy, rather to deliver us from false simplicities, and from all 'movements', charismatic or political. He who runs cannot read it, only he who stays

[1] Evans, C. F., op. cit., p. 97.
[2] *We are the Pharisees*, pp. 6, 7.
[3] Ibid., p. 64.

and wrestles. And our longings for synthesis, for some universal philosophy embracing all faiths and civilizations are thwarted by 'the scandal of particularity'.

And here is the secret of Christianity. It depends on history, on 'rough, crude, history'. This was where Hoskyns parted company with Will Spens, for whom Christianity might still have been true had Jesus not lived. 'On the basis of a purely critical examination of the New Testament documents (the historian) can reconstruct a clear historical figure, which is an intelligible figure; and he can, as a result of the reconstruction, show that the emergence of the primitive Church is also intelligible.'

That quotation is found near the end of *The Riddle*. The book begins, and this the reviewer in *The Times Literary Supplement* found astonishing, with the Nicene Creed in Latin :

> When the Catholic Christian kneels at the words *incarnatus est* . . . he marks with proper solemnity his recognition that the Christian religion has its origins neither in general religious experience, nor in some particular esoteric mysticism, nor in a dogma. He declares his faith to rest upon a particular event.[1]

Hoskyns is aware that at this point there are two problems. The lesser is that the historical Jesus is not necessarily congenial to our time, one whom we may easily domesticate.

Hoskyns was inclined to take every opportunity of emphasizing the crudeness of the Gospels. Jesus is presented as 'a superstitious wonder-worker. He performs two cures with the use of saliva and certain manual acts. He spits upon the tongue of the stammerer, placing his finger into his deaf ears; he spits into the eyes of the blind man, and lays his hands upon him. Such a use of saliva was well known in antiquity.' Jesus muzzles the demons of the storm —this is the literal translation of the serene English, 'Peace! be still!' In John 6 when he talks of eating the flesh of the Son of Man and drinking his blood, the Greek verb '*trogein*' could be rendered 'to munch'. Hoskyns dwells often on the humiliation of the Jesus of history. 'The salvation of God occurred not in one who possessed plenary power or lived in the light of an open vision of his glory; it occurred in human faith and temptation and in a single, isolated

---

[1] *The Riddle of the New Testament*, Sir Edwyn Hoskyns, Bart., and Noel Davey. 3rd edn. (Faber and Faber 1947), p. 9.

figure.'[1] An unpublished paper accounts for the 'lost' ending of Mark on the assumption that the disciples' desertion of Jesus was so scandalous that it had to be suppressed. The Son of Man, the Son of God, died in abject misery and utter foresakenness. Here is God incognito. 'Verily thou art a God that hidest thyself, O God of Israel, the Saviour.'

But the greater problem is that though we must insist on a historical Jesus and in events which happened as truly as my eating breakfast this morning, the documents which report the history are far from scientific or objective, they are infuriatingly silent at vital points, which would not merely inform our curiosity but guarantee our belief, and they are entrammelled with myth and weird and unsophisticated theology which is sometimes an affront to our intelligence. When the history is the heart of the matter why is so much of completeness and accuracy denied us?

Hoskyns would answer that the theology controls the history, and that the uniqueness of the Bible lies in the fact that before all else it demands a decision.

> The visible, historical Jesus is the place in history where it is demanded that men should believe, and where they can so easily disbelieve, but where, if they disbelieve, the concrete history is found to be altogether meaningless, and where, if they believe, the fragmentary story of his life is woven into one whole, manifesting the glory of God and the glory of men who have been created by him.[2]

Hoskyns was perturbed by the neglect of Biblical Theology. His visits to Roman Catholic libraries at Rome and elsewhere disappointed him in those days, when the modernists had been condemned and Vatican II had not even been seen and greeted from afar. He was most courteously received, but saddened to think that the riches of Roman Catholic scholarship were not dedicated to the study of the Scriptures. Library walls were covered with St Thomas Aquinas and the Schoolmen and there might be one modest case of very traditional works on the New Testament. At Marburg, he met a student who was writing a thesis on the Holy Spirit. Hoskyns

[1] Ibid., p. 176.
[2] *The Fourth Gospel*, Edwyn Clement Hoskyns, ed. Francis Noel Davey. 1947 edn. (Faber and Faber), p. 85.

said, 'I shall want to know what you have to say about the Holy
Spirit in the New Testament.' 'Oh no!' said the student, 'I daren't
include anything about that, it would be much too dangerous.' But
some Roman Catholics were prepared to wait. In fifty years the
work of the reactionary Biblical Commission of 1905, under which
blight they lived, would be forgotten.

Work as a School Certificate examiner depressed him because of
the superficiality of much biblical teaching in schools. The received
opinions of liberalism were repeated again and again. And not all
tripos candidates were much better. Some of them were incapable
of appreciating that the elder brother in the parable had a case, that
the scribes and Pharisees *were* righteous, that Christianity was *not*
simply a religion of the heart, but made inexorable demands in the
flesh and the actualities of living. One candidate wrote: 'Jesus in
his ethical teaching transferred the emphasis from doing to being.
The righteousness which is in the heart is for him the fulfilment of
the law.' Hoskyns commented to Davey: 'I wonder what these
young men really make of the bloody, concrete scene of Crucifixion?'

Hoskyns, then, moved from a religion of experience to one of
revelation through history received by faith. He dreaded the escape
into spirituality, which was causing the Anglo-Catholics to ignore
historical and critical issues and, indeed, ethics; 'devotion' was more
important to some of them than either truth or behaviour. The
Scriptures should be interpreted 'critically rather than mystically'.
The threefold ministry has no independent 'mystique'. It is
authoritative and valid only because, so it is believed, it is 'organi-
cally linked to the witness which the apostolic eyewitnesses once
bore to the obedience of Jesus'. As for Will Spens, Hoskyns felt
that he was in danger of putting himself in the place of Almighty
God, because his solution to the problems of Christianity depended
so much on his own subjective responses and his sense of what was
fitting. 'After all,' said Hoskyns once to Davey, 'the humiliation
of Christ described in Philippians 2 might lead us to think that it
were more fitting that Christ should be born of fornication rather
than of a pure virgin, the self-abnegation would have been greater'.
Shortly afterwards it was Christmas, and Hoskyns sent Davey a
card with a prayer for 'a great deepening of faith at this time'. As
Kenneth Pickthorn once said, Hoskyns was 'incapable of assuming

that what he wanted for the times was what the Lord always intended'. He required something objective, greater than himself, in which to believe, and where the Church confirmed the biblical revelation, speculation might be, if not mortified, suspended. The tradition, too, was given and he took it gratefully and passed it on. He used to say that there were only two miracles. The rest might be theological interpretations of events which could be otherwise accounted for, and in any case, we must live not by signs but by faith. But the birth and resurrection of Jesus were unparalleled events, the entry of a unique person into the world and his departure out of it. Here, we are governed, not by the Bible alone, but by the Creeds, which select from Scripture those events by which we are saved.

The Cambridge Faculty of Divinity and the Years Since

'Is a theological faculty in a university true to its subject-matter, if it never be permitted to stray beyond a purely historical description of the Church in primitive and other times, or if it be permitted to stray, to stray only into speculative theology?'[1]

So Hoskyns to Karl Barth. And there is no doubt that he had the Cambridge Faculty in mind, for his theology was very different from that of his colleagues. For most of his time, they were dominated by Lady Margaret's Professor, Dr J. F. Bethune-Baker, who was not only a scholar of great learning and distinction, but very anxious that theology should be brought into the twentieth century, even though he sustained a Cambridge tripos that was purposely grounded in the study of Scripture in the original tongues and the history of the first five centuries. Hoskyns's disagreement with him is illustrated by a sentence from one of the Corpus sermons delivered as early as 1927:

> The Lady Margaret Professor of Divinity recently defined the immediate task of Christian theology to be the re-expression of Christian faith in terms of evolution. I would venture to suggest that the task of the Christian theologian is rather to preserve the

[1] *Cambridge Sermons*, p. 218.

Christian doctrine of God from the corrupting influence of the dogma of evolution at least as that doctrine is popularly understood.[1]

Many felt then and would feel now that Bethune-Baker, though a less vivid personality, more the traditional Cambridge savant, conceived and shaped in academe, prone to donnish sarcasm, was the more enlightened, the more aware of what was happening in the non-theological world and of the need to see God, if there be a God, in relation to the whole universe. In 1963, another Cambridge theologian, J. S. Bezzant, stated the issue in words which Bethune-Baker would doubtless have approved:

. . . there is no general or widely accepted natural theology. I know that many theologians rejoice that it is so and seem to think that it leaves them free to commend Christianity as Divine Revelation. They know not what they do. For if the immeasurably vast and mysterious creation reveals nothing of its originator or of his attributes and nature, there is no *ground* whatever for supposing that any events recorded in an ancient and partly mythopoeic literature and deductions from it can do so.[2]

Relations between Hoskyns and Bethune-Baker were not acrimonious, nor was there lack of charity, simply a difference of standpoint, which the following anecdote illustrates. The day that Hoskyns's youngest son was born, he met Bethune-Baker in Grange Road and dismounted from his bicycle to tell him the good news. 'Another priest for the Church of England,' he said. 'By the time he is old enough to be ordained', retorted the Professor, 'there will not be a Church of England.' And Bethune-Baker did say that he was selling every one of his theological books on retirement, and was described by Edward Wynn of Pembroke, later Bishop of Ely, as a 'destroyer of vocations'.

Hoskyns was usually in a minority of one in the meetings of the Faculty Board. There is an instance of an argument which will not endear Hoskyns to Free Churchmen. Bethune-Baker wanted the University Sermon, hitherto confined to Anglicans, to be open to preachers from the Free Churches. There was a great desire to

---

[1] Ibid., pp. 34–5.
[2] Bezzant, J. S., in Vidler, A. R., ed., *Objections to Christian Belief*. (Constable 1963), p. 107.

invite the revered Presbyterian from Westminster College, Dr Anderson Scott. Hoskyns had been alerted about this and had consulted Will Spens. When his turn came to express an opinion at the Committee, in addition to naming two Anglicans, he said, 'I should like to propose the Abbot of Downside.' 'Oh no, no, no!' said Bethune-Baker, 'I didn't mean that, I didn't mean that.'

The Faculty with its liberal regime, tended to be self-perpetuating. In 1932, the senior Divinity Chair, the Regius Professorship, fell vacant. This, in spite of its name, is not a Crown appointment, but is elective. The man voted in, though not according to W. R. Matthews, who was an elector, with very great conviction, was Charles Raven, a Canon of Liverpool, with a brilliant Cambridge record, and already famed as preacher, ornithologist, and liberal theologian.

In his life of Raven, F. W. Dillistone gives a characteristically able and illuminating account of the theological contrast between Raven and Hoskyns. In the one quotation which must suffice, he does it with reference to *Mysterium Christi*:

> . . . whereas Charles's theological interests had been aroused as he became aware of the wonder of *the world,* most of the contributors to *Mysterium Christi* had begun and sustained their theological concern by responding to the wonder of certain *words* and of the events to which the words bore witness.[1]

Where Dillistone is wrong is in his assertion that 'there was a remarkable polarization of theological teaching between Charles at Christ's and Hoskyns at Corpus'. Few theologians either senior or junior took sides, and there was no confrontation of parties or of persons.[2] When Hoskyns died less than five years after Raven's inauguration, Raven wrote a gracious obituary for *The Times*. In Hoskyns's lifetime, it was Bethune-Baker and his sense of isolation in the Faculty, which disheartened and frustrated him.

But Raven did not find Noel Davey *persona grata*. Some complained that Davey's lectures were unintelligible, and Raven disapproved of the University Sermon. The result was that his University lectureship was not renewed, and in 1942 he became Rector of Coddenham in Suffolk. He was happy there until, in

[1] Dillistone, F. W., *Charles Raven*, p. 208.
[2] See Vidler, A. R., in *The Guardian*, 12 February 1975.

1944, he joined Dr Lowther Clarke at the S.P.C.K. Never again was teaching to be the main business of his life.

To Raven, Davey, (and Hoskyns), became symptomatic of 'the great blight' which had attacked theology with the advent of Barth and those who seemed to narrow down God's revelation to the biblical events. He had hoped that he and his friend, Oliver Quick, had formulated a theology which could reconcile the whole of human life and thought in what Quick said were the two great sacraments, the Universe and the Person of Christ. Now came this new dialectic of paradox, strangeness, discontinuity, of a God who is in some sense a visitor to the world if not an invader from an alien realm, rather than one who is immanent, already in the world, even if 'the world' knows him not. All was made to rest on a decision of faith concerning one narrow point of history, while human endeavour seems to be discouraged because it is twisted by sin, and the long struggle of mankind towards a new order is doomed to failure from the start. And Raven himself felt isolated; not in the Cambridge Faculty of Divinity where he had control, but in the Christian world at large and especially among the younger exponents of biblical theology, who seem to have been marked by a more than usual arrogance—and perhaps also among scientists, for whom physics reigned supreme and eclipsed biology, which was considered 'soft' in comparison with that dynamic juggernaut.

Here we see one of the great divides of twentieth century theology. Time has moved on and the lines are not drawn where they were, but in spite of the passing cult of Teilhard de Chardin, about whom Raven wrote his last book in 1962, biblical theology has not been without its victories, some of them strange. Hoskyns would be astonished at some of those who might be more in his succession than Raven's. He would have been delighted by the setting free of scriptural scholarship in the Church of Rome. But the 'liberation theology' of Latin America uses biblical categories and paradigms, and the language of crucifixion–resurrection rather than of creative evolution, while many of the radicals of the 1960s were followers of Bultmann and denied knowledge to make room for faith, a faith so tested as to be able to contemplate the slogan 'the death of God'. On the other hand the past decade has seen a swing back to conservatism, a biblical exegesis armed with great learning which seems somehow never to engage with the radical questions. There is a strange new complacency abroad among many Christians of the West, which is astonishing when a 'theology of crisis' might seem to be demanded by the signs of the times. But British Christians are trying to feel their way back to security, while the spiritual vigour of Africa, for instance, springs from a point of history very different from ours, where what we may fear as Armageddon seems like Exodus.

Hoskyns's theology is vulnerable at several places. He had the gift which an old Cambridge don, F. A. Simpson, thought indispensable for a historian of being able to think of six impossible things before breakfast; but sometimes this led him into fancy. In a conversation with Stephen Neill, he said that he had seriously considered whether the reference in Hebrews 4.8 was not to Jesus Christ rather than Jesus-Joshua—'If Jesus had given them rest . . .' That is indeed an intriguing thought and true to Hoskyns's understanding, though the more obvious interpretation is surely what the biblical author intended.[1]

W. F. Howard had no difficulty in showing that the word *trogein* in John 6, which Hoskyns was so excited to regard as a very crude word for 'to eat', was perfectly common and normal in spoken Greek.[2] James Barr in *The Semantics of Biblical Language* (1961) singles out what Hoskyns and Davey have to say about *aletheia* in *The Riddle of the New Testament*. Kittel commended their treatment of this word. They claim that whereas for the Greek *aletheia* meant very much what the English 'true' means to us—'something genuine and not counterfeit, without emphasis on any particular standard by which a statement may be judged true or false, the Hebrew in his certainty of a transcendent God fixed upon him as the standard of truth'. Barr totally disproves this. Hoskyns and Davey are reading 'the pregnant and theological usages' in such New Testament phrases as 'the truth as it is in Jesus' back into the Old Testament and the Septuagint, and claiming that this is the distinctive contribution of the Bible as a whole.[3]

---

[1] Neill, Stephen, *The Interpretation of the New Testament 1861–1961*. (OUP 1964 p. 213. Neill antedates Hoskyns's 'Barthian conversion', though the process began when he read the second edition of the *Römerbrief*.

[2] See Howard, W. F., *Christianity According to St John*. (Duckworth 1943), Appendix, Note D, p. 205, where Hoskyns is not named.

[3] Barr, James, *The Semantics of Biblical Language*. (Oxford 1961), p. 19 ff

Hoskyns believed that the Bible was governed by theology. In his lectures, assuming the Papias tradition that Mark's Gospel rested on the reminiscences of Peter, he would imagine Peter being asked by some early enquirer, 'What do you mean by the forgiveness of sins?', and telling the story of the paralytic in reply. But is there one controlling theological *motif* of the whole of Scripture, as Hoskyns asserts in his eloquent passage about the scarlet thread?[2] Does he not impose a unity on the Bible, contrived from his own understanding of 'the Christ-event', which though supported by his studies is conditioned by his own temperament, his Catholic convictions, and the Protestantism of the Prayer Book and his German friends?

Those who do not find him congenial might seize above all on 'the scandal of particularity', which narrows down, in a way the New Testament does not, the significant moments of God's action to an infinitesimal fraction of the whole of time, and, as Dennis Nineham has said, 'seems to give to long periods of history what I might perhaps call a certain vacuous character'.[3] Hoskyns might well be unrepentant and argue that he does not deny the importance, indeed the crisis, of the whole of history and the life of man, but that it is all understood through God's act in Christ, and by the following of the way of crucifixion–resurrection in each aeon of the Universe.

Nevertheless, during his lifetime, such reservations as those of Oliver Quick, summarized by Donald MacKinnon, had their point:

Where the theological attitudes that Hoskyns's work seemed to encourage were concerned, Quick feared the extent to which they might encourage men to treat Christianity as a closed system and blind themselves to the manifold richness and complexity of God's working in this world, including the achievement of constitutional democracy.[3]

---

[1] See above, p. 68.

[2] Nineham, Dennis, *The Use and Abuse of the Bible.* (Macmillan 1976), p. 92, quoted from a lecture printed in the *Bulletin of the John Rylands Library,* Vol. 52, No 1, Autumn1969, pp. 186–7.

[3] Donald MacKinnon in an unpublished study 'Oliver Chase Quick as a theologian' written in 1974 and revised 1978, which he has kindly shown to me. In *The Gospel of Divine Action,* (Nisbet 1933) Quick has a critique of Hoskyns (pp. 107ff.) in which he regards him as the leading contemporary English exponent of Barthianism.

Many scholars have felt that Davey's essay on 'The Fourth Gospe and the Problem of the Meaning of History' is the least satisfactory feature of a work which was a landmark of theological expositior and is still to some extent unique in its combination of critica analysis, use of the Fathers, and theological penetration. R. V. G Tasker, for instance, had much to say in its praise . . . 'the most thoroughgoing *theological* commentary on the Gospel in English . . . strong linguistically and rich in its use of patristic commentaries and liturgical references . . . the masterly analysis of previous criticism of the Gospel'. But then the disapproval begins.

> The question Did Lazarus rise from the dead? we are told cannot be answered by a simple 'Yes' or a simple 'No', but we are not told how it ought to be answered. The plain man, however, knows that a historical fact either did or did not happen; and unless the writer of the Fourth Gospel is writing fiction, he will assume that the author really believed that Lazarus was raised.[1]

C. H. Dodd also was uneasy about the imprecision in dealing with the problem of historicity and his biographer, F. W. Dillistone, thinks that Dodd's monumental work on *Historical Tradition in the Fourth Gospel* (1963) may have been undertaken in order to try to repair this defect.[2]

Dodd certainly succeeds in showing that there is authentic history in John's source. But I am not sure that it is possible to be more precise than Hoskyns and Davey on specific problems such as the raising of Lazarus. Tasker's bulldozing may speak for the plain man; it cannot satisfy the scholar or indeed any reflective person who tries to reconcile the synoptic and Johannine traditions, which seem incompatible at this point. Is it possible for any honest scholar to say more than Davey does in the concluding words of the offending chapter?

> However positively we must maintain that there is no evidence that the fourth evangelist invented episodes or Sayings of Jesus out of the air, it remains equally certain that his perception of the meaning of history forces him to set the history he narrates

[1] Tasker, R. V. G., *Church Quarterly Review*, CXXX, July–Sept. 1940, pp. 318ff.
[2] Dillistone, F. W., *C. H. Dodd, Interpreter of the New Testament*. (Hodder and Stoughton 1977), p. 165.

in the widest possible theological context, in the full light of his perception of Jesus, and with the fullest regard for the theological implications, not only of isolated episodes and fragmentary sayings, but of the whole apostolic gospel. Whatever was the actual chain of events by which the crucifixion of Jesus was set in motion, his death was veritably brought about by his claim to hold out the eternal life of God to men and women, a claim which he made in declaring the advent of the Kingdom of God, and entry into the Kingdom of God through obedience to his call. Therefore, if this is the inevitable implication of the historical acts of Jesus vindicated and made perceptible to men by his resurrection from the dead, it follows that the fourth evangelist is doing no more than justice to the history behind him when he recounts the raising of a man from the dead with such circumstance and repercussions that it appears unmistakably to be the vital turning point of the gospel of *God* who *so loved the world that he gave his only begotten Son, that whosoever believeth in him should not perish but have everlasting life.*[1]

Perhaps the inaugural lecture of Christopher Evans when he became Lightfoot Professor at Durham vindicates this approach twenty years on. He speaks as a genuine successor to Hoskyns when he says :

On the one hand . . . the Christian gospel is contained in an event which is genuinely historical and in a life authentically human; the very fact that its investigation has gone hand in hand with the development of historical science itself, to which it has made its own significant contributions, is a strong indication of this. On the other hand, however, it escapes a purely historical description, and the historical method does not suffice to penetrate to its heart.[2]

Hoskyns did penetrate to the heart of the gospel. This is the secret of a greatness, which when all criticisms have been admitted, speaks still from the Cambridge of near half-a-century ago and with an awesome power. For he was in no doubt that the gospel demands conversion; not only change of heart and direction of life but

[1] *The Fourth Gospel*, pp. 127–8. On this problem see below pp. 113–4.
[2] Evans, C. F., op. cit., p. 99, from his Durham inaugural, 'Queen or Cinderella ?'

change of mind, the reversal of values. This is what the New Testament means by faith—not assent to certain propositions, reasonable or not, nor, in the words of his wartime author Donald Hankey, 'betting your life there's a God', but the power to see in the crucified and risen Jesus, so obscure and strange to us, so much a failure by our standards of good as well as of self-interest, the Light of the World. Let Hoskyns speak for himself from that great commentary, which, grappling in the deeps, at times carries us to heights of glory :

> Faith is not a separable fragment of human behaviour, nor is unbelief a detachable thing done in the midst of other things. Faith is not a wish that remains unfulfilled, nor is unbelief the refusal to stretch out towards some distant goal. To believe is to apprehend human action, all human action, in its relation to God; not to believe is not to recognize the only context in which human behaviour can be anything more than trivial. The man who believes apprehends that every visible human act requires to be fulfilled by the invisible, corresponding and creative action of God. The man who believes recognizes that all human behaviour is by itself and in itself incomplete. The man who believes knows that God fills up this incompleteness and that, in filling it up, he makes of the human act a thing that has been wrought in God. This is the love of God.[2]

The Last Days

From 1936, Hoskyns did no more work on the fourth Gospel, which had occupied him for the previous thirteen years. He was tired out with toil and responsibility—President of Corpus and Dean of Chapel, Director of Theological Studies, with pupils every night, University Lecturer and examiner, Canon Theologian of Liverpool, and then of Derby, in demand for courses in dioceses and parishes, member of the Advisory Council of the President of the Board of Education, which produced the Haddow and Spens reports, and needed in international conferences of theologians, both for his

---

[1] *The Fourth Gospel*, p. 208.

Sir Edwyn Hoskyns two years before his death in 1937

Noel Davey as Director of S.P.C.K.

own contributions and to translate the Germans. And he had no secretary until the Michaelmas term of 1936, when he paid for one himself. This helped him greatly.

Towards the end of the Easter term of 1937, he made his colleagues anxious by some very odd behaviour. He gave all the candidates in one of the papers of the tripos the same mark. He was in danger crossing the road. All of a sudden he seemed to have aged.

On Sunday, 20 June, he celebrated the Eucharist in Corpus Chapel and made no mistake—for the only time in the experience of one of the Fellows, who said that this 'gave Clement back to him'. In the evening, he had nothing but soup for supper, and was seen by his doctor, to whom he handed 'an important note', which was just scribble. But he looked out of the window and saw the delphiniums and said that the blue reminded him of Our Lady.

That was to be his last night at home. He had a final, loving conversation with his wife, but slept uneasily and woke deranged. He was driven to London to see a specialist, who sent him to a mental home in a southern suburb. He refused food and drink and deteriorated rapidly. Pneumonia set in, and a week later, in the afternoon of Monday, 28 June he died, still six weeks short of his fifty-third birthday.

His friends and pupils grieved sorely. A. E. J. Rawlinson, the New Testament theologian, then Bishop of Derby, burst into tears in his study when he heard the news. Gerhard Kittel wrote, in a memorial page of the German translation of *The Riddle*, of a 'bitter sense of grief', but also of 'gratitude both for the theological depth and understanding and also for the human kindness, which God presented to us in Sir Edwyn'. And Hoskyns had left behind a widow and five children, the eldest but fourteen, the youngest still a baby. Lady Hoskyns in time found the faith which overcame her stunned, bewildered questioning, and surrendered him to the God whose gift he was, and to whom he belonged. For the Requiem, Gordon Selwyn chose the hymn 'Praise to the Holiest', Lady Hoskyns, 'The strife is o'er'.

He lies in Grantchester churchyard, his second son, the fifteenth baronet, now beside him, and, on the stone, the words:

CRUCIFIXION RESURRECTION

Crucifixion – Resurrection

The Theme of the Church[1]

The Church has always a dagger at its heart, for it cannot long escape from its own theme, the theme which it is bound to proclaim —Christ Crucified. But we must not forget that even this theme is not something imposed by the Church upon the world, it is not some peculiar truth: it is rather that by which men are enabled to see clearly the tribulation which underlies their own selected place of security, whatever it may be. Every visible 'Christ' upon which they think they can stand, every '-ism' which we so passionately proclaim, every 'movement' which we join, every truth *we* enunciate, every scepticism of which we are so proud when we have cynically detached ourselves from all 'movements', all the pride of our aloofness and freedom from the superstition of every church and every conventicle, all our scepticism of science, not to mention our scepticism of theology—all these positions which we occupy pass like the gospel story from Galilee to Jerusalem, from life to death.

But, though compelled by its theme to see and to announce this movement from Galilee to Jerusalem and to see it everywhere, the Church does not thereby make nonsense of human life; the Church is not so *unwise,* not so irrational, not so lacking in understanding what the will of the Lord is. For precisely at the point where it is confronted by crucifixion it proclaims resurrection. It proclaims Christ Risen, it announces a new heaven and a new earth, it announces consolation in tribulation. It makes sense of the nonsense, for, knowing that all visible things are done in parables, it proclaims the glory and righteousness of God, and it sees his glory and his righteousness made known where our glory and our righteousness manifestly break down.

Did we say that the Church makes sense of the nonsense? No, a thousand times no. *It* does not *make* sense, as though once again it were manipulating and propaganding: it simply sees that the sense is everywhere, because it sees, beyond human sin and inadequacy

[1] Hoskyns, *Cambridge Sermons,* pp. 91–94.

which is everywhere, not a void, not nonsense, but the fullness of the glory of God.

And so, though the Church seems so often to be moving towards cynicism and scepticism and irrationalism, at the supreme point, at Jerusalem where the Lord was crucified, the whole world—please notice, the *whole world*—comes back to us in all its vigorous energy, shining with the reflected glory of the God who made it and us, and with the reflected love of the God who has redeemed both it and us.

It is therefore precisely our failure, our sin, and finally our death which prevents us from supposing that we are sufficient of ourselves, and which make room for the glory of God.

The theme of the Church—Crucifixion–Resurrection—is therefore the song which is sung, whether it be recognized or not, by the whole world of men and things in their tribulation and in their merriment. This is the gospel of the Church; the gospel, because it is the gospel—of God. There is no question here of bringing men within the sphere of the truth, for they are already there. God is not the God of the Jews only, but of the Gentiles also, of the anti-clericals and the communists, of all the 'movements' which tingle with resentment against the Church. He is also the God of the superior, detached person who, like Gallio, pins his faith neither on the Church nor on its opponents.

Yet, though the Church cannot bring men within the sphere of the truth since they are already there, it can, if it be true to the theme by which its pride is destroyed, enable men to see the truth in which men are standing. The Church can make sense of the pandemonium and the nonsense of the conflict between religion and irreligion; it can even make sense of the superior person who has removed himself from the conflict, by shewing that he too is a parable of the peace of God which passeth all understanding, and that he is a parable precisely when, at the last moment, he, too, is swept into the turmoil and finds that after all he has taken a side, and that peace and rest really do pass all understanding, because they are not found even in him.

PART ONE
Propounding the Problem

CHAPTER 1

The Intention of this Book

The title and sub-title of this book are designed to show its scope. Here are two well-known words—'Crucifixion' and 'Resurrection' —each of which has been interpreted in many differing ways, linked together as closely as two words can be linked, 'Crucifixion– Resurrection'. And this (so the sub-title affirms) is a proper description of a study of New Testament theology. A title like this must necessarily be taken to anticipate the book's conclusions. The reader who perseveres to the end may reasonably expect to find the interdependence of the words Crucifixion and Resurrection demonstrated and defined. He might also reasonably expect to find the concepts attached to these words examined separately as well as in their mutual dependence. If this study of New Testament theology is objective, are we to understand by 'crucifixion' anything more than an affirmation, or at most perhaps a statement, that Jesus died the common death of a criminal convicted of sedition under the Roman Empire? Or does crucifixion legitimately, or necessarily, describe the essential condition of Christian faith and life? Does it, indeed, provide a key to the meaning of the whole nature and context of human life in the world? Or again, are we to understand by 'resurrection' an event within history—unprecedented, perhaps, but none the less fully historical? Or does resurrection refer more properly to every moment of history, as well as to the 'end' of history (whatever that may mean) and all this because the New Testament apprehension of resurrection is inseparably bound up with the crucifixion of Jesus?

This book has been written with the intention of surveying a vast, and sometimes highly controversial subject, by means of a study of the New Testament writings. Its object will be to let those who wrote the New Testament speak for themselves, and to try to facilitate understanding of what they are saying. However unsystematized and unselfconscious that may have been, it is *their* 'theology' *then*, not ours today, that will be under examination. Of course, such an intention requires of the modern student an un-

89

attainable objectivity, and exposes him at once to the mercy of his critics, whose criticism, moreover, must certainly not be disarmed by the frank recognition that he is attempting the impossible. And of course, if the modern student is to communicate with his own readers with any measure of success, he will have to try to couch his exegesis in terms congenial to modern minds—which will at once expose him to the danger of ceasing to write as a historian. To this danger he must never willingly succumb. For, even if the study of the New Testament as history has rightly led to the conclusion that that history raises problems that cannot be solved historically and must be treated theologically, the study of New Testament theology none the less remains a historical discipline. It requires the student to discover, if he possibly can, by means of the ideas, concepts, or arguments actually crystallized or reflected in what they wrote, their sentences and periods, how those men thought about the event by which they believed themselves to have been created as Christians, and by which their Christian understanding, experience, and relationships were consciously controlled.

The student therefore has to make one fundamental assumption, namely that, as they left the hands of their authors, the New Testament writings seemed to them to make sense. At least at that moment, these men must have supposed that they had written reasonably, intelligibly, and in accordance with the gospel which had compelled them to faith in Christ, which required them to live in the fellowship of the Church, and which seemed to them to disclose the real meaning of life in this world. That assumption has determined the method of this book. Whenever possible, the way in which the relevant material has been laid out has been suggested by those parts of the New Testament where it lies most conspicuously to hand. This means moving about the New Testament selectively as the progress of the inquiry seems to demand. It has seemed undesirable to attempt either a systematic treatment of each book or author in turn, or an equally elaborate discussion of every topic considered: the latter course would have made the book needlessly repetitive, the former would have altered its character altogether. For in the last resort this book is designed to be a study, not so much of various, identifiable, and individual conceptions or experiences of the gospel, as of the gospel itself. Nevertheless, it is confidently hoped that the selection of material dictated by a tentatively framed and gradually unfolding argument will be seen, when followed through to the end, to have been sufficiently ubiquitous and penetrating to give any conclusion that may have been reached a cumulative force.

The New Testament writers have just been described as 'men'— not as evangelists, or apostles, or pastors, or votaries of a new religion—since they have their eyes open to the whole world human beings live in, and to nothing less. The significance of this will force itself upon us from time to time. It is recalled now for this reason. Although the 'rationalization' of life, and of the world, with which these men lived, was very different from the 'rationalization' with which we live today, both are reactions to what remains in essence the same life in the same world. No doubt the more or less 'unscientific' mythology in which their thinking was done differed radically from the more or less 'scientific' mythology in which we do ours. But, in spite of certain disparities on the surface, the radical rhythms and patterns of human life and of its natural environment remain for us very much what they were for them. They knew for instance that food is necessary to sustain life but that it cannot maintain it indefinitely; they had come to distinguish between satisfaction and satiety. They were well aware that relations between parents and children are normally subject to strain (Mal. 4.6; cf. Ecclus. 48.10), although they may not have explained this psychologically. They were as torn as we are between conflicting loyalties. They cherished memories of a happier and simpler past, and hopes for a just and more righteous future, and even if we are too disillusioned to look backwards or forwards with much nostalgia or expectation, we can enter into their bitter frustration with the present. And they perceived—perhaps more sensitively than we do—the propensity of human beings to put themselves at the centre of their own lives and of the whole creation, and to evaluate everything in terms of their own narrow interests, convenience, and well-being. These are only random examples. But they suggest that there may be common terms of reference here; that insofar as we are able to reconstruct the thoughts and conceptions of these men of long ago in terms of the essential rhythms and habitual patterns of life, we shall have found a constant by means of which we may to some extent bridge the gulf that separates us.

To illustrate the scope of this book

Crucifixion–Resurrection is our subject. On what ground may we expect it to take us? And where shall we start? *The Riddle of the New Testament* began by quoting the Nicene Creed—in fact by quoting most of the section referring to the life of Jesus Christ on earth, ending with the words:

> And was crucified also for us under Pontius Pilate.
> He suffered and was buried.

If this summary of the birth, ministry, and death of Jesus served to map out the area for a historical study, why should a theological essay not start from the clause immediately following:

And the third day he rose again according to the Scriptures . . . ? And why should this book not have been entitled, very much more simply, *Crucifixion AND Resurrection*?

Such a title was rejected not simply because credal Christianity has been much blown upon lately.[1] That conjunctive 'and' raises all kinds of problems. It might suggest, for instance, that the 'resurrection' of Jesus Christ was merely an additional occurrence. During the course of this book the accounts of the 'resurrection appearances' of Jesus will call for examination, and it may very well be concluded that they can be properly linked, to this effect, by an 'and' —and, indeed, that they justify our construing in this sense the '*et resurrexit*' of the creed, which is, after all, an almost word-for-word quotation from St Paul (1 Cor. 15.4). But we shall find that, in the New Testament, the resurrection of Jesus 'on the third day' is much more than an occurrence or a series of occurrences. It controls the whole material of the New Testament, and could be said to make of it the gospel of God. It is a strange, a unique, tying together of these two words that is described by this use of 'and', resembling the use of the 'thens', the 'wherefores', and the 'therefores', by means of which the apostolic writers link with the death the resurrection and exaltation of Jesus, or the lives to which his

---

[1] It was in fact at least as much a subject of criticism at the time when *The Riddle of the New Testament* was written. The reviewer (anonymous) of the *Times Literary Supplement* rebuked the authors for opening a book about the New Testament with a quotation from the Nicene Creed.

followers are called (Phil. 2.9; Col. 3.1–12). If the task of this book is carried through successfully we shall be in a better position to paraphrase such conjunctions with some hope of adequacy, for they derive their force, not from ancient colloquial usage (according to which they may have been entirely casual and otiose) or even from ancient rhetorical usage (by which, as so often today, their meaning may well have defied syntax and logic alike), but from the juxtaposition of the words, or concepts, or definitions of faith, they conjoin—Crucifixion, Resurrection. Who put these together? Why, so put together, are they forced upon us? It may help us to see the extent of this problem if we turn right away from credal statement to a starting-point that is not already complicated by theological interpretation. Let us begin with the physical context of the journey undertaken by Jesus when he set his face to go up to Jerusalem (Luke 9.53). Here is an account of it.

From Galilee to Judaea and Jerusalem—to the ordinary reader such a journey has no more particular significance than any movement from the provinces to the metropolis. Physically, it is merely a progress from one place on the map to another. But to a scientific observer—for instance, to a trained geographer—there is a vast distinction between these two places, a distinction that is quite different from the antithesis between town and country. The Galilee region and the plain of Esdraelon are volcanic, basaltic larvas from vents in the Safed area having overflowed the limestone country. These eruptions are normally considered to have been contemporaneous with the faulting that went to form the great 'rift' of the Jordan valley. On account of its alkalis, volcanic soil is, of course, proverbially rich, and consequently the contrast between the Galilee district and the limestone plateaux further south is especially striking. The arid environs of Jerusalem are due to its 'karst-like' limestone plateau structure, and to the absence of soil, except in restricted areas, which is the normal characteristic of such terrain. The perennial drainage, such as it is, is mostly underground, and the seasonal heavy rains and torrents wash away most of the surface soil.[1]

There we have an objective description of a very striking physical contrast. We might easily conclude that this countryside has no very

[1] From a letter the precise source of which is unacknowledged in the original.

obvious reference either to theology in general, or to the subject of this book in particular. But now compare Sir George Adam Smith's less technical account of the same contrast, noting that although his language is more poetic, it is none the less occasioned by the same physical facts.

To her dependence on the Lebanons Galilee owes her water and her immense superiority in fruitfulness to both Judaea and Samaria. This is not because Galilee has a greater rainfall—her excess in that respect is slight, and during the dry seasons showers are almost as unknown as in the rest of Palestine. But the moisture, seen and unseen, which the westerly winds lavish on the Lebanons, is stored by them for Galilee's sake, and dispensed to her with unfailing regularity all round the year. They break out in the full-born rivers of the Upper Jordan Valley, and in the wealth of wells among her hills. When Judaea is dry they feed the streams of Gennesaret and Esdraelon. In winter the springs of Kishon burst so richly from the ground, that the Great Plain above Tabor is a quagmire; even in summer there are fountains in Esdraelon, round which the thickets keep green; and in the glens running up the Lower Galilee the paths cross rivulets and sometimes wind round a marsh. In the long cross valleys, winter lakes last till July, and further north the autumn streams descend both watersheds with a music unheard in Southern Palestine. In fact, the difference in this respect between Galilee and Judaea is just the difference between their names— the one liquid and musical like her running waters, the other dry and dead like the fall of your horse's hoof on her blistered and muffled rock.[1]

In spite of our desire for objectivity, the geomorphology of Palestine presents the movement of Jesus from Galilee to Jerusalem as a movement from life to death. Is this geographical analysis purely coincidental, trivial, external, and irrelevant? Why should the terrain through which Jesus travelled on his way to the cross be significant for the understanding of his death and resurrection? Are we not leading up to a ludicrous example of reading into our material what cannot possibly be there; of searching round for

[1] *The Historical Geography of the Holy Land*, George Adam Smith. (3rd edn. 1895), pp. 417f.

purely fortuitous analogies in order to universalize a narrowly limited theme; indeed, of anthropomorphizing the natural order for the sake of externalizing an emotional experience, after the fashion of the romantic poet lyricizing his egotism in the ripples of a lake? Or does the very structure of the Holy Land provide a fitting frame and background for the events that are recorded as having taken place there? And does it therefore raise, in a peculiarly acute form, the problem of theology and the meaning of faith?

Before we label this approach 'fantastic',[1] two points deserve consideration. First, the whole concentration of the New Testament upon the life and death of Jesus Christ demonstrates the conviction of those who wrote the Gospels and Epistles that in that event, conceived to be altogether unique, they had come to understand the meaning of all history and of the whole of human experience. Parts at least of the actual historical context are essential to our understanding of the gospel—for instance, that Jesus was a Jew, who lived and died when his country was under the yoke of a triumph of empire-building almost coterminous with the whole known world. But, if so, where are we to draw the line outside which his immediate context ceases to have particular relevance to the meaning of his life and death? Can we say, for instance, that the physical environment of the last journey of Jesus is irrelevant simply because (which may perhaps be demonstrable) none of the New Testament writers seems to have thought it so?[2] The problem of particularity will remain with us throughout this book.

Again, even if we grant that the suggestion of life moving to death presented by the physical environment of the journey to Jerusalem is there, in the form of this almost over-dramatic contrast, have we really explained the fact that the same contrast runs in some measure, but with no such meaningful direction, right through the physical world? In our own environment, indeed, it will not be difficult to find hints and intimations of the antithesis of life and death which maps out the scope of the gospel. At almost

---

[1] A word favoured by some receivers of *The Riddle*, who did not appear to understand that to propose an illustration does not necessarily mean that its significance is to be regarded as proven.

[2] Not even the author of the fourth Gospel, we must suppose, though after reading Adam Smith's description of the geographical contrast between Galilee and Jerusalem we may well pause again at the paradox implied in John 4.10–15 and 19.28.

every point, the promise, indeed, the assurance, of 'life' may start out at us from our environment—just as it may force itself upon us from many other angles of our experience. But here also the promise may suddenly be stultified, the assurance be ruthlessly and wantonly belied, the cup proffered us, over-brimming, be snatched away barely tasted by our lips—or, and this is equally significant, they may not! And all this—as, in spite of their orthodox upbringing, more than one Old Testament writer perceived—confronts us without any apparent rhyme or reason. That might argue no more than that our environment is impressed with a meaningless pattern of bitter-sweet, of the rough with the smooth, of living and dying: an idiot pattern, which we encounter, intensified, in our human relationships and, most maddeningly of all, in our own lives. But what impresses us when we study the geomorphology of Palestine is that the deliberate progress of Jesus from fertile Galilee to barren Jerusalem provides, as it were, the environmental counterpart to the 'theme of descent' (cf. Phil. 2.6–8) which, according to the New Testament, he appears to have traced out deliberately in moving to the cross. What throws light at last upon the amorphous and outrageous scandal of life and death written all over our experience but typified most acutely of all in that particular geographical contrast is not merely that the Man who is said to have met death with life passed through a countryside known in some sort to us also. It is that he moved deliberately from the parable of life to the parable of death as he directed himself to the 'point' where there was no sign or hope of life at all: to what is presented as the point of absolute negation—and in so doing revealed the pattern of living that made sense to his disciples of this whole welter of life and death: the pattern of living by which, for them, the whole of life seemed to be brought to that same 'point', where resurrection is made known, faith born, eternal life bestowed, God's purpose revealed. Our illustration, of course, proves nothing—except, perhaps, the difficulty of keeping credal language out when the apostolic apprehension of Jesus Christ is under consideration. But this, at least, may be claimed for it. It is entirely in keeping with the exposition of the natural order attributed to Jesus in the Gospels that it is seen to point, vertically, to the Kingdom of God come with power precisely when it is seen to point, horizontally, to the death of the Son of Man.

The meaning of faith seems to have been defined for us in the absolute negation of crucifixion. Let us look further at the nature of faith, taking our next illustration from our own impressions of religious experience. Christians are accustomed to speak of faith in God's 'mighty acts'. Many would declare—no doubt, quite rightly—that their faith is based upon the supreme 'mighty act' of God's salvation, the event of the life, death, and resurrection of Jesus Christ: and, leading up to this act or proceeding from it, many other secondary but directly related 'mighty acts', in the history of Israel, for instance, and in the history of the Christian Church. This conception, that God has intervened, and will, no doubt, intervene again, in the course of human history, in such a way as to make his intervention clear to men of faith, must be taken very seriously. There is ample precedent for it, in the New as well as the Old Testament; and it is, indeed, a conviction by no means confined to Jewish or Christian experience. Yet the faith with which the New Testament writers are ultimately concerned is not so much faith in past, isolated, acts, recognizable as having been wrought by the hand of God, as faith that the non-exceptional pattern and incident of life—what might be called the very commonplace of life—is the primary 'material' of God's Kingdom. The problem of faith in this sense perhaps becomes most noticeable when piety, devotion, or good works are in question.

For instance, let us suppose that we engage ourselves in an act of worship, dressed up with all the prestige of a great civilization. In a moment of insight (or is it perversion of insight?) we see that what we are doing *is*, in spite of its supernatural trimmings, a very human action. At such a moment as this, we are put to the test. For, if we understand rightly what we are doing and saying, this very human action is, none the less, the revelation of God. This identification is the truth upon which human faith depends.

Or again, we read the Scriptures; and as we do so—this is the great discovery of a historically-minded age—we know that the books we are reading are very human, and very fallible. Yet here also it is required of us to say: 'This *is* the word of God.' And, if we know what we are doing, this copulative *is* must stand. For here also our faith is being put to the test.

Or we do a good action to a poor man. To that action we apply all the wealth of 'religious' affirmation, taking care to remove every vestige of theological superstructure, and asserting that this action *is* that upon which, when all is said and done, we stand before God and man as good. But, in a moment of perception, we know that this also is a human, a very human, act, complicated with all kinds of human motives of a most subtle nature. Yet here again it is required of us that we should preserve that copulative *is*. This *is* the love of God and, if we know what we are doing, that *is* must stand.

At each of these points the verb 'to be' confronts us with the problem of existence; and at each of these points we stand poised between blasphemy and faith.

Consider these four instances from another angle. Does the first seem to be carrying us along towards some supposedly 'catholic' identification of religion with 'rites and ceremonies'? Does the second, in spite of our contemporary liberalism, seem to be leading up to a declaration of some supposedly protestant fundamentalism? Does the third seem to be preparing us for a commendation of 'spirituality' wider, perhaps, in its basis even than orthodox Christianity, whether Catholic or Protestant or both together: or the fourth for an affirmation of 'the truth' over against all specifically religious acts of worship, devotion, or piety? Surely not, for kindness to the poor is no more human than the exercise of religion or dependence upon a sacred book, or perseverance in prayer. We cannot set one over against the other as though salvation consisted in selecting one aspect of human behaviour and pronouncing it to *be* the truth. Each *is*, and there is no pre-eminence. For God has bound these things together in a strange manner, so that the Catholic is what the Protestant is, and *vice versa*. The Catholic does not busy himself with the Mass and leave the Bible to the Protestant. Nor does the Protestant who observes his Bible withdraw from the fellowship of the Church. Nor do either neglect their prayers—or the poor.[1] In each case the 'is' required by faith em-

---

[1] The rough notes by Hoskyns, which have been worked up into this illustration, continue as follows: 'To do this is to descend to Mr Thwackum, the divine who never mentioned "goodness", or to Captain Blifil, who showed that grace did not involve acts of generosity. But when we have discarded Mr Thwackum and Captain Blifil, we dare not fall into the arms of Dr Square, the philosopher; nor dare we, though this is, strangely enough, a greater temptation, re-instate the man of the hill who, having passed through the classics, left them behind for the Scriptures.

braces an act exposed as utterly and unmistakably human—a human act emptied of all pretence to be, in any humanly-determinable sense, anything more whatever. Should this not be clear to us if we have considered the gospel of Jesus Christ, crucified and risen? And yet, so impenitently human are we, that we tend to select one, or another, of these four occasions (no doubt out of an infinite number of occasions for the identifying 'is' of faith), and to give it pre-eminence in our own religious scheme. And not only so, but we are tempted to make it a test of the 'faith' of others, as though *we* rather than *God* were the arbiter of faith and competent to signalize the proper *locus* of that *is* by means of which men are required to confess their faith.

What does all this mean? It is not, surely, simply a further measure (if one were needed) of our desperate 'human-ness'. Rather it demonstrates that the grace of God—for that, in theo-logical language, is what we are trying to talk about—meets our humanity at its most admittedly human, where it is most consciously disillusioned, most warily emptied of pretension—and this, over the whole wide range of our experience, and without justifying any 'logic' or 'order' or 'hierarchy'. Differentiations of that sort are also seen, in the moment of insight, to be very, very, human indeed. And this perhaps demonstrates as well the baffling 'logic' and 'order' and 'hierarchy' of God, which level men out just where the force of our 'experience' tempts us to be most selective and exclusive; compel-ling us to 'faith' that God makes sense precisely where the intolerant and mutually-competitive patterns of life as we know it are revealed as most senseless. If so, the 'oddity' of which, as men in the world, we become aware, lies not so much in the exceptional 'revelations' or 'mighty acts' of God (though no doubt the language in which Christians try to describe them must seem 'odd' to non-Christian ears) as in the pattern and structure of life, when considered apart from the limitless purpose and achievement of God. For this reason the 'rough edges', the 'loose ends', the paradoxes, the apparently

---

Yes, Henry Fielding has, for any Englishman, stopped for ever by his exhilarat-ing ridicule, in the famous chapters of Book III of *Tom Jones*, a dichotomy between truth and behaviour, between grace and goodness, and he has raised the problem of the sacred Book. But in a sense, Fielding is the beginning of the trouble, because he formulated the revolt against theology, and won the day so completely that we hardly realize that he did it far too easily.'

irreconcilables in life as we experience it, may be found particularly suggestive for our present task, since they seem to cry out for, and may perhaps point towards, a solution outside themselves.

Our illustrations have induced us to leap a long way forward. That was their intention. A glance at the geomorphology of Palestine has at least suggested that we should consider whether the relevance of the movement of Jesus to death, to crucifixion, can have any limits within the range of our human experience. And this tentative glance at the nature of faith, requiring an affirmation of that copulative *is* precisely where God seems most remote from the starkly human, suggests that we should consider whether there are any limits—again within the range of our human experience— to the relevance of the resurrection of Jesus. At the same time, we shall have to consider whether these two questions are not intimately related to each other, at the 'point' signified by the title of this book.

The scheme to be followed

A third, and last, illustration may help us to lay out the method proposed. Imagine yourself newly arriving from Mars, in the stratosphere above London. It is night, and for some reason all domestic lights are blacked out and the masked head-lights of the cars are unseen. Only, by a whim of the Minister of Transport, all the trains running in and out of London are brilliantly illuminated. There they go, to and from an obscure centre delineated by their termini, within which nothing moves visibly and where they can never meet. As new arrivals to Earth, we have no previous knowledge of what is there, no precedent from which to argue what it all may mean—this ceaseless movement towards something that remains invisible and unachieved, this equally ceaseless issuing out from it, but not of it.

We cannot see the 'point' at which life is said to have met death in Christ, and we have no precedents whatever from which to reconstruct it. But can we discern 'movements'—not physical or chronological movements, but movements of thought, of argument, of experience, of insight, which may lead us towards the understanding of his crucifixion? And can we discern 'movements' away from that invisible 'point', 'movements' occasioned by it, which may help us to understand his resurrection? And will such an inquiry help us to understand the central and all-embracing position which 'Crucifixion–Resurrection' seems to have occupied in the minds of those who wrote the New Testament?

It is the intention of this book to undertake this inquiry in four stages. First, we shall examine the place of the death of Jesus in the New Testament, and the significance there ascribed to it: secondly, some outstanding themes that run right through the New Testament will be considered, in order that any interpretation or reinterpretation of them occasioned by the crucifixion and resurrection of Jesus may be observed. Up to this point we shall be chiefly concerned with what we have called 'movements' *towards* crucifixion, but already the reverse 'movements', *from* resurrection, will be disclosing themselves. Thirdly, we shall look at the resurrection appearances, and then try to assess, in various ways, the concepts of crucifixion and of resurrection which set in motion the apostolic formulation and application of the gospel. Finally, while trying to keep studiously within the boundaries of objective criticism, we shall deliberately attempt to consider, by reference to the New Testament, some of the ultimate problems of human life which press upon us today; in spite of the fact that, so far as we know, none of the New Testament writers ever considered these problems directly, or in the way in which we are bound to state them. Whether any conclusions that may seem indicated will, or will not, satisfy modern readers is not our present concern. For the object of this fourth part, as of the whole book, is not to offer an apology for the Christian faith but to explicate 'Crucifixion–Resurrection' in terms of the New Testament.

CHAPTER 2

The Problem of the Death
of Jesus

The material contained in the first three Gospels can be gathered together and its general meaning described in such a way as to present no final and acute problem either for theology or for faith. That is to say, the material can be so described that human life is seen to reach its goal and come to rest in the visible, analysable, historical figure of Jesus, in his words and in his actions. It can also be claimed that this concentration upon the life of Jesus does full justice to the orthodox doctrine of the incarnation and discloses its meaning. Nor, in fact, does such a procedure do violence to the plain meaning of the Gospels, for the evangelists are careful to select incident after incident illustrating the movement from disease to health, from distress to happiness, from tumultuous chaos to peace, and from yearning desire to its satisfaction; and, lest their meaning should be overlooked, they from time to time add generalizations that set these incidents in a wide, spacious, and all-embracing framework: 'Jesus went about all the cities and the villages, teaching in their synagogues, and preaching the gospel of the kingdom, and healing all manner of disease and all manner of sickness among the people' (Matt. 9.35; cf. 4.23). 'And he entered, as his custom was, into the synagogue on the sabbath day, and stood up to read. And there was delivered unto him the book of the prophet Isaiah. And he opened the book, and found the place where it was written,

> The Spirit of the Lord is upon me,
> Because he anointed me to preach good tidings to the poor:
> He hath sent me to proclaim release to the captives,
> And recovering of sight to the blind,
> To set at liberty them that are bruised,
> To proclaim the acceptable year of the Lord . . .

And he began to say unto them, Today hath this scripture been fulfilled in your ears. And all bare him witness, and wondered at

the words of grace which proceeded out of his mouth' (Luke 4.16–
22). This passage seems to govern and explain everything this
author has to say about the life and work of Jesus, for in the Acts of
the Apostles, which we may presume to come from his hand, when
he looks back on what he had written, he again summarizes its
meaning in similar form: 'Jesus of Nazareth, how that God
anointed him with the Holy Ghost and with power: who went
about doing good, and healing all that were oppressed of the devil;
for God was with him. And we are witnesses of all things which
he did both in the land of the Jews and in Jerusalem' (Acts 10.38–
9). 'Jesus of Nazareth, a man approved of God unto you by mighty
works and wonders and signs, which God did by him in the midst
of you, even as ye yourselves know' (Acts 2.22). Jesus is therefore
the 'Prince (or, Author) of life' (Acts 3.15).

When once this general framework is recognized and taken
seriously, the isolated, separate episodes and sayings recorded in the
gospels cease to be isolated or episodic. The Beatitudes, for
example, do no more than bring out into the open what is everywhere implied. The poor are blessed, mourners are comforted, the
meek enter into their inheritance, those who hunger and thirst after
righteousness are filled and so satisfied. Men stand within the
mercy of God, see him, are his children and enter his kingdom
(Matt. 5.2–9; cf. Luke 6.20–3). The sabbath, too, provides an
opportunity for doing good and saving life (Mark 3.4), since it is
the day when men and women are loosed from the bonds of Satan
(Luke 13.16), and the peace which it proclaims is established in the
peace that Jesus proclaims and gives: 'Come unto me, all ye that
labour and are heavy laden, and I will give you rest. Take my yoke
upon you, and learn of me; for I am meek and lowly in heart: and
ye shall find rest unto your souls. For my yoke is easy, and my
burden is light' (Matt. 11.28–30). The labourers may be few, but
with the effective compassion of Jesus the harvest has veritably
come: 'But when he saw the multitudes, he was moved with compassion for them, because they were distressed and scattered, as
sheep not having a shepherd. Then saith he unto his disciples, The
harvest truly is plenteous, but the labourers are few. Pray ye therefore the Lord of the harvest, that he send forth labourers into his
harvest' (Matt. 9.36–8; cf. Mark 6.34). And so the expansion and
extension of this life-giving ministry is entrusted to the disciples of

Jesus. Their work too is defined as effective compassion, for they are the servants of all: 'He . . . began to send them forth by two and two; and he gave them authority over the unclean spirits' (Mark 6.7; cf. 9.38–40). 'If any man would be first, he shall be last of all, and minister of all' (Mark 9.35). Surely, here at last the goal of human life has been reached as it had been defined in the Old Testament summaries of the commandments that God has laid upon his people. Here is the consuming love of the one God, and here too is the true and exhaustive love of the neighbour (Deut. 6.5; Lev. 19.18; quoted in Mark 12.29–31). 'And . . . they were all amazed, and glorified God, saying, We never saw it on this fashion' (Mark 2.12). 'He hath done all things well: he maketh even the deaf to hear, and the dumb to speak' (Mark 7.37). 'Blessed are your eyes, for they see; and your ears, for they hear. For verily I say unto you, that many prophets and righteous men desired to see the things which ye see, and saw them not; and to hear the things which ye hear, and heard them not' (Matt. 13.16–17; cf. Luke 10.23–4).

It is impossible to exaggerate the emphasis which, in every fragment of the gospel material, is laid upon the audible and visible fact of what Jesus said and did, that is to say, upon his life. And for this emphasis the evangelists cannot be held solely responsible. Unless the records are altogether untrustworthy, for Jesus himself the importance of what he said and did lay in its event. He demonstrated his teaching by putting it into practice; and he demanded that those who heard him should do the same. And so men saw and heard, and were enlisted in, an activity of compassionate mercy defined as obedience to the will of God. Nor are this extreme sensitiveness to the poor and afflicted, and this confident power of relief, concerned merely with physical and material poverty and distress. Affliction of spirit is everywhere depicted or assumed. It may be rough language that describes men as possessed by evil spirit, but it requires no serious modernization to become intelligible. Jesus leaves the demoniac, or lunatic, 'clothed and in his right mind' (Mark 5.15). And there is, moreover, a distress in human life deeper and far more widespread than physical, or even mental, disease; deeper, too, and more widespread even, than poverty. Men did, and do, long for a righteousness that seems everywhere to escape them, till they are persuaded that the object of this search is hidden and inaccessible in the righteousness that belongs only to God. This sceptical despair, which in the biblical literature is named sin, is also met and driven out by Jesus. He does not merely hold out the hope of some future salvation. He breaks the bonds of sin, and sets men free. In all this, the analysis of human life that underlies the gospel records is so deep, and the answer given to its problems so effective, that it would seem that Jesus speaks not only for his contemporaries, but for all time. If this be so, his life is not of relative but of final importance, and the record of it carries conviction in a manner different from all other known biography.

From this concentration of attention upon the works of Jesus meeting and relieving the material, physical, mental, and spiritual needs of men, there seems to emerge a picture of the life of Jesus that is at once convincing, satisfying, attractive, and orthodox. Are we not driven to say that with his definition of himself as son of man he provides a definition of all proper human life, not by some generalized, speculative argument or by some delicate romantic intuition, but by the living of an individual human life in obedience to the will of God? And must we not go on to use the venerable language of revelation and say that his life is the revelation of the life that men ought to live as sons of God, a life compassionate to the poor and weak, and hostile only towards pride and pretence and prejudice? And is not this the onslaught of God upon all the powers of evil that possess the world; an onslaught that need cause men no fear, for its purpose is to set them free from the bondage of false conventions about themselves and from fearsome delusions about God; an onslaught, moreover, which, though of absolute and eternal moment (since man is made for eternity), is comprised, nevertheless, in a series of observable engagements whose actual fact is at once the means, the occasion, and the assurance of victory? And must we not say finally, with those who heard his words and saw his deeds, that he 'hath done all things well'—and mean more perhaps than they did because we recognize in his life the reflection of the positive and absolute goodness of God, the manifestation of the righteousness to which the prophets pointed, for which the law was framed, of which the patriarchs had dreamed, and in which creation itself reaches its goal? This may seem to be romantic language. But is it more than the first three evangelists intended, and the fourth evangelist declared and formulated when he spoke of the

flesh of Jesus as the place where the word of God was made known
and his glory manifested, and when he summed up the meaning of
the mission of the only-begotten Son of God—his ministry of healing, liberating, binding up the suffering, comforting those that
mourn, seeking the lost, serving the poor—in the one word love,
and was then able to comprehend in the same single word the whole
duty of man and the nature of God? All this then *is* the love of
God. And it means neither more nor less than : 'No man hath seen
God at any time; the only-begotten Son, which is in the bosom of
the Father, he hath declared him' (John 1.18); no more in the end
than : 'He that hath seen me hath seen the Father' (John 14.9). Is
there really any more to say than to proclaim this, anything more
to do than to hear and obey? Is there any further orthodoxy beyond
the doctrine of incarnation, any further definition of the Church
than that it is the extension of the incarnation? And, far more
important than the substantiation of the language of orthodoxy, is
not this picture true to the Gospels and convincing to the modern
reader? Why should anyone speak of problems of theology, or of
acute problems of faith? For does not this description of the life of
Jesus adequately embrace also his death and apparent abandonment
by God? If the mainspring of the teaching of Jesus concerning the
love of God towards sinners is that God wills to liberate men from
sin by absorbing their violence in a love that is infinitely forgiving,
and thus, by showing men the truth of his love, to lead them to
faith based on a true knowledge, and so to that imitation from
which righteousness proceeds, there is no point at which God
resists evil. And so the death of Jesus merely demonstrates how
terribly destructive man is in his blindness, since he not only fails
to recognize human goodness, but crucifies it as unfit to live, and
therefore shows, too, how desperately man needs the love of God.
The catastrophe of the crucifixion is repudiated by God and
declared to be irrelevant and ultimately insignificant by the resurrection, in which the inherent and intrinsic goodness of the life of
Jesus is ratified and confirmed. The essential revelation of the love
of God manifested in Jesus was therefore already complete, and his
death is no criticism, but rather, if anything, an additional affirmation of it. This explanation of the crucifixion is not a creation of
modern theology. It is clearly stated in the speeches of Peter in the
opening chapters of Acts. There the problem of the death of Jesus

is resolved by laying it to the charge of those Jews whom Stephen had denounced as 'betrayers and murderers' (Acts 7.52). 'Whom . . . they slew, hanging him on a tree. Him God raised up the third day, and gave him to be made manifest, not to all the people, but unto witnesses that were chosen before of God, even to us, who did eat and drink with him after he rose from the dead' (Acts 10.39–41; cf. 2.23–4; 3.15; 4.10; 5.10–32).

If the death of Jesus need not be thought of as in any way limiting the efficacy of his life, it also need not be thought of as putting a terminus to the historical manifestation of the love of God. Is it making an unreasonable claim to say that the Church that springs from his life and was created by it continues to perform the same works and to teach the same truths as he himself wrought and taught; or that his disciples continued, and continue, his life; or that the Church remains in the world as the continuation of his incarnation? For the Church exists to reconcile men to God, to preach his power and his wisdom, to comfort and relieve the afflicted, to mediate God's effective satisfaction of human needs. This is no empty boast, justified only by an arbitrary romanticization of church history. There is no doubt that with the life of Jesus a new factor entered the world, a new spirit or quality entered the hearts of men, which brings forth recognizable fruit. This new factor, or spirit, or quality, may well explain the use of the future tense in the sayings of Jesus, and prove how clearly he saw through his own death to the imminent and effective work of his disciples, an insight precisely formulated in the fourth Gospel: 'Verily, verily, I say unto you, he that believeth on me, the works that I do shall he do also; and greater works than these shall he do; because I go unto the Father' (John 14.12).

The circumstances and manner of the death of Jesus may thus be shown in no way to disturb the general picture of his life. In the history of Jesus there appeared an event which, by its literal fact, brings a new and real salvation to men. And this salvation is perpetuated for all time through the life and work of the Church. To speak therefore of an acute problem of history and of an acute problem of faith is nervous language, and belongs to a sense of tension precisely where all tension has been removed.

There can, then, be no proper description or analysis of New Testament theology that is not rooted and grounded in the observation of event, that does not proceed with as great a realism as Shakespeare:

> Tell me where is fancie bred,
> Or in the heart, or in the head:
> How begot, how nourished.   Replie, replie.
> It is engendered in the eyes
> With gazing fed . . .[1]

or that does not, perhaps with greater modernity, include under the term 'history' not merely what strikes the eye, but those inner motions of the heart and mind which form the proper material of psychological investigation. Nothing that edges away from the analysable world of event and experience, and that makes of them no more than shadows of reality, shadows, or similitudes, or reflections, or signposts—nothing, in fact, that serves to direct attention elsewhere—can be true to what every New Testament writer is asserting. Nevertheless, there is a problem of New Testament exposition, just as there was a problem presented to Shakespeare by his own realism:

> . . . and Fancie dies,
> in the cradle where it lies:
> Let us all ring Fancies knell.
> Ile begin it.
>   Ding, dong, bell.
> *All*. Ding, dong, bell.[2]

The New Testament writers become increasingly aware that it is the very material upon which their eyes are fixed, and the very experience with which their hearts are filled, that raise problems that are entirely final and ultimate. There is a certain 'grossness' in event and in experience that must not be hidden by the fair ornament of romantic theology, or obscured by simply naming it spiritual. 'Flesh and blood cannot inherit the kingdom of God' (1 Cor. 15.50)—'The flesh profiteth nothing' (John 6.63). There is a problem of knowledge that is not solved by the manner in which men observe and see and know. There is a problem of the meaning of history that is not solved by the mere description of what is seen

---

[1] *The Merchant of Venice*, Act II, sc. ii.
[2] Ibid.

and experienced. There is a problem of ethical behaviour that is not solved by distinguishing between what is good and bad, or even by the doing of good works. And, underlying all these problems and embracing them all, is the problem of defining the 'ego' of the man who observes and experiences and thinks and does good actions to the neighbour.

These are, no doubt, difficult matters. But they cannot be dismissed as Tristram Shandy dismissed them:

> My good friend, quoth I, — as sure as I am I and you are you –
> And who are you? saith he.
> Don't you puzzle me, saith I.[1]

They cannot be dismissed, because it is precisely these questions that are raised by the actual historical figure of Jesus, by the authority with which he speaks, by the nature of his teaching and action, and, most clearly, by the fact of his death and by the circumstances in which it took place. They are, moreover, not questions that are imposed upon the New Testament; they form its subject-matter. Therefore, tempting though it is to construct from the synoptic material a convincing historical figure in which all these problems are avoided or provided with an easy, straightforward historical solution, because the consolation of an effective dispensation of the healing and reconciling love of God has been achieved within the framework of visible history, such a course is entirely unauthorized by the New Testament writers. Although they accuse the Jews of murder, they cannot let it be supposed that the death of Jesus is an irrelevant end to a life already completely significant. Jesus was delivered 'by the determinate counsel and foreknowledge of God,' (Acts 2.23; cf. Luke 24.27, 44–8)—'according to the scriptures' (1 Cor. 15.3–4). In the end, that is to say, the New Testament writers are agreed not only that the death of Jesus was the culminating fact of his life, but that his life is only perfectly understood in the light of it. This is not at all simple, but they do not regard it as difficult in the sense that it requires some peculiarly mature intelligence to understand it, as though it were the last chapter of some intricate philosophy of religion or of human life in general; rather, they conceive of it as so closely bound up with the nexus of human life that there is no understanding of Jesus, or, indeed, of men and

[1] *Tristram Shandy*, Vol. VII, ch. xxxiii.

women, unless it be grasped from the outset. How they ever came to think in this fashion, and to think so confidently in this fashion, is the problem, not only of New Testament exegesis, but of all biblical theology. For in the end the problem of New Testament theology is no new problem. It is the problem of the book of Job, of the Psalter, and indeed of the whole history of Israel as it was seen through the eyes of the prophets of Israel. And the New Testament writers seem to be aware that this is the necessary background for the understanding of Jesus of Nazareth. For they set his death, not only in the context of divine necessity, but in the setting of that necessity as it had been defined in the Old Testament Scriptures.

But the death of Jesus presents not only a theological but also a historical problem. Is it really possible to explain his death historically as occasioned merely by the blindness and wantonness of the Jews? If his life, as it has been described, carries conviction to the modern reader and almost compels imitation, how is it that it did not carry the same conviction to the Jews and compel them to imitation? Has there been such an evolution in human behaviour that the reaction of men, no doubt under the influence of Christianity, is more reliable now than then? This comparison would be a very bold one to make with any period or section of humanity. But, in view of the historical evidence of the enlightenment and humanity of rabbinic Judaism during the time of Jesus, it appears perilous in the extreme. For this reason alone it must be asked whether the Jews can be made solely responsible for the death of Jesus: whether, that is to say, the crucifixion was indeed an unjustifiable act of folly; whether it was not murder at all but an entirely sane and necessary execution of justice. For if, as would in fact appear, what Jesus said and did, and what he of set purpose claimed to be, were held by him to be of final importance on the plane of history as literal facts, it must be seriously considered whether the accusation of the Jews that he was 'perverting our nation, and forbidding to give tribute to Caesar, and saying that he himself is Christ a king' (Luke 23.2) was not wholly justifiable.

According to the synoptic tradition, Jesus was condemned by the Sanhedrin because he affirmed that he was 'son of God', and so persisted in blasphemy. He was handed over to death by Pilate because he refused to deny that he was the king of the Jews, and so persisted in sedition. Crucifixion was, moreover, the common legal punishment of criminals of the worst sort, robbers, and those who rebelled against the Roman *imperium*. The evangelists, it is true, present both these verdicts as transparently absurd, but it is certain that they would never have been delivered, and, what is more, that these charges would never have been brought, had there not been circumstances that were peculiarly aggravating. The sadducean hierarchy was far too anxious to keep on good terms with the Roman government to present it with difficult problems of administration and order—unless they appeared to its members important and urgent. A Roman governor in Palestine was far too anxious to avoid rousing national feeling to cast round for opportunities to crucify, on the charge of treason, a manifestly good and harmless man—so long as he really was harmless. Indeed, the record of Jesus before Pilate illustrates this anxiety. Nor is it only in the narratives of the trials that Jesus is set in opposition to the Jewish authorities and to the imperial government. It is clear that the literal words when coupled with the actual deeds of Jesus carried with them implications that inevitably involved him in collision with the Jewish church and the Roman administration. For, in ascribing ultimate importance to his liberation of men from the bondage of tradition, of mental and physical disease, and of sin; in claiming that through these actions God was exercising his mercy; and in defining what he was doing as the ultimate salvation of God; Jesus provoked the question 'What manner of man is this?' (cf. Mark 4.41; 1.27), and provoked it in such a way as to raise in a peculiarly acute form the problem of blasphemy. This being so, the Jewish hierarchy could neither welcome him as a human if somewhat unorthodox teacher, nor avoid him as a harmless fanatic. As the guardian of the people against blasphemy, it was bound to pay careful attention to what he said and did, to examine him and, if found guilty, to condemn him. Long before he came to describe the final trials, the fourth evangelist formulated the issue, and surely formulated it correctly : 'For this cause therefore the Jews sought the more to kill him, because he not only brake the sabbath, but also called God his own Father, making himself equal with God' (John 5.18). Similarly, in proclaiming the kingdom of God, Jesus used language that was by its very definition seditious. And, more than this, the proclamation of the kingdom was the proclamation of a call demanding an obedience that made a real impact upon society. Men were impelled to leave their work, their families, and their homes, to follow Jesus. The crowds came out to meet him as he entered Jerusalem, and, if the records are trustworthy, gave him a royal welcome. And Jesus would not silence their cries, just as later he would not deny that he was king.

It accordingly appears that Jesus could not be permitted to continue his work without its implications being questioned. Both in the religious and in the political field he was causing a revolution that seemed to cast doubt upon the authority of contemporary Judaism on the one hand and of the Roman *imperium* on the other. And when approached and challenged with this, he made no apology, but let what he did speak for itself.

It is true, of course, that side by side with this apparent religious and political rebellion Jesus threw into question and repudiated those who supposed him to be erecting a religious morality superior to, and in competition with, the older religion and ethics, and inaugurating a kingdom that was to rival and supersede the kingdom of Caesar. What he said and did was in his eyes the fulfilment of all that Judaism, its Scriptures, its priesthood, its law, and its prophets, meant. And for him there was no tension at all between the kingdom of Caesar and the kingdom of God. But, just as his teaching had to be formulated in action, so that action had to present itself to men in the real situation in which they were placed. He could not adopt language that would have seemed to his judges harmless, without denying the reality of the world and destroying the truth of his gospel. No doubt, their presuppositions were wrong. No doubt the high priest did not perceive what his office really meant, just as Pilate, the representative of Caesar, did not see what the function of Empire really was. Jesus came to show men the truth about all these things. But, granted their presuppositions, it is difficult to see that they did not pass right judgement.

Jesus, it has been said, threw into question and repudiated those who interpreted his words and actions literally. This does not, however, mean that he intended them to be understood as allegories or symbols. It remains true that the literal event of his actions was supremely important: and it is in this setting of acceptance and repudiation, put as it were midway between them, that the prediction of suffering and the actual facts of the passion became essential

112

to the understanding of what Jesus said and did. When Peter sees that he is in some sense the Christ, Jesus apparently rejoices in the confession that his words and deeds have provoked, and attributes it to a revelation from the Father. But when Peter, a moment later, betrays that he apprehends the truth he had confessed as belonging within the continuity of visible history, he is at once rebuked in the strongest language. So Jesus advances to Jerusalem accepting the confession of Peter and the acclamations of the crowd, yet predicting his own rejection and death. The kingdom of God 'cometh not with observation' (Luke 17.20), or, as the fourth evangelist says, the kingdom of Jesus does not spring from or originate in this world (John 18.36). And so, it is necessary for him to suffer. He has a baptism to be baptized with (Luke 12.50). This emphatic discontinuity is, moreover, reflected in the course of the ministry itself. The life of Jesus that had begun with an activity of compassionate power continues in retirement and in an almost complete absence of works of mercy. The ministry that had begun with so great an exuberance of eloquent teaching ends in almost complete silence, broken only by the grim controversies with the scribes and Pharisees and by almost equally grim words spoken only to the disciples. Finally, therefore, Jesus not only questioned the literal interpretation of words and deeds upon the literal event of which he had laid such stress, but almost entirely gave them up and stood dumb and helpless before his judges.

There is, therefore, a historical problem presented by the fact of the crucifixion. No description of the life of Jesus can be satisfactory that does not explain his condemnation by the Jews or Pilate's handing of him over to death, or that does not make the behaviour of both Pilate and the Jews intelligible. But there is a further problem that concerns the manner in which the evangelists wrote their history. If it be true to say that the evangelists regarded the actual, continuous history of the life of Jesus as the sphere in which the love and mercy and royalty of God were completely made known and revealed, why should they not have been content simply to write history? Why should they not, that is to say, have been content to let the bare facts speak for themselves? The problem of the historicity of the Gospels is not a problem raised merely by our modern scepticism or by our supposedly precise knowledge of what is historically credible and what is not. The problem of the historicity of the Gospels is raised by the Gospels themselves, and by their literary analysis. It is a real problem; and it is acute not only in the fourth Gospel. The problem of historicity is a biblical problem that is not set to rest merely by speaking of legends and myths and of the tendency to heighten the miraculous. It is not even set to rest by saying, in the case of the evangelists, that they were concerned more with edification than with the writing of history. There is a larger problem here. The evangelists are free to alter history and to rearrange it; they move into the miraculous apparently for the same reason as their Old Testament predecessors. They seem to be aware that the history with which they are concerned presses beyond history, and that its meaning demands this further pressure. The recognition that history requires non-historical description does not mean that the biblical historians have lost their bearings and have strayed into a dim, shadowy, undisciplined, world. Their procedure simply questions the final ability of the historian to master his material. This questioning is of prime importance. It cannot be dismissed as a regrettable lapse from truth, unless describable history itself is, or has become, truth.

Now where is all this leading? It might at first sight seem that we should have to recognize that the life of Jesus was, as St Paul described it in writing to the Philippians (Phil. 2.6–8), a steady and progressive descent of humiliation reaching its known and recognized climax in the scene of the crucifixion. We might have to conclude that the whole material is ordered and arranged by the evangelists so as to secure this movement of descent. We might have to reckon with the possibility, not merely that this was the meaning of Jesus's life, but that he recognized that it was so, and himself ordered his ministry to make it clear. So precise a framework is, however, open to very serious historical objections, for it assumes a conscious direction of his life from the very beginning, which is not, in fact, borne out by the way in which the evangelists do actually record the ministry. And yet it would surely be to misunderstand the New Testament writers to suppose them to mean that the story of the passion in the Gospels, or the theme of crucifixion in the Pauline Epistles, or the theme of sacrifice in the Epistle to the Hebrews, or the picture of the lamb of God in the Book of Revelation, were a kind of excrescence upon the life of Jesus. To all the New Testament writers, the death of Jesus and the manner of its occurrence were entirely relevant to his historical figure. They were not additions to an otherwise complete or incomplete picture of his life. This is clear in the fourth Gospel, where each episode as it is recorded is in a sense complete in itself, and the passion narrative introduces no new themes that have not already been not only treated but to some extent exhausted. The themes may be, and indeed are, more transparent in the narrative of the passion, but they are not new themes. This is true not only of the fourth Gospel but also of the synoptic Gospels. For, strange as the language at first sight seems to be in the narrative of the upper room, its themes are present throughout these Gospels, and are only formulated at the end with greater precision and with greater expectation of understanding. Indeed, when Luke determines, as it would seem, to expand the teaching given in the upper room, he collects it from teaching that had been given earlier in the Marcan narrative, and, perhaps in another setting, in some other source available to him.

It is now once again necessary to formulate the problem with which this book is concerned. It may be, of course, that the New Testament writers are wrong, and that there was no intimate connection between the circumstances of the death of Jesus and the previous events of his life. It may be, further, that there was no inherent relationship between the circumstances of the death of Jesus and the history of Israel, as it was seen and described by the prophets of Israel; and that there was no inherent relationship between the circumstances of the death of Jesus and those dim apprehensions of reality that underlie the Old Testament sacrificial system. It may therefore be that there is no proper basis for the Christian doctrine of the atonement in the ministry of Jesus seen as a whole, but only a basis for the doctrine of the incarnation. For the moment, however, if the New Testament is to be understood (quite apart from its relevance to the modern world) it is precisely this relevance of the death to the life that requires careful investigation. For a weakness of analysis here might damage the whole understanding of primitive Christianity. What therefore requires further analysis is not the narrative of the passion, but the actual teaching and actions of Jesus before the passion. In addition an attempt must be made to understand (again without attention to the modern world) what was the mainspring of the Pauline

Epistles, and why the apostle regarded the situation in, say, the Corinthian Church, as so unsatisfactory and unchristian. It must also be asked why the author of the Johannine writings also regarded the situation of the Church in his day as so blasphemous, and how it ever came about that the Epistle to the Hebrews, and the Book of Revelation, could be addressed to primitive Christians at all. We must remember that these primitive Christian writings did not emerge *from* the Church but were, rather, addressed *to* the Church. It seems that it was this relevance of the death of Jesus, not merely to his own life, but to the life of the Church, that the Christians misunderstood, and that it was precisely this widespread misunderstanding that made these apostolic men feel that a gulf was opening out between the Christians and the Lord whom they worshipped. That a situation should ever have arisen in which Christians were addressed with such authority and seriousness requires some explanation.

CHAPTER 3

The Death of Jesus in the Pauline Epistles

In the synoptic Gospels it appears, though only at first sight, that the predictions of the death and resurrection of Jesus, and the assertions of their divine necessity, form an irrelevant addition to an activity of Jesus in word and deed that is in itself complete and in itself of ultimate importance. In the Pauline Epistles there is no such appearance of discontinuity. In describing what the Church must be and what every Christian must think and do, St Paul is as urgently concerned with the living of real human life in the world as the first three evangelists are when they set out in their Gospels the visible and describable life of Jesus. Real, visible, good works are just as essential to St Paul's gospel as they are to the synoptic picture of Jesus Christ. Indeed, when the good works that St Paul requires of the Christians are analysed, they are seen to be identical with those attributed by the evangelists to Jesus, for they too can be summed up in the one word 'love': 'He that loveth his neighbour hath fulfilled the law. . . . Thou shalt love they neighbour as thyself. Love worketh no ill to his neighbour: love therefore is the fulfilment of the law' (Rom. 13.8–10; cf. 1 Cor. 13).

But, whereas the evangelists pass straight to their story of the good works of Jesus, St Paul is unable to move so easily to his subject-matter. There is a necessary prolegomenon to the confident imperative of moral behaviour which he addresses to the Church. St Paul sees the whole of human life, and in particular the life of the Church, and with even greater urgency his own life, through the mirror of the death and resurrection of Jesus. He can see human life from no other angle and in no other perspective. It is this angle, this perspective, this mirror, that give St Paul his unity and consistency of analysis, perception, and apprehension: that drive the urgent moral imperatives to the end of what he has to say; and that enable him to hear without flinching the imperative of the universal law of God defining all men as sinners and obliterating all arrogant distinctions between them. No doubt, it is possible to deny the unity and consistency of the Pauline Epistles. They have been broken up and dismembered. They have been divided into theology and ethics. A subtle evolution has been detected in them. St Paul's ethical demands have been pronounced to be of permanent importance, whereas his theology or Christology and his exegesis of the Old Testament have been discarded as incompatible with his ethical perception and as stamped with his own strange, nervous, abnormal personal history and experience. But it may be asked whether these quick judgements concerning what is valuable and what is not valuable in what St Paul said and wrote really belong to the proper business of the commentator. Manifestly, St Paul thought that he was talking sense and not nonsense, and did not think that he was writing partly sense and partly nonsense. Indeed, the Epistle to the Romans, for example, becomes little short of a psychological monstrosity if its author did not think that what he was saying was throughout relevant and intelligible to those for whom it was written. He may, of course, have exaggerated their powers of comprehension, but that does not exonerate us from the responsibility of trying to understand at least the main points of his argument, and their coherence, even though they be found in the end to be altogether irrelevant to the modern world.

The problem of the Pauline Epistles is to discover why the death of Christ was of such importance to St Paul that he never escapes from it. To judge from his reference to the time when the Galatians first heard the gospel, it formed the subject-matter of his missionary and evangelical preaching: 'O foolish Galatians, who did bewitch you, before whose eyes Jesus Christ was openly set forth crucified? This only would I learn from you, Received ye the Spirit by the works of the law or by the hearing of faith? Are ye so foolish? having begun in the Spirit, are ye now perfected in the flesh?' (Gal. 3.1–3). That is to say, the crucifixion of Jesus is the place where life in the Spirit takes its origin, where faith begins, where the works of the law are of no avail, and, by a strange paradox, where there can be no perfection in the flesh. The whole of the first Epistle to the Corinthians is governed by the same steady theme. St Paul has in front of him a picture of the church in Corinth, drawn partly from the reports he has had from members of the house of Chloe, and partly from letters he has received from Corinth; partly from his knowledge of the Corinthian church, and partly, no doubt, from his knowledge of Christians everywhere, since we may presume that the problems that faced the church in Corinth were, fundamentally at least, neither unique nor peculiar. It is therefore possible to form a fairly accurate picture of the Corinthian church as it strikes St Paul's eye.

It is at first sight a very pleasing picture. They are serious-minded Christians. Indeed the problems that arise are a consequence of this seriousness, not a lapse from it. For example, these Christians take seriously the fact that they are spiritual men and women, and, precisely because they are spiritual, the physical aspect of marriage seems to them unworthy of their new spiritual life. Similarly the doctrine of 'resurrection', involving, as it did, the resurrection of the body, seems to them unworthy of the faith by which they stand, and they have grave doubts whether the word 'resurrection' can be a Christian word at all. Probably they would far rather speak of immortality. No doubt there are lapses from morality within the Christian church in Corinth, and one rather glaring case is causing them considerable difficulty. But, being Christians, they hesitate to proceed with any roughness towards a man who has fallen into sin, because, feeling themselves to be strong, they think it is better for him to remain in their midst in the hope that he may borrow from them something of their strength. In any case, so long as he remains in their company there can be hope of his repentance. This strong faith, able to bear the sinner in their midst, also enables them to move freely in a pagan society without danger of their being contaminated by its idolatry. They know that idols are nothing. And therefore they are free to use the temples as restaurants and to feed on meat that has been sacrificed to idols. No doubt not all the members of the church in Corinth were so strong as this. There were weak Christians. But they were weak *Christians*. The strong not unreasonably hope that they too will borrow something of their strength. At any cost it is important that those who are strong in faith should exhibit this strength, in order that the weaker Christian may be enabled to mount from weakness to strength by their example. And there is a grand liberty of prophesying; there is no distinction here between men and women. For the women at Corinth prophesy with as great an eloquence and fervour as the men do, and the veil marking the distinction between the sexes is, at least at times of prayers, significantly removed. Nor is it only prophecy that shows how gifted the Corinthian church is. They speak with tongues, and there are some there able to interpret what is said. They perform miracles of healing. There are teachers in their midst; men, too, able to take pastoral and administrative responsibility (1 Cor. 12.28–9). Moreover, the whole church is imbued with a splendid sense of freedom: freedom from convention, freedom from their past manner of life, freedom in their relation one to another and, indeed, in their relation to God, for they know him and are therefore able to distinguish between good and evil, and so they can be said to know the truth and to possess wisdom. To all, the moment of their conversion has been the turning point of their life. Consequently the man who baptized them stands in a specially intimate relationship with them, as the human means of their conversion from slavery to freedom. Nor is their respect limited to those who have baptized them. In spite of their independence and freedom they are not unable to appreciate the work of apostles and of outstanding men who have from time to time visited their churches. Peter has been there and has left behind him men devoted to his memory. Apollos has also taught in their midst, and on some he has left an indelible impression. Nor are they unable to appreciate the apostle who has founded the church in Corinth. But there are some among them who are suspicious of these great men, apostles though they are. There are some who are simply Christians; who belong to no party, since they belong only to Christ.

Though there are no doubt in the Corinthian church (as St Paul hints) a few who are well born and a few who are rich, nevertheless the majority of the Corinthian Christians are poor men and women. A heavy responsibility to support their poorer brothers and sisters therefore lies upon the more wealthy among them. This being their prime responsibility, it is not surprising that the collection which St Paul is anxious to take for the poor saints in Jerusalem should receive rather lukewarm support. After all, the Corinthians are human. This humanity appears in another context. There are limits to what could be demanded of them. One of these limits is abstention from fornication. Brothels were not in the ancient world what they are in the modern. They were to some extent a protection of the virtue of married life, and in any case a normal part of the social life of a great city. In spite of their spirituality the Corinthians

120

cannot condemn brothels altogether, or suppose that a relationship with a harlot has any moral or spiritual effects that are permanent. Their defence of the practice of fornication does not mean that they are accustomed to practise it, but merely that they are doubtful about excluding from their midst those who are unable to do without it. And indeed, can a purely physical action seriously damage spiritual life?

There is something extremely moving in this Corinthian piety, moving by its determination to be bold and free in its whole conception of Christianity, and also in its human-ness. But St Paul is moved neither by the one nor by the other. It is not that he criticizes this or that point, or that he urges the Corinthian Christians to a stricter piety, or to an even greater freedom from convention where convention still survives. He questions the whole temper of the Corinthian church. He questions their whole theory of knowledge and their whole conception of ethics. But he does not do this because he has some superior philosophy of religion, or another epistemology, or a different standard of moral values. He pronounces the quality of Corinthian Christians to be unchristian at every point because the Corinthian Christians, in overlooking the death of the Christ, leave no room for the power of God. And so, with all its gifts and energy and spirituality, the church in Corinth has ceased to be the steward of the mysteries of God. Accordingly, before ever he comes to deal with this or that point, St Paul devotes four whole chapters to the definition of that wisdom and that power which proceed from the wisdom and power of God as set forth and made accessible to men in the crucifixion of the Christ, and which belong only to those who have the mind of Christ. And with extreme delicacy he works out what this means, not as yet in an attack upon the Corinthians, but by transferring the problem to himself and Apollos and the rest of the apostles. If the Corinthian church is wise and strong and honourable, it is because the apostles are fools and weak and despised; because they hunger and thirst and are naked and are buffeted, and have no certain dwelling place; because they are the filth of the world and the off-scouring of all things. But St Paul's purpose in writing all this is not primarily to describe what apostles are but to warn the Corinthians of what they are in grave danger of not being. For if the Corinthians are what they are because the apostles are what *they* are, then the Corinthians will not be effectively wise and strong and honourable unless they share in this apostolic humiliation. As St Paul says, he has transferred the problem to himself and Apollos 'that in us ye might learn not to go beyond the things which are written, that no one of you be puffed up for the one against another. For who maketh thee to differ? and what hast thou that thou didst not receive? but if thou didst receive it, why dost thou glory, as if thou hadst not received it?' (1 Cor. 4.6–13). They have thought to reign in God's kingdom without apostolic humiliation, and St Paul shatters their comfortable position: 'would . . . that we . . . might reign with you'. Why should St Paul be cynical? Whatever the answer to this question may be, he holds on to what he has said throughout the Epistle, and holds on to it because he is determined to define the whole activity of the Corinthian church in terms of the crucifixion of Christ. And what this means is that 'God chose the weak things of this world, that he might put to shame the things that are strong; and the base things of this world, and the things that are despised, did God choose, and the things that are not, that he might bring to nought the things that are: that no flesh should glory before God' (1 Cor. 1.27–9).

Spiritual gifts, freedom, liberty, knowledge—St Paul agrees that to possess all these is the mark of the Christian Church. But they are not to be understood so simply as the Corinthians suppose. He has the same sense of freedom as the Corinthians have (1 Cor. 9.1); like them he knows that there is but one God and that an idol is nothing (1 Cor. 8.4); and moreover, he speaks with tongues more than any of them (1 Cor. 14.18). But whereas the Corinthians stand on their freedom and knowledge, and on their possession of outstanding, brilliant spiritual gifts, St Paul has no such confidence; and he is deprived of this confidence not by some especial sense of personal moral and intellectual weakness, not by any doubt regarding the importance of visible marks of exuberant piety, but by the very nature of the gospel with which he has been entrusted. He cannot stand before God on his knowledge, or on his freedom, or in virtue of his gifts, for two reasons. First because such a relationship to God would reintroduce precisely that claim upon God from which he has escaped. He stands under God's knowledge of him, not upon his knowledge of God (1 Cor. 8.3; 13.12). And secondly, because the whole Corinthian conception of knowledge and freedom, and their pride of piety, open up an impossible gulf between the strong Corinthians and their weaker brethren who possess no such impregnable knowledge (1 Cor. 8.13), who are in their social relationships not free as wives or as servants (1 Cor. 7.10–11; 20–4), and who are not possessed of outstanding spiritual gifts (1 Cor. 12.22). Knowledge, such as the Corinthians boast in, puffeth up: their liberty, by a strange paradox, leads them to thrust others into the worst kind of slavery, the slavery of idolatry (1 Cor. 10.29), and to deny to St Paul his freedom (1 Cor. 9.4–5). Their confidence in the way of piety leads them to neglect a more excellent way (1 Cor. 12.31).

As St Paul exercises it, this criticism of the Corinthian Christians has no ordinary ground. He does not write as a man peculiarly sensitive to the appearance of pride and arrogance in human relationships; or peculiarly, almost abnormally, sensitive to the claims of the poor, the weak, and the foolish. Or rather, his sensitiveness has a very particular ground and occasion. He writes as an apostle of Jesus Christ, and it is this position that causes him to write as he does. Liberty, as the Corinthian Christians understand it, is incompatible with a gospel that is declared in a setting of crucifixion and death, incompatible with an apostleship that consists in exercising freedom by being under bondage to all (1 Cor. 9.19), incompatible with their proper position as men who have been brought into freedom by the death of the Christ whose bondservants they are (1 Cor. 6.20; 7.23). Knowledge, as the Corinthians understand it, is compatible with the wisdom of men, with the characteristic wisdom of the Greeks as St Paul knew and experienced it, that is to say with a wisdom that leaves the man who knows still master in his own house, still undisturbed by the knowledge of God (1 Cor. 1.25; 2.3–4). But it is altogether incompatible with the foolishness in which the wisdom of God has been revealed through the death and resurrection of the Christ, incompatible also with the fear and trembling of the apostolic preaching: 'If any man thinketh he knoweth anything, he knoweth not yet as he ought to know' (1 Cor. 8.2).

The conscious sense of strength of the leaders of the Corinthian church, and the consequent distinction between the strong and the weak, contradict the whole picture of the Christ whose servants they claim to be, more glaringly, perhaps, because less subtly. The weak brother, for whose sake Christ died, is perishing through their knowledge, and therefore in sinning against the brethren and wounding their conscience they are sinners against Christ. It follows from all this that their ethical position is by no means so secure as they suppose, not so secure that they can support in their midst a case of glaring immorality without danger to themselves, not so secure that they can visit brothels without contamination. There are acts from which they must flee, men whom they must exclude from the Church. But here again St Paul is not speaking as a mature man of the world, aware of the instability of weak human nature and of the vast ramifications of the power of evil. The Corinthian Christians must be rid of these things because, bought by the death of the Christ, they belong to him body and soul. They cannot therefore give their bodies to a harlot (1 Cor. 6.15). The Christ has been sacrificed, and they must therefore keep the new passover feast by excluding from the Church all that represents the old leaven (1 Cor. 5.7–8): 'Put away the wicked man from among yourselves' (1 Cor. 5.12). Nor in all the various problems connected with marriage can St Paul think as they think. He is more human than they are, but there crosses all his humanity a far greater sense of the urgency of the call that is laid upon them, and of the completeness of the claim that Christ makes upon them. Christ's claim thrusts both the marriage relationship, and its more spiritual equivalent apparently preferred by the more spiritually-minded among them, into a position not ultimate but penultimate: 'For the fashion of this world passeth away' (1 Cor. 7.31) and 'The time is shortened' (1 Cor. 7.29). The eschatology of St Paul is undeniably difficult, but it is a Christian eschatology. When the Church stands under the law of the death of Christ it is set inevitably at the end of history, not at the beginning of an evolution in history. To St Paul, this whole situation has vast implications for Christian behaviour and makes the problem of marriage acute. But this is far removed from what is normally understood by asceticism. Moreover, the attitude of the Corinthians to those who baptized them, and to the apostles who have taught them, is not free from the all-pervading misunderstanding of the nature of the gospel under which they stand. It is not merely that their different loyalties inevitably cause divisions in the Church, not merely that they throw into the foreground an altogether undefined, and therefore arrogant

Ego: I am—I am—I am—I am. In turning apostles into great men they have set them jostling one against another, and have failed to see in them the folly and weakness of the Christ; have failed to see that they are, as it were, appointed to death and made a spectacle unto the world (1 Cor. 4.9). And, having failed to see this, they also fail to see in the apostles the stewards of the mysteries of God. On the other hand, those who claim to distinguish between the apostles and the Christ, and who assert that they belong only to him, fall perhaps into an even greater arrogance of piety. For apostles are the ministers through whom they believed: they labour as the Lord gave to them, separated neither from him nor from one another (1 Cor. 3.5–9). They work together, but the husbandry is God's, the building is God's, and it is he who gives the increase.

It is clear from all this that the references to the death of the Christ with which St Paul punctuates the Epistle are in no sense casual; in no sense do they lie on the periphery of what he is saying. Every aspect of Corinthian piety is described, criticized, and judged in the light of Christ's death, and throughout St Paul not only speaks as the apostle of Christ Jesus but (as he himself had said) is determined to know nothing among them but Christ, and him crucified (1 Cor. 2.2). At two points in this Epistle, St Paul brings the chronological background of what he says right into the foreground. At one point it is perhaps inevitable that he should do this, because he has to defend the word 'resurrection' as a Christian word. But at the other point, his description of the Lord's supper, he drags the chronological background into the foreground. When once the Corinthians have questioned the word 'resurrection' as suitable to describe the hope of the future, St Paul sees that they are doing far more than jib at a word. The sting of death is not death, but sin; and the strength of sin is that it is disobedience to the known and formulated law of God. All men are therefore under the condemnation of God. To St Paul this whole situation is not met by a bare belief in immortality, and certainly not by a belief in the immortality of the soul. To discard the word 'resurrection' means to St Paul to move away from the horror of sin at the very point at which it is most essential that it should be taken seriously. He can therefore contemplate death—that is to say, contemplate sin—only at the place where its horror has been removed, and so he opens the section in which he treats of 'resurrection', not with 'resurrection' at all, but with that which he had first of all proclaimed to them, and which he had not initiated but received, namely that Christ died for our sins according to the Scriptures and that he was buried (1 Cor. 15.3–4). The answer to that death was not the immortality of the soul but the resurrection of Christ according to the Scriptures (1 Cor. 15.4). There and there only is the sting of death removed and the power of sin overcome. 'Thanks be to God which giveth us the victory through our Lord Jesus Christ' (1 Cor. 15.57). Of course, in riveting the word 'resurrection' upon the Christians, St Paul does not for one moment mean to supersede the doctrine of the immortality of the soul with some strange and intolerable doctrine of the resurrection of the flesh. Indeed, he definitely excludes it (1 Cor. 15.35–44). In the light of the death of the Christ, his concern is to set no limit to the power of God, and to open up, over the death of the Christ and through his resurrection, the hope, nay the certainty, of a new creation in which sin is destroyed and all will be changed.

When treating of the word 'resurrection' it was perhaps inevitable that St Paul should have written much as he did. But when he had to speak of the coming together of the Corinthians 'in assembly' (*en ecclesia*) there would seem no obvious necessity for him to mention the death of the Christ. The Corinthians themselves had no idea at all that the two were connected, though we, no doubt influenced largely by what St Paul actually said, find the connection very natural. The Corinthians are thinking in terms of fellowship one with another, presumably supposing that the mere fact of coming together must be 'for the better'. St Paul, however, has no belief that a mere act of fellowship ministers to good. Indeed he roundly asserts that they are coming together for the worse, and points out that the Lord's supper is in Corinth an occasion when the distinction between rich and poor is not obliterated but actually heightened (1 Cor. 11.17–21). Here again, however difficult it may be, St Paul sets the whole congregation of Corinth under the death of the Christ, under his body and blood, and declares that only so can their coming together be for the better (1 Cor. 11.26–34).

This analysis has been based upon one only of the surviving Epistles of St Paul. But, when subjected to a similar analysis, the remaining Epistles yield the same results. St Paul everywhere subjects human behaviour in general, the behaviour of the Church, his own experiences, to the same scrutiny. And everywhere this scrutiny is conditioned by, and undertaken in, the light of what he has seen in the death of Jesus and of what he believes in the light of the resurrection of Jesus from the dead. Indeed, it is this that sets St Paul in motion not only as preacher and as missionary but also as a writer of letters to those who have been converted by his agency or who, though converted by others, require the assistance of his insight, just as he requires the encouragement of their understanding. St Paul is no isolated person. He stands in the full stream of time and history, overwhelmed, as other men are, by the wealth and abundance of human experiences of joy and sorrow. In the midst of all this, he knows that he has seen the truth and is confident that what he has seen is relevant not merely to himself, as though he were some peculiar person, but to all men, and that it is recognizable by all who believe in Christ Jesus, crucified and risen. Like all the other New Testament writers, he knows he is moving along a narrow path with two precipices falling away, one on each side of him. But more clearly than any of these men, except perhaps the author of the Johannine writings, he knows precisely what these two dangerous precipices are. He has heard the imperative of the law of God accessible to the Jew in the Ten Commandments, and also accessible to the Gentile in the unwritten law that exercises a sure criticism of idolatry and immorality through a certain innate awareness of the heart and conscience. He knows moreover that this imperative of God is inescapable and unavoidable; that the divine commands are issued in order that they may be obeyed. He knows therefore that in this obedience lies the ultimate destiny of men. But these are the demands of God, and when men hear them as they really are, with their full implications, they are crushed by them, crushed so completely that there emerges an equality in human life, an equality that breaks down all distinctions, even the distinction between Jew and Gentile. This equality is, however, not an equality of salvation. It is an equality of judgement. No man is justified by the works of the law (Gal. 2.16): that is to say, no man can stand securely before God by virtue of what he has done in obedience to the law declared by Moses or recognized by the conscience.

At this point there opens up a most attractive territory of religion, the territory of faith in the mercy of God. If it be impossible to obey the decrees of God, and if all men are equal in sin and equally under his judgement, why should men not luxuriate in this most religious equality and in this most comfortable relationship to God? To be under judgement is no secular, hopeless, or irreligious position: why should men not continue in sin, in order that grace may abound (Rom. 6.1)? God's judgement cannot be his last word, in spite of his demand that men should obey him. Why therefore should men not trust in his mercy and love—and go on sinning?

To St Paul this is no fruitful territory at all; it is a stark precipice of destruction. And it is so, not because he is after all, in the last analysis, a Jew who knows that the moral struggle cannot be avoided or discontinued, but because he is a Christian and because the death of the Christ cannot by any possible manoeuvre of theology be reconciled with an acquiescence in sin or with so comfortable a doctrine of the love of God. Still less can the death of the Christ be thought of as irrelevant for the Christians. They have been baptized into his death (Rom. 6.2–18), that is to say, they are involved in his onslaught against sin. They have crucified the flesh with its passions and lusts (Gal. 5.24). They bear about always in the body the dying or mortification of Jesus (2 Cor. 4.10).

If this attractive road to the love of God towards sinners be forbidden, is it not possible to turn in an opposite direction and luxuriate not in sin but in the righteousness of the Christian Church, and to claim that this righteousness is the righteousness demanded by God? Is it not possible to assert that there has appeared in human life a tangible, concrete, behaviour that is finally adequate, in which true justice is done, not only to the moral optimism of Judaism, but also to the actual language of St Paul? Are we not bound to take his words seriously, and to claim that through the obedience of Christ there has entered the world a real crucifixion of the flesh with its passions and lusts, a genuinely successful onslaught upon sin? And are we not therefore able to speak of a new visible order of society in which sin and suffering are done away, and from which the sting of death has consequently been removed? Are there not two requirements only that are necessary for the emergence of an entirely adequate and final reign of peace and righteousness, of faith and love as an organic structure: that Christians must take their faith seriously, and that the Church must be enlarged until all men and women are embraced within it?

Much that St Paul says would seem to be compatible with this grand view of the future, and with this splendid doctrine of the Church. St Paul does certainly assert that the Christians can and do now live, not unto themselves, but unto God (2 Cor. 5.18): and he does confidently describe what that life is in the real world of human relationship (Rom. 6.11). Not for one moment does he think that he is here making impossible demands. But any interpretation of the Pauline Epistles that makes of the visible, analysable Church a thing subsisting in itself, or even a thing depending upon its faith, does veritably come to rest in a false interpretation of all that St Paul is saying. That indeed is for him the second precipice, as stark and menacing as the first.

'There are men,' Disraeli once said, 'whose phrases are oracles; who condense in a sentence the secrets of life; who blurt out an aphorism that forms a character or illustrates an existence.' Such a man was St Paul. If we are to understand him, we are bound to take seriously those pregnant sayings in which, sometimes in an aside and half unconsciously, he crystallizes his meaning and defines the existence about which he is talking. When he says, for example, 'we have this treasure in earthern vessels' (2 Cor. 4.7); or 'we walk by faith, not by sight' (2 Cor. 5.7); or 'the things which are seen are temporal: but the things that are not seen are eternal' (2 Cor. 4.18); or 'flesh and blood cannot inherit the kingdom of God' (1 Cor. 15.50); or 'by hope we were saved: but hope that is seen is not hope' (Rom. 8.24), St Paul is drawing a line of demarcation that in the end rules out a direct identification of the Church with the life about which he is speaking. He does the same when, at surprising moments, he falls into pure eschatology (1 Thess. 4.13–18), or sets what he is saying as it were inside a bracket and defines the whole by adding, outside the bracket, the phrase, 'in the spirit' (Col. 1.8; Eph. 2.14–22), or 'in Christ Jesus' (Rom. 6.11; Eph. 2.6–7), or 'in Christ' (Col. 1.28), or 'in the Lord' (1 Cor. 15.58; Eph. 6.1), or 'in Christ Jesus our Lord' (Rom. 8.37–9). Nor indeed is the severe line of demarcation difficult to understand, if it be recognized that the death of Jesus does lie at the heart of his whole exposition of the gospel and of the nature of the Church. For how could he first set the Church in the context of the life of Jesus in the flesh, define it as the body of Christ and see in its obedience the reflection of the obedience of Christ, and then go on to tear away the whole ground of identification by making of the visible Church, or of his own life, a wholly successful thing? Of course he does nothing of the kind. He defines the Church by its relation to the death of the Christ. The Church is a persecuted Church : this is the theme of the Epistle to the Philippians (Phil. 1.29–30; 3.10–19), but it is a theme that underlies all the Epistles (2 Cor. 4.8–9). To St Paul this is not a regrettable situation; rather it is the mark that the Church is the Church of Christ. Nor is the suffering of the Church due merely to external persecution. Its origin lies far deeper. The Church's knowledge is a dark knowledge (1 Cor. 13.12; Phil. 3.13); its prayers are uttered *de profundis*, out of the depths of weakness and ignorance, (Rom. 8.26); its moral behaviour is a dire struggle most adequately described by the analogy of war, of athletic competition, of boxing and wrestling (Eph. 6.11, 12; 1 Cor. 9.24–7). Only one activity of the Church can stand uncriticised, and that is its love and charity to the weak and the poor, and this activity is the natural corollary to the uncertainty and insecurity of every single Christian (1 Cor. 13.2–3; Gal. 6.1–5). Before this sole adequate behaviour, every act of heroic morality, every claim to knowledge, every spiritual gift, every exalted experience (2 Cor. 12.7), must bow in the humiliation of not having reached the goal. This almost unbearable description of the Church is summed up by St Paul in the language of sacrifice : 'I beseech you therefore, brethren, by the mercies of God, to present your bodies a living sacrifice' (Rom. 12.1). A passage like this cannot be explained as arising from his 'personal experience', as occasioned, perhaps, by some physical or other abnormality in himself—tempting though such a course might be. St Paul writes as he does, consistently, because this is what the death of the Christ means to him, and because he is persuaded that this *is* the meaning of that death. He sees and describes the Church in this manner because he sees it in and through Christ.

But St Paul has much more to say than this. The place of weakness, when it is also the place of obedience to God, is the place where the power of God is made known and exercised (Phil. 2.8–11). The death of Christ is therefore the place of resurrection. God raised him from the dead. The very weakness and folly of the obedience of the Christ is therefore the *locus intelligentiae*, and

130

not only the place of understanding, but the place of faith : 'he was crucified through weakness, yet he liveth through the power of God. For we also are weak in him, but we shall live with him through the power of God towards you. Try your own selves, whether ye be in the faith' (2 Cor. 13.4–5). This faith rings through the Pauline Epistles. Grounded upon the resurrection of Christ, it provides a final definition of the Church in its humiliation, just as it defines his own apostolate. 'If then ye were raised together with Christ, seek the things that are above, where Christ is seated on the right hand of God' (Col. 3.1)—'If we died with Christ, we believe that we shall also live with him' (Rom. 6.8). In the end St Paul can so lay hold of the truth expressed in the death and resurrection of Jesus that he can assert it without mentioning death or resurrection : 'When I am weak, then am I strong', or when he says that the Lord said to him, 'My grace is sufficient for thee : for my strength is made perfect in weakness' (2 Cor. 12.9–10).

The narrow path along which St Paul is moving can now be precisely defined. The life that is lived in the faith of Christ is not weak or foolish in the sense that it has no precise direction, or involves no clear and definite behaviour or manner of thinking. St Paul does not exhort men to believe in the love and mercy of God in such a way that their faith enables them to continue in sin that grace may abound. A strict discipline of thought and action underlies everything that he writes. To overlook this is to make nonsense of his Epistles. But he does not so exalt the manner of life and thought as to make of it an adequate, concrete, visible, analysable life sufficient in itself. To explain St Paul's Epistles along either of these lines is to miss their whole meaning. There is an ethic of faith and there is a knowledge of faith; and it is about these things that he is talking. And he is talking in this fashion because he takes both the death and the resurrection of Christ seriously. The one lays an imperative on human life, an imperative that must be obeyed; the other sets a limit to this obedience lest it should become so great a matter of boasting as to rule out the action of God.

It will therefore be seen that to St Paul the death and resurrection of Christ are not two events that lie side by side on one and the same plane. Nor are they two things, as it were, laid by God upon the plane of history as a kind of addition to normal human life. There is, as the Reformers perceived, and as the Catholic Church has always recognized by making the sacrifice of Christ the pivot of worship, a veritable *theologia crucis*. Nevertheless, when this has been said, it still remains obscure, for the meaning of theology and the meaning of the cross have still to be ascertained. But it is possible to reach two preliminary conclusions : first, that, however it is to be explained, the death of the Christ is central in St Paul's manner of thinking, just as it governs his ethical teaching; and secondly, that it does not seem possible to explain this merely as the outcome of a highly developed sense of 'finiteness' or 'createdness', as though the line of demarcation were simply drawn between what is finite and what is infinite, or between the creature and the Creator. St Paul's deep sense of personal sin and of personal guilt would by itself make either of these two explanations of his language inadequate.

But are these preliminary conclusions true only of St Paul, and that because his understanding of Christ, his experience as a Christian, his whole view of life, were exceptional, abnormal, unique? This question requires that we should now turn to the writings of the other great New Testament theologian, the author of the fourth Gospel.

CHAPTER 4

The Death of Jesus in the Fourth Gospel

To St Paul, the death of Jesus Christ was central. But St Paul was accustomed to hammer out his theology in the first person singular. And St Paul was an exceptional man, of unusual history. Does his particular experience account for his concentration on Christ's death, and explain his choice of metaphors—in writing, for instance, 'When the commandment came, sin revived and I died' (Rom. 7.9); or in reliving his deliverance 'out of the body of this death' (Rom. 7.24); or in protesting to the over-confident Corinthian Christians, 'I die daily' (1 Cor. 15.31)? Was his view of the death of Christ in fact abnormal, derived perhaps from some inherited pathological tendency? No doubt his grasp of the gospel was clear and profound. But some personal obsession of his own, not really essential to the gospel, might have caused him to work out its implications, for those in his care as well as for himself, in terms of life and death. Again, morbidity may be not unconnected with a natural egotism. Was St Paul aware of some such egotism in himself, and did he deliberately and consistently seek to root it out—as he would say, to put it to death (Rom. 8.13; Col. 3.3), to mortify it? Might this explain his continual harking back to the metaphor of death and to the thought of Christ's death on the cross —even though he believed the sickness of his soul to have been healed, and the 'old man' in him to have been dethroned? Was it for some such reason as this that he would not treat the death of Christ simply as an event in history, but made it part of his ethics, of his philosophy, even of his own personal religion?

It is time to turn to the Gospel according to John. Our first impression is reassuringly different. Here, it would seem, we are not to be exhausted by autobiographical testimony. The author nowhere writes in the first person singular, except when, with a diffident 'I suppose', he emphasizes the limitations of his own achievement (John 21.25). Here we detect no tendency to introspection and—apparently—no personal preoccupation with the physical death of Jesus. It is not only that the author has burnt himself out of his book. In this Gospel we feel that the great Christian experience of the glory of the death and of the atonement has shone through the tragedy. The 'flesh' of Christ is not, as it is for St Paul, the 'flesh of sin'—existence 'in the likeness of sinful flesh' (Rom. 8.3). It is the means through which the Father is revealed (John 14.9), and through which eternal life is given to men. Those who 'eat the flesh of the Son of man and drink his blood' eat 'the bread which came down from heaven' and 'live for ever' (John 6.52–8). Only in respect of its formal pattern can Christ's road to death in this Gospel be called a *via dolorosa*.[1] In other respects it more resembles the triumphal progress of a king to his throne. Throughout the narrative—and above all, throughout the narrative of the passion—Jesus is the master. This is made clear when Jesus speaks of the Good Shepherd's laying down his life for the sheep (John 10.11–15)—'Therefore does the Father love me, because I lay down my life, that I may take it again. No one taketh it away from me, but I lay it down of myself. I have power to lay it down, and I have power to take it again. This commandment received I from my Father' (John 10.17–18). But the same freedom and willingness to die appear in the account of the Washing of the Disciples' Feet (John 13, especially vv. 3, 4, 12), where Jesus is represented as defining and explaining his imminent death. Even when the officers and soldiers draw near to arrest him, Jesus 'goes forth' and in fact *gives* himself up (John 18.4). When Pilate says to him, 'Knowest thou not that I have power to release thee, and have power to crucify thee?' Jesus answers, 'Thou wouldest have no power against me, except it were given thee from above' (John 19.10–11). Whatever this may mean, it is not Pilate who is in control. At the moment of death, Jesus cries, 'It is finished'—that is, it is accomplished, completed, done (John 19.30)—a cry of

---

[1] So Dr C. H. Dodd: 'The way from Galilee to Jerusalem is a *via dolorosa*, in all gospels, and apparently in the *kerygma* which lies behind them' (*The Interpretation of the Fourth Gospel*, p. 384). Dr Dodd shows that 'this symbolic value of the journey to Jerusalem' is so deeply embedded in the scheme of the fourth Gospel that it recurs as well within each of the 'seven episodes' which (he believes) make up what he calls 'The Book of Signs' (John 2.1–12.50). But he also observes that this section 'is so constructed that each several episode contains in itself the *whole* theme of the Gospel: Christ manifested, crucified, risen, exalted, communicating eternal life to men' (op. cit., p. 386).

victory and joy. Then 'he bowed his head, and gave up his spirit'—master to the very end.

Cannot we now define the place of the death of Jesus in the fourth Gospel, without any more ado? Shall we not say that, although as a historical fact it was so central to the Christian gospel that it could not be set on one side, in the fourth Gospel it is significant chiefly as being the act by which Christ ushered in the order in which Christians are privileged to live? Must we not suppose that, with time and the maturing experience gained through faith and piety and fellowship, the apostles' daring—and opportunist?—proclamation of the saving death of Jesus, and St Paul's brilliant—but eccentric?—theologizing of it, came to be thought irrelevant to the apprehension of the gospel that had come to be regarded as totally 'spiritual'? And indeed, with the fourth Gospel, do we not really move into a religion of the Spirit? No doubt, this is brought about by Christ. To him we owe it that we recognize our potential relation with God, that we apprehend our need of the truth and grace from eternity offered to men. To advise us of our happy situation, and to convince us of our need, it was necessary that the Word should become flesh. And because, when that took place, it happened that his contemporaries, and above all his own countrymen, would not 'hear his word', it was necessary that the Son of man should die, and die of his own free will. Not for a moment may the incarnation be thought irrelevant, or the death on the cross unreal. But now that they have taken place and had effect, can they not be allowed to drop away behind us as mere vestiges in time of the travail through which our spiritual religion was brought into being, and forgotten even, as her pangs should be forgotten by the mother of a new-born child? It is in this Gospel that Jesus says: 'The hour cometh, and now is, when the true worshippers shall worship the Father in spirit and truth; for such doth the Father seek to be his worshippers. God is a Spirit: and they that worship him must worship in spirit and truth' (John 4.23–4). Have we not here the *fiat* for a supreme religion of humanity, modelled upon the manhood of Jesus—man liberated from superstition and convention, sure of himself, master in his own house, communing with his creator as spirit with Spirit? Can we not therefore describe the gospel of man's liberation like this—Jesus dying voluntarily; by his death dispelling the clouds created by human ignorance and assuring men of the love that has always embraced them and that always will embrace them; inaugurating, in so doing, a spiritual communion with God which is proved, in the sequel, to be undisturbed by the incident of death; inaugurating, consequently, a religion of which the preoccupation, from beginning to end, is eternal life in the Spirit; in which the record of the death of Jesus is retained only because he did in fact die? It is a grand and highly attractive picture. And in each of its components there is an element of truth. But is it a true picture of the religion of the fourth Gospel? Or is the death of Jesus written into every part of this Gospel, with ubiquitous design, because, for the evangelist as well as for St Paul, the death of Jesus is all-embracing in its significance and achievement, the only key to the understanding of life and the only means of true living, the 'necessary condition of the life of the world'?

The object of the preliminary stage of this inquiry may now be more precisely stated. We have to try to discover how the fourth evangelist himself conceived the Christian religion and the demands it made upon those who professed it in his day; and in particular whether he regarded the relation between the death of Jesus and Christian faith and religion as merely casual or whether he thought of that death as both indispensable for the understanding of the truth of God and also uniquely creative of true life according to God's will. It will be suitable to begin our inquiry by returning to this predicted worship of the Father, 'in Spirit and in truth'.

According to the fourth Gospel, when Jesus cleansed the temple, driving out the sheep and oxen required for its sacrifices and disrupting the busy money-changing and marketing that this form of worship made inevitable, the Jews asked him for a sign, to justify what he was doing. Jesus answered: 'Destroy this temple, and in three days I will raise it up.' The evangelist notes: 'But he spake of the temple of his body' (John 4.19–22). This 'sign' and its interpretation give us an insight into his mind. He appears to be thinking both of the destruction of a building and of the dissolution of human life—the death of Jesus; both of rebuilding a demolished temple and of the resurrection of the body—the resurrection of Jesus. If we are right to suppose that this bears upon the prediction of true, spiritual worship—'The hour cometh, and now is, when the true worshippers shall worship the Father in spirit and truth . . .' (John 4.23–4)—it must be right to infer much more than that such worship will be initiated *after* Jesus is risen from the dead. The strong suggestion is that this worship will come about partly as a result of his rejection by his own people—the evangelist was perhaps thinking of the Scripture that the Lord would 'suddenly come to his temple . . .' (Mal. 3.2–4)—and of his death at their hands, for the narrative is deliberately set against the backgrounds of sacrifice and passover. Moreover, the prediction presumes not only the destruction of the temple and the end of animal sacrifices, but also God's presence in the midst of those who believe in Jesus, and the removal of sin. Consequently, both the death of Jesus and his resurrection are here bound up with the true, spiritual worship which will be offered in his risen body, the Church, and in a closer relation than that of being consecutive 'incidents' in the course of history.

Having described the Cleansing of the Temple, and noted that Jesus was referring to 'the temple of his body', the evangelist suggests that at the time no one, not even those who followed Jesus, had the slightest idea what this sign meant. He goes on : 'When therefore he was raised from the dead, his disciples remembered that he spake this; and they believed the scripture, and the word which Jesus had said' (John 2.22). What in fact he means here by 'the scripture' need not now detain us.[1] Of more immediate importance for our inquiry is the implication that the resurrection of Jesus (necessarily referred to as an event still future) will provide the context in which what Jesus said will be remembered by his disciples in such a way as to lead to their understanding 'the scripture' and believing 'his word'. We are reminded of other such notes made by the evangelist. We have been told, for instance, with some

[1] Psalm 69 – one of the 'Suffering Servant' psalms – has just been quoted (John 2.17; cf. Ps. 69.9), and the evangelist may have in mind the fulfilment of the hope expressed in the last eight verses ; or perhaps he was thinking of the general witness in the Old Testament to the resurrection, or of its general prediction of the vindication of the Messiah. See, however, R. H. Lightfoot, *St John's Gospel*, p. 130.

circumstance, that: 'On the last day, the great day of the feast, Jesus stood and cried, saying, If any man thirst, let him come unto me, and drink. He that believeth on me, as the scripture hath said, out of his belly shall flow rivers of living water.' Here, also, a 'prophetic' statement involves understanding 'the scripture' and 'believing' in Jesus. But now the evangelist comments: 'This spake he of the Spirit, which they that believed on him were to receive: for the Spirit was not yet given; because Jesus was not yet glorified' (John 7.37–9). Again, having described how the multitude went to meet Jesus as he approached Jerusalem, crying out, 'Hosanna: Blessed is he that cometh in the name of the Lord, even the King of Israel', and how Jesus rode on a young ass 'as it is written, Fear not, daughter of Zion: behold, thy King cometh, sitting on an ass's colt', the evangelist notes: 'These things understood not his disciples at the first: but when Jesus was glorified, then remembered they that these things were written of him, and that they had done these things unto him' (John 12.12–16). Understanding how Scripture is in fact fulfilled, faith in Jesus or in his word—these will result from his resurrection from the dead, or from the gift of the Spirit after he has been 'glorified', or from the disciples' remembrance after his 'glorification'. But what is to be understood, the *subject* of faith, is presented as part and parcel of the ministry of Jesus in the flesh. It has, as it were, already been fully stated in history.

This conception of the history of Jesus is substantially confirmed in what is said about the Holy Spirit in the 'Farewell Discourses' (John 14.15–17, 25–6; 15.26–7; 16.7–15). The scope of the Holy Spirit's teaching is, first of all, retrospective: to recall to the disciples all that Jesus has said to them; to bear witness to Jesus, simultaneously with the witness they will furnish out of their companionship with him, and in corroboration of it; and to convict the world 'in respect of sin, and of righteousness, and of judgement', that is, according to the historical reactions of the majority to Jesus when he came among men as man. And it is wholly derived. The Holy Spirit will guide the disciples into all truth, but 'he shall not speak from himself; but what things soever he shall hear, these shall he speak'. There is no doubt a reference to events still to take place. It is said that 'he shall declare . . . the things that are to come'

But this seems to mean, first of all, that through his guidance the disciples will understand such events as the passion and crucifixion, and the resurrection appearances, *as these occur*; at more than one point in the narrative of these events, the gift of the Spirit is referred to. If the statement looks even further forward than this, to particular events and experiences in the future, in which Christians will be involved as human beings, the implication remains that, through these events and experiences, the Holy Spirit will deepen their understanding and strengthen their faith in Jesus Christ. In any case, what is postulated is a new order *brought about by* the 'departure' or death of Jesus: a new order in which those who believe in him know themselves confronted with the last things of God, having with them, and within them, the spiritual witness to his presence (John 14.15–20), and consequently the assurance of the salvation and eternal life which he bestows.

Are we now moving away into a religion of the Spirit—or perhaps of the 'Christ-Spirit'? If so, we are certainly not being removed from the history of Jesus. Indeed, we are being pressed back upon that history. The Spirit is 'the Spirit of *truth*'. This we are told three times, with an insistence which reminds us that Christian worship will be 'in Spirit and in Truth'. The Spirit's function is, indeed, to reveal the truth of God. But the field of his revelation is always the truth of God *in Jesus*; the truth which has been observed by the disciples though not at the time fully apprehended by them. 'He shall glorify me: for he shall take of mine, and shall declare it unto you. All things whatsoever the Father hath are mine: therefore said I, that he taketh of mine, and shall declare it unto you.' What is meant by the 'all things whatsoever the Father hath' which are now 'his'? Whatever else, this at least: the potential witness to God of all that human beings experience. The words have been thought to echo, and elucidate in terms of the Spirit, the Matthaean and Lucan saying: 'All things have been delivered unto me of my Father: and no one knoweth the Son, save the Father; neither doth any know the Father, save the Son, and he to whomsoever the Son willeth to reveal him' (Matt. 11.27; Luke 10.22). The sum total of the revelation of God appears to be vested in the Son: and to be made perceptible to men only through the agency of the Spirit sent by the Father—the Holy Spirit, that is, the Spirit of

God.[1] But the part played in all this by Jesus, who possesses all that the Father has given him, is no merely passive one. The Father will send the Spirit as a result of the prayer of Jesus (John 14.16). And this prayer is not a mere matter of 'asking'. It involves all that is summed up in his prayer of 'consecration' or 'dedication' (John 17), including what is there implied as an interpretation of his imminent death and of his motives in laying down his life. Indeed, Jesus himself will send the Comforter (John 16.7), who will come 'in his name' (John 14.26). This Comforter is outside the competence, the perception, the cognizance of the world—as of the disciples before Jesus rose from the dead—but, in the new order of which

---

[1] In the Farewell Discourses, the authentication of the fulfilment of Old Testament Scripture is not explicitly stated to be the function of the Holy Spirit, as might perhaps be inferred from the passages examined on p. 138 above. The Jews, however, were traditionally sensitive to the possibility not only of false prophets but of the false interpretation of prophecy (e.g., Deut. 13.1–5; 18.15–22). It would seem that Christians like the fourth evangelist, for whom the Scriptures were essentially God-given means of revelation (cf. John 5.39), regarded the authority to fulfil Scripture, creatively and finally, as among the 'all things" given by the Father to the Son; and were therefore careful to represent the experience of coming to see how Scripture was fulfilled in the words and actions of Jesus, and in his death and resurrection, not as the outcome of human opinion, but as divinely guaranteed. The synoptic evangelists were content to record 'a voice out of heaven', or to speak of direct revelation by the Father. For instance, according to Matthew, when Simon Peter is led by what Jesus is saying and doing to declare: 'Thou art the Christ, the Son of the living God,' Jesus says to him: 'Blessed art thou, Simon Bar-Jonah: for flesh and blood hath not revealed it unto thee, but my Father which is in heaven' (Matt. 16.16, 17). The underlying argument seems to go like this. Peter, being supposed to have some familiarity with the Old Testament, or at any rate with the kind of expectation it had engendered in first-century Judaism, has recognised, in the historical person of Jesus, the fulfilment of scriptural revelation. But this at once involves him in a judgement outside his competence as a man, for it has as its subject the truth of God. Therefore, in so far as the conviction that has led him to this declaration approximates to the truth of God, it must result from insight given him by God. The fourth evangelist has no parallel to such direct revelation except in the case of Jesus himself (who alone descended out of heaven: John 3.13, 31; 8.23), and perhaps of John Baptist, where he recalls the synoptic account of the baptism of Jesus to explain how the Baptist recognized Jesus as the Son of God, although, like those he was baptizing, he did not know him. He is sensitive both to the problem of the revelation, in time and space, of the God whom 'no man hath seen at any time' (John 1.18), and to the danger that human subjectivity may run riot with the Christian gospel (John 16. 29–31). He therefore sees all human apprehension of the truth *objectively*, and tends to describe it as the work of the Spirit, while insisting, with an equal objectivity, that there is no revelation of God except in Jesus Christ. In the final resurrection narrative there emerges, however, a direct apostolic recognition of the risen Jesus (John 21.7, 12. see pp., 284f below).

Jesus speaks, the disciples know him: 'for he abideth with you and shall be in you'. From this reference to the Holy Spirit, however, Jesus at once passes, first to his own coming again to his disciples, next to his presence with them, when they will see him (though not as the world saw him) and will live because he lives (John 14.16–19), and then to the fulness of the Christian revelation of God: 'In that day ye shall know that I am in my Father, and ye in me, and I in you'; and to the Christian hope: 'He that loveth me shall be loved of my Father, and I will love him and manifest myself unto him . . . we will come unto him, and make our abode with him' (John 14.20–3). This conjunction—the Father, Jesus, those who believe in Jesus—is the substance of the revelation and the hope mediated by the Spirit. From this alone issues the worship of the Father in spirit and in truth.

To touch the fourth Gospel at any one point is to touch it at every point. Inevitably, we have been led to broach questions to which we shall have to return. So far, what would seem to have been established is this. For the fourth evangelist, understanding and belief on the part of the disciples of Jesus and his Church—appear, in the event, to be consequent upon his resurrection, his 'glorification' (which we have not yet attempted to define), and his gift of the Spirit. What the relation between these three concepts may be, we cannot yet say with any greater particularity; except, perhaps, that the evangelist appears to think of them as concomitant or concurrent, as associated together rather than as 'events' following upon each other in sequence (as the author of the Gospel according to Luke and the Acts of the Apostles might seem to do), yet certainly not as alternatives producing identical results. But this at least can be said without any qualification: the history of Jesus remains central. Here is the content of the word that is to be understood, the source of the faith that is to be created. And the most open and sustained teaching about this understanding and this faith is delivered in the context of his imminent death when, 'before the feast of the passover, Jesus, knowing that his hour was come that he should depart out of this world unto the Father, having loved his own which were in the world . . . loved them unto the end' (John 13.2).

In the evangelist's mind the resurrection, the 'glorification', of Jesus, and his gift of the Spirit are held closely together. But how does he relate each, or all, of these concepts to the death of Jesus? In this Gospel there are certain words which the evangelist seems to have chosen and used, almost or quite deliberately, in order to hold his fundamental ideas as closely as possible together. It may be useful to look at three of these words in some detail.

The first is the word *hupsoo,* a word which has two well-authenticated meanings: to raise up, locatively, and to exalt in the sense of magnify. It is used four times in the fourth Gospel, in three different passages (3.14; 8.27; 12.32–4). Commentators have frequently supposed that the author chose this word precisely because of its double meaning. It lay ready to anyone's hand who might wish to refer both to the physical lifting up of Jesus on the cross and to his metaphorical exaltation in glory. Perhaps the author hit on this usage because of the Palestinian word which may be taken to lie behind the Greek, and which means not only to be 'lifted up' but even to be 'crucified'.[1] Or perhaps it was through some sudden recognition of the way in which the lot of the Suffering Servant was fulfilled on the cross (Isa. 52.13).[2] However he came to adopt it, the author clearly had both meanings of the word in mind. But which of them, if either, was uppermost?

To make our task more difficult still, it seems very likely that when he first used this word the author was deliberately concealing his meaning.[3] Nevertheless, whether he baffled his readers or not, the death of the Son of man might well be supposed to be, *for the Christian author,* the primary reference of the analogy 'as Moses lifted up the serpent in the wilderness'. And the second occurrence of the word seems to confirm this impression. It is in a speech addressed to the Jews: 'When ye have lifted up the Son of man . . .' This must be a reference to the crucifixion, however obscure it might have seemed to those whom Jesus is described as addressing, for the argument is that Christ's 'going away' will be not suicide (John 8.22) but murder (John 8.27). And the third and fourth times the author uses the word he deliberately fastens the parable of the grain of wheat to Christ's death on the cross: 'This he said, signifying by what manner of death he should die.' Here he must

---

[1] C. K. Barrett, *The Gospel according to St John*, p. 9.
[2] In the LXX Greek, *Idou sunesei ho pais mou, kai hupsothesetai, kai doxasthesetai sphodra*: cf. Barrett, op. cit., p. 179; C. H. Dodd, op. cit., p. 375.
[3] So Dr Dodd, op. cit., p. 306.

mean us to understand that the multitude took the word to refer to the death of the Son of man, for he records that they answered him, 'We have heard out of the law that the Christ abideth for ever: and how sayest thou, The Son of man must be lifted up?'

So far, so good. But it is precisely this last instance that sets us wondering whether the author has only the crucifixion in mind. Throughout this Gospel, those who make judgements about Jesus —even his own disciples—are usually right in one sense but, in a deeper and more ultimate sense, wrong. Here, the multitude suppose that Jesus is speaking of the death of the Messiah—and are offended at the suggestion that he should die. Of the exaltation of the Son of man they have no inkling. We are reminded of the offence caused to the disciples of Jesus by his insistence that they must 'eat the flesh of the Son of man and drink his blood' if they are to receive eternal life, and of his words to them on that occasion : 'Doth this cause you to stumble? What then if you should behold the Son of man *ascending where he was before?*' (John 6.61–2). In view of this we are forced to ask again whether in each case the author does not clearly wish us to think of the 'exaltation' of the Son of man, as well as of his death on the cross. And with this in mind we notice that on each occasion the result of the 'lifting up' of Jesus is clearly described. Men will receive faith and eternal life (John 3.15); will be given knowledge of the truth about Jesus—that is, apprehend his true relation to the Father (John 8.28); and will be drawn to him (John 12.32). Now in this Gospel faith, knowledge, and full fellowship with Jesus Christ are fruits of his resurrection. They are demonstrated historically, first at the empty tomb, when 'the other disciple . . . saw and believed' (John 20.8); and in the appearances to the disciples—and in particular to Thomas, who confesses, 'My Lord and my God' (John 20.28), while it is the beloved disciple, again, who says, 'It is the Lord' (John 21.7); then in the apostolic mission to the world (John 20.31). These fruits had been anticipated in Christ's prayer on the eve of the crucifixion, both in respect of his disciples (John 17.6–19) and of his Church (John 17.20–6). The suggestion is that, from the first, when the author referred to the death of Jesus, his thought moved on inevitably to his resurrection and exaltation; and not only this, but that the author saw in the essential pattern of the ministry, in any threat of death or movement towards death, in any semblance of faith or glimmering of understanding, an anticipation of the event of Christ's death and resurrection.

The use in this Gospel of a second word, the noun *hora*—'hour' or 'time'—seems to point in the same direction. On three occasions we read 'his hour is not yet come' (John 2.4; 7.30; 8.20).[1] The first occasion is the Marriage at Cana. Here the reference appears as deliberately cryptic as the first use of the verb 'lift up'.[2] Yet the whole incident is described as a 'manifestation' of Christ's 'glory', as a result of which 'his disciples believed in him' (John 3.11). On the second and third occasions the Jews are seeking to kill Jesus. Now it would seem that the author has in mind the 'hour' of his death. But as the 'hour' of the death of Jesus in fact draws near, causing his 'soul to be troubled' (John 12.27), Jesus acclaims it as the 'hour' of his 'glorifying' (John 12.23, cf. 13.1; 17.1). We may compare, for instance, the emphatic 'now' in the utterance: 'Now is the Son of man glorified, and God is glorified in him; and God shall glorify him in himself, and straightway shall he glorify him' (John 13.31). The commentators tell us, a little easily perhaps, that 'the hour of Jesus refers to his death on the cross and exaltation in glory',[3] and that 'the word "glorify" denotes the death, the resurrection, and the return of Jesus to the Father'.[4] What exactly does this composite reference imply? Had the outcome of the gospel taken such hold of the evangelist's thought that he could not mention the death of Jesus without hastening to remind his understanding Christian readers of Christ's exaltation? This need not be supposed to suggest that the death of Jesus, and all that went before it, had become for the evangelist merely incidental to the exaltation, and therefore describable only in terms of the exaltation.[5]

---

[1] We may add to these John 7.6,8 where, using a different word, Jesus says 'my time is not yet come'.

[2] See p. 142 above.

[3] Barrett, op. cit., p. 15; Hoskyns, *The Fourth Gospel*, p. 188.

[4] Hoskyns, op. cit., p. 323.

[5] That this analysis of the author's way of thinking is not extravagant is confirmed by a note of Dr Dodd's: 'The question may be raised, whether even the banal *anabainein eis Ierosoluma* (go up to Jerusalem) (2.13; 5.1; 7.10,14), though it is an expression that every pilgrim to the temple had occasion to use, may not have had for this writer a suggestion of the *anabasis* (going up, ascension) of the Son of man (3.13; 6.62; 20.17)' (op. cit., p. 385n.). When it is remembered that on each of these occasions Jesus is said to have been going up to Jerusalem *to a feast*, and that his death and resurrection are set at the heart of the feast of the Passover, this seems even more probable.

Modern Christians who expound a gold or jewelled cross as the symbol of resurrection sometimes tend to evacuate the crucifixion of its physical reality and historical urgency. But it is not in that direction that the evangelist is going. It is not that at the mention of death he hurries on to speak of exaltation, but that when events might lead him to speak directly of Christ's glory he obstinately refers to his death. Before the first 'sign' which Jesus did, manifesting his glory, we have the caution, 'My hour is not yet come' (John 2.4). The glory of Jesus, it would seem, cannot be revealed except in anticipation of the 'hour' which saw him die. The argument at the end of the final discourse on the night before the crucifixion (John 16.29–33) is by no means untypical. His disciples say, 'Lo, now speakest thou plainly, and speaketh no proverb. Now know we that thou knowest all things, and needest not that any man should ask thee: by this we believe that thou camest forth from God.' To them, the hour of direct communication appears to have arrived, for they now believe themselves to be confronted by, and, indeed, to be actually apprehending, the revelation of the truth of God. At once Jesus answers, 'Behold the hour cometh, yea, is come, that ye shall be scattered, every man to his own, and shall leave me alone.' An event in history, what we call the passion of Christ, his isolation and death, will have a catastrophic effect upon his disciples, and throw their new-found confidence entirely into question. Yet this is no merely negative demolition in the interests of agnosticism or cynicism. *The Father is with him.* And his words have been spoken to them so that they may receive peace and the joy of Christ's victory. His words *are* the means of 'glory', but neither apart from, nor on this side of, his death.

A similar argument seems to underlie the evangelist's careful use of a third word, *semeion*, 'a sign'. This word has a central place in the vocabulary of the fourth Gospel, occurring no less than seventeen times. It is possible that the evangelist chose it because of its use in the Greek version of the Old Testament—particularly in Isaiah and Ezekiel—or because it might help him to communicate with those who had a smattering of Greek philosophy, or some acquaintance with popular Greek religion[1]: it was a word with various, sometimes quite technical, connotations, and we know that the evangelist was both sensitive to the allusiveness of words

[1] For the background of this word, see Barrett, op. cit., pp. 63ff.

in themselves and also careful to build upon the allusions that they already held for his readers. Whether he was aware of the use of *semeion* in the Christian tradition preserved for us in the synoptic Gospels is at present a matter of discussion. Certainly the word appears there in two groups of sayings, both of them apparently directly concerned with the expectation of the 'last things', that is, at any rate in a broad sense, 'eschatological'.

Mark, followed by Matthew and Luke, records that when Jesus foretold the destruction of the temple buildings, his disciples asked him privately, 'When shall these things be? and what shall be the sign (*semeion*) when these things are all about to be accomplished?' (Mark 13.4). The answer given by Jesus develops into a discourse about the 'last things'. He warns them that the end is not yet, even though false prophets come and lead men astray with 'signs' (*semeia*) and 'wonders' (Mark 13.22—a reference to Deut. 13.1–3). They must continually watch against the coming of the Son of man 'in clouds with great power and glory' (13.26). Matthew and Luke reproduce Mark's introduction to this discourse almost exactly, though Luke blunts the eschatology of the disciples' question (Luke 21.7), and Matthew sharpens it—'What shall be the sign of thy coming, and of the end of the world?' (Matt. 24.3). Luke however postulates 'great signs from heaven' (Luke 21.11) and, ready as always to embellish his point with snatches of Old Testament apocalyptic, 'signs in the sun and moon and stars' (Luke 21.25; cf. Isa. 14.12; 34.4). Matthew, however, adds to Mark's prediction of the coming of the Son of man, 'Then shall appear the sign (*semeion*) of the Son of man in heaven' (Matt. 24.30). From this it seems clear that 'the synoptists . . . preferred to reserve the word *semeion* for those eschatological events which mark the near approach of the end',[1] though the central point in their expectation is 'the Son of man coming in clouds with great power and glory' (Mark 13.26; Matt. 24.30; Luke 21.27 cf. Dan. 7.13–14). Yet it is only in Matthew that we read outright of the 'sign of the Son of man' as the answer to the disciples' request for a sign.

The other references to 'signs' in the synoptic Gospels are in answer to requests for signs made by the scribes and Pharisees (Mark 8.11–12; Matt. 16.1–4; Luke 11.16; Matt. 12.38–40; Luke 11.29–30). In Mark and in one of the Lucan instances the answer

---

[1] Barrett, op. cit., p. 64.

is that no sign shall be given. But in the other three instances there is added 'except the sign of Jonah', and it is asserted that this 'sign of Jonah' will be realized in the Son of man.[1]

The prediction of the destruction of the temple which ushers in the great apocalyptical discourses in Mark and Matthew and Luke reverberates through the passion according to Mark (Mark 14.58; 15.29). As we have already seen, the fourth evangelist also uses the word *semeion* in connection with the predicted destruction of the temple. *But he reverses the order of the argument.* It is not that, Jesus having foretold the destruction of the temple, the disciples ask when this shall take place and what sign will be given of its taking place. In the fourth Gospel the Jews (here recalling the scribes and pharisees in the synoptic Gospels) ask for a 'sign' to justify his cleansing of the temple. They are at once told of the destruction of the temple of his body and its raising up in three days. On another occasion recorded in this Gospel, when he is telling the Jews that the work of God is to believe on him whom God has sent (John 6.30), and that he is 'the true bread from heaven', Jesus is pressed for a sign. On that occasion also his answer runs to the thought of the death and resurrection of the Son of man : 'The bread which I will give is my flesh, for the life of the world' (John 6.51). Yet neither on these nor on any other occasion, does the evangelist actually call the death and resurrection of the Son of man 'a sign'.

Ask for 'a sign', so that you may see and believe—and the evangelist directs you to the death and resurrection of Jesus. Yet he refers to 'many other signs' which 'Jesus truly did in the presence of his disciples'; and states that his purpose in writing 'these' is in order that his readers may believe that 'Jesus is the Christ the Son of God; and . . . believing . . . have life in his name' (John 20.30–1). Is this a summary of the argument of his whole book? And if so, did he think of everything that Jesus did as a 'sign'? These

---

[1] It is immaterial for the present discussion whether the analogy of the Son of man with Jonah consists in his being three days dead and buried and rising again, or in the call of repentance uttered in the Christian *kerygma* (see note on p. 180 below). The point is that already in the synoptic tradition the belief that Jesus himself is the answer – Jesus crucified and risen from the dead – is superseding the request for a *sign wrought by him* – a request in the earliest tradition perhaps universally denied.

147

questions are difficult to answer because the word seems to be used in very different ways.

Several times, for instance, the fourth evangelist uses the word in the plural to conjure up situations reminiscent of those described in the synoptic Gospels, when the crowds thronged Jesus because of his works of compassion. 'Many believed on his name, beholding the signs which he did' (John 2.23). 'No man can do these signs that thou doest, except God be with him' (John 3.2). 'A great multitude followed him, because they beheld the signs which he did on them that were sick' (John 6.2). 'When therefore the people saw the sign (perhaps we should read "signs") which Jesus did, they said, This is of a truth that prophet that cometh into the world' (John 6.14). 'Of the multitude many believed on him; and they said, When the Christ shall come, will he do more signs than those which this man hath done?' (John 7.31). 'How can a man that is a sinner do such signs?' (John 9.16). 'John indeed did no sign; but all things whatsoever John spake of this man were true. And many believed on him there' (John 10.41).

Yet side by side with this recapitulation of situations and reactions well known to readers of the synoptic Gospels, we have a devastating criticism of those apparently moved to 'belief' by these signs. 'Jesus did not trust himself unto them, for that he knew all men . . .' (John 2.24). 'Except a man be born again, he *cannot see* the kingdom of God . . . Art thou the teacher of Israel, and understandest not these things?' (John 3.3–10). 'Jesus therefore perceiving that they were about to come and take him by force, to make him king, withdrew again into the mountain himself alone' (John 6.15).

The significance of this paradoxical record seems to be this. These things which Jesus did, which the evangelist calls 'signs', are real works of compassion or mercy, like the 'mighty works' described in the synoptic Gospels. They create 'belief' in Jesus, even to the extent of relating him to God, or to the Kingdom of God, or of identifying him with 'that Prophet' or 'the Messiah'. And so they should, and must. But to treat them as 'mighty acts' in themselves, suggesting that the Kingdom of God has come with power simply in their enaction and multiplication, is wholly to misapprehend their meaning. Such reactions on the part of the multitudes exposes them to the irony voiced by Jesus to the nobleman at Cana : 'Except ye see signs and wonders, ye will in no wise believe' (John 4.48); or to the equally searching analysis of their motives : 'Ye seek me, not because ye see signs, but because ye ate of the loaves, and were filled' (John 6.26). Neither a faith founded upon 'signs and wonders' as the ultimate basis of belief, nor a discipleship founded merely upon a recognition of the material effects of the 'signs' wrought by Jesus, can survive the judgement of the Word of God. So, when the period of the doing of 'signs' (John 2.1—12.50) draws to a close, before the complete restraint from the working of signs that marks the Passion narrative—'We must work the works of him that sent me, while it is day : the night cometh, when no man can work' (John 9.4)—the inadequate 'faith' of the Jews is finally examined, declared to be no faith at all, and shown to fulfil Isaiah's prediction of Israel's disbelief and consequent rejection : 'But though he had done so many signs before them, yet they believed not on him : that the word of Isaiah the prophet might be fulfilled, which he spake, Lord, who hath believed our report? And to whom hath the arm of the Lord been revealed? For this cause they could not believe, for that Isaiah said again, He hath blinded their eyes, and he hardened their hearts; Lest they should see with their eyes, and perceive with their heart, and should turn, and I should heal them' (John 12.37–40).

The evangelist goes on to observe that Isaiah 'spake of him (Jesus) . . . because he saw his glory'. Isaiah's prophetic insight anticipated in some measure the apprehension of those disciples of Jesus who, when Jesus was glorified, would receive the Spirit and believe (John 7.39).[1] It is these that the evangelist has in mind when, in his prologue, he foresees the response effected by the Word incarnate : 'We beheld his glory' (John 1.14); and when he points out the effectual significance of the changing of the water into wine and, by implication, of all the 'signs' of Jesus : 'This beginning of his signs did Jesus in Cana of Galilee, and manifested his glory : and his disciples believed in him' (John 2.11). It is not that he wishes us to understand that true belief did in fact emerge *before* the death of Jesus and the reception of the Spirit.[2] It is, rather, that he is contrasting two kinds of belief. On the one hand there is a belief generated in the crowds by the mere fact of the

[1] See p. 137 above.
[2] See p. 138 above.

'signs', by evaluation of them as visible or observable achievements, in isolation—a belief that is soon proved by the crowds' subsequent actions to be no belief at all. On the other hand there is a belief generated through the understanding of the death of Jesus by the light of his resurrection from the dead, a belief which, once their meaning is rightly perceived, these 'signs' also must be declared to generate.

With this deliberate contrast in mind the evangelist has apparently selected a number of 'signs',[1] and worked them into his narrative. He may well have known them as 'episodes' in the tradition he had received, or in written sources—most of them are paralleled in the synoptic Gospels. But he will not allow his readers to consider any of them in isolation. The Marriage of Cana, with the Cleansing of the Temple, leads directly into the discourse with Nicodemus, which ends with the dark references to the death and resurrection of Jesus and exposes Nicodemus—and, by implication, the 'believing' Galilean crowds—to judgement. The Healings of the Nobleman's Son and of a Cripple in Jerusalem lead directly into the long speech to the Jews (John 5.19–47) about the identity of the Son's work with the Father's, and about the Son's authority —a speech in which the raising and quickening of the dead is described as the 'greater work' which the Father shows the Son, while the 'hour' when 'the dead shall hear the voice of the Son of God . . . and live' is confidently foretold because 'as the Father hath life in himself, even so gave he to the Son also to have life in himself'. This speech, which provokes the Jews to reveal their murderous intentions, also ends in judgement—the judgement of the Jews who believe not the writings of Moses. The Feeding of the Five Thousand and the Walking on the Sea lead into the discourse of the Bread of Life,[2] and this in turn leads directly to the mention of the death and resurrection of Jesus, to the sifting out of belief and unbelief (this time in the disciples), and to a further

---

[1] Perhaps we may distinguish eight such 'signs': The Marriage at Cana (2.1–11); the Cleansing of the Temple (2.13–22) – not a 'miracle', but certainly a significant act; The Healing of the Nobleman's Son (4.46–54); the Healing of a Cripple in Jerusalem (5.1–8); the Feeding of the 5,000 (6.1–14); the Walking on the Water (6.15–21); the Healing of the Man born Blind (9.1–12); the Raising of Lazarus (11.1–49). The word 'sign' is used, in the singular, with direct reference to one of these, only three (2.11; 4.54; 12.18), or perhaps four (6.14) times.

[2] See below, pp. 166ff, for a more detailed examination of this discourse.

attempt to kill Jesus. The Healing of the Man born blind is developed dramatically in such a way as to expound the great theme of Jesus as the light of the world, leading up to the reaffirmation : 'For judgement came I into this world, that they who see not may see; and that they which see may become blind' (John 9.39). And immediately afterwards Jesus declares that he is the Good Shepherd who freely lays down his life for the sheep, and freely takes his life again (John 10.7–18). The Raising of Lazarus, it is true, does not lead into a discourse. But it poses the issue of life from the dead, at the command of Jesus, with great clarity and circumstance. And it is at once followed, not only by the final consultations of the Jews to put Jesus to death (John 11.53; 12.11), but also by Jesus's open declaration of the manner and meaning of his death (John 12.20–36).

To analyse the 'signs' or 'miraculous works' of Jesus apart from the whole flow of the complex and carefully formulated argument of the gospel would be artificial. But certain tentative conclusions may now be advanced.

As has often been noted, the two central themes of the gospel are 'light' and 'life'. These two themes find their dramatic climaxes in the last two 'signs'—the Healing of the Man born blind, and the Raising of Lazarus. The evangelist's intention, however, is not fully explained by saying that he is concerned with the revelation of God (light) and with eternal life (life). The author is concerned, and desperately concerned, about *apprehension* of the truth of God, and about the *place* where the truth of God is to be apprehended. The theme of life is inseparable from the anticipation of death. But in laying out both these themes, light (manifestation) as well as life, he presses forward to the 'hour' of the death of Jesus. It is tempting to suppose that, because the evangelist is trying to lay bare by means of these 'signs' what is fully revealed in the death and resurrection of Jesus, the word 'sign' has been chosen as insisting that all his actions 'look forward' to death and resurrection. Certainly, when he describes the Raising of Lazarus, the evangelist appears to be writing with the death and resurrection of Jesus in the forefront of his mind. Should we therefore speak of the death and resurrection of Jesus as itself the supreme 'sign' or, by contrast with the signs worked during the ministry, as the 'truth' to which they have pointed?[1] Either way, the point of the evangelist's careful contrast between two kinds of 'belief' would be missed. The death of Jesus is the 'place', the sole 'place of understanding', because it is there that his resurrection is made known. All the 'signs' of Jesus —all that he said and did, when truly understood—are seen to point to this sole 'place of understanding'. But this is not all. Immediately they are seen to point to the death and resurrection, they themselves are seen to confront men with the glory of Jesus, as directly and fully as do *his* death and resurrection. The death of Jesus *is* the place of understanding. But to those whose eyes have been opened (the theme of light) everything Jesus said or did appears translucent, bearing witness to his glory. As a fact of history, no one 'saw' this glory until he was 'risen from the dead' (cf. John 2.22). 'No man hath seen God at any time' (John 1.18). Sight like this is brought about by the Spirit, who had not yet been 'given' (cf. John 7.39). But revelation in Jesus Christ is not merely subjective: 'he that hath seen me hath seen the Father' (John 14.9). The meaning of what he does, and says, is neither established nor excluded by whether or not men in fact apprehended the truth in this or that episode, saying, discourse, or act. Therefore, once the truth in Jesus has been revealed in his death and resurrection, each episode, saying, discourse, or act is now seen to be significant, and cries out to be described as creating belief and manifesting his glory to the believer. What forces itself upon the evangelist, and drives him beyond the bounds of strict logic, is not so much that those who subsequently believed, failed at the time to apprehend the 'glory' in the events in which they took part—he is well aware of that— as the fact that what he could only call real belief was created even in those who did not have the courage to profess that belief! The fulfilment of Isaiah's prediction (John 12.37–40) sums up the out-come of the whole ministry to the Jews—yet immediately it has been solemnly recorded the evangelist adds: 'Nevertheless even of the rulers many believed on him; but because of the Pharisees they did not confess it, lest they should be put out of the synagogue:

[1] Dr Barrett, for instance (op. cit., p. 65) writes boldly 'in fact the death and resurrec-tion are the supreme *semeion*'. But a moment later he adds: 'Yet it is not a *semeion* and is not called a *semeion*, because it is not merely a token of something other than itself: this event is the thing which it signifies, not a *semeion* but *aletheia* (truth).' As the succeeding pages will attempt to show, it may be doubted whether this statement would have satisfied the evangelist.

for they loved the glory of men more than the glory of God' (John
12.42–3). The 'signs' of the Word of God *are* what they signify.
The truth apprehended at the sole point of crucifixion itself presses
upon men from every point in the life of Jesus, because every point
is significant of his death.

How all this may be; how we are to describe the relation between
the death and resurrection of Jesus and his historical actions;
whether we can understand the 'signs' recorded in the fourth
Gospel without raising the meaning of the eschatological associations which the word appeared to have in the synoptic Gospels; and
what all this telescoping of history really meant to the evangelist,
and might mean to us—all these questions wait for answers. But
we are now in a position to check some of the impressions we have
formed of the place of the death of Jesus in the synoptic Gospels
and the writings of St Paul. In spite of the preoccupation of the
fourth Gospel with 'life'—indeed, because of it—we find more
consistent references to the death of Jesus in this than in any other
New Testament document. Here also, the death of Jesus is linked
closely—we are forced to say, inseparably—with his resurrection.
But there is no evidence that it has become a mere formality of
thought; the reality of the death, and its urgent immediacy in the
whole context of his mission to the Jews, are far more constantly
insisted upon by the fourth evangelist than by any other New
Testament writer. The examples we have considered; the use of the
same word to signify the crucifixion and exaltation of Jesus; the
insistent looking for the 'hour' which comes only with his death,
for the 'glory' which can be apprehended only with his 'glorification', the prediction of the Spirit which, until he dies, is withheld
by that grim 'not yet' because the Spirit can be given only if he goes
away—all these point in one direction. The fourth evangelist is
deeply concerned with the problem of history. He will never allow
history, that is, actual occurrence, to slip into some secondary place.
But for him history is not a succession of distinguishable points in
time, each with a separable, self-contained, significance of its own,
such as you might evaluate, one by one, according to the extent of
their various contributions to truth, religious experience, ethics, or
what you would. There is one point at which men have been confronted with the meaning of every point of history, and some men
have apprehended something of this meaning through the Spirit.

But the unique significance of this one point does not now diminish, rather it raises, as it were to infinity, the significance of every other point. Looking back with the eyes of *faith,* it is impossible to describe any point at which Jesus Christ confronts men except in terms of glory and belief.

CHAPTER 5

The Humanism of the Fourth Gospel

That the author of the fourth Gospel regarded the death of Jesus Christ as the 'place of understanding' to which the whole ministry of the Word of God should have pointed those who witnessed it, and which, indeed, found its true significance in so pointing, may now be tentatively assumed. But are we perhaps still evading the issue? Does he not show us a 'human' Jesus, serene and undisturbed by the humiliation through which he wills to pass? And does not his spiritual gospel pave the way for a Christian humanism that may rest secure in the belief 'that the resurrection is past already' (2 Tim. 2.18); or at any rate liberate itself from St Paul's heavy conviction that the Christian life must be lived along the razor-edge traced out by the death of Jesus Christ? In any case, even if the literal follow-ing of the example of Jesus Christ, and the sincere imitation of the 'life for many' which brought him to the cross, is a necessary factor in Christian humanism, does not the fourth Gospel reject St Paul's arbitrary determination to see the imperative, 'Jesus Christ, and him crucified', written over the whole of life in this world? Surely here at least the fourth evangelist will give modern man a little en-couragement and help?

Unlike some modern men, but like the other New Testament theologians and writers, the fourth evangelist derives that under-standing of God's will for man which we may rightly call his humanism, from his apprehension of the relation between Jesus 'the Son' and his 'Father'. That relation conditions all that he records. If considered in a little more detail, it will soon be found to force us back upon the death and resurrection.

'Thou wouldest have no power against me, except it were given thee from above' (John 19.11). The mastery which Jesus shows in the fourth Gospel is not something that he possesses in his own right, or has achieved for himself. At the very point at which he is said to have insisted most plainly that he had authority over his own life, he attributes that authority to his Father's ordinance: 'This commandment received I from my Father' (John 10.17–18).

In the same way, his actions are not rightly understood if they are thought to issue from any essential liberty of his own, as though he could act without any reference outside himself (John 5.19–30). This is also true of his words: 'I spake not from myself, but the Father which sent me, he hath given me a commandment, what I should say and what I should speak. And I know that his commandment is life eternal . . .' (John 12.49–50). The Son's relation with his Father is wholly conditioned by his Father's commandment and his own response to it. Think of him (so the fourth evangelist would have us do from the first) as Messiah (John 1.41)—yet, from the holding of this office he derives neither self-determining privilege nor power. The acts, the words, the judgement through which he exercises his messiahship, even his ability to retain or yield up his life, are subject to his Father. But subjection is not subordination. As Jesus prepares for the supreme moment of his passion, and the theme of 'commandment' reaches its climax, a very different word transfigures his obedience: 'But that the world may know that I *love* the Father, and as the Father gave me commandment,' he says, 'even so I do' (John 14.31).

To modern ears this use of the sacrosanct word 'love', to signify unswerving obedience to a commandment issuing in death, may seem startling, unnatural, and forbidding. However, the word is in our text not by chance but by deliberate choice. It leads us straight to the central axis of related thought around which the author's mind consistently moves. Indeed, if we examine its use a little more closely, it will do more than give us a deeper insight into the relation between the Father and the Son. It will show us that modern sentimental idealism, however refined, can never by itself explicate for us the statement made twice in the First Epistle of John,[1] that 'God is love' (1 John 4.7–16); still less the inversion of that statement: 'Love is God'.

In the synoptic Gospels, a voice 'out of the heavens' had declared: 'Thou art my beloved Son, in whom I am well pleased' (Mark 1.11 and parallels); and again: 'This is my beloved Son, hear ye him' (Mark 9.7 and parallels). Whatever else their allusion, these acclamations must be taken to recall the words of Isaiah: 'my

---

[1] The Gospel according to John and the First Epistle of John may very probably not be from the same hand. They are none the less from the same workshop, and cannot be fully studied without reference to each other.

chosen (in the Greek version, "beloved") in whom my soul de-
lighteth' (Isa. 42.1). In the fourth Gospel, the story of Christ's
baptism is referred to (John 1.23–34), but not described; and no
account is given of his transfiguration. But throughout this Gospel
there are references to the Father's love for the Son (John 3.35;
10.17; 15.9; 17.23–4–6). And at the only point at which 'a voice' is
said to speak 'out of heaven' it is in answer to the great affirmation
of unwavering allegiance with which the Son, aware of imminent
death and troubled in soul, brushes aside his own suggestion that
he should pray to be saved from 'this hour', 'Father, glorify thy
name. There came therefore a voice out of the heaven, saying, I
have both glorified it, and will glorify it again' (John 12.27–8). The
conclusion seems inescapable. This is the evangelist's interpretation
of that prophetic and synoptic 'in whom I am well pleased'. He
wishes his readers to receive it in the context, not of spectacular
apocalypse but of Gethsemane. In his narrative there is no account
of rent heavens or descending dove, of glistering garments or over-
shadowing cloud. What is heard, some take to be thunder, others
the voice of an angel (in contemporary cosmology a phenomenon
equally terrifying but equally natural). Yet this should have been,
for the multitude, as it ought to be for the Christian reader, the
declaration not only of how the Father receives the faithful appeal
of his servant out of mental anguish, agonizing uncertainty, and
impending death, but also of what the Father makes of the unique,
messianic, obedience thus summed up. 'Now is the judgement of
this world; now shall the prince of this world be cast out' (John
12.31). Indeed, the Son's cry out of the depths and the Father's
response to it have already been anticipated in this Gospel: 'Therefore doth the Father love me (i.e., this is why the Father loves me),
because I lay down my life that I might take it again' (John 10.17).
The key both to the Father's love for the Son and to the Son's
messiahship is supplied in the Son's readiness to die—and to live!
To perceive this at the point of impending death is to become aware
that it has been pressing upon the reader all through the gospel
narrative. But, if the Father's authentication of the Son's readiness
to die in obedience to his commandment is described as 'love', so
also (as we have seen[1]) is the Son's obedience to the Father. And,
lest this mutual relation of love should be thought to be a closed

[1] P. 156 above; John 14.31.

circle of interaction, this same word 'love' is also directed outside it. The Father, who has loved the Son since 'before the foundation of the world' (John 17.24); who loves the Son 'because he lays down his life that he may take it again' (John 10.17); '*so loved the world, that he gave his only begotten Son, that whosoever believeth on him should not perish, but have eternal life*' (John 3.16).

Here our circle of mutual love is broken in order to create a second circle; and broken, it would seem (if we may illustrate it by the phrase of another New Testament writer) 'by the determinate counsel and foreknowledge of God' (Acts 2.23). The Son, whose love for the Father is shown in his obedience to the Father's commandment and his readiness to die, 'knowing that his hour was come that he should depart out of this world unto the Father, having loved his own which were in the world . . . loved them unto the end' (John 13.1). Again the circle is broken, again with reference to his death, and again creatively. For 'unto the end' means that Jesus loved his own not only 'to the very end of his life' but also 'completely', 'with entire self-sacrifice'.[1] His love, indeed, is like the Father's: 'Even as the Father hath loved me,' he says, 'I have also loved you' (John 15.9). And he goes on: 'Abide ye in my love. If ye keep my commandments, ye shall abide in my love; even as I have kept my Father's commandments, and abide in his love' (John 15.9–10).

What are these commandments? They are summed up in Christ's own (new) commandment 'that ye love one another' (John 15.12–17; cf. 13.34). And immediately, almost as though the author was aware of our modern proclivities and afraid that this commandment would be understood sentimentally, 'love' is again defined in terms of death: 'Greater love hath no man than this, that a man lay down his life for his friends' (John 15.13). Of whose love is Jesus now speaking? Of his own love, no doubt; but also of the love which Christians must have for each other. They are to love each other exactly *as he has loved them* (John 13.34). Such love may therefore be called upon to express itself in quite literal imitation of his love for them. When he described the Good Shepherd, he described the

---

[1] Professor Barrett, op. cit., p. 365, hears an 'eschatological echo' in the phrase, and comments: 'the hour of Jesus, the hour of his suffering, was an anticipation of the last events'. If there is an eschatological echo here, this is a signal understatement.

type of all Christian pastors.[1] Like other participants in the drama of Christ's ministry as recorded in this Gospel, Thomas spoke far more truly even than he feared when he said to his fellow disciples : 'Let us also go, that we may die with him' (John 11.6). We do not need to read of the consummation of Peter's love for the sheep of Jesus (John 21.15–17), of the death by which he would glorify God (John 21.19), or to turn to the Acts of the Apostles, to realize that these interlocking circles of mutual love never blur away into harmless metaphor and platitudinous good-fellowship. At no point can this love be divorced from broken flesh and poured out blood. If the disciples keep his commandment, that is, love him (again the two descriptions are identical, compare John 14.15 with John 14.21), Jesus will pray the Father and they will be given the Spirit; he himself will love them and manifest himself to them; above all, the Father himself will love them and abide with them (John 14.15–21, 23) : 'In that day ye shall know that I am in the Father, and ye in me, and I in you' (John 14.20). But essentially the same promise attaches to those who believe on Jesus through their word (John 17.20). For them too his prayer is 'that they may all be one; even as thou, Father, art in me, and I in thee, that they also may be in us' (John 17.21). And upon them too, upon their unity, their love for each other—which is, as it were, the expression in them of the Father's love for the Son—as upon the unity and love of the first disciples, does the witness to the world of God's love for the Son depend (John 17.22–3; cf. 17.26, also 13.35).

There is no doubt about the centrality and the reality of death in the love thus ascribed to Jesus and called for in those who follow him. Yet (we are told), if his disciples had 'loved him' in the days of his flesh (John 14.28), they would have rejoiced at the news of his death, his going to the Father—for 'the Father is greater than I'. At that time, the stupendous promise in his death was hidden from them. Like the Jews, they stumbled at such sentences as these : 'I lay down my life that I may take it again . . . I have power to lay it down, and I have power to take it again' (John 10.17–18). It was

---

[1] John 10.12,13 suggests that the evangelist has Christian pastors in mind; or at least so-called pastors who have proved themselves unworthy of their Christian calling. Presumably Jesus does not speak outright of 'shepherds' because, like the sheep, these must go in and out 'by him' (John 10.9). At the least, they must share his intention and purpose.

reserved for those perhaps symbolized in 'the disciple whom Jesus loved' to understand that the declaration of power to take his life again, with all the fruits that that bestows upon men, does not remove from death—for Jesus or for his followers—either its inevitability in God's ordering of the world, or its essential instrumentality in the achievement of God's purpose for the world, or its desperate and bitter reality in man's experience in the world, although it does remove its ultimacy and therefore its soul-destroying sterility.

The twin metaphors of 'keeping a commandment' and 'loving' have introduced us to the theme we know from study of the synoptic Gospels as the *dei pathein*.[1] This theme is given out in the Gospel according to Mark in the repeated insistence of Jesus that the Son of man *must*, or *shall, suffer many things*: 'be rejected by the elders, and the chief priests, and the scribes, and be killed' (Mark 8.31); 'be set at nought' (Mark 9.12); 'delivered up into the hands of men, and they shall kill him' (Mark 9.31); 'delivered unto the chief priests and the scribes; and they shall deliver him to the gentiles and they shall mock him, and shall spit upon him, and shall scourge him, and shall kill him' (Mark 10.33–4). Three of these assertions of suffering so imminent as to be already beginning (Mark 9.31) are followed by the affirmation of resurrection: 'and after three days (he shall) rise again' (Mark 8.31; 9.31; 10.34). The 'must' that leads to death *and* life 'for many' is said to be laid upon the Son of man not only by the Old Testament scripture (Mark 9.12–13; 14.21; cf. 1 Cor. 15.3–4) but also by the will of the Father (Mark 10.45; 14.34–6). Such repeated assertions, no less evident in the Gospels according to Matthew and Luke than in the Gospel according to Mark, reinforce the theme of descent[2] which makes the whole ministry of Jesus a *via dolorosa,* a pilgrimage in increasingly obvious humiliation and isolation, in which Jesus looks forward to the baptism which shall terminate his 'straitening' (Luke 12.50) and predicts for his disciples a comparable baptism and tribulation (Mark 10.39); in which, in fact, he calls them to take up his cross (Mark 8.34).

In the fourth Gospel this theme of descent is so universal that it has been suggested that each of the several 'episodes' into which

[1] *Dei pathein* is Greek for '(he) must suffer'.
[2] Cf. Chapter 2, particularly p. 114, above.

the ministry appears to divide is a deliberate recapitulation of it.[1] However this may be, the theme goes far deeper than any formal pattern on the surface. For it derives, not from the *external tension and conflict* between Jesus and the Jews (although, as we shall see, that tension is related to it) but from the absolute unity of Father and Son. At every point the human authority, even of Jesus, has to be evacuated of all semblance of an ultimately human origin. Consequently, although Jesus is introduced as 'the Messiah', the messianic title 'Son of man' is used simply to mean one who is man. Hence also the paradoxes in which this Gospel abounds—the paradox, for instance, contained in such statements as 'My Father worketh even until now, and I work' . . . 'the Son can do nothing of himself but what he seeth the Father doing' (John 5.17–19). That any action originates with the Son, or belongs to the Son in his own right, is rigorously excluded. It is not for the Son to bear witness to himself, or to judge others (John 5.30–1). Yet his judgement and his witness are true because they *are* the Father's (John 8.16–18), *and this has to be said*. The Son can, and must, deny any suggestion that he is speaking for himself, but he cannot deny his Word, since it is the Word of God. Similarly, Jesus 'sends'—but because he himself is 'sent'. If he is received in the persons of those whom he sends, it means that the Father who sent him is received in them (John 13.20).[2]

Finally, to take a further example from among the many that could be picked out of the prolific consistency of this Gospel, Jesus 'receives not glory from men' (John 5.41) yet—as the hour of his death draws near—he calls upon the Father to glorify him, in order that he may glorify the Father (John 17.1). But he has already glorified the Father upon earth, having done the work which he has been given to do! What remains, except that he should exercise the authority given him over all flesh—by giving those whom the Father has given him eternal life? And how is this to come about? How are these men to know the only true God and Jesus Christ whom he sent, except through the Father's glorifying of the Son with the Father's own self; that is, with the glory which the Son had with the Father before the world was (John 17.2–5)? Thus the

[1] See note (1) p. 134 above.
[2] Like much else in this Gospel, this argument echoes a saying recorded in the synoptic Gospels; cf. Mark 9.37.

words are, as it were, tossed about from Father to Son and from Son to Father. But this is not a game. It is a desperately serious demonstration in flesh and blood. On the one hand, the ultimacy of any human claim or power or assessment or opinion must be ruled out as finally as the fact of death rules out every possibility of men and women persisting in living, through some inherent right or ability of their own. On the other hand, the supremacy and immediacy and entire relevance of the Word of God become flesh must be constantly recorded and proclaimed, enacted and commended, for his whole purpose in the world is to offer eternal life from God.

On the one hand, therefore, Jesus is running right in the teeth of all the self-romanticizing thought and fantasy natural in man, and this he cannot do automatically or without cost to himself. It imposes upon him a necessity of self-abnegation such as can be adequately expressed only in actual death. But this self-abnegation dominates and characterizes his life so that almost as soon as he confronts the Jews he begins to speak of 'going away' from them (John 8.21), representing his whole ministry, as it were, as a progress towards death. Yet, on the other hand, *his already* are the words that create faith and life, the deeds that bestow grace and life, the presence that is incompatible with death because he is the source of life. And the fact that his whole ministry is at the time vain and futile—in that it produces, at the time, no full faith, no entire acceptation of grace, no total identification with his death— is not evidence of any failure on his part, *as man*. It is, rather, the grim measure of his human isolation before God. Something like this the evangelist is struggling to communicate when he records that 'Jesus . . . said, When ye have lifted up the Son of man, then shall ye know that I am he, and that I do nothing of myself, but as the Father taught me, I speak these things. And he that sent me is with me; he hath not left me alone; for I do always the things that are pleasing to him.' He goes on—for he is now describing the point at which faith does indeed begin—'As he spake these things, many believed on him' (John 8.28–30). But faith has not yet begun; nor is it yet clear to human eyes that the Father has sent the Son and has not left him alone. It is not long before some of these 'believing' Jews are being accused of seeking to kill him (John 8.31–7, etc.).

In itself, this pendulum-swinging between faith that is no faith and frustrated desire to kill is not an invention of the fourth Gospel. Essentially, it is to be found in the contrasted reactions of wonder and suspicion in the synoptic accounts of the Galilean ministry (e.g., cf. Mark 2.12 with Mark 2.6–7). The author of the third Gospel, thanks either to the insight of his principal source or to his own literary genius, prefaces the ministry of Jesus with an incident which, running from incipient acceptance to a murderous attempt to throw him down from a hill, seems intended to sum up the argument of the whole Gospel (Luke 4.16–30)—just as a novelist may sometimes make a beginning with a narrative symbolizing the course of his whole story.[1] In the fourth Gospel the 'wonder' is apt to be described, not once but habitually, as faith (e.g. John 2.22; 4.41–53; 8.31; 11.45; 12.11), while the 'suspicion' is repeatedly sharpened into intent to kill (John 5.18; 7.25–44; 8.59). But what the author is thus doing is to lay bare what is inevitably involved in his subject-matter. The whole is characterized —and apparently stabilized—by death; the whole is potent with eternal life.

These Jews, who suspect Jesus of blasphemy (just as the Pharisees did, according to Mark), in *wrongly* thinking that he is making himself equal with God (John 5.18; 8.53) and *devilishly* attempting to put him to death, in fact testify to the point at which alone the glory of the Father will be revealed in him. In *wrongly* thinking that he is contemplating suicide (John 8.22), they testify to his obedient acceptance of the death which is at once his Father's will and the means of life for the world. In all this, their opposition to his coming not to judge but to bring, and confer, eternal life, at once provides the eventual and actual occasion of eternal life, and subjects *them* inevitably to judgement and to death. All this is on the widest canvas. 'Salvation is from the Jews' (John 4.22), but the chief priests deny the heart of Jewish history and vocation : 'We have no king but Caesar' (John 19.16). Yet, if Pilate unwittingly forbids the expunging of the contrary truth (John 19.19–22), it is Caiaphas, the high priest for that year, who proclaims truly, but also unwittingly, that 'one man should die for the people' (John 11.49–51; 18.14). And the supreme reason for the Jews' rejection of Jesus, namely, the brief term of his life on earth, which they suppose to be inconsistent with the abiding of the Christ for ever

[1] For instance, as Thomas Hardy did in his *Tess of the d'Urbervilles*.

(John 12.34), is in fact the supreme ground for true faith (John 12.35–6a).[1] All this may seem to be a masterly exercise in irony, but the evangelist is not indulging in it for literary effect. At every point his thought runs directly to the death of Jesus because that appears to him, everywhere, to be the logical implication, the condition even, of his words and acts and presence on earth. Yet at every point his thought runs also to the resurrection of Jesus which, giving faith, giving life, does not remove death from the evangelist's subject-matter, but reveals its true glory—whatever that may mean.

This collision between the Jews and their Messiah is vitally important to the evangelist, yet throughout he is primarily concerned with the relation between the Father and the Son. The controversy leads, on both sides, to death. But that is, as it were, only the outward and visible repercussion of an essential tension that, in this Gospel, goes far deeper. For in this Gospel even the faith of the disciples, and even the faith of the Church which they appear to foreshadow (John 6.60–71; 16.1–4, 29–32), constantly come under criticism and are shown to be no faith at all.[2] In the paradoxes of that commandment to lay down his life which *is* the Father's love for the Son, and of that obedience unto death which *is* the Son's love of the Father, the author appears to be trying to describe a relation which only the obedient death of the Son can rightly convey and which must therefore be constantly referred to his death. In the sequence of negatives in favour of the Father, round which these discourses revolve, the 'I' of the Son is voluntarily evacuated of all the self-direction and self-sufficiency of which life (as opposed to death) naturally speaks to us. Thus, the positive use of the first person is, on the lips of Jesus, safeguarded from all suspicion of human egotism. And now the Son can, and must, utter the 'ego' which it is indeed blasphemy to take in vain.

---

[1] At this point Jesus finally hides himself from the Jews, whose unbelief is solemnly affirmed with quotations from the prophet Isaiah. He is not, however, here evading death: it is the Jews who disappear from the scene, to re-enter only in order to shout for his death. Nevertheless, even at this point, the author has to note that 'many of the rulers believed on him' (John 12.36b–43).

[2] In view of the author's insight, it would be hazardous to suppose that John 20.31: 'these are written that ye may believe that Jesus is the Christ', etc., has any bearing at all on the question whether this Gospel was written for Christians or for non-believers.

Even so, this utterance is carefully set at the very point of death : 'When ye have lifted up the Son of man, then shall ye know that I am he[1]' (John 8.28). But—and here we are perhaps beginning to move towards a fuller understanding of the relation between lifting up on the cross and exaltation in glory—because the theme of descent, the making nothing of himself that the Father's name may be glorified, is propounded from the beginning of this Gospel, it can be reversed within the Gospel. The evangelist does not ignore the order of his argument. The great positive statements beginning 'I am . . .' are not introduced until the relation between the Father and the Son has been fully adumbrated.[2] They then follow one another with no suspicion of human egotism, with no suggestion that a man is 'making himself' God. They are, as he is, nothing more, or less, than the Word of God. Now Jesus can say to Philip : 'He that hath seen me hath seen the Father' (John 14.9).[3]

Yet the death of Jesus is not thereby left behind, as a fact of history without significance beyond its event. In the immediate context (John 14.1–12), Jesus is speaking of his approaching death, precisely in order to show how very much more it is than death as men know and fear it. It would seem that, just because his speech is wholly conditioned by the fact of his death, he can speak positively and serenely of eternal life from and with God. The synoptic evangelists had written, as two propositions : 'The Son of man must suffer . . . and after three days rise again.' The author of the fourth Gospel writes : 'The Son of man must be lifted up.' He reaffirms both these propositions *in one word*. In so doing he does not smooth away the paradox, but rather intensifies it. He does not restrict its scope to a narrow sequence of events, but rather seeks to enlarge upon the tremendous, simultaneous, significance of what he has seen, or come to see, as a single event.

Furious controversy often foments the making of final judgements and the frenzy to kill. We might therefore ask whether, in spite of his life-giving purpose, the accounts of the polemical arguments between Jesus and the Jews were not bound to issue in

---

[1] Or 'I am I am'. The reader will rightly recall Exodus 3.14.

[2] The first 'I am . . .' statement is at John 6.35 : the relation between the Father and the Son is substantially set out in chapter 5.

[3] It may be observed that even if, as Professor Bultmann has suggested, this statement requires no demythologization, it none the less presupposes a complete *theologia crucis – et resurrectionis*.

approximations to his death—particularly in view of the historical sequel to his ministry and the years of bitter dispute between Jews and Christians which preceded the writing of this fourth Gospel, and in which the evangelist himself had very probably taken part. Shall we find the same tendency when the context is not rejection but acceptance; for instance, in the argument of which the climax is the first group of 'I am' statements: 'I am the bread of life . . .' (John 6.35–48; cf. 41–51)?

For these statements, the reader has been prepared by the account of the Feeding of the Five Thousand—a 'sign' so effective that Jesus had to withdraw, not this time to escape from death at the hands of the crowds but because 'they were about to come and take him by force, to make him king' (John 6.14–15). It is therefore introduced against the broad background of the general human need for food, and the satisfaction of that need—and of what happens, in such circumstances, to the man who provides a hungry multitude with bread. The crowds had 'followed' Jesus because of 'the signs which he did on those that were sick' (John 6.8). Next day they will 'follow' him, not now because of the signs they had seen before, or even because of this new sign *as a sign,* but because he gave them a good meal (John 6.26). The discourse that follows, in which the 'I am the bread of life' statements occur, is therefore set—like others in this Gospel—in the context of the fickle, misapprehending 'belief' and enthusiasm of the Galilean crowds, familiar to us from the synoptic Gospels, as well as in the universal human experience within the natural order (cf. John 2.23—3.12). We may expect it to offer an interpretation of that experience and, in so doing, to point the way towards true belief. We may also expect to learn from it more about the function of Jesus since—in what looks like a deliberate divergence from the synoptic accounts of the Feeding—we have been told that it was Jesus himself who distributed the bread, rather than his disciples.[1] And we must not ignore such other 'background' considerations as the evangelist thinks relevant—for instance, that 'the passover, the feast of the Jews, was at hand' (John 6.4)—even if we are rightly beginning to

---

[1] A similar intention, perhaps no more justified in historical fact, seems to lie behind the statement that Jesus was 'baptizing' and the immediate correction of it that follows (John 4.1,2).

wonder whether there were in his mind any limits at all to the relevance of his subject-matter, wherever he approached it.

The discourse opens with the words: 'Work not for the meat which perisheth, but for the meat which abideth unto eternal life, which the Son of man shall give you: for him the Father, even God, hath sealed' (John 6.27). At first sight this might seem straightforward enough. It might be nothing more than the correction of the idea that Jesus is come to supply material benefits and to be made an earthly ruler. The gift of the Son of man is eternal life. This it is for which they should have sought him. All this is sufficiently usual. But, before we follow the discourse further, there is an echo in these words which may perhaps give us pause and make us turn back to another passage that emerges from the thought of human dependence upon food: 'The disciples prayed him, saying, Rabbi, eat. But he said unto them, I have meat to eat that ye know not. The disciples therefore said one to another, Hath any man brought him aught to eat? Jesus saith unto them, My meat is to do the will of him that sent me, and to accomplish his work' (John 4.31-4). There seems to be an allusion here which leads us once again to the thought of the Son's essential 'work' of 'loving' the Father in carrying out his will (John 5.36; 14.31), of 'glorifying' the Father on earth (John 17.4). According to the Scripture (John 19.28), that 'work' will be accomplished on the cross (John 19.30), at the time anticipated in the setting of the scene for the sign of the Feeding of the Five Thousand—the slaying of the Passover lambs.

It is for Jesus alone to do the Father's will, and to accomplish his work. But even as he introduces this theme, the evangelist shows his inability to confine the scope of what is accomplished by Jesus to what is achieved in his ministry on earth. From the mission to the Samaritans which Jesus here inaugurates with apparent success, the evangelist's thought runs on at once to the apostles' mission in the world, and comes to rest, for the moment, in the same mission as it involves the Church in in his own day. It seems that he cannot think of that mission apart from what Christ has perfectly performed. The work is one, since only its completion by Jesus achieves the accomplishment of all that has prepared for it, and of all that arises out of it (John 4.35-42). And in the discourse which follows the Feeding of the Five Thousand the evangelist seems less concerned with the work of Jesus than with the work of those who obey his commandment. There is, in each case, a parallel between what is required. *His* meat is to do the Father's will; indeed—the closest possible identification—*to work the Father's work* (John 5.17). *Their* meat also is 'the work of God' (John 6.29). But there is also a significant disparity: *their* work, not his, is described as faith. They must believe 'on him whom he (God) has sent' (John 6.29).

The multitude then asks for a sign, citing the manna eaten by their ancestors in the wilderness during the exodus—bread from heaven (John 6.31; cf. Ps. 78.24). This introduces yet another frame of reference, but the Old Testament narrative is recalled only in order that there may be no doubt that the true bread from heaven is the bread which comes down out of heaven and gives life to the world (John 6.33). Patently, the bread which Moses gave did nothing of the sort, since their ancestors who ate it, died (John 6.58). Here, within the culminating framework of an Old Testament story *now truly* fulfilled in Jesus, the 'I am the bread of life' statements are made, whilst it is repeatedly asserted that coming to Jesus, believing on him, (John 6.35); beholding Jesus, believing on him, (John 6.40); believing him (John 6.47); eating him (John 6.50), means no more hunger and thirst, since it bestows eternal life.

Jesus, come down from heaven, the Word made flesh, *is* the bread of life, the bread that gives eternal life to the eater. This is entirely in keeping with the author's insistence—already noted—that the words of Jesus, his acts, his presence, should have been, and indeed *are*, the ground of true faith; *although in the event there was no true faith found*. But the discourse now takes a most significant turn. 'Yea', says Jesus, 'and the bread which I will give you is my flesh, for the life of the world' (John 6.51). Here, no doubt with the Christian Eucharist in mind, but also and primarily with the crucifixion in mind, the concentration upon bread becomes a concentration upon flesh and blood, the flesh and the blood of the Son of man which men must eat and drink if they are to have life in themselves. 'For my flesh is meat indeed, and my blood is drink indeed. He that eateth my flesh and drinketh my blood abideth in me, and I in him' (John 6.55–6). The Son of man gives himself, offers himself, in order that those who feed on him, who work the work of God in believing on him, may be identified with him. And since he has power, through the Father's commandment, to lay down his life and to take it again (John 10.17–18), Jesus goes on : 'As the living Father sent me, and I live because of the Father; so he that eateth me, he also shall live because of me.' Those who are identified with Jesus in his death are, *because of him and through his resurrection,* raised in accordance with the Father's will. Thus, and only thus—in the view of this Gospel—is eternal life bestowed; and here only—in Jesus, in his words and actions, and finally in his offering of himself—here only is the basis of true human faith in God, free from the possibilities of self-deception and delusion.

This discourse originated in the general experience of human-kind—the eating and drinking which must be carried on daily if life is to be maintained, which can satiate, but which can never satisfy. Christ's presence and action makes out of this experience a 'sign'—the sign that he is the fulfilment of the *more* fundamental need perceptible in this experience, satisfying that for which there is no earthly satisfaction. But, real though his presence is, and vital, ultimate, and uniquely free from corruption as is the possibility of faith that it offers, and truly as that faith must be said to bestow eternal life, even Jesus is wholly misunderstood if his coming is thought to make the final things of God's salvation available *within history.* The bread that gives eternal life will never be assured for men by their making him an earthly king. What Jesus has come to effect can be defined and accomplished only through his death and through that feeding upon him in faith which is identification with his death. So the discourse brings to those who read it the offer of eternal life, but only in confronting them with the crucifixion. And therefore the discourse moves immediately to the unresolved climax of every discourse in this Gospel. It has exposed those who are said to have heard (or who read) it to the alternative of faith or judgement, according to their reactions to the words of Jesus. The disciples murmur (John 6.61), and stumble. Many of them 'go back' and 'walk no more with him' (John 6.66). Although Peter rightly—but still with almost com-plete lack of comprehension—confesses that they have no one else to go to, since Jesus has 'the words of eternal life' (John 6.68), it is now openly declared that one of the twelve will betray him (John 6.71).

Is it possible that the movement of thought shown in this dis-course is exceptional? As a Christian, the evangelist must have been familiar with the Eucharist and, we may assume, with various 'backgrounds'—the Manna in the Wilderness, the Feeding of the Five Thousand—against which its meaning was perhaps expounded. Is it this familiarity that has led him to carry his argument through until those who believe are shown to be forced back upon the death of Jesus, not only as the ground of their hope of 'eternal life' but also as summarizing the obedience with which they must seek identification?

That his reasons are more far-reaching is strongly suggested by the evangelist's tendency, noticeable throughout his Gospel, to discern in the mission of the Church in his own day the direct results of the ministry of Jesus. In this connection it may be useful to consider three passages in all of which, probably without conscious cross-reference, the thought runs to the 'fruit'[1] of the Son's 'work' on earth : the interlude in which, as the Samaritans are approaching at the bidding of the Samaritan woman, Jesus tells his disciples that the fields are already white unto harvest (John 4.34–8); the speech which begins with the saying about the grain of wheat falling into the earth (John 12.23–6); and the discourse[2] on the eve of the crucifixion introduced by the last of the 'I am' statements : 'I am the true vine . . .' (John 15.1—16.33). These three passages are the only instances in the fourth Gospel of the use of the processes of nature, evident in the gardens and fields of a rural civilization, to set forth the teaching of Jesus. In the synoptic Gospels these processes provide a number of 'parables', generally described as demonstrating the Kingdom of God. In the fourth Gospel it is above all their fruitfulness that illuminates the purpose for which Jesus has come into the world. Indeed, just as the evangelist can hardly record the words of Jesus without recording the beginnings of true belief, even when the time of true belief is still 'not yet', so too he anticipates the effectual carrying out of the purpose of Jesus, even while the disciples have still to be scattered in fear, doubt, and despair.

First, the sight of the Samaritans coming out of the city to see Jesus is the formal occasion for his words about the harvest (John

---

[1] John 4.36; 12.24; 15.2,4,5,16. The word does not appear elsewhere in this Gospel.
[2] The last words of John 14.31 and certain formal parallels between 13.31 – 14.31 on the one hand and 15.1 – 16.33 on the other, make it usual to regard this part of the Gospel as comprising two discourses.

4.29–30), though thematically they follow from the thought of the 'work' which he has to accomplish, and which he will declare accomplished on the cross (John 4.34). The passage ends: 'I sent you to reap that whereon ye have not laboured: others have laboured, and ye are entered into their labour.' Here, as so often in this Gospel, there seem to be various 'planes of interpretation': the woman bearing fruit in the harvest of her own people; the work of the prophets, and especially of John the Baptist, completed in the work of Jesus; the apostolic mission based upon the mission of Jesus. But the argument seems to come to rest when the evangelist 'addresses his contemporaries and exhorts them to reap the harvest, so that the others who have laboured become . . . less John and the prophets of Israel than Jesus and the apostolic generation'.[1]

Again, the far-reaching saying about 'the grain of wheat falling into the earth' follows close upon the Raising of Lazarus and all the repercussions produced by it, the anointing at Bethany, and the Entry into Jerusalem. It is introduced with great circumstance by the account of the request of the Greeks to see him, and the words: 'The hour is come, that the Son of man should be glorified.' Indeed, it contains, as no other single saying does, the heart of the gospel. 'Except a grain of wheat fall into the earth and die, it abideth by itself alone; but if it die, it beareth much fruit' (John 12.23–4). That might be the text for the whole passion narrative, now declared to have begun. But almost immediately the thought widens from Jesus to the disciples, and through them to the Church: 'he that loveth his life loseth it, and he that hateth his life in this world shall keep it unto life eternal. If any man serve me, let him follow me; and where I am, there shall also my servant be; if any man serve me, him will the Father honour' (John 12.25–7). The hour of the death of Jesus is come, and the discourse will shortly give way to the solemn declaration of Israel's failure to believe and consequent rejection.[2] But this is already the hour of glorification, and the coming of the Greeks (like that of the Samaritans) seems to foreshadow the fulfilment, *in the mission of the Church*, of the Old Testament expectation of the time when God's Name would be honoured and feared by the gentiles (Pss. 103.15; 113.3–4; Isa. 59.19; Mal. 1.11). The death of Jesus is infinitely fruitful. It is

---

[1] Hoskyns, op. cit., p. 247.
[2] See pp. 149, 157, above.

central, unique, and all-embracing, the sole and sufficient work of God which he will accomplish on the cross. Yet its positive result is none the less the fruit unto life eternal (John 4.36) which the disciples will gather in by following him and 'hating' their lives after his example (John 15.25–6). *Their lot in this world may be identical with their master's, for they must follow his example if they are to serve him.* But any fruit they may bear is his fruit, borne by them only because they abide in him.

Again, on the eve of the crucifixion, in the context of the imminent death of Jesus, and in the setting in which the synoptists record the Last Supper, the fourth evangelist shows us Jesus concentrating his thought upon the disciples he has chosen and appointed to 'go and bear fruit that will abide' (John 15.16), and through them on those who will later believe through their word. Here we have the statements : 'I am the true vine, and my Father is the husbandman', 'I am the vine, ye are the branches' (John 15.1–5). The thought of the death of Jesus does not lose its centrality (cf. John 15.13), but in the ensuing discourse he speaks more openly than ever before of the persecution, the hatred, and the tribulation, that his disciples will encounter in this world. Side by side with this the thought of resurrection begins to become more explicit, for this is the hour of glorification. Jesus now speaks openly of the Comforter whom he will send to his disciples, and of his own coming to them again. But the shadows become darker and more sombre as he speaks of the approaching light. Like those that go before, this final discourse ends with the possibility of rejection. At the moment when the disciples believe they at last understand him, he tells them that they will soon all be scattered, every man to his own home (John 16.29–33). A tribulation more searching than their external tribulation at the hands of men has already begun— the tribulation which is the abiding condition of faith, and which no doubt reflects the necessary condition of his own obedience to his Father in this world. This is how the Father, the husbandman, cleanses the branches that bear fruit (John 15.2), if they abide in the true vine, Jesus. And in so abiding, and bearing much fruit, like him they also will glorify the Father (John 15.8).

We may now venture certain preliminary conclusions regarding the humanism of the fourth Gospel.

At the centre of the evangelist's understanding of the world and of life in the world stands the human figure of Jesus—what he actually said, and did, and how he lived and died, in history. His words should create belief, his works generate true life in those who believe, yet his death conditions both the revelation of the truth and the communication of the power in his words and works.

The death of Jesus cannot be explained simply as the result of the hatred of hostile men—gravely significant and horrifyingly real as their opposition was. The obedience of Jesus 'unto death' is the necessary expression in history of the relation between the incarnate Son and his Father.

Again, his death accomplishes the work of God and overcomes the world. But those who believe in him are not thereby released from tribulation in this world. Rather, they are called to life like his, in the immediacy of death: to life to be lived 'unto death' as their master's had been. And their relationship with their master involves them in an inward tension that is far more exacting than external tribulation—in their case, the tension which is the necessary condition of faith.

The humanism of the New Testament is defined, and indeed created, by the human life of Jesus. It does not manifest itself in perfect visible achievement, such as the men of this world may wonder at and admire; nor yet does it formulate itself in a licence of self-expression uncontrolled by any law outside the will of man. It is, from the point of view of this world, a perfection of 'brokenness' that finds its supreme statement on the cross. A study of the fourth Gospel therefore confirms the essential insights we have found in the writings of St Paul, and makes it impossible for us to dismiss them as arising from St Paul's own personal constitution. Nevertheless, it remains true that the abiding impression made by the writings of the fourth evangelist is one of life, peace, joy, victory, and glory. Accordingly any final estimation of his humanism must wait until we have tried to discover what it meant to him that Jesus is 'the resurrection and the life.'

APPENDED NOTE

In this chapter we have found Jesus presented as fulfilling, through his creative word and in his death, the witness of whole categories of human experience. It is important to notice that this presentation is not limited to the 'I am' statements, and is too deeply involved in the evangelist's material to be regarded as belonging only to the framework of his thought.

It should be observed that, with one exception, all the 'I am' statements, whatever their associations in Greek thought, belong to the vocabulary of everyday life. Their religious or philosophical associations are essential for understanding their full meaning, and may well have partly determined their choice. We must certainly suppose, for instance, that when the evangelist writes 'I am *the real vine*' he is hoping to communicate his meaning the more successfully by using such language as that which a Platonist might have employed to express 'the idea of vine'.[1] His material was given by the *whole* world as he knew it. Nevertheless, the fundamental allusions in his predicates lie far deeper down,—and, para-doxically, far more obviously on the surface—in common experience. Not only Greeks in the first and second centuries of our era, but men and women of many cultures, in many ages, have been familiar with vines, doors, roads, and shepherds, both in their physical environment and as part of their religious or ethical imagery. It is normal to be concerned about 'the truth', whatever dialectic we may use when trying to argue towards it. It would be abnormal not to be fully aware of the phenomena of light and life, and of the patterns they commonly impose upon almost all forms of existence. The one exception is the word ridiculed by the Athenians when St Paul uttered it at Athens (Acts 17.18–32): 'the resurrection'. In the fourth Gospel this word, which cuts right across the ordinary experience of human existence, *must* be coupled with 'life' when applied to Jesus, since he is the source of life (John 7.38), 'who quickeneth whom he will' (John 11.25; cf. 5.21–9).

But it would be wrong to regard the 'I am' statements as con-trolling the pattern of the evangelist's thought. Like the 'signs', they vary greatly in the extent of their elaboration. 'I am the light of the world' (John 8.12), on the one hand, might be placed appo-sitely almost anywhere in this Gospel, for it summarizes one of its major themes—yet there is little in the immediate context to show why it should have been introduced where it is. On the other hand, the statements, 'I am the door', 'I am the good shepherd', both twice repeated, draw into themselves the whole significance of the

[1] Cf. C. H. Dodd, op. cit., p. 173.

'parable' which has just been told; indicate, with grasp and depth, the scope of the passion now close at hand; and then disappear altogether from the scene! The evangelist has no more ordered his narrative around these statements than (as we have seen) around a limited number of carefully chosen 'signs'. Rather, the pattern of his thought is consistently determined by his understanding of Jesus in relation to the whole world of his own experience, to the hope of Israel, to the disciples who accompanied him, to the Church which sprang from their word. From time to time this understanding finds crystallization in an 'I am' statement. But where no such statement emerges, Jesus stands, all-embracingly, at the centre of the argument, as our brief consideration of the references to the fruitfulness of the processes of sowing and harvesting have shown. Yet here also he consistently anticipates the hour of his crucifixion which is the hour of his glorification.

CHAPTER 6

The Old Testament Setting of New Testament Theology

So far, all that has been asserted is that the New Testament writers, and presumably therefore the outstanding exponents of the meaning of Christianity to the primitive Church and to all who were willing to hear them speak, regarded the death and resurrection of Jesus as strictly relevant to human life considered as a whole. This relevance did not concern merely the end of life, or certain fragments of it, nor was it merely a kind of general prolegomenon to thought and action. For these men, the death and resurrection of Jesus conditioned the life and thought of the Church at every point. They were, moreover, persuaded that the salvation of human society, and indeed of the world, depended upon the recognition and apprehension that human life was so conditioned. This belief and conviction made them speak and write, and made them evangelists. To modern readers of the New Testament this relevance is not at all obvious, and, to judge from the tension between writers and readers that is everywhere apparent in the New Testament, and from the hints it contains of an even greater tension between those who spoke and those who heard, between what was said and what was apprehended, it does not seem that the modern reader is in any way unique in his aloofness. The modern reader may, of course, be right. There may be no *theologica crucis*; at least there may be no *theologica crucis* sufficient to bear the weight that is being put upon it in the New Testament. But, even so, we are not thereby absolved from the necessity of trying to understand it; and, if we are to understand it, we must be prepared to follow the New Testament writers along their own road rather than to be perpetually marshalling them along a road which we have chosen for them. Otherwise we are bound to make them dumb and nonsensical and therefore unintelligible, in spite of the fact that at times they may seem to be saying remarkably good things. It is the framework in which these good things are said that ultimately matters, and it is this framework that is so very difficult.

176

No New Testament writer supposes for one moment that what he is saying is at all intelligible unless men are in fact standing where the prophets of Israel and the Old Testament Scriptures have compelled them to stand. All the New Testament writers assume that human life has already been defined in the Old Testament. They require their readers to take this definition seriously. They affirm that there is no other description of life capable of providing a setting in which they can speak or be understood. If this be so, it is manifestly important to understand what this definition in fact is, quite apart from any judgement whether the definition be in any way right or even tolerable.

The most primitive preaching of the gospel, so far as it may be recovered from the writings of St Paul and the Acts of the Apostles, began by setting the death and resurrection of Jesus in the context of the Old Testament Scriptures. 'For I delivered unto you first of all that which also I received, how that Christ died for our sins according to the scriptures; and that he was buried, and that he hath been raised on the third day according to the scriptures . . .' (1 Cor. 15.3–5). The third evangelist concluded his Gospel with the picture of Jesus opening the Scriptures to his disciples, interpreting to them in all the Scriptures beginning from Moses and the prophets the things concerning himself, namely, that it behoved the Christ to suffer and to enter into his glory, and saying to them, 'Thus it is written, that the Christ should suffer, and rise again from the dead the third day; and that repentance and remission of sins should be preached in his name unto all the nations, beginning from Jerusalem' (Luke 24.25–7, 32, 44–7). And the same writer holds on to this picture when in Acts he describes the preaching of Peter and Paul to Jews and to Gentiles. As his custom was, St Paul went into the synagogues of the Jews and reasoned with them out of the Scriptures, 'opening and alleging, that it behoved the Christ to suffer, and to rise again from the dead' (Acts 17.2–3). The speeches in the opening chapters of Acts fall into a consistent form. Jesus is proclaimed as the Christ, his death and resurrection are set on the background of a network of Old Testament passages, and then on the basis of what has been said repentance is required of those who hear (Acts 2.14–40; 3.12–26; 8.26–39; 10.34–43; 13.16–42).[1]

No doubt the speeches in Acts are Lucan compositions. No doubt

[1] See the analysis by Dr Martin Dibelius in his *From Tradition to Gospel*, London 1934.

his selections of Old Testament passages are largely his particular selections. None the less, the confidence with which he refuses to isolate the themes of crucifixion and resurrection, and the confidence with which he throws back upon Jesus himself the insistence upon the importance of the general Old Testament background, are most surprising. Nor is the author of the Acts of the Apostles unaware of the difficulties for his Gentile readers involved in this procedure. For, in recording or making the speech of Paul on the Areopagus at Athens, he reserves the intermingling of language that is peculiarly Jewish and Christian to the end, and precisely at that point feels bound to record the mocking that is evoked by the demand that men should repent by the reference to a day of judgement, and most of all by the notion of death and resurrection (Acts 17.30–2). The citation of the Old Testament Scriptures is not designed by this writer to provide a secondary line of apologetic relevant only to Jews; it is rather the primary setting in which alone it is really possible for him to speak of the death and resurrection of Jesus, and it provides also the ground for the exhortation to repentance and of the theme of forgiveness of sins. It is therefore impossible for him, in writing for Theophilus, and through him for the Gentile world, to leave the Old Testament behind him as though it were relevant only to the earlier period of Christian history when the problem of the conversion of Jews drove all other problems into the background, or to that still more remote period when Jesus spoke only to Jews.

Nor is the author of Luke and Acts in the least exceptional in his behaviour. In addressing the Church in Rome, which may be presumed to have been predominantly Gentile, St Paul asserts at the very beginning that the gospel of God concerning his Son Jesus Christ was 'promised afore by his prophets in the holy scriptures' (Rom. 1.2), and throughout his long epistle never strays far from what had already been written in the Old Testament. Similarly, his letter to the Galatians, who by definition were Gentile pure and simple, is a veritable mosaic of Old Testament allusions and expositions. Indeed, precisely at the point where he refers to their original conversion and to what he had first said to them, he goes, it would seem, out of his way not only to quote the Old Testament in order to make clear to them what had then occurred but to do so in such a manner as to obscure the simplicity of their conversion altogether

178

(Gal. 3.6–14). Yet to say this is clearly to misunderstand St Paul, for he could not have written as he did unless the passages he selected had appeared to him transparently relevant. No doubt the Galatians had not understood his teaching, for otherwise they would not have regarded circumcision as a step forward in the progress of piety. But, in trying to understand St Paul, we can hardly take refuge in what seemed to him downright stupidity, and then proceed to blame him for complicating the situation by introducing in the course of a few sentences three references to the book of Genesis, one to Leviticus, two to Deuteronomy, and one to the prophecy of Habakkuk. St Paul is not playing with his converts, or trying to puzzle them. He is wrestling for their souls by trying to kindle in them some theological perception in order that they may not be at the mercy of the last plausible visitor to Galatia. This is, at least, the situation as St Paul saw it; the situation in which he makes his remarkable, but nevertheless confident, appeal to the Old Testament. And he has been impelled to do so by the necessity of explaining why they owed their conversion to his open proclamation of Christ crucified before their eyes (Gal. 3.1).

Nor is it really otherwise with St Mark and with the fourth evangelist. The former, although writing, as both tradition and the character of his book assert, for non-Jewish readers, begins his Gospel by combining two Old Testament passages and by reintroducing Old Testament prophecy in the figure of John the Baptist, whose dress and behaviour recall the prophet Elijah; and ends it by presenting the crucifixion of Jesus on the background of the description of the persecuted poor in the Psalter. The latter, though moving in a Greek-speaking, Greek-thinking society, in order to explain the meaning of what Jesus is, requires his readers to follow him into the world of Judaism, to Jerusalem, to the temple, and to the temple at the time of the great feasts; and he dins into their ears the language of the Old Testament Scriptures, not because it is his own native literature (though it may have been so), not even because these Scriptures 'have eternal life', but because it is they that 'bear witness' of Jesus (John 5.39). He exhorts his readers to believe what Moses wrote, because so only will they believe, or indeed understand, what Jesus said (John 5.4). And finally, when he comes to retell the story of the death of Jesus, he sets it not merely historically but theologically on the background of the

Passover (e.g. John 13.1; 19.14; 19.36). Why should he thus have endeavoured to tear the Greeks up by the roots and plant them in a foreign soil? Surely he is no more playing with his readers than St Paul is. Nor can it be seriously maintained that he is compelled to write as he does because he is limited and confined by the necessity of writing accurate history.

Although the setting of the death and resurrection of Jesus in the perspective of what had already been said in the Old Testament is universal in the New Testament and reaches back to the earliest strata of the synoptic Gospels accessible to us;[1] and although this background is extended to cover all that is recorded of the life of Jesus and everything too that Christians are expected to do and think, the manner in which the Old Testament is used is by no means everywhere the same. In the first place there is a remarkable difference between the way in which Jesus himself is represented as appealing to Scripture and the way in which the evangelists assert its fulfilment. When Jesus, for example, cites the 110th Psalm, in which David is represented as recognizing a monarchy beyond and above his own, in order to throw into question altogether every notion of the Messiah that sets his royalty in a line with David's, he is not primarily asserting his own Messiahship but defining the context in which the whole conception of the Christ must be understood (Mark 12.35–7; Ps. 110.1). And—here is the point—it is the Psalter that had already provided the proper definition. Again, the condemnation of Capernaum, 'And thou, Capernaum, which art exalted to heaven, shalt be brought down to hell', by echoing the prophet's condemnation of Babylon, makes of the judgement of God against everything that is exalted in itself and has ascended 'above the heights of the clouds' and has made itself 'like the most High' a present judgement (Matt. 11.23; Luke 10.15; Isa. 14.13–15). But the ground of the judgement of God has already been perceived and defined by the prophets of Israel. Or again, when it is

---

[1] It belongs to all four distinguishable 'sources', e.g. (Mark 12.10; 11; 14.27, 28; 15.34), 'Q' (Matt. 12.39, 40; Luke 11.29, 30); Special Matthew (Matt. 26.52–4); Special Luke (Luke 22.37; 23.46). The reference in Q to the sign of Jonah may, in its Lucan form, be no more than an allusion to the repentance of the Ninevites, but the sign of the Son of man is a future, not a present, event, 'so shall also the Son of man be to this generation', and to Luke the Christian preaching of repentance depends upon the death and resurrection of Jesus.

recognized that the requirement of prayer, 'But thou, when thou prayest enter into thine inner chamber, and having shut thy door, pray to thy Father which is in secret, and thy Father which seeth in secret shall recompense thee' (Matt. 6.6) echoes what had already been required of Israel, 'Come, my people, enter thou into thy chambers, and shut thy doors about thee: hide thyself for a little moment, until the indignation be overpast' (Isa. 26.20), it must also be recognized that the seclusion demanded by Jesus is similar. Here is no 'pride of prayer', not even the seclusion of quiet, confident solitary prayer and meditation. Here, rather, is a tremulous retirement in the midst of the impending judgement of God, a veritable prayer *de profundis*. But the definition of the whole situation in which prayer takes place is a definition already provided by Old Testament prophecy. With this definition of prayer we may compare the retirement of Elijah described in 1 Kings 17.18–19, and the behaviour of Elisha in the presence of death described in 2 Kings 4.33. Or again, when Jesus comes to speak of the safety of his disciples, 'Behold, I have given you authority to tread upon serpents and scorpions, and over all the power of the enemy: and nothing shall in any wise hurt you' (Luke 10.19), he does so in the language of the Psalter, 'Thou shalt tread upon the lion and adder; the young lion and the dragon shalt thou trample under foot' (Ps. 91.13); and by so doing he defines and shows forth the nature of the salvation of God as the psalmist had already defined it, 'Because he hath set his love upon me, therefore will I deliver him . . . I will be with him in trouble', and introduces a conception of exaltation wholly different from that of Capernaum, 'I will set him on high, because he hath known my name' (Ps. 91.14, 15).

Such passages represent far more than a mere citation of Old Testament texts, far more than an allusion to Old Testament language, far more than the application of Old Testament prophecy to substantiate the claims of Jesus. This is a wholly creative handling of the Old Testament: a creative handling that proceeds from a sure and certain understanding of it. In narrating the life and death of Jesus, the synoptic evangelists cast their narratives in words that recall Old Testament prophecy; they introduce citations to show explicitly its explicit fulfilment; and they were, no doubt, led to do so by a tradition originating in the practice of Jesus himself. But there is a marked distinction between their pedestrian discovery of some degree of literal identity between the events they describe and Old Testament prophecy, and the confident assurance with which Jesus seizes upon a phrase of Scripture, evokes its vast theological background, and then shows thereby not only what current events are and what they mean, but also how the Scriptures themselves become an event, and receive their final meaning in what is taking place. To Jesus the Scriptures are luminous with the light of the Kingdom that has come nigh; to the evangelists they are quarries for proof-texts calculated to edify or to convince. The synoptic evangelists seem hardly to have understood Jesus's use of Scripture. They quote *because* he did, but not *as* he did.

But it is not so with St Paul. In the Old Testament he sees resolved the problems with which he himself is faced, not as a body of legal precedent to which appeal may be made, upon which arguments may be based, and from which conclusions may be reached, but as the word of God whose concrete application is pereceived only in the present. So when the Hebrews passed through the Red Sea, ate the manna, and drank of the rock, these things 'happened unto them by way of example: and they were written for our admonition, upon whom the ends of the world are come' (1 Cor. 10.11). The true situation, foreshadowed by the situation of the Hebrews in the desert, is that of the Christians held in the tension between this world and the next. When St Paul recalls that Abraham's faith was reckoned unto him for righteousness (Rom. 4.3; Gal. 3.6), he is making no rabbinical appeal to a biblical story in order to justify, out of the law, liberty from the law. Abraham displays God's promise of a righteousness through faith and not by the keeping of the law; but the faith about which Paul is arguing, and the promise in which he is glorying, are not the ancient facts, either as precedent or as historical event, of Abraham's faith in God's promise, but the faith which is revealed through Jesus in whom the promises of God are fulfilled. 'Now it was not written for his sake alone, that it was reckoned unto him; but for us also, unto whom it shall be reckoned, who believe on him that raised Jesus our Lord from the dead, who was delivered up for our trespasses, and was raised for our justification' (Rom. 4.23–5). Paul does not mean that Abraham was a Christian before his time. He is not interested in Abraham as an isolated historical figure. What he does mean is that the story of Abraham is full of meaning for Christians and that it has now for the first time come into its own. Again, he is concerned with what the Christians are, with the possibility of faith that is theirs, and with the fulfilment of the promises of God in the death and resurrection of Jesus. The story of Abraham provides him with the framework of theology in which he can show the Christians the truth about themselves.

But what is to be said of that long drawn out wrestling with the law that forms the background and the foreground of so much that St Paul says? Not for one moment can he dismiss the law as though it were merely a ritual which has been outgrown at the coming of Christ. Fundamentally, the law means to him the Ten Commandments. The entire Old Testament, as he sees and understands it, is concerned to rivet the commands of God upon the whole area of human behaviour. The law stands related to the promises of God. This relationship also is the theme of the Old Testament. The law does not obliterate the promise of God and never did so (Gal. 3.17). It was 'our tutor to bring us unto Christ' (Gal. 3.24). The relation between law and promise must not, however, be thought of as a chronological sequence, as though law merely preceded the coming of Christ and could be discarded when he came; for it is at his coming that the law is for the first time seen as it really is. 'Is the law then against the promises of Christ? God forbid : for if there had been a law given which could have made alive, verily righteousness would have been of the law. Howbeit the scripture hath shut up all things under sin, that the promise by faith in Jesus Christ might be given to them that believe. But before faith came, we were kept in ward under the law, shut up unto the faith which should afterwards be revealed' (Gal. 3.21–3). What is done away is not the commandments of God. They remain as stern as ever. Indeed, they have now become to Paul more stern, more unbending, even more inescapable. What has been done away, obliterated, annulled, discarded, is the belief that the commandments of God do, or ever can, give life. They have been shown to be commandments of death, and for that very reason they can now be pronounced to be holy and just and good (Rom. 7.12). The divine requirements are not trimmed to human capacity; they are the expression or revelation of the holy and just and good will of God. Only when men hear the law as the word and commandment of God, and pay attention to its vast implications, do they know what the will of God is and, consequently, know what sin is: 'I had not known what sin is, but through the law' (Rom. 7.7) – 'But when the commandment came, sin revived, and I died' (Rom. 7.9). Therefore, insofar as the Jews thought of the law as life-giving and supposed that they lived by it, they misunderstood its function: 'For, being ignorant of God's righteousness, and seeking to establish their own, they did not submit themselves to the righteousness of God' (Rom. 10.3). And so, when the Galatian Christians proposed to advance towards Judaism, it did not mean to St Paul that they were advancing under the law of God. Having seen the truth in Jesus, they already stood under the law and will of God far more seriously than did the Jews (Gal. 4.4). But it did mean that they were in grave danger of advancing to a position where they would be led to think that they were standing *on the law* and not *under its condemnation*. This security of position is, however, precisely what is denied to men by the law itself. There is no security of achievement. Men cannot rest in their obedience, stand on what they have done, and be thereby what God has created them to be (Rom. 3.19–20). 'The commandment, which was unto life, this I found to be unto death: for sin, finding occasion, through the commandment beguiled me, and through it slew me' (Rom. 7.10–11).

This definition of human life is, as Paul sees it, the definition required by the law, by the prophets of Israel, and indeed by the whole Old Testament Scripture (Gal. 3.22). But the purpose of this biblical definition of visible and analysable human life is not to introduce despair or foster cynicism just at the point where its greatest nobility can be discerned, namely when men determine to obey the will of God. The commandment was 'unto life'. What this means has also been defined in the Old Testament. The place where sin is recognized is the place where men yearn and cry out for the salvation that God alone can provide, and where men are driven to the faith by which they live. And so the Old Testament definition of faith is achieved in the context of recognized and acknowledged sin: 'Blessed are they whose iniquities are forgiven, and whose sins are covered. Blessed is the man to whom the Lord will not impute sin' (Ps. 32.1–2; quoted in Rom. 4.7–8). The Old Testament is the record of the history and experience of men acquainted with law; it is therefore also—and this is a most characteristic and surprising deduction—the record of an acute and passionate yearning for the mercy, and forgiveness, and salvation of God. St Paul sees in this relationship between law and faith the essential emphasis of Old Testament prophecy.

This insight of Paul is a creative insight, for it overlooks, or sees behind, the record of Israel's confidence in itself and in its law; it overlooks, or sees behind, Israel's condemnation of others and assuredness of its own vindication. But Paul's insight is not creative because it is set in motion by his peculiar imagination or by his own power of discriminating selection; it is creative because what the Old Testament is in the end talking about has become an event. Paul has seen the salvation of God meeting a human insecurity far more acute than that which had normally been described in the Old Testament. He has seen the salvation of God meeting the insecurity not of disobedience, but of obedience. 'But now apart from the law a righteousness of God hath been manifested, being witnessed by the law and the prophets; even the righteousness of God through faith in Jesus Christ . . . whom God hath set forth to be a propitiation, through faith, by his blood' (Rom. 3.21–5). 'Being found in fashion as a man, he humbled himself, becoming obedient even unto death, yea, the death of the cross. Therefore also God highly exalted him' (Phil. 2.8–9). As has been said,[1] it is in the light of this event that Paul defines the Church as the body of Christ: 'We are pressed on every side, yet not straitened; perplexed, yet not unto despair; pursued, yet not forsaken; smitten down, yet not destroyed; always bearing about in the body the dying of Jesus, that the life also of Jesus may be manifested in our body' (2 Cor. 4.8–10). And he sums up his own position thus: 'O wretched man that I am! who shall deliver me out of the body of this death? I thank God through Jesus Christ' (Rom. 7.24–5). But the framework in which Paul sees the death and resurrection of Jesus, and by which he is able to define the Church and his own position as an apostle, is the theological framework in which human life has already been set in the Old Testament.

The relation between law and promise, and between sin and grace, is, then, not a chronological relationship, even though it may be expressed chronologically. Law, because of its importance to produce a secure righteousness, is, rather, the context in which the promise of God is apprehended and in which faith is born. So

[1] See p. 130 above.

Abraham, in the hopeless position of knowing his own body and Sarah's womb to be already dead, believed in hope against hope and staggered not at the promise of God that he should be the father of many nations (Rom. 4.18–20). Sin is the situation in which grace is recognized. So a boy, living under the restraints and restrictions of a pedagogue, receives in that position, and because of that position, his first serious intimations of freedom (Gal. 3.24–5; cf. 4.1–3). But St Paul sees all this, not as any studious rabbi might have done, through much study of the Scriptures, but in Christ. And for this reason he sees that human life defined as under law and slavery and sin—defined, in fact, as the Scriptures do define it—presents a far more acute problem than it could have presented to any rabbi, however learned in the Scriptures. Hitherto, it had always been possible to resolve the tension of human life by explaining it as a tension caused by sin and guilt and therefore removable by righteousness and repentance. But in Christ this resolution of the problem is forbidden. For, though Christ did no sin, he was nevertheless under law, under its curse. In Christ therefore the tension of human life became more, not less, acute; and, as St Paul saw it, this was in order that the problem of life might be resolved only by the manifestation of the power and wisdom of God, who raised Jesus Christ from the dead. At this supreme point Paul does not escape from the Old Testament, for he sees the humiliation and death of Jesus still in the framework of the prophetic, Old Testament, biblical definition, of human life as awaiting the salvation of God. For Paul, Jesus has no meaning apart from that definition of life. Moreover, God reveals himself only to those who in Christ are recognizably in the same tremulous position.

Even so, we have not yet accounted for the precision and confidence of St Paul's insight. The theological, scriptural, framework of his faith does not seem either to explain the precision of his moral analysis, or the confidence of his moral demands. Law and sin still appear as generalizations that go perilously near to robbing men of every incentive to right conduct, and the description of Jesus as one who 'did no sin' still remains elusive and aloof and dogmatic, if not romantic. The sinlessness of Jesus is, however, the pivot round which St Paul's thought moves, and very particularly it conditions his precise moral analysis and his confident moral demands. Therefore all hope of understanding what he said must be surrendered if the sinlessness of Jesus be dismissed as a dogma, or as a piece of romanticism, or even as an undigested fragment of Christian tradition. No doubt St Paul does leap at the place where it could most of all be wished that he had proceeded more logically and at a slower pace. But why does he leap? And why is he so confident? Here again it is worth while to explore whether he is not at this point also moving within an Old Testament frame of reference, and whether his apparent leap is due to his, perhaps unreasonable, confidence that Christians at least will understand him.

In the Old Testament sin is summed up as idolatry, and the supreme sin of Israel as 'whoring after other gods'. That is to say, the sin from which all sins spring and in terms of which all sin must be reckoned is the service of something other than God. When St Paul says that covetousness is idolatry, he presses the definition far further than any Old Testament writers had done, but he is in no way going outside the terms of the older definition. The final dethronement of God occurs not when men turn to the external worship of dumb idols (for these are, as St Paul knows, and as every strong Christian knows, and as every Jew certainly knew, nothing) but when men so enthrone themselves as to draw, or to attempt to draw, all things to themselves and to judge all other people by reference to themselves. This is the lust of the flesh of which St Paul so often speaks and in the light of which he interprets the tenth commandment: 'Thou shalt not covet': and interprets it in such a manner that it finally strays beyond the relation of a man to his neighbour or to his goods and embraces also his relation to God. For when a man's ego becomes established at the centre of the universe it both excludes the neighbour from his proper position and dethrones God by making piety itself minister to self-glorification. And so 'covetousness, the which is idolatry' (Col. 3.5) does not define a particular kind of sin; it defines sin altogether. This precision of meaning given by Paul to sin and to unrighteousness is, of course, not peculiar to him among New Testament writers. The author of the First Epistle to John, after exhorting his readers to love of the brethren, because without it the love of God is a lie, ends with the startling words, 'Little children, guard yourselves from idols' (1 John 5.21). Surely he does not mean to sum up all that he has been saying by warning them against frequenting temples. Again, the fourth evangelist, perhaps the same writer, describes the Jews as men who 'receive glory one of another' and who because they 'seek not the glory that cometh from the only God' (John 5.44) are deprived of the possibility of faith. Similarly, the rejection of God is illustrated in the synoptic Gospels by the parable of the Rich Fool who said to himself : 'Soul, thou hast much goods laid up for many years: take thine ease, eat, drink, be merry' (Luke 12.19), and by the terrible exposure of the piety of the Pharisees: 'Ye are they that justify yourselves in the sight of men; but God knoweth your hearts: for that which is exalted among men is an abomination in the sight of God' (Luke 16.15). Such behaviour is an inverted exposition of what is demanded by the law as it had been formulated in the Old Testament: 'Thou shalt love the Lord thy God with all thine heart, and with all thy soul, and with all thy might' and 'Thou shalt love thy neighbour as thyself' (Deut. 6.5 and Lev. 19.18, quoted in Mark 12.30–1).

But St Paul's language about lust and desire and covetousness and idolatry is not to be explained as due to the pressure of the moral analysis of the Old Testament to its logical conclusion. The Old Testament does, it is true, provide him with his vocabulary and so with a framework of thought and expression, but it is his picture of Jesus that brings all the scattered fragments together, sets his thought in motion, and enables him to formulate precise and positive moral imperatives which can and must be obeyed.

In the death of Jesus he sees the theme of the Old Testament as an event, for there has occurred the dethronement of covetousness and idolatry, a dethronement so complete that it is not sin but sinlessness that has now been defined in human flesh and blood, and defined in such a manner as to involve those series of moral imperatives with which a Pauline epistle normally ends. Finally, the dethronement of covetousness in Jesus makes him the place where the glory of God is made known : seeing it is God, that said, Light shall shine out of darkness, who shined in our hearts, to give the light of the knowledge of the glory of God in the face of Jesus Christ' (2 Cor. 4.6)—'That every tongue should confess that Jesus Christ is Lord, to the glory of God the Father' (Phil. 2.11). And so the death and resurrection of Jesus, thus understood, govern St Paul's definition of the Church as the body of Christ: 'always bearing about in the body the dying of Jesus, that the life also of

188

Jesus may be manifested in our body' (2 Cor. 4.10—in the following verse Paul substitutes 'in our mortal flesh' for 'in our body'). Thus, what seemed at first sight to be a wild leap on St Paul's part is found to be not a leap at all but a steady requirement of Old Testament moral theology, which had become luminous to him through the event which was Christ Jesus.

It is not, however, the purpose of this chapter to attempt to recover either the precise meaning that the Old Testament possessed for St Paul, or the precise meaning which he saw in the death and resurrection of Christ when they had been related to what had been said in the Old Testament, or the precise meaning which he saw reflected back upon the Old Testament through the mirror of the Christ. The preceding argument has been primarily concerned with far simpler matters. It has been concerned to show that the Old Testament Scriptures did, in fact, provide St Paul with a theological framework or context or setting with which he was able to work in expounding the death and resurrection of Jesus. That he was also to use the same framework to define the behaviour of Christians in their actual lives suggests that he did not, in fact, isolate the death of Jesus and separate it from his life, but saw rather in his death the meaning of his life, and consequently also the meaning of the Church, and ultimately the meaning of all human life.

St Paul undoubtedly claimed to have penetrated the meaning of the Old Testament Scriptures. But he did not turn to them as the rabbis did. He was no rabbi. He was no exegetical expounder of Scripture. He did not, that is to say, proceed as though the Scriptures held in themselves the key to the proper ordering of human life. The Scriptures were no concern of his except as the means of expounding the gospel. Nor did he, like some venerable scholastic, armed with a complete and mathematical system of reasoning, construct from the Scriptures an edifice of biblical theology. St Paul was no scholastic. He was never bound by scriptural analogy. The stories of Abraham's faith, or of Israel's wanderings in the desert, might serve to illustrate an unquestioned fact; they could never be referred to as tribunals for the decision of a doubtful point of faith or morals. In deciding upon the character of Christian behaviour and faith, it was never a matter of weighing probable interpretation against probable interpretation, and then abiding with provisional confidence by the more probable. Even when his interpretation is most allegorical, as when, for example, he interprets Abraham's sons as two covenants (Gal. 4.22–31) or insists upon the importance of the singular 'seed' over against the plural 'seed' (Gal. 3.16), his interpretation is wholly created by the matter in hand, by the antithesis between those under law and those under grace, and by the fact that, since there is but one Lord, there cannot be a diversity of revelations, as though God's promises could be performed in a plurality of complementary parts. Otherwise he would not pass without hesitation or excuse from the story in Genesis to a passage in Isaiah which is utterly irrelevant except as a means of bringing out a further point in his antithesis (Gal. 4.27). Nor would he, if he were simply expounding the promise made to Abraham, rule out in a single phrase a whole theology of mediation in order to assert that God is one, and then sum up his argument by saying that the Scripture hath shut up all things under sin (Gal. 3.20–2).

If St Paul were neither exegete nor scholastic, still less can he be set down as a scholar or dismissed as a bad scholar according to modern standards. Of course, he was learned in the Scriptures. He had been a pharisee of the pharisees; and this may perhaps be detected in his allusions to traditional Jewish expansions of the text of the Scriptures—as, for example, when he speaks of Ishmael 'persecuting' Isaac (Gal. 4.29), or when (if his hand is to be detected in the Epistle to the Ephesians) he alters the words of the 68th Psalm from 'received gifts' to 'gave gifts' (Ps. 68.18; Eph. 4.8), or when he refers to the rock 'following' Israel (1 Cor. 10.4). But he never permits his learning to obtrude itself upon his preaching of the gospel. He does not burden his readers with rare and subtle information or make spectacular dissertations to dazzle them with his skill. He has been deprived of the right to exhibit erudition, and of the power of rhetoric that rests upon information, by the subject-matter of the gospel with which he has been entrusted and by the needs of his hearers. Consciously, at any rate, he maintained no thesis that might be expected to evoke a counter-thesis from some other school of theological thought or biblical exegesis. Even the Epistle to the Romans, which was avowedly written for the 'strong' in implied contrast to the 'weak', was no essay in speculative theology, or compendium of esoteric, mystical *gnosis,* or catena of proof-texts from the Old Testament Scriptures, but a desperate attempt to set out the resolution of the universal problems that

assail the 'weak' as they grow to 'strength'. St Paul wrote as one
convinced of the meaning of human life, in order that other men
might live in truth. It is misleading to speak of him even as a
pastor. He wrote as a man. He stood precisely where his readers
stood, except that he knew that he had been more seriously dethroned than they had been. In this situation, he used the Scriptures
when he had need of them. Were it not so: did he expound the
Scriptures merely in order to establish them, interpret them merely
in order to exalt them, teach them merely in order to impose them
upon his readers; were he, in short, a Rabbi devoted to the Old
Testament for the sake of the Old Testament, his writings would
be no gospel, but propaganda. For their ultimate authority would
be, in that case, not the Christ, but the Scriptures; their final object
belief, not in him, but in them. Salvation would be not only of the
Jews but for the Jews, and Jesus would be no more than a witness
to a truth written already in a book.

That this would be a caricature of St Paul's use of Scripture a
passage in which he defines the purpose of the Old Testament will
serve to show. He is writing of the duty of a Christian to please his
neighbour that he may edify him for his good. The manner of
pleasing is illustrated by the example of Christ who 'pleased not
himself; but, as it is written, The reproaches of them that re-
proached thee fell on me. For whatsoever things were written
aforetime were written for our learning, that we through patience
and through comfort of the Scriptures might have hope. Now the
God of patience and of comfort grant you to be of the same mind
one with another according to Christ Jesus: that with one accord
ye may with one mouth glorify the God and Father of our Lord
Jesus Christ' (Rom. 15.2–6).

The comfort offered by the Scriptures, and the patience or endurance necessitated by life in the flesh and required by the
Scriptures, serve to establish the Christian in the hope of his calling.
But patience and comfort both proceed from God, and Scripture is
the means of comfort only because it explains the patience of Jesus
in whom the underlying theme of the Scripture is realized and who
is the perfect example of life in hope. For St Paul, learning means
learning Christ; knowledge is knowledge of him; imitation is imitation of him. The Scriptures are an invaluable and necessary means

of understanding Jesus, and St Paul turns to them again and again for help. But they are not the only means, and St Paul is much too intent upon the exposition of the gospel not to seek help from elsewhere when he can find it.

CHAPTER 7

The Scope of Biblical Theology

The steady insistence of the New Testament writers that what they have to say, and very specially what they have to say about the death and resurrection of Jesus, is intelligible and believable only on the background of what had already been said in the Law of Moses, by the prophets of Israel, and in the Psalms—'If they hear not Moses and the prophets, neither will they be persuaded, if one rise from the dead'—(Luke 16.31) is, however, open to serious misunderstanding. The appeal to the Old Testament seems to conflict with the freedom which is the peculiar and persistent theme of the New Testament, a freedom which St Paul contrasts with the slavery of the letter and the burden of the law. In speaking of the Old Testament framework of New Testament theology, are we not imposing a literary standard upon primitive Christian thought which cripples, confines, and damages the freedom of the spirit to move unfettered by an ancient manner of thought and experience, however grand its literary expression may have been? Is not therefore this emphasis on the importance of the Old Testament at least exaggerated and perhaps perverse? And after all, does not a modern historical and critical study of the Old Testament itself make it impossible for us at least to take seriously the weight that is placed upon it by Paul and by the evangelists and by the author of the Epistle to the Hebrews, and presumably also by Jesus himself? Is there such a thing as a consistent Old Testament Theology capable of providing a steady method of thought or a steady interpretation of anything? It would indeed seem that the opposite is rather the truth, that the Old Testament has no consistency at all, that it is undisciplined and fragmentary, a text-book of primitive beliefs suitable for the use of anthropologists and of those who are embarking upon the study of comparative religion. The claim that it provides a necessary introduction to all human thought and conduct altogether, and that it provides an introduction that can never be outgrown or made irrelevant, would seem unjustified by the analysis of the Old Testament to which we are accustomed.

A priori, all this would seem to be sound common sense. There remains always a certain uncomfortable feeling that, however great and important a book the New Testament may be, its allusions to the Old Testament and its business with it are slightly ridiculous and form its weakest strands. That is to say, the New Testament is thereby 'dated'. And yet, when this uneasiness is voiced, it is clear that there is some misunderstanding between us and primitive Christianity, something that prevents us from seeing in the Old Testament what the apostolic Church had been led to see. But perhaps the misunderstanding lies deeper. Perhaps we are blind to what the prophets of Israel and the prophets of Christ had seen in human life and experience. In any case, our historical sympathy at least is weak at this point, for it remains an undoubted fact that the Old Testament not only provided the vocabulary of the apostolic Church—that is at once clear to anyone who takes up the Greek version of the Psalter after reading the Greek New Testament—but also gave the Church its power of speech. The New Testament eloquence is really unintelligible apart from the eloquence of the psalmists and prophets of Israel. There is a biblical pattern of insight that holds both Testaments together, and this pattern is not something imposed upon nature and history but something inherent in the natural order and in the visible behaviour of men and women. When we speak of the Old Testament literature we are not really dealing with a set of ideas forced upon a recalcitrant world. We are dealing with something seen everywhere, and seen so clearly that men break into speech. The Paul who interprets the Old Testament is the Paul who interprets human behaviour. What cripples and fetters and kills is not a literature but an apprehended pattern in the very structure of the universe. This is the eloquent realism of the biblical literature, a realism that forces upon prophets and apostles the problem of salvation and the problem of truth.

This biblical realism is nowhere more transparent than in the broad sweep of the third to the sixth chapters of the Second Epistle of Paul to the Corinthians. Men are not 'sufficient' of themselves (2 Cor. 3.5). This was the truth that had been seen and announced by the prophets of Israel and in the law of Moses, announced by the prophets who had seen the Israelite monarchy tumble in ruins, announced in the law of Moses when the springs of human behaviour had been perceived and confronted by the law of God and by his righteousness. The condemnation of Israel, which is also the condemnation of the self-sufficiency of all human behaviour and of all human knowledge, is the sentence of death—'the letter killeth' (2 Cor. 3.6). At first it would seem that St Paul is speaking only of a written law, only of a letter that could easily be destroyed, and by the destruction of which life and freedom and the power of the spirit could easily be proclaimed. But that would be to misunderstand Paul altogether. 'The ministration of death, written and engraven on stones' (2 Cor. 3.7), did not cease to be operative simply by being disregarded because it is merely something external. That is not what Paul is saying. Sin is not ended by neglecting the prophets of Israel, and the law of Moses, nor yet by proclaiming some inner spiritual truth that makes human sin and human ignorance irrelevancies. To Paul, the ministration of death is glorious: glorious because it is God's condemnation and not a human condemnation at all. This is indeed the ground of hope, the only setting in which the Gospel of the love of God can be proclaimed and apprehended. The speed with which St Paul moves from the contrast of letter and spirit to the contrast or paradox that is written in the flesh and blood of the Christians shows what is his proper theme (2 Cor. 3.9ff). The treasure remains in earthen vessels. The apostles of Jesus Christ are pressed on every side—yet not altogether driven into a corner; perplexed—yet not so as to end in despair; struck down—yet not destroyed: always bearing about in the body the mortification of Jesus (and now with the mention of the name Jesus the language of paradox yields to the language of divine purpose) in order that the life also of Jesus may be manifested in our mortal flesh (2 Cor. 4.7–11). Having reached this assertion of divine purpose, Paul can name this whole situation of death a light affliction (2 Cor. 4.7), not because it is, humanly speaking, light, any more than the yoke that Jesus places upon his disciples is, humanly speaking, light or easy (Matt. 11.10), but because its purpose has been apprehended as the purpose of God. Nor are the afflictions of which St Paul speaks merely external persecutions. Persecution itself is a sign of a far deeper disturbance and poverty. The disturbance is the whole concrete, observable situation in which human life is, in fact, lived: a disturbance that is intolerable if the ministration of death be the final truth of God, and his

condemnation his last word; if there be no treasure, but only
earthen vessels whose end is to be broken. St Paul comes back
again in chapter 6 vv. 8–10 to the same paradox :

as deceivers	—and yet true;
as unknown	—and yet well-known;
as dying	—and behold, we live;
as chastened	—and not killed;
as sorrowful	—yet always rejoicing;
as poor	—yet making many rich;
as having nothing	—yet possessing all things.

Paul had begun with the contrast between letter and spirit; he ends
by pressing the letter of Scripture into the very marrow of human
life. And there he proclaims the love of God. No doubt this language seems, and is, rhetoric. But it is rhetoric in its true sense of
eloquence. Paul is made eloquent by the real situation as he sees it :
'Our mouth is open unto you, O Corinthians, our heart is enlarged'
(2 Cor. 6.11). His forceful manner of speech is strictly to the
purpose of the matter in hand, being evoked by that by which Paul
himself is created and controlled. If the Corinthians do not understand what he is saying, their failure to apprehend is due, not to the
fact that Paul is thrusting them into a narrow groove, but to the
circumscribed nature of their own affections, of their own perception. It is not merely that they do not know the Scriptures, but that
they do not understand the nature of human life. They still suppose
that the exceeding greatness of the awaited power is of themselves
(2 Cor. 4.7), and they do not yet know the terror of the Lord (2 Cor.
5.11). They have still to learn what Paul had learned : When I am
weak, then am I strong (2 Cor. 12.10).

This is the biblical setting in which the death and resurrection
of Jesus is proclaimed, and in which Paul can speak of letter and
spirit, of flesh and spirit, and of death and life (2 Cor. 5.15). If this
setting be forgotten or misunderstood, the New Testament language about the death and resurrection of Jesus *does* degenerate into
mythology, for it loses its basis in the Old Testament, and has
therefore lost its basis in the frank recognition of the actual poverty
of human life when men live 'unto themselves' (2 Cor. 5.15) or 'of
themselves' (2 Cor. 4.7), regarding life as a thing in itself expecting

its own inherent perfectibility, as the goal of their own achievement or the source of their power.

In the eighth chapter of the Epistle to the Romans, where the movement of St Paul's eloquence is governed by the contrast between flesh and Spirit, he throws out a sentence which comes, almost casually, from the very heart of his analysis of human life. He is speaking of the sufferings of the present time, contrasting them with the glory that shall be revealed, and speaking also of the expectant longing of the creation (he is presumably thinking of men rather than of the natural order). He sees that men are by themselves subject to vanity. At every point they fail to reach the goal which their imagination lays hold of. And he sees that this groaning vanity affects the Christians just as it affects those outside. But—and here is the point—St Paul refuses to treat this present situation as outside the purpose of God: as a secular, or meaningless, or untheological situation. That human life should be, in and by itself, subject to vanity is not to be explained as an independent free action of the will of men. Neither can this whole situation be explained simply as an aberration of the will of men. In the last analysis this vanity—experienced in these sufferings of the present time—is the God-given witness to the truth that human life is not a self-sufficient thing, satisfactorily or unsatisfactorily rounded off in itself. No; the creation was subjected to vanity *by God himself* (Rom. 8.20), in order that its very vanity might witness to his fulness and in order that men might live in confident hope, the hope of freedom and redemption. We are saved in hope, not in sight (Rom. 8.24); human freedom is not a concrete, visible, thing. What is concrete, visible, and analysable is the incomplete character of present experience, or, as Paul boldly says, its vanity: and it is precisely this that is the ground of faith and hope. Here again this whole eloquent, theological, and positive interpretation of the vanity of human life is set in motion by St Paul's faith in the death and resurrection of Jesus Christ (Rom. 8.11). Faith is as necessary in understanding the death of Jesus as it is in apprehending his resurrection (Rom. 5.2). This is the theme of the law and the prophets. Only in the general setting of sin and death are the death and resurrection of Jesus at all intelligible: 'He that raised Christ Jesus from the dead shall quicken also your mortal bodies through his spirit that dwelleth in you' (Rom. 8.11).

The importance of all this lies in the fact that to Paul the biblical analysis of human life, its fundamental apprehension of sin and death, is not a view of life imposed upon a recalcitrant stuff capable of some other, non-biblical, interpretation. St Paul swings to and fro, from the prophets and the law to the matter of human life as it stands naked and clear before his eyes; and from the actual situation to the words of the prophets and the condemnation of the law. The two are fitted together and inseparable. The concrete situation is as much the word of God as were the words of the prophets of Israel and of the law of Moses. And so knowledge is less an observation of the world than a being observed by it: a being thrust under the power of sin and death in order that there the judgement of God may be perceived, and that there, through faith in Christ Jesus, the love of God may be recognized and apprehended. 'The love of Christ constraineth us—he died for all, that they which live should no longer live unto themselves, but unto him who for their sakes died and rose again' (2 Cor. 5.15). This is the word of reconciliation committed to the apostles as ambassadors of Christ. And this word of reconciliation is not a philosophy of religion, but a veritable intreaty of men by God; it is as though 'God were intreating by us' (2 Cor. 5.18–20). The world is therefore not something dead—to be observed, analysed, and described; or into which research is to be conducted; or upon which a religious or irreligious interpretation can be put; or which is capable of being manipulated in the interest of this or that religious, or irreligious, philosophy. The world, and the history and experience of men, are God's creatures. For this reason they are eloquent of truth. It is this universal truth that was perceived by the prophets of Israel and has been summed up in Jesus Christ crucified, nay rather risen, and present in the Church which is his body. Death and resurrection, slavery and freedom, flesh and Spirit, lie woven in the structure of a universe which everywhere bears witness to the tension which is the witness of God to himself. The scope of biblical theology is therefore unlimited.

St Paul's procedure throughout his Epistles now becomes far more intelligible, and his use of metaphor and analogy far more important. St Paul had an easy command of happy and forceful metaphor. He could clinch an argument with a concrete image, the lump of clay in the hands of a potter (Rom. 9.20–1), or the triumphal procession of a victorious Roman general (Col. 2.15). Certain analogies he used frequently, as when he likens the Church to the human body, or to a building or temple. These habitual analogies may reflect his normal method of teaching (cf. 2 Cor. 6.16). Some of them have a scriptural basis, some of them have not. But a large number of his metaphors and analogies seem quite spontaneous. They are suggested either by the matter in hand or by the ordinary sights and topics of the world in which he lived, and he uses them in a manner that cannot be dismissed as due to a certain facility of literary illustrative technique. He fastens the attention of his readers on a common object or person—an athlete, for example—and employs him to show the effort and discipline that are required of a Christian. Then, moved by a further relevance in the analogy he has chosen, he presses on to reinforce his exhortation with an antithesis between the corruptible rewards of human endeavour, the wreath for which the athlete strives, and the incorruptible hope of the Christian (2 Cor. 9.25). The analogy is more than an illustration, far more than an aid to Christian teaching. There is in the analogy itself, a creative factor. Similarly, the mention of drunkenness, in the course of a straightforward requirement that the Christians should have no fellowship with the unfruitful works of darkness, itself creates the antithetical exhortation that they should be 'filled with the Spirit' and that, instead of rioting, they should sing and make melody to the Lord (Eph. 5.18–19). Or again, in the passage considered above, so simple a matter as the letters of commendation which his opponents have used to secure the right to address the Corinthians, leads St Paul to speak of the Corinthians as 'our epistle, written in our hearts, known and read of all men'. Then at once, as though to justify this turn of rhetoric, he goes on to speak of the essential distinction between the old and the new order or covenant : '(Ye are) made manifest that ye are an epistle of Christ, ministered by us, written not with ink, but with the Spirit of the living God; not in tables of stone, but in tables that are hearts of flesh' (2 Cor. 3.1–3). How quickly he passes from the fact that letters of recommendation are necessary in ordinary social life to the final commendation of his work as an apostle of Christ and of God! Or again, twice St Paul uses the common metaphor of leaven to show how dangerous to the whole Church one sinner or wrongheaded person may be (Gal. 5.9; 1 Cor. 5.6). On one of these occasions he has, however, much more to say about leaven. 'Purge out the old leaven, that you may be a new lump' . . . he begins. And then a further meaning of his metaphor strikes him, and he continues: 'even as ye are unleavened. For our passover also hath been sacrificed, even Christ; wherefore let us keep the feast, not with old leaven, neither with the leaven of malice and wickedness, but with the unleavened bread of sincerity and truth' (1 Cor. 5.7–8). Presumably only a Jew would understand the force of this transition, depending as it does on the association of unleavened bread with the Passover, but it shows how uneasy Paul is in a purely secular world, and how for him the ordinary things of the world in which he lived are fraught with theological and with christological meaning. To Paul a world that comes to rest in itself is a meaningless world, a world that has lost its capacity to speak and to interpret itself.

So far it would seem that St Paul does no more than fly with all possible speed from the concrete world around him to the meaning that lies in part beyond it and in part in opposition to it, but to which it bears witness. There is, however, a far more complicated, and far more important, movement to be discerned in the Pauline epistles. St Paul does not simply pass from an external fact to its theological or christological meaning, and stop there. Again and again he passes back again, from the theological meaning to the external fact, as though, when it has been seen in its relation to God, it has for the first time received its full importance and proper dignity.

Circumcision, for example, is manifestly a visible fact, and it points to that inward circumcision of the heart in the spirit and not in the letter, which latter it is that makes a man properly a Jew (Rom. 2.29). Having reached the meaning of circumcision Paul does not proceed to treat the fact of circumcision as meaningless and unimportant. On the contrary, when its Godward meaning has been perceived, circumcision is itself an important thing, for it testifies to the righteousness that comes only from God (Rom. 3.1–21). What is done away with is the blasphemous notion that the act of circumcision is in itself an act by which salvation is guaranteed to the Jew, and by the absence of which a man is left without hope of salvation. The tension between the circumcised Jew and the uncircumcised Gentile is the really important theological fact (Rom. 3.29–31).

The double movement—from the visible fact to the truth by which it is embraced, and back again from the truth to the visible fact, the meaning of which has now been apprehended—can be most clearly observed when Paul (or those directly influenced by his teaching) are discussing the essential relationships between human beings; and even here it is important to notice that the double movement appears quite spontaneous and not at all laboured or forced.

In the course of an exhortation to Christian behaviour, the relation between husband and wife is described, but almost at once the argument leaps to the relation between Christ and the Church, not as though this further relationship had merely been suggested by the human phenomenon of husband and wife or as though it were being argued from an actual human relationship to a conjectural spiritual relationship, but in order to define what husband and wife ought to be to one another in the light of the relation between Christ and the Church (Eph. 5.22–33). The writer is not here introducing the analogy of marriage in order to explain a mystical doctrine. On the contrary, at the mention of marriage he springs to the reality in Christ that determines Christian marriage and discloses the meaning of marriage altogether.[1] In the same Epistle the relation of slaves to masters and of masters to slaves leads the writer at once to the recognition that Christians are slaves of Christ and that the Master to whom all Christians owe their final allegiance is in heaven, that is to say, to the reality which the human phenomenon of slavery suggests and by which it is itself defined and its practice governed (Eph. 6.5–9). In another Epistle the fact that some men are slaves whilst others are free does not cause St Paul to distinguish between these two classes of men as though the latter were theologically important but the former not. Both are important for Christian truth : 'Let each man abide in that calling wherein he was called. Wast thou called being a slave? care not for it; but if thou canst become free, use it rather. For he that was called in the Lord, being a slave, is the Lord's freed-man : likewise he that was called, being free, is Christ's slave. Ye were bought with a price; be

[1] For the argument of Ephesians 5.22–33 see below, pp. 250–4.

ye not the slaves of men. Brethren, let each man, wherein he was called, therein abide with God' (1 Cor. 7.20–4). What St Paul means is that the fact that the call of God has taken place both in slavery and in freedom dignifies both freedom and slavery. When Paul says, 'Be ye not the slaves of men', he certainly does not mean that slaves must repudiate their bondage—the whole passage forbids us to understand him thus—but that all men, including slaves, must in the last resort serve God only. As with domestic relationships, so with the wider, more expensive, authority of the State. There are to St Paul no such things as mere secular 'powers' and 'authorities'. No doubt the visible authority of the Roman empire compels submission, and men refuse it obedience at their peril. Such obedience is obedience in fear of the wrath that descends upon them should they disobey. But to Paul there is a deeper ground of obedience to the State. Obedience is an important experience in human life, for it is here, in the payment of 'dues', tribute, custom, fear, honour—in fact the payment of all things—that men are able to learn what obedience to God really means and what is finally 'due' to him. But now what is finally due from men to God can be summed up in the one word 'love', and when thus summed up it is a due which can be paid to no earthly visible ruler but which, nevertheless, makes sense of the obedience due to an emperor and his officers and makes of it an obedience 'for conscience sake' (Rom. 13.1–8).

St Paul's use of metaphor, illustration, and analogy is far more than a matter of literary or catechetical technique, far more than an ornament of his prose. The world in which he lived was God's world, engraved even in its most unlikely parts with the marks of its relation to him and of its creation by him. The world spoke to St Paul incessantly of God and of Christ, and it spoke to him not merely in its general form but in the details of its laws and of its behaviour. A woman released from the lifelong bond of marriage by the death of her husband and thus enabled to enter into a new marital relationship (Rom. 7.1–6); an heir passing from the slavery of infancy to the lordship of his inheritance and to his position as son (Gal. 4.1–7); the wages that are paid and must be paid to servants for the work they have done (Rom. 6.23)—all these things preach the gospel. But they preach the gospel only because they speak of the reality that has been made known in Christ, which is mirrored in them, and of which they are, as it were, shadows. The reality that is shadowed and engraved in the actual concrete phenomena of human life does not lie beyond human life. It ceases to be a goal in the future or a starting-point in the past. It turns round from the beginning and from the end, and, laying hold of the essential facts and relationships of present experience, it establishes them by revealing the Godward meaning which they in fact have and which gives them their very existence. And then, when this is apprehended, they are proclaimed no longer as shadows but as acts that are done in Christ. So St Paul's continued insistence that all things must be done in Christ, or in the Spirit, or unto the Lord, means that the gospel shows how human life can be truly lived and reveals its true meaning. When therefore he speaks of being 'all things to all men', of becoming as a Jew to the Jews, as without law to them that are without law, and as weak to the weak (1 Cor. 9.20–2), he is guilty of no doubtful subtlety or adjustment, but is declaring his confident belief that in Christ all these states of life are for the first time perceived in their true perspective and are therefore states in which men can live unto God.

St Paul's eyes had been so opened to the world in which he lived that he everywhere saw the theme of the gospel with which he had been entrusted. It is in this, surely, as in his use of the Old Testament,[1] that he is to be recognized as the disciple of his master, born it may be out of due time, but nevertheless reborn to be the apostle of Jesus Christ and to see the world as he had seen it, and to see his death and resurrection in this all-embracing, cosmological setting. The suspicion that St Paul was writing no more than the story of his own life, and that his own life had got in the way of his subject, breaks down on a strict analysis of what he actually wrote. Paul was neither a second founder of Christianity nor the creator of Christian theology, nor did he for the first time make of Christianity a religion of redemption, nor did he make a myth the foundation of his religion and so pervert the Church. The question, 'Who founded Christianity, Jesus or Paul?' is a false question implying a false antithesis, posing a false dilemma. Like Paul, Jesus saw the truth of the power of God in the context of his hearers' actual lives. He spoke of vineyards and harvests and shepherds and birds, of the flowers at his feet and the vultures soaring over his head, and he

[1] See above, p. 182.

spoke of these things in such a way as to recall the language of the Old Testament. Both the natural world and the Old Testament had already been woven together in the context of Palestinian life, and the Old Testament had already taken the natural world seriously and provided it with theological meaning; had already associated theological truth with natural phenomena. Therefore Jesus did not resort to a somewhat remote body of Scripture in order to formulate his teaching, so that it was hard for all except the few who were learned enough or lucky enough to stumble upon the key. Everything was grist to his mill. Not only the Old Testament, but the ordinary facts of his environment, and the notable and notorious events of his time, provided him with the means of proclaiming truth—the fall of a tower in Siloam, for example, or the political incident of a man who journeyed into a far land to get a kingdom. To his eyes, the world around him and the events of human life were luminous with the truth of God. Just as Paul sprang from the world around him to God, and, in the light of the truth thus glimpsed, came back to the metaphor of human life and confirmed it by showing its real meaning, so the parabolic method of Jesus— and it must not be forgotten that the parabolic method covers also the attitude of Jesus to his own actions—establishes the world that enables him to formulate his message. The fact that the visible world is eloquent of God gives it its ultimate meaning: no longer can it be thought of as a thing in itself, separated from God, for discerning eyes can see the truth of God wherever they look. And so, even in the details of their form and substance, the fundamental things and relations of life are confirmed as having an intrinsic parabolic significance. Eating and drinking, a feast, a marriage ceremony, the reality of marriage, children, brotherly love, filial devotion, seed-time, growth, and the eventual fruits of the harvest, labourers in a vineyard, and above all the temporary arrest of the general movement to death by an act of healing, all these things point by their very occurrence to the Kingdom of God by which they are made good or fulfilled, are productive of faith, and serve to define what the attitude of men should be to God and to each other. The teaching and action of Jesus therefore seem to establish the visible world by a simple mystical insight into its inherent meaning. Its form, indeed, is so analogous to that of the unseen spiritual world that, if only men had eyes to see, the very stones should cry out the praise and truth of God.

There is without doubt an underlying similarity between the view of the world ascribed to Jesus and St Paul's view of the world. If the metaphors they select are different, this difference is occasioned simply by the fact that Jesus belonged to the country and St Paul to the town. Consequently, the language of Jesus is largely pastoral and natural, whereas that of St Paul is derived from the relationships of a highly complex civilization. But, unless the most arbitrary and Rousseauesque distinction is made between 'nature' and man who is a part of nature, this difference is quite superficial. And when it is remembered that each is using the background of his own surroundings, the identity of their usage is perceived in the very disparity of their material. To suppose Jesus to be preaching a movement 'back to nature', on the ground that there alone God is to be perceived, would be as complete a misunderstanding as to suppose that, because St Paul saw the power of God breaking out in wrath over the complex structure of human civilization, he would not have perceived the power of God in the 'natural' world had he been summoned to live in more direct contact with it. But the similarity between the usage of Jesus and the usage of St Paul does not consist merely in the fact that both turned to account the whole context in which they lived. Nor does it consist merely in an employment of analogy so prodigal that the ordinary distinctions that have been erected between good and bad are destroyed, and Jesus can see in the astuteness of a dishonest bailiff as he prepares to face the results of dismissal a pointer to the right use of material things in a rapidly passing age, and St Paul the truth about God and man in the behaviour of a drunkard. Their message, the meaning which they disclose in what is around them, is concerned with the same ultimate things—things that are common to all human life. Life and death, rich and poor, husband and wife, eating and drinking, father and son, parents and children, the relation of the things of God to the things of Caesar—these are profound themes lying at the very heart of human existence. These themes, through their different social contexts, are equally the concern of the apostle of the Gentiles and of his Master, just as they had been the concern of the prophets of Israel. The same urgent imperative of God speaks through the concrete world of human history and experience to the prophets of Israel, to Jesus, and to St Paul.

It would seem that visible human life is hereby finally affirmed and established and made good. If the world is altogether para-bolic, if it speaks by its intrinsic and inherent nature of the things of God, if it points beyond its actual significance to an ultimate meaning in God, and if this meaning is revealed by the unclouded insight of Jesus, an insight shared by those who have received his Spirit, does not this constitute so complete an affirmation of the world that human life does veritably come to rest and that its tension is once and for all resolved? Fortified by the promise of Scripture, all who are given eyes to see do perceive the meaning of the world and the meaning of history and of human experience, and do make sense of their lives. Why is this not the teaching of the New Testament, just as it is the teaching of the Old Testament? Why is this affirmation of the world crossed by an ultimate nega-tion? Why is the subject-matter of the Gospels and of the Epistles disturbed by the central position occupied by the death of Jesus, the visible importance of which seems to question the whole efficacy of his positive actions? Why does the tension of human life not only persist but become even more acute than it had been under the old covenant? And why above all does the ethical distinction between good and bad actions remain and become even more clear cut in spite of the meaning that is assigned to all human behaviour—in spite, that is to say, of the apparent blurring of the distinction between what is evil and what is good in the interest of the higher righteousness of him who maketh his sun to shine on the good and on the bad? How is the nervousness of the Pauline Epistles to be explained? What explanation can be given of the positive attitude of Jesus to his own death? What is to be said of that emphasis upon the death of Jesus that calls into question the final efficacy of his avowedly perfect life, and that affirms this inefficacy to be in the end the most significant fact about his life; to be indeed its perfection? How can these questions be explained without jettisoning the whole affirmation of the visible world and of human life which it has been the purpose of this chapter to assert must not be weakened or denied? This is the problem of the theology of the New Testament.

PART TWO

*Some Outstanding Themes of
the New Testament*

Introduction

The books of the New Testament could never have taken the form they did take, had there not existed, behind the act of writing, an eloquence of speech and behaviour that had been set in motion by the general structure and normal occurrences of human life. Neither St Paul, nor the evangelists, nor the author of the Epistle to the Hebrews, nor the prophet whose work underlies the Apocalypse, nor the moralist who addressed the Church in the Epistle of James, nor the apostolic man who wrote the First Epistle of Peter, could have written or spoken as he did unless he had been persuaded that the visible form and structure of human life bore necessary witness to the invisible truth of God. In this these men were not innovators; nor did they feel themselves to be so. Possessing the prophetic literature of the Hebrew people and of the Jewish Church, they knew that what they observed had already been seen, that what they said had already been uttered, and that the demands they were bound to make had already been urged. But—and to overlook this is to overlook everything—they knew that, as a consequence of what had recently occurred and of what was taking place in their midst, they were compelled to observe more closely, to speak more plainly, and to make even more pressing demands upon those without as well as those within the Church.

These men believed in Jesus. This was the most important fact about them, for it meant that they had not arrived at their crucial and personal perception by some general process of reasoning or induction. Nor, so far as is known, did they, as a consequence of their faith, compress their insight into a system of theology or into a cosmic philosophy, or even into a comprehensive system of ethics. At times, indeed, there can be detected a certain friction or irritation when they are confronted by these things, whether in the teaching of the Jewish Rabbis or in the wisdom of the Greeks. Nor is this at all trivial or irrelevant, for, unless the records are altogether untrustworthy, the teaching of Jesus was both conditioned and, in a sense, exhausted by, particular matters in hand: by particular events, by the business of the countryside or of the neighbouring towns, by current topics of conversation, or by some evident scandal of conduct. This concrete limitation of the teaching and action of Jesus—this firm setting in life—must not, however, be misunderstood. Neither his teaching nor his action was in any way haphazard, for he permitted none of these things to remain valuable merely for illustration, allusion, or description. They were facts of creation, and judgement, and salvation; and they were so because God had provided them with their only proper frame of reference and their only proper range of application. This property of the action and teaching of Jesus was, so far as we are able to judge, consistent. Belief in Jesus therefore required an especial capacity of insight, and brought into being a quite final respect for what can be observed in the straightforward events of human life.

The New Testament may seem bewildering in its variety and complexity. Nevertheless, in spite of this, it displays a remarkable unity of direction and emphasis. The various authors are drawn irresistibly towards certain major themes, from which they never altogether escape or indeed for one moment wish to escape. Where there is complexity in the New Testament it is due far more to the fact that human life is a very perplexing affair than to the necessity of mastering some inherently difficult, unfamiliar, and ancient technique of thought and expression. The New Testament writers speak seriously, for example, about marriage, about eating and drinking, about the relation between father and son, about the necessity and the difficulty of living under government, about money, about good people, about soldiers, about teachers of religion, about death, and, very particularly, about the importance of poor and distressed men and women. It follows that an analysis of what is said in the New Testament about some of these familiar facts and problems of human behaviour may turn out to be of very great importance for an understanding of what is said there about human life altogether, and in particular about the death and resurrection of Jesus.

CHAPTER 8

The Poor – and the Poverty of Jesus

'They that are whole (R.V. mg. "strong") have no need of a physician, but they that are sick' (Mark 2.17). The most outstanding and characteristic feature of the historical figure of Jesus, as it is set forth in the Gospels, is his extreme sensitiveness to poor and diseased men, women, and children. The evangelists portray him impelled towards the poor by the divine necessity of his mission. His eye singled them out from the midst of the crowds that pressed upon or followed him; his ear heard the cry of their appeal; he had compassion upon them, touched them—and healed them. The evangelists are also careful to narrate a reverse and complementary movement of the poor towards Jesus. This movement too is depicted as taking place according to the will and purpose of God. And so, the twofold rhythmical motion reveals the pattern of divinely ordered behaviour the meaning of which is finally summarized in the Prologue to the fourth Gospel : 'He came unto his own . . . as many as received him, to them gave he power (A.V. mg. "the right" or "privilege") to become the sons of God (John 1.11–12).

St Mark had already provided his readers with a selection from the many episodes in the life of Jesus that underlie the summary in the fourth Gospel; for at the very beginning of his narrative he plunges them into scene after scene of quite desperate human need.[1] He requires only a few verses in order to define the public ministry of Jesus as an authoritative ministry for the relief of human distress. Briefly and rapidly he records how evil spirits, fever, leprosy, and paralysis yield to Jesus's command. Later, however, this context is extended and emphasized till it frames the whole narrative. Wherever men are hard pressed, whether by a storm or by the stern requirements of an inhuman religious tradition, Jesus moves towards them with effective compassion. If they starve, he gives them to eat. If they are blind, he makes them see.

But these scenes of relieved distress are not narrated merely to define the ministry of Jesus. They serve also to define the behaviour

[1] Mark 1.21—2.12.

that is required of his disciples. Even the series of charitable acts of Jesus himself is prefaced by the call of those fishermen whose business it now is to become fishers of men and whose activity of fishing is afterwards more nearly defined as healing the sick and casting out evil spirits (Mark 6.13).[1] Their ministry, like his, is conditioned by the necessity of giving to the poor: 'Freely ye received, freely give' (Matt. 10.8). Though he himself provides for the hungry, nevertheless his word to the disciples is 'Give ye them to eat' (Mark 6.36), and it is not his loaves and fishes but those they have procured that he blesses and breaks. Moreover, the movement of the crowd to Jesus evokes also a corresponding expectant movement towards his disciples (Mark 9.18). And, if this is at first disappointed, it is not permitted to remain so long, as Luke is careful to record in the opening chapters of Acts (Acts 3.10–11; 9.32–43). For the author of the Epistle of James, to heal the sick is a necessary activity of the Church (James 5.14–15), and for St Paul the power to do so is a gift that he can assume is being exercised among the Christians at Corinth (1 Cor. 12.28).

The vocation to be a disciple of Jesus therefore means that men are called to extend and imitate his work of relieving human suffering and need wherever and in whatever form it manifests itself (John 14.12). The action of Jesus and the movement of the crowds towards him evoked, in his disciples, a corresponding and effective movement towards the poor and, in the crowds, a corresponding and effective movement towards the disciples. Indeed, charity towards the poor must have been the most characteristic visible mark of the primitive Church. Nevertheless, care of the poor is never portrayed in the New Testament as though it were some new and strange human activity that appeared first in Galilee and afterwards spread outwards with the expansion of the Church. The compassionate action of Jesus and his disciples rests—and it is the purpose, for example, of the parable of the Good Samaritan to assert this—upon a widespread, deep-seated, human capacity that answers to widespread and deep-seated human needs. Indeed, the work of the physicians not only provided the evangelists and the other New Testament writers with a rich and relevant vocabulary[2] but also enabled them to set the action of Jesus and of his disciples

---

[1] Cf. the added ending of this Gospel, 16.17.
[2] E.g., the Greek word translated *salvation*.

in a general context of the relief of distress. And more important than this: the action of Jesus and of his disciples sums up and reveals what is involved in the prophetic definition of the function of Israel in the world:

> Ho, everyone that thirsteth, come ye to the waters, and he that hath no money: come ye, buy, and eat; yea come, buy wine and milk without money and without price . . . And nations[1] that knew thee not shall run unto thee (Isa. 55.1–5).

and what is involved in the requirements of the Deuteronomist concerning 'the stranger, and the fatherless and the widow' (Deut. 14.29, etc.), and in the language of the Psalter when it speaks of deliverance of the poor and needy (e.g. Ps. 82.4), and in the poetic description of Job's charity:

> I delivered the poor that cried,
> The fatherless also and him that had none to help him . . .
> I was eyes to the blind,
> And feet was I to the lame.
> I was a father to the needy:
> And the cause of him that I knew not I searched out.
> (Job 29.12–16; cf. 31.16–22).

It is not at all difficult to extract from the Gospels an impressive series of charitable actions of Jesus, and to reinforce them by an equally impressive series of parables and sayings of his concerning the relief of poor and suffering men and women. Nor, having done this, is it difficult to relate this selection of characteristic actions and words, on the one hand to what the disciples of Jesus afterwards did and said, and on the other hand to what had previously been done in Israel and required by the Law and the Prophets, so as to show that both in ancient Israel and in the primitive Church the latent instinct for charity that is common to all men took unique form in a wide range of concrete acts of mercy. If this be so, it may well be claimed that the life of Jesus not only realized and epitomized the characteristic righteousness that had been required of Israel by the prophets, and not only supplied an authoritative standard of conduct for Christians, but also provides for all men

[1] To read the plural 'nations' with the LXX seems to secure the fundamental meaning of a difficult Hebrew passage.

a final example of human charity—an example which in fact constitutes a command. In any case, it cannot be doubted that all the New Testament writers do invest the care of the poor with an ultimate sanction and embrace it in an ultimate divine imperative.

The question must now be raised whether, in spite of all this, the theme of charity, as it is set out in the Gospels and elsewhere in the New Testament, is in any way exhausted by such an analysis. Is it possible that an analysis of this kind may be so seriously inadequate that it obscures what was most characteristic of primitive Christian faith and leads to a grave misunderstanding even of the importance in the Church of effective acts of charity? The question concerns the theology of the New Testament and the purpose of the ministry of Jesus and of his disciples. Is the truth about God that he purposes to supply man's needs? And was the purpose of the work of Jesus and of his disciples to restore to man, spoiled in some way or another, or lacking in some physical or mental necessity, that health and wealth which God created them to enjoy? Or to put it another way—is the truth about the life of Jesus that it must be set in the context of the creative work of God if it is to be understood? And is the gospel preached by him properly defined as the revelation that God wills men to participate in his work by working fruitfully in his vineyard and disposing of the fruit that God gives them to the physical, moral, and spiritual advantage of those who are clearly in need, that is to say, to the advantage of the poor?

It is therefore necessary at this point to call attention to very difficult and surprising aspects of the teaching and action of Jesus as recorded in the Gospels, to which as yet no reference has been made. These are the blessings pronounced upon the poor because they are poor; the frequent withdrawal of Jesus from the crowd; the poverty and distress of Jesus himself; the miraculous language in which acts of healing are described; and the anti-miraculous sayings of Jesus.

In composing his Gospel, the author of Matthew arranges his material so as to introduce the public ministry of Jesus with a generalized summary of acts of healing: 'and they brought unto him all that were sick, holden with divers diseases and torments, possessed with devils, and epileptic, and palsied; and he healed them' (Matt. 4.24). This is followed immediately by the Beatitudes: 'Blessed are the poor in spirit . . . Blessed are they that mourn . . .' (Matt. 5.3ff). Whether this paradox is intentional, or whether it is simply due to the juxtaposition brought about by the introduction of a 'second source', is irrelevant. The point is that the evangelist's material contains two contrary judgements upon the significance of the fact of poverty and distress. Poor, diseased men and women are first objects of charity; they are then pronounced to be of supreme significance in their poverty and in their distress. In arranging these two judgements side by side, or in allowing them to remain side by side at the beginning of his Gospel, Matthew does no more than consciously or unconsciously set before his readers that poverty and distress which can, and have been, and must be relieved, and that poverty and distress which remain as a permanent appeal to the power and mercy of God because, being a hungering and thirsting for the righteousness that is required by God, and in that sense a poverty of spirit not of body, they can be satisfied only *in heaven* or by the transformation of all things (Matt. 5.12). The sensitiveness to this ultimate poverty and to its vast theological significance is, from beginning to end, the fundamental theme of the New Testament. This it is, indeed, that alone gives any final meaning to acts of healing or philanthropy.

Acts of healing are never described in the Gospels as though they were 'things in themselves' whose meaning is exhausted in the physical action. If so their importance would lie only in that they can and must be repeated. The acts of healing that are recorded in the Gospels are *evangelical* acts. That is to say, they are described as taking place within the framework of the heralding of the gospel of God. They are prefaced by the prophetic and eschatological mission of the Baptist, who sums up in himself, and voices, the urgent prophetic and eschatological hope of Israel; and also by a precise statement of the essential themes of the preaching of Jesus in Galilee :

> He came into Galilee,
> preaching the gospel of God,
> and saying, The time is fulfilled,
> and the Kingdom of God is at hand : repent ye,
> and believe in the gospel.
>
> (Mark 1.14–15)

Within this framework of faith in the power and mercy of the living God, men are turned about from sickness to health; within this framework also the demand is made by act and parable and aphorism that the poor must be relieved. Though these acts of charity are not identified with the Kingdom of God, they nevertheless lie within its range and are signs by means of which it can be apprehended and believed in, for they contain, hidden within them, the pattern of the will and power of God. Sometimes, as in the record of the healing of the paralytic (Mark 2.1–12), the rhythm of an incident brings the pattern so near to the surface that it seems, as the evangelist records it, almost to be engrained visibly upon it. The paralytic has no power of movement. As though he were a corpse, four men are required to bring him to the house where Jesus 'spake the word' to the crowd gathered within and without. First Jesus observes the faith or confidence without which the paralytic would not have reached him. The man is healed by the power and at the command of Jesus, carries his bed, and goes out to his home publicly in the presence of the crowd. The rhythm of the episode is therefore: impotence—faith (directed towards one who is able to respond to it)—health. But it is Jesus himself who observes and presumably emphasizes the crucial act of confidence apart from which the man would have remained where he was. Yet there is much more than this in the episode. The attention of Jesus is concentrated upon a far deeper distress and impotence. Before ever the paralysis is done away with, he asserts not only his authority to proclaim the release of men from this deeper, greater slavery, but also that the physical healing will take place in order that the greater distress may be recognized and the greater healing known.

Finally, the narrative calls attention to the blindness of the scribes and the misunderstanding of the crowd. The former argue; the latter are amazed—but their amazement is caused by the doing away of paralysis, for which alone they glorify God. In the perspective of the gospel the behaviour of the crowds betrays unbelief, that of the scribes blasphemy.

Disease, confidence, health—sin, faith, salvation. The rhythm, or curve, or pattern, or form that can be seen and analysed most clearly in the narrative of the healing of the paralytic is present everywhere in the records in the Gospels of the healing of disease by Jesus—as it is, indeed, in the structure of a physician's work, which explains why the medical vocabulary penetrates so deeply the language of the New Testament. There is therefore no reason to suppose that the 'meaning' or form of an episode of healing was something imposed upon a straightforward act of charity by the evangelists under the influence of the later faith of the Church, as though it were some foreign thing. The call to faith lies in the structure of human life. This is what Jesus saw, and what he saw as supremely evident in his own acts. It may well be, however, that the evangelists were enabled by the later faith of the Church, or by the insight of apostolic men, or through the unforgettable eloquence of St Paul, or by the combined direction of all these, to see clearly what neither the scribes nor the crowd saw, and what the disciples had at first been unable to understand. They saw the rhythmic pattern of effective human charity as Jesus saw it, and stood, as he did, completely within it. An act of charity evokes faith, and is evoked by it. St Paul exhorts the Church, as Jesus commanded his disciples, to do acts of charity, because acts of charity are not only an incentive to faith but an effective parable of it. When this is recognized it is not surprising that the whole corpus of Pauline epistles is written in the knowledge and experience of a poverty that is beyond human relief. Without this knowledge and experience the gospel is no gospel and faith is not faith. Neither is it surprising that the author of the fourth Gospel should have narrated acts of healing as he did.

Jesus stands within the action of charity[1] towards the poor. He gives, they receive. But his acts are not silent acts; they are accompanied by speech in which he makes known a final poverty and a final charity. The comprehensive word in which this poverty is summed up in the Old and New Testaments is 'sin' (in Christian dogmatics the word is retained, but there is added to it the adjective 'original'). The comprehensive phrase that sums up the final relief is 'the Love of God'—the genitive is, in this case, of course subjective, not objective. This is the philanthropy about which the whole biblical literature is talking in the end—and at the beginning! As

---

[1] It would be convenient to use the word 'charity' only for actions which can be observed and described, or for actions the consequences of which are capable of analysis, and to reserve the word 'love' for that of which such charity is the effective parable. But any attempt to adhere consistently to so rigid a distinction would destroy the theological structure of life and experience, which it is the purpose of the New Testament writers to preserve and make known.

the Christ, the Son of God, and as the eschatological Son of man, Jesus stands within the final act of God's salvation. For this reason, the evangelists present him to the primitive Church, and to the Jews, and indeed to all men, as the fulfilment of prophecy. For this reason, in the synoptic Gospels, the narrative of the baptism of Jesus immediately precedes the record of his work. For this reason the narrative of his work is interrupted by that of the transfiguration. For the same reason, in the fourth Gospel, these strictly theological interruptions cease to be episodes, and take manifest control of the whole narrative. For the moment, however, it is necessary to draw attention to all this only in order to explain the nature of that poverty which provides the evangelists with their most important subject matter, and to explain how it comes about that those who have been thrust recognizably into a final poverty (harlots and publicans, for example) move more easily towards Jesus than do the Pharisees, and are therefore nearer to the Kingdom of God; why the persecuted Church of the apostolic age is represented as almost visibly within the range of the love of God; and why those who hunger and thirst after righteousness are pronounced 'blessed'.

Here again, however, what is said in the New Testament about poverty is no new thing. The passages previously selected[1] in order to illustrate the acute sensitiveness towards the poor and the distressed, and the urgent demand for their relief, that mark the literature of the Old Testament, had to be misquoted in order, in passing, to obscure and even remove from sight the theological framework in which the demand was made and the distress defined. The hunger and thirst of which 'Isaiah' speaks is satisfied only within the 'everlasting covenant' that God will make with his people (Isa. 55.3). The nations will 'run' not merely to an Israel that exercises a reasonable and necessary charity towards those who are hungry and thirsty and have no money, but to the Israel that has been 'glorified' by God (Isa. 55.5). Similarly, the deliverance of which the Psalmists speak, and for which they yearn in confident hope, is the deliverance from that oppression and poverty from which they can perceive no means of escape: 'Thou wilt compass me about with songs of deliverance' (Ps. 32.7). Similarly again, the 'humanitarianism' of the Deuteronomist, who re-created and re-formed the customs of Israel and required the care of the fatherless

[1] See above, p. 213.

and widows and orphans, was called forth by the ultimate distress
of Israel itself : partly by the memory of the oppression in Egypt,
but more particularly by the nearer experience of the collapse of the
monarchy and, consequently, of political and religious security
(Deut. 28.36–7). The joining of the Levites, too, to the fatherless
and widows and orphans shows that even a reform of Israelite
religion threw up unexpected problems of charity, for it created
dispossessed and poverty stricken clergy! Lastly, the whole point of
the Book of Job is that not until Job recognized that he himself was,
and had been, as poor as the poor he so charitably served was he in
a position to understand the meaning of his own words and actions :

> Therefore have I uttered that which I understand not . . .
> I had heard of thee by the hearing of the ear;
> But now mine eye seeth thee,
> Wherefore I abhor myself (R.V. mg. 'loathe my words'),
>   and repent
>   in dust and ashes.   (Job 42.3–6)

This does not mean that readers of the Book of Job are to suppose
that Job then ceased to care for the poor, any more than that readers
of other parts of the Old Testament are intended to draw the deduction that because a reform of religion brought into being new
objects of charity, no reform of any kind ought to be even con-
templated, still less embarked upon. Had that been so the rise of
Judaism would be unintelligible.

If the picture of Jesus moving towards the crowds, and especially
towards poor and diseased men, be of such vast theological importance, what is to be said of the theme of withdrawal? And if his acts
of healing and the general care of the poor be veritably an effective
call to faith and an effective and intended indication, in the structure of human experience, of the love of God, what is to be said
about their elimination? If his public speech was an integral factor
in and accompanying his public action, what is to be said about his
characteristic silence in the passion narratives? Even the comparatively smooth run of the record of the work in Galilee is, in the
synoptic Gospels, held up by checks and stops, so that the movement towards the crowds is importantly reversed. The evangelists
relate that Jesus 'went out, and departed into a solitary place, and

there prayed . . .' (Mark 1.35); that, with his disciples, he 'departed into a desert place by ship privately . . .' (Mark 6.32); and that, alone, he 'departed into a mountain to pray' (Mark 6.46). At times the necessity of acts of charity seems to be unwillingly thrust upon him. Finally, all acts of healing are eliminated. In the Marcan narrative it is not recorded that the ear of the high priest's servant was healed. Matthew preserves this reserve. The author of the fourth Gospel does the same, though he has named the man. Luke alone here disturbs the form of the Marcan tradition, but even he records no other act of healing in Jerusalem. The fourth evangelist proceeds differently; though he too records no powerful act of healing after the raising of Lazarus, no speech to the crowds after the concluding summary of the public ministry (John 12.36–50); and his narrative, also, preserves the characteristic theme of withdrawal (John 6.15).

The breaks in the curve and form that occur in the earlier parts of a Gospel—and they are not caused only by the fact of opposition and persecution—might not be treated very seriously, were it not that they do but prepare the way for, and anticipate, a complete reversal of rhythm. Therefore they cannot be explained only as marking pauses or rests in a fruitful but exhausting mission, or as occasioned by the necessity of concentrating upon the teaching of the disciples. Nor is the emphasis upon Jesus praying altogether explained by the necessity of interceding for others, for the crowds or for the disciples, or even for a renewal of physical energy to preach and to heal the sick. All these are, of course, part of the picture of Jesus in the synoptic Gospels. But they may be emphasized to such an extent as to obscure the fact that in all these a contrary rhythm is coming to the surface of the narrative: a rhythm which silences the preaching, puts an end to the describable acts of charity, and finally allows Jesus to remain alone, engulfed by the extremity of final poverty. Such an extremity of final poverty had long before compelled the psalmist to cry, 'My God, my God, why hast thou forsaken me?' (Ps. 22.1). The prayer of Jesus not only belongs within the range of this poverty, but finally defines it, and having defined it, awaits the answer that God alone can give. The author of the Epistle to the Hebrews has preserved this extremity of prayer (Heb. 5.7).

Even more clearly and more necessarily than the record of the acts of healing do the narratives of the passion lay bare both the meaning of poverty and the meaning of faith; and this is so in all four Gospels. For this reason, the evangelists assert most explicitly, in the concluding sections of their narratives, that what they have to record took place in accordance with the will of God and under the pressure of divine necessity.[1] He who relieved the distress of the poor must himself await the relief that no man can give. The sceptical proverb 'physician heal thyself' formulates, as Luke perhaps knew, the final problem of theology and faith (Luke 4.23). The author of the fourth Gospel formulates that problem by an even bolder paradox. Jesus, who offers water that shall be 'a well . . . springing up unto eternal life' (John 4.14), when all things were accomplished, 'that the scripture might be fulfilled, saith, I thirst' (John 19.28).

The theme of withdrawal from the crowd and from acts of charity has assumed in the Gospels larger proportions than could at first sight have seemed possible. It is no doubt attractive to suppose that the contradictions in the Gospels constitute but another illustration of the intrusion of the later faith of the Church into the historical tradition; or, in this case, of the later doctrine of the secret Messiahship of Jesus. But this is really to misunderstand the essential themes of a gospel. The evangelists are compelled to set out what poverty really is in order that they may expose the grounds upon which faith in the love of God is in the end resting. They have understood this, and consequently acts of healing and their elimination both revolve round the same theme. Indeed, it is in the light of their elimination that they are most properly understood. A theological understanding of the life of Jesus, just as of the faith of the Church, may indeed have to move backwards from the story of his death to the record of his work in Galilee. For this reason, it would appear, the author of the fourth Gospel places at the beginning of his book the words: 'Behold the Lamb of God, which taketh away the sin of the world' (John 1.29–36). However this may be, it is the ultimate poverty of Jesus and the answer to that poverty that form the conclusion of the Gospels and formulate the eloquence of St Paul:

> Have this mind in you, which was also in Christ Jesus: who, being in the form of God, counted it not a prize (R.V. mg. 'a

[1] Cf. pp. 159–62 above.

thing to be grasped') to be on an equality with God, but emptied himself, taking the form of a servant, being made in the likeness of men; and being found in fashion as a man, he humbled himself, becoming obedient even unto death, yea, the death of the cross. Wherefore also God highly exalted him, and gave unto him the name which is above every name; that in the name of Jesus every knee should bow, of things in heaven, and things on earth, and things under the earth, and that every tongue should confess that Jesus Christ is Lord, to the glory of God the Father. (Phil. 2.5–11)

For ye know the grace of our Lord Jesus Christ, that, though he was rich, yet for your sakes he became poor, that ye through his poverty might become rich. (2 Cor. 8.9)

For I determined not to know anything among you, save Jesus Christ, and him crucified. And I was with you in weakness, and in fear, and in much trembling. And my speech and my preaching was not with enticing words of man's wisdom. (1 Cor. 2.2–4)

For, I think, God hath set forth us the apostles last of all, as men doomed to death : for we are made a spectacle unto the world and to angels, and to men. We are fools for Christ's sake, but ye are wise in Christ; we are weak, but ye are strong; ye have glory, but we have dishonour. Even unto this present hour we both hunger, and thirst, and are naked, and are buffeted, and have no certain dwelling-place; and we toil, working with our own hands : being reviled, we bless; being persecuted, we endure; being defamed, we intreat : we are made as the filth of the world, the offscouring of all things, even until now. (1 Cor. 4.9–13; cf. 1 Cor. 1.27–8)

The Epistle to the Hebrews, the First Epistle of Peter, and the Apocalypse show that St Paul was not alone among New Testament writers in this respect.

But we behold him who hath been made a little lower than the angels, even Jesus, because of the suffering of death, crowned with glory and honour, that by the grace of God he should taste death for every man . . . For in that he himself hath suffered being tempted, he is able to succour them that are tempted. (Heb. 2.9–18)

Wherefore when he cometh into the world, he saith, Sacrifice and offering thou wouldest not, But a body didst thou prepare for me; In whole burnt offerings and sacrifices for sin thou hadst no pleasure : Then said I, Lo, I am come (in the roll of the book it is written of me) to do thy will, O God . . . By which will we have been sanctified through the offering of the body of Jesus Christ once for all.   (Heb. 10.5–7, 18)

Wherefore Jesus also, that he might sanctify the people through his own blood, suffered without the gate. Let us therefore go forth unto him without the camp, bearing his reproach.   (Heb. 13.12–13)

For hereunto were ye called : because Christ also suffered for you, leaving you an example, that ye should follow his steps. (1 Pet. 2.21; cf. 4.1)

Worthy is the Lamb that hath been slain to receive the power, and riches, and wisdom, and might, and honour, and glory, and blessing. (Rev. 5.12)

These are they which came out of the great tribulation, and they washed their robes, and made them white in the blood of the Lamb. (Rev. 7.14)

If what is being said in the New Testament about poverty is to be understood, the records of the charitable acts and words of Jesus must now be examined once again. For it would now appear that, while these charitable acts and words clearly evoked the faith of the primitive Church and the theological perception of those who formulated its Scriptures, they did so because it was possible to regard them in an order directly contrary and opposite to that of their chronological and historical occurrence. It was the circumstances of his death—the behaviour of the crowds, of the authorities, Jewish and imperial, above all of Jesus himself—and those things that took place immediately afterwards, that enabled the apostles to understand what Jesus had previously said and done. Moreover, at the same time, the scope of their understanding was extended backwards far beyond the events of the immediate past.

For they perceived that the truth seen in the passion of Jesus embraced and illuminated the whole story of Israel in general and in detail. Finally, abandoning all thought of chronological and historical sequence, they were enabled to stand within human life with eyes wide open to the faith that is required by its fundamental structure and rhythm.[1]

In the stories of the charitable acts of healing so frequently repeated, especially in the first halves of the synoptic Gospels, the 'biblical humanism' is presented in miraculous form. Sometimes the familiar stories of the miracles of Elisha provide the background of its description, more frequently the evangelists make use of the more easily recognizable curve of the almost universal manner of narrating miracles. The single words, moreover, in which the good actions of Jesus are summed up, are words coined in the rough mint of popular, uncultured, and even superstitious religion. The works of Jesus 'who went about doing good, and healing all that were oppressed by the devil' (Acts 10.38) are 'mighty works, signs, and wonders'. These English words, however, in some degree smooth out the roughness of the original Greek—and indeed of the Vulgate also:

> Ye men of Israel, hear these words:
> Jesus of Nazareth, a man approved of God unto you
> by mighty works (R.V.mg. powers) and wonders and signs,[2]
> which God did by him in the midst of you... (Acts 2.22).

This summary may be presumed not to represent, any more than does the summary in Acts 10.38, an isolated and peculiar opinion of Luke concerning the material he had put together and edited in the first volume of his work on the 'Beginnings of Christianity'. Nor can the three words be reasonably held to cover some neatly arranged and separate groups or levels of miraculous episodes—as though, for example, the call of Levi and the healing of an epileptic boy were *mighty works,* the feeding of the five thousand and the

---

[1] In this context, it is not irrelevant that a technical and critical analysis of the process by which the Gospels reached their present form seems to suggest that, in correspondence with the emphasis in the preaching of the primitive Church, the narrative of the passion was first shaped and then drew to itself other episodes and controlled their form and arrangement.

[2] *Virtutibus et prodigiis et signis* – Vulgate: *dunamesi kai terasi kai semeiois* – the original Greek.

raising of the widow's only son at Nain *signs,* but the walking on the sea and the stilling of the storm ('nature miracles') *prodigies.* These nice distinctions may be convenient, but they are altogether foreign to the form and meaning of a Gospel. The distinction that is fundamental in the Gospels of Matthew and Luke, and may also be so in the Gospel of Mark, is that between the miraculous acts of which Jesus is the object, and those of which he is the subject : his birth and resurrection on the one hand, his charitable actions on the other. God is, of course, beginning and ending, Alpha and Omega, but what lies betwixt and between, the rest of the alphabet, is by no means simple, nor is it capable of straightforward description. Miraculous language is not discarded, but—and this is surely very surprising—it is wholly made use of to describe acts of charity. It is removed from the service of vague supernaturalism and pressed into the service of the revelation of the one God, who had made himself known in Israel and was now making himself known to all men. The use of miraculous language in the Gospels to describe non-miraculous and non-unique acts of charity—'by whom do your sons cast them out?' (Matt. 12.27; Luke 11.19; cf. Matt. 7.22–3) – requires some explanation. And no explanation is satisfactory which, by speaking of legends and myths and symbols, etc., suggests that the language of miracle need not be taken seriously. How important this language is in the Gospels can be seen in its steady retention by the author of the fourth Gospel, as for example, in the account of the Raising of Lazarus (John 11).

If a psalm be, as Martin Buber has said, a cry, not a poem, and if prophecy be an appeal, not a direct allocution, then all acts of physical healing, all acts of human charity are, as has been seen, appeals for a greater and permanent healing, cries for a greater and permanent relief. Seen in the perspective of the death of Jesus, in which the cry of the psalmists and the call of the prophets are gathered up into a concrete, historical, silent event, his charitable acts are supremely appeals to the love and mercy of God, for they neither are, nor are set forth as, final answers to the problem of human poverty. There is not the slightest hint in the Gospels that those who were healed by the powerful action of Jesus became thereby exempt from the ravages of disease or hunger or distress or poverty, or were thereby rendered immortal, or even that those whose sins had been forgiven were thereby released from the power of sin. As appeals to the love of God, the charitable acts of Jesus needed miraculous description no more than did the prayer of the publican. When, however, they are seen in the perspective of the effective answer of God to the poverty of Jesus—when, that is to say, the passing of men from disease to temporary health is seen in the light of his resurrection—their last meaning and truth can be understood only if they are described in the language in which Israel and all other peoples have been compelled to express their bitter experience that the observable world is unable to answer its own final problems. Herein lies the necessity of the human language of miracle. For this reason the prophet Isaiah presented himself and his boys Shear-jashub and Maher-shalal-hash-baz as 'signs and wonders' (Isa. 8.18; cf. 7.3; 8.3); for the same reason Luke the evangelist presented the charitable acts of Jesus to Israel, to the Church and to the world, as 'mighty works, wonders and signs'. And for the same reason the author of the Epistle to the Hebrews described the confirmation of the apostolic gospel 'God also bearing witness with them, both by signs and wonders, and by manifold powers, and by gifts of the Holy Ghost, according to his own will' (Heb. 2.4).

The language of miracle is, however, as dangerous to theology as it is necessary to faith. This danger is from time to time voiced in the Gospels, as it is by St Paul. The anti-miraculous sayings of Jesus are called forth when his charitable actions are treated by the crowds as things in themselves, and when they therefore cease to provide an incentive to faith and obscure rather than show forth the final answer of God to the fact of poverty.

> An evil and adulterous generation seeketh after a sign;
> and there shall no sign be given unto it,
> but the sign of Jonah the prophet.
> (Matt. 12.39; cf. Mark 8.12; Luke 11.29; John 6.14–15, 27)

CHAPTER 9

Father and Son – and the Dereliction of Jesus

'He that hath seen me hath seen the Father' (John 14.9). Dr Karl Barth once said:[1] 'Theologians had to learn to think no longer abstractly and scientifically, but *ecclesiastically,* as bound to the Church, and by that to reckon the scientific character of their work. And the Church had on its side to think and act *theologically.*' Yes of course! But how can theologians think ecclesiastically, and how can the Church act theologically, unless they know that they are both bound together to the world as it is, and that they both stand together within its structure and rhythm? How can God be named Father and Jesus Christ his Son, unless what it means to be a father and what it means to be a son have first been correctly observed, and unless the existence of all men—yes, and of all women too—be in some way or other bound up with the relation of a father to a son and of a son to a father. If this be not so, theology is deprived of its basis in the concrete world, and the Church is wholly deprived of its capacity to speak intelligibly.

According to the humanism of the Bible, men cannot be thought of as individuals complete, or aiming at completion, in themselves : they cannot be depicted in isolation, or as portraits in frames. Israel did not develop a technique of sculpture or painting. It abhorred idols whether of men or of gods. It developed no secular political theory, and it produced no philosophy of existence, that is, of the existence of this or that thing, of this or that person, or of this or that god. The world and human life spoke to Israel neither of existence nor yet of individuality, but of relationship—the relationship between the world and its creator, between men and men, and between men and God. As the new Israel, the primitive Church thought and acted likewise. Consequently, for the Church as for Israel the relation between father and son was of quite fundamental importance. If, therefore, the New Testament is to be understood,

[1] In a letter to the *British Weekly.*

it is necessary to be quite clear about what had been observed as being most characteristic of this relationship.

The definition of Jesus as the Son of God, and the consequent rider that God is his Father, underlie all the books of the New Testament. These were the fundamental dogmas of primitive Christian theology and ethics. In the fourth Gospel they drive all other definitions into second place. There Jesus is primarily neither Messiah or Christ, nor Son of man, nor Lord: he is Son of God. And God is primarily neither King, nor Judge, nor Master: he is the Father who sent into the world his Son, Jesus: 'God so loved the world, that he gave his only begotten Son, that whosoever believeth on him should not perish, but have eternal life' (John 3.16). 'As the Father hath sent me, even so send I you' (John 20.21). In thus formulating the work of Jesus, the author of the fourth Gospel is laying no violent hands upon the tradition that lies behind him, nor is he saying what St Paul had not said already, or what is not said, for example, in the Epistle to the Hebrews.

Mark not only presents Jesus to his readers at the beginning of his Gospel as the Son of God, but is careful to assert that this is not to be understood as a speculative opinion or idea about him. He is pronounced by the voice from heaven to be 'the Beloved Son of God,' and since in him God is 'well pleased', his behaviour as the Son is of supreme significance (Mark 1.9–11). This authoritative definition controls the whole run of the Marcan narrative. It conditions the faith of the apostles: 'This is my Beloved Son: hear ye him' (Mark 9.7). It defines the unbelief of the Jewish authorities: 'They will reverence my son . . . and they took him, and killed him, and cast him forth out of the vineyard' (Mark 12.6–8). It provides the language in which the centurion explains the impression made upon him by the manner in which Jesus had died: 'When the centurion, which stood by over against him, saw that he so cried out (R.V. mg.) and gave up the ghost, he said, Truly this man was Son of God (A.V., R.V. 'the Son of God'; R.V. mg. 'a son of God') (Mark 15.39).

St Paul opens his Epistle to the Romans with an address in which the current epistolary form, 'Paul—to all who are in Rome—greeting', is expanded so as to define precisely the gospel that had been promised afore by the prophets and was now entrusted to him:

The gospel of God . . .
concerning his son Jesus Christ our Lord,
who was born of the seed of David
    according to the flesh,
who was declared to be the son of God with power,
    according to the spirit of holiness . . .   (Rom. 1.1–4)

From what is said at the beginning of the Epistle to the Ephesians
it is clear that the language round which the Marcan narrative of
the Baptism had been constructed also formed the groundwork of
primitive Christian preaching.

Blessed be the God and Father of our Lord Jesus Christ,
who . . . having foreordained us unto adoption as sons
through Jesus Christ unto himself, according to the good
pleasure of his will,
to the praise and glory of his grace,
which he freely bestowed upon us in the Beloved.
                                          (Eph. 1.3–6)

Here the position of the believers as sons is conditioned by their
relation to the Beloved Son of God; and moreover, the whole interlocking relationship of the Son to the Father and of the sons to the
Son is comprehensively defined as according to the good pleasure of
the will of God.

Nor does the writer of the Epistle to the Hebrews introduce what
he has to say in any different fashion, or with any different emphasis.
Like St Paul he combines what God had spoken through the prophets with what has now at the end of these days been spoken by
his Son (Heb. 1.1–2); and then goes on to contrast Jesus with the
angels :

For unto which of the angels said he at any time,
    Thou art my Son,
This day have I begotten thee?
and again,
    I will be to him a Father
    and he shall be to me a son?
    (Heb. 1.5; 2.9; cf. 3.5–6, etc.)

The New Testament is not a literature that is spread out before us primarily for our enjoyment or for our research. The Biblical 'word' is the spoken word. At times the artistry of the Bible, as for example in the Lucan writings and in the Matthean Gospel in so far as it is the product of editing, may obscure the directness of what had been said. Nevertheless, even then the rough spoken word remains always recognizable. Speech is directed to those who are willing and able to hear, and the effective spoken word is fundamental and original; it moves out towards, and presses into its service, the things that lie at the root of human experience. It is therefore not surprising that the relation between father and son should have played so large a part in providing the rough material of primitive Christian preaching. There is, however, another reason for the pre-eminence of this theme. The apostolic preaching was, no doubt, concerned with the direction in which human life was moving, and in which it ought to move—with its goal, or purpose, or aim. But it was far more seriously concerned with its place of departure and with its origin. This was not because those who addressed the Church were conservative or reactionary—or radical devotees of the simple life—but because they were persuaded that the goal or purpose of human life lies hidden in its origin. This place of departure must therefore be made known. Within wide limits it is possible for men to select and manipulate the direction in which they propose to move, but it is not possible for them to select their place of departure. The directness and originality of New Testament speech is largely due to the directness with which it speaks of the origin of human life, and to the directness of the requirements for human behaviour that follow from this definition of origin. Here the relation between father and son provided the New Testament writers with more than an analogy or illustration or parable. Lying at the foundation of human life, it lay also at the heart of their theology and faith.

The essential rhythm of the relation between father and son governs the argument of the eighth chapter of the fourth Gospel. The chapter is otherwise unintelligible. It is first assumed that men betray by their behaviour the stock from which they have come, 'Ye do the works of your father' (John 8.41). Then, as a rider to this, their conduct is governed by their origin : 'If ye were Abraham's children, ye would do the works of Abraham' (John 8.39). Lastly, an intimate and recognizable bond of union exists between those who share a common father: 'If God were your father, ye would love me: for I came forth and am come from God' (John 8.42). Following this rhythm, the conclusion is inevitable. The scheming of the Jews to commit murder is of more serious and ultimate importance than they were aware of: 'Ye are of your father the devil, and the lusts of your father ye will do. He was a murderer from the beginning' (John 8.44).[1] The same argument appears in a passage in the Gospel according to Matthew. When the scribes and Pharisees admit that those who slew the prophets were their fathers, Jesus calls attention to the seriousness of this admission; for, in spite of the care they bestow on the tombs of the prophets and in spite of their assertions that they would not have acted as their fathers did, their acknowledgement of their descent constitutes an inevitable witness to their own future murderous behaviour, 'Behold, I send unto you prophets, and wise men, and scribes: some of them shall ye kill and crucify; and some of them shall ye scourge in your synagogues, and persecute from city to city' (Matt. 23.29–36).[2]

In the biblical literature, and especially in the New Testament, it is congruity of conduct that marks the relation between father and son and defines the fact of sonship. Mere physical descent is trivial, if it does not carry with it a behaviour that tallies with and reproduces the behaviour of him who is named father. Thus St Paul can argue that, since Abraham's faith was the most characteristic fact about him, the children of Abraham are those who walk in his steps and reproduce his faith (Rom. 4; cf. Matt. 3.9; Luke 3.8; 19.9). No doubt, he expects that his physical descendants will be more likely to believe in God and to hope when all seems hopeless than those who are not privileged to be his descendants; yet, when he sees faith and hope displayed among those whose forefather Abraham is not *according to the flesh*, he does not hesitate to pronounce them children of Abraham. A merely biological description of sonship is therefore at best inadequate and may obscure its essential nature.

These are, of course, strictly theological arguments. But they are relevant only because they are based on the observation that the key

[1] Cf. the argument in John 5.19–38.
[2] In the parallel Lucan passage (Luke 11.47–50), the argument is obscured.

to the understanding of the thought and action of any given person lies primarily in his parentage. So securely does this analysis of human conduct lie behind the New Testament writers that they do not have to explain how it could come about that an unknown father could be known through the behaviour of his son. New Testament theology rests on this observable fact in much the same way as the Semitic idiom, *sons of peace, sons of evil,* etc., etc., denotes the manifestation of what would otherwise remain an abstraction.

The relation between father and son is not, however, described as a dumb transmission of life and behaviour. It is a tradition or handing over of teaching and commandment. The father commands: the son obeys. Obedience is therefore the characteristic note of sonship. A son reproduces the behaviour of his father because he hears and obeys. The biblical writers therefore depict no straining after emancipation. It is not the duty of a father to train and prepare his son for a time when he will be free to develop his own character, follow his own desires, and work out his own destiny. Nor is it the duty of a son to free himself from the honour due to his father or from the bond by which he is linked to the man who has given him life. The freedom of a son lies in his recognition of his parentage, not in emancipating himself from it. Here again, it is in the fourth Gospel that this rhythm of sonship, this rhythm of obedience, is most precisely formulated.

> The Son can do nothing of himself, but what he seeth the Father doing.   (John 5.19)
>
> I can of myself do nothing; as I hear I judge . . .
> I seek not my own will, but the will of him that sent me.   (John 5.30)
>
> As I have kept my Father's commandments, and abide in his love.   (John 15.15)
>
> The word which ye hear is not mine, but the Father's who sent me.   (John 14.24)
>
> If therefore the Son shall make you free, ye shall be free indeed. (John 8.36)

The necessity of filial obedience provides the subject-matter of the

232

parable of the Two Sons narrated in the Gospel of Matthew, 'Whether of the twain did the will of his father' (Matt. 21.28–31). The obedience of children to their parents is therefore, as St Paul says, the most necessary fact of their upbringing: 'this is right'; it is a 'commandment' (Eph. 6.1–3); it is 'well pleasing unto the Lord' (Col. 3.20). Nor is the honour due to parents a temporary virtue belonging to childhood alone. It must not be disturbed, even by the specific requirements of religious piety (Corban!—Mark 7.11). And so, in the prophecy of Jeremiah, the obedience of the whole house of the Rechabites to the commands of their father provides a standard of obedience by which Israel as the disobedient son of God is put to shame and judged.

> We will drink no wine: for Jonadab the son of Rechab our father commanded us, saying, Ye shall drink no wine, neither ye, nor your sons, for ever: neither shall ye build house, nor sow seed, nor plant vineyard nor have any: but all your days ye shall dwell in tents; that ye may live many days in the land wherein ye sojourn. And we have obeyed the voice of Jonadab the son of Rechab our father in all that he charged us. . . . Because ye have obeyed the commandment of Jonadab your father, and kept all his precepts, and done according to all that he commanded you, therefore thus saith the Lord of hosts, the God of Israel: Jonadab the son of Rechab shall not want a man to stand before me for ever. (Jer. 35.6–7, 18–19)

Thus, in the biblical literature there is built up upon the biological and organic relation between father and son, and upon the sociological fact of the reproduction by sons of the behaviour of their father, a vast pyramid of filial obedience that has its apex in the obedience of men to God. In the universal fact of birth the Jew was confronted by the fact of his creation by God; and in the command that he should honour the immediate source of his existence he was confronted by the honour due to the final source of his existence. The Jews included the fifth commandment in the first Table of the Law, of which the subject-matter was God. Filial piety and obedience were therefore no mere social virtues grounded in tradition and convention; they were the necessary response of the creature to the Creator and the means by which the invisible and living God makes himself known among men. When Israel is declared to be the son of God, the title describes no mystical experience; it voices the call to obedience given to Israel in order that the origin and destiny of all life might be revealed (cf. Exod. 4.22–3; Hos. 11.1). The obedience of Israel reveals the fatherhood that is beyond history and beyond all biological analysis. The disobedience of Israel, which is described in the New Testament, would have left men deprived of the knowledge of their true origin and of their proper behaviour, had it not been for the sonship and obedience of Jesus : 'He that hath seen me hath seen the Father' (John 14.9).

There is here set before us a splendid panorama of human life, in which the human relation between father and son is provided with ultimate significance in the divine structure of creation. Here is a grand and catholic coherence of orderliness. But is this the theology of the New Testament? And is this all-embracing doctrine of obedience the moral teaching of the New Testament? And if it were, can human paternity bear the theological weight that is being put upon it?

It is tempting to interpret the New Testament mystically, to think of the visible world as encircled by an invisible world to which it corresponds at every point, so that it is possible to pass from the visible world to the invisible, from sight to faith, without any disturbance or uneasiness. The fundamental structure of human life would then be provided with a meaning so final and authoritative that it could be permitted to run its course easily without doubt, question, or disturbance. Of this congruence of sight and faith the relation between father and son might be taken to provide an admirable illustration; for its rhythm could be said to correspond so exactly with the relation between God and man as to provide a wholly adequate parable of it; a parable that is, moreover, also a standard by which the conduct of all fathers and of all sons can, and must, be regulated.

The security of the relation between fathers and sons which the theological movement from sight to faith requires is, however, in no way a theme of the New Testament. When the coherence and correspondence between the relation between fathers and sons and the relation between God and man is seen and drawn out, it is rather the consequence of faith, not the prolegomenon to it; 'he shall go before his face in the spirit and power of Elijah, to turn the hearts of the fathers to the children' (Luke 1.17; cf. Mal. 4.6; Ecclus. 48.10). Indeed, in the New Testament the fatherhood of God is frequently depicted as invading and disturbing the human relationship of father and son. The rich pattern, or rhythm, of the relationship between the two is seen first in the fatherhood of God and in the sonship of Jesus; it is not seen first in the normal behaviour of men. 'Call no man your father on the earth, for one is your Father, which is in heaven' (Matt. 23.9).[1] The word 'father' is here declared to rest uncomfortably upon all human fathers, even upon the best. As teacher, he is compelled to surrender his responsibility to a pedagogue; as responsible for his son's piety, he yields to the Rabbis. His authority cannot be compared with the authority exercised by a centurion. Even the importance of the physical fact of paternity must be vastly exaggerated if it is to answer the problems of the origin of his son's interests, desires, and capacities. Similarly, and perhaps in part as a consequence of this, the behaviour of sons providing at best a thin, shadowy anticipation or analogy of the obedience of Jesus to God, as shown by the behaviour of both the sons in the parable of the Prodigal Son. So great is the strain between the latent implications of the relation between father and son and what actually takes place in human life that the analogy breaks on the lips of Jesus. Immediately the thought of procreation leads to the thought of man as the son of God, it becomes evident that no human father and no human son can stand under its scrutiny. Where is the man who can represent with his will, as father, the will of God? And where is the man whose obedience substantiates the thought of him as son of God? And so, although (as has been seen) the relation between father and son does provide an important and recurring theme in his parables, Jesus nevertheless also moves by word and action so quickly and firmly away from this human relationship that its security is altogether disturbed in order that its meaning may be established. For example, his call is so rough, so urgent, and so insistent that he

---

[1] It is possible that this saying refers to the use of the word 'father' for a teacher, for it is sandwiched between two sayings beginning, respectively, 'be not ye called Rabbi' and 'neither be ye called masters', and to call a Rabbi 'Father' was not unknown in Judaism. But since the different, active, form, 'call no man father . . .', suggests that the three sayings have been drawn together by an editor, it seems preferable to understand this saying in the fundamental sense it must have had if it stood alone.

requires that the fifth commandment be broken in its own interests, 'If any man cometh unto me, and hateth not his own father . . . he cannot be my disciple' (Luke 14.26; cf. Matt. 10.37). Not less rough are the forebodings of the consequences of discipleship: 'Brother shall deliver up the brother to death, and the father his child; and children shall rise up against parents, and cause them to be put to death' (Mark 13.12). Here submission to the will of God breaks in upon and disturbs the obedience of son to father and the love of father to son.

This disturbing, reverse, movement must be taken seriously if the Gospels are to be interpreted at all. It is not merely that they contain here and there a 'hard' saying. These hard sayings correspond with and explain the action of Jesus himself. On his lips the word 'father' means God; it has no other meaning. His obedience as son is obedience to the will of God; no other obedience complicates or obscures or even simplifies the directness of his words and actions. His primary definition of the family concerns those who 'shall do the will of God' (Mark 3.34–5), and his primary blessing rests upon those that 'hear the word of God and keep it' (Luke 11.27–8). The primary and only source of his authority is his father in heaven. There is no other Jesus of history discernible in any record that has come down to us. This means that the historical figure of Jesus is no rounded-off and complete human life to which there corresponds some second, mystical, glorified Christ, perceived and recognized by faith. The obedience of Jesus to the will of his father provides the only key to his words and actions and to his death. In the historical figure of Jesus faith in God presses into human life and announces its presence by disturbing the self-sufficiency of human relations at their very foundations.

Throughout the New Testament, the theme of the relation between father and son quite clearly provokes a series of contradictions. Since the same contradictions reappear when other themes are being dealt with, there is very good reason to think that the realism of primitive Christian preaching consisted precisely in the fearlessness with which these contradictions were formulated and proclaimed. If this be so, they provide so important a problem of New Testament exegesis that, at the risk of repetition, another attempt must be made to define and, if possible, to explain them. The foundation of everything that is said in the New Testament

236

concerning the relation between father and son is provided by the normal structure of human life. The relationship is governed by a certain pattern of behaviour. When, however, this pattern is observed, it is also observed broken into fragments by the actual behaviour of fathers and sons. Tyranny takes the place of the proper exercise of authority, obedience lacks conviction, the freedom that is not secured by obedience is therefore sought for elsewhere, and, most serious of all, the problem of origin remains unanswered. Yet, in spite of this, the pattern is not surrendered. It is ineradicable and indestructible. There is an authority that can require and support obedience; there is a freedom to be found in obedience; and there must be an answer to the problem of origin. And so the pattern that has emerged from the fact of paternity, but to which the relation between fathers and sons does not correspond, strays to seek a home in other congruous, but non-physical relationships. The language of father and son, and the pattern of behaviour involved in this language, are used to describe the relation between a king and his people, between an emperor and the peoples who are united under his authority, between a teacher of religion and his disciples, between a nation and its god, and finally, with a cruel scepticism about human life, it is used as a basis of mythical speculation concerning the relation between the gods themselves.

To judge from the writings that have survived from primitive Christianity, the Church was acutely sensitive to this general restlessness. But it was not engulfed by it. The Church had been presented with a relationship in which what the natural order yearned after but could not satisfy was fulfilled. It is this theme of fulfilment that in the New Testament governs everything that is said—the fulfilment, not only of what has been promised in the Old Testament, but of the yearning of creation itself. The Christians were therefore able to return to the quite straightforward language of father and son. They had seen an obedience exercised in response to an authority that was not tyrannical; they had seen an obedience wrought out in freedom, not in slavery; and they were persuaded that in the relation of Jesus to God as son to father, the ultimate ground and origin of human life had been revealed. The relationship between father and son is here neither moralized nor philosophized: it is fulfilled. Jesus did not become the son of God by obeying him, nor could his union with his father be explained as a 'metaphysical' union.

In all this New Testament theme of fulfilment there is of necessity a negative factor, for there is almost universal blasphemy rearing its head everywhere in human thought and conduct. In the New Testament this blasphemy is recognized and exposed. Human paternity and human sonship can never in and by themselves answer the problems raised by the facts of their existence. They can, that is to say, never be their own fulfilment. Blasphemy consists in the conscious or unconscious claim that human behaviour is able to fulfil the truth to which by its very structure it bears witness.

> Then the old man
> Was wrath, and doubled up his hands and said :
> 'You will not, boy! You dare to answer thus!
> But in my time a father's word was law
> And so it shall be now for me . . .'[1]

Against this self-sufficiency the negative rhythm of the New Testament is always directed. This is its theological purpose and meaning. Nor is this negative rhythm limited to the words and actions of Jesus. It remained an integral element in the witness of the primitive Church. So much is this the case that it would almost seem that the language of father and son is altogether removed from a description of the normal relation between parents and children and is exhausted in its use to describe the relation between God and Jesus and between God and those who believe in him through his Son. This was, and presumably still is, the gospel of the Church. But to stop at this negation would certainly be to misunderstand what is said in the New Testament.

The deep throb of existence was the matrix of the life and teaching of the Church, and to this matrix the Church of necessity returned; but it returned purged of idolatry.

> Whatsoever ye do in word or deed, do all in the name of the Lord Jesus, giving thanks to God and the Father by him . . . Children, obey your parents in all things. (Col. 3.17–20)

> Children obey your parents—in the Lord . . . And, ye fathers,

[1] Tennyson, *Dora*.

provoke not your children to wrath: but bring them up in the nurture and admonition of the Lord. (Eph. 6.1–4)

And so the pattern of life reappears more clearly defined and more confidently demanded when human conduct has been deprived of its self-sufficiency.

CHAPTER 10
Marriage – and the Isolation of Jesus

'This mystery is great; but I speak in regard of Christ and of the Church' (Eph. 5.32). There is one category of human experience, one fundamental personal relationship, which does not merely illustrate the radical poverty of the individual man or woman in isolation. The universal incompleteness manifest in the fact of sex, and the potential fruitfulness of the union which it demands, inevitably raise problems far wider than the mutual concentration of two human beings. What is the meaning of this union (whether life-long or ephemeral); what should its status be in, or over against, society? It is easy, and banal, to say that the phenomenon of sex complicates the whole pattern of life; very much more difficult to decide upon its fundamental character, essential as it is both to community and race, yet awkward not least because it poses the essential paradox of the particular and the general.

Sex has obtruded itself, often literally, even more often metaphorically, into religion, as witness monasticism on the one hand, and fertility rites on the other. Should not the religious uses of the metaphor of sex, at any given time, help us to understand what general significance it is thought to have? It is at first sight disappointing that in the Bible the particular relationship of a man and a woman should seem no less intolerant of analysis and generalization than it has shown itself to be almost everywhere else in recorded human experience. No biblical writer treats of it systematically, as requiring explanation—there are no biblical records of sex-instruction or of preparation for marriage. Yet what really matters is that in the Bible marriage is assumed to have certain characteristic implications which are taken to be self-evident; and that thus apprehended, it is confidently used to expound, in the Old Testament the relation between God and his people, in the New Testament the relation between Christ and his Church.

Marriage encourages the hope of fruitfulness. It is often an occasion of joy. Here are two possibilities of theological illustration by means of analogy, neither of which the Bible neglects. But

240

marriage has two further implications, which seem to have impressed the biblical writers even more. Both are in origin physical. The first is the implication of *unity*. In their union, man and woman evidently supplement each other. Their potential fruitfulness reveals the essential insufficiency of each alone: only the two together can be thought of as fully one. The second implication is that of *commitment*. This is manifest more obviously, but by no means exclusively, in the submission of the woman to the man. Their unity is fruitful because of their mutual self-abandonment.

The writers of the Old Testament refuse to allow that sexual union can be rightly understood if its implications are supposed to be merely ephemeral or purely physical. This does not mean either that the standards of sexual behaviour in Old Testament times were exceptionally high, or that these writers idealized or romanticized marriage. Prohibitions of adultery and coveting were not included among the Ten Commandments without good cause, nor were the provisions of the Law elaborated to protect an institution that needed no defence. In the Bible, as in more modern literature, we read of the infidelity and promiscuity of husbands and wives. There too we read of the sacred prostitution through which fertility was perhaps sought for a nation and its soil or stock, or the identification of worshippers with their goddess or god. Those were days when polygamy and concubinage were common—days, too, when the social structure was built up, without question, round the male, the wife 'belonging' to the husband as a piece of his property.[1] Moreover, the times demanded an over-riding concern for human fruitfulness. For most people, the object of marriage must have seemed to be the begetting of children rather than the comfort each should have of the other. Why should a barren wife be kept any longer than an unprofitable servant? What ought perhaps to amaze us in the Bible is the extent of the protest against such pragmatic conceptions of marriage. The good husband, like Elkanah, hopes that he is better to his barren wife than ten sons (1 Sam. 1.8), while the wife so lauded in the Proverbs has virtues congruous with a lifetime of loving care, intellectual as well as physical or material (Prov. 31.10–31). Old Testament Judaism, indeed, would not tolerate any ultimate cynicism about marriage. If the Jewish people's

---

[1] One of the Hebrew words (*ba'al*) commonly translated 'husband' could rightly be rendered 'owner', 'lord', or 'master'.

greatest contribution to the dignity of human life has lain in their conception of the family, that conception is rooted in the idea of the personal commitment of husband to wife and wife to husband, and in a deep appreciation of the creative potentialities of this relationship when governed by self-giving and love.

That this is a just impression is confirmed by the fact that such a conception—as an intimate and enduring personal union—underlies the use of marriage in the Old Testament to describe the relation between God and his people—a use strikingly different from that evident in some of the religions among which Judaism developed. The intimate union between God and Israel—sometimes described as a union between God and Jerusalem—is such that any traffic with other deities in prostitution (Exod. 24.15; Deut. 31.16; Ps. 73.27). The continual faithlessness of God's people therefore invites the conclusion that the people whom God has betrothed to himself as a bride has behaved as an adulterous wife, as a harlot indeed (cf., e.g. Hos. 1.2; 3.1); or, worse still, as an 'imperious whorish woman', in the phrase of Ezekiel, not plying for hire, as a harlot does, but giving gifts to all her lovers and bribing them (Ezek. 16.30–4). It was therefore natural, by an extension of the same metaphor, to represent her exile and the destruction of the holy city as evidence that God had divorced Israel, and discarded her, for her sins (Jer. 3.1–5; Isa. 50.1–3), just as the Hebrew husband might divorce his wife, and put her away, for adultery. But the pathetic prophesying of Hosea, apparently through the medium of his own disastrous marriage; the reproaches, whether stern or pleading, of Jeremiah and the Second Isaiah; the blistering scorn of Ezekiel—all these have one object only, to press home the assurance that God remains unchanged in his free choice, and that a penitent Israel will be forgiven and restored, *because the covenant made of old with his people by God must be everlasting* (Hos. 14.1–8; Jer. 3.14–15; Isa. 54.1–8; Ezek. 16.60–3): 'for thy Maker is thy husband; the Lord of hosts is his name: and the Holy One of Israel is thy redeemer; the God of the whole earth shall he be called' (Isa. 54.5). These prophets use the analogy of a marriage, first broken and then restored, partly, no doubt, to convict Israel of infidelity, but primarily to demonstrate God's more than human faithfulness and loving-kindness.[1] In response, they express their

[1] Cf. Ulrich E. Simon, *A Theology of Salvation*, p. 171.

hope of Israel's redemption in the idealized picture of a virgin-bride purified and made beautiful for her husband. Accordingly, although they reserve the analogy of betrothal or marriage for the relation between God and his people—perhaps under the figure of the city which is their mother, or of the remnant in which they will be preserved and restored—they demand a corporate faithfulness, obedience, and love, so exacting that each individual man or woman in Israel is fully involved in it: in a word, a human 'submission' that will match the exclusive faithfulness and zeal of God. Perhaps because relics of fertility rites still survived uncomfortably near at hand, the bond between God and Israel is never in the Old Testament expressed in terms of marriage between the individual soul and God. Nevertheless, the oft-quoted words of Jeremiah describing the new covenant when 'they shall all know me, from the least of them unto the greatest of them' (Jer. 31.30–4) illustrate the implications of the national marriage bond. That the prophets use the man-with-woman relationship in this way suggests that, in spite of the failures, the imperfections, and the impermanence of many human marriages in their experience, this human relationship seemed to them most truly and fully achieved in permanent union and exclusive, mutual, commitment.

A similar belief is assumed in the New Testament. According to the Gospel of Mark, some Pharisees once raised the question of the character of marriage by asking Jesus whether divorce is lawful. Jesus is said to have answered by means of a catena of texts from Genesis. The origin and purpose of marriage derives from God—'from the beginning of the creation, male and female created he them'. Marriage may disrupt the relation between parents and children—'for this cause shall a man leave his father and mother, and cleave to his wife'—but it creates a unity that brings the previous, self-sufficient, independence of its participants to an end—'so then they are no more twain, but one flesh'. That is the crucial point, and Jesus clinches it with words of his own. Since the new unity of the man and the woman is effected by God through his ordering of creation, it is something that men may not seek to destroy—'what therefore God hath joined together, let not man put asunder' (Mark 10.6–9; cf. Gen. 1.27; 5.2; 2.24). Afterwards, 'in the house,'[1] Jesus goes further than the Old Testament had done

[1] See p. 181 above.

when he declares that if either party divorces the other and marries again he or she is guilty of adultery.[1] 'Whosoever shall put away his wife, and marry again, committeth adultery against her: and if she herself shall put away her husband, and marry another, she committeth adultery' (Mark 10.10–12). Man and woman have an equal responsibility and obligation to preserve the bond of marriage. In spite of the famous Matthaean 'exceptive clauses' (Matt. 13.32; 19.2), divorce is alien to this teaching, a second best, instituted for the hardness of men's hearts (Mark 10.5; Matt. 18.8). Disregard of their mutual commitment, by husband or by wife, or repudiation of it, makes nonsense of their potential unity. That is the horror of adultery.[2]

Similarly, the apostles teach the equal obligation and opportunity of both partners within the marriage bond (1 Cor. 7.2–4; 1 Pet. 3.7). St Paul, though not specifically excluding polygamy (1 Cor. 7.2), confirms the impression that monogamy is coming to be generally assumed,[3] and that a deepening appreciation of the nature of man and woman, and of what union between them can bring about, is making the exaltation of permanent and exclusive monogamy inevitable. He too expounds 'the twain shall become one flesh', in order to expose the horror of fornication—'he that is joined to a harlot is one body' (1 Cor. 6.16). Perhaps he is using rhetoric to drive his point home, but the cause of his concern is revealing. It is his sense for the totality of human personality and the seriousness of all human action. Although he speaks readily enough of flesh and spirit, of body, mind, and soul, he will not permit any essential dichotomy or trichotomy of man or woman, in such a way as would give the act of sexual union no more than mechanical or sensuous significance.

Here, then, in the New Testament, we seem to have a consistent conception of marriage. It is characterized by unity—permanent, and exclusive, achieved through the commitment of each to the

---

[1] It must be noted that the strikingly parallel saying common to Matthew and Luke (Matt. 5.32; Luke 16.18) restricts responsibility to the man.

[2] Are the Matthaean 'exceptive clauses' in fact significant of a modification in a gospel precept too hard even for Christians? Or are they a recognition that no precept will protect against destruction what adultery has already destroyed?

[3] Of Mark 12.18–27 and its parallels, Dr Henry J. Cadbury has said: 'this is perhaps the first place in the Bible where monogamy is most definitely assumed' (in SPCK *Theological Collections 3, The Miracles and the Resurrection*, p. 93).

other, in total self-giving; should we not say, in authentic love? No doubt it is true that 'the New Testament does not profess to set forth any new law or theory of marriage'.[1] But can we not describe what is there held up for us as the crystallization of the Old Testament insight into the potentialities of marriage, not as a law, and certainly not as a theory, but as the ideal created by a real perception of human need and by a real experience of human altruism? If so, is this not in itself a conspicuous achievement of New Testament humanism?

Such a conclusion is seriously defective in at least one respect— that it can be reached only by ignoring part of the evidence. For it leaves unconsidered certain sayings, attributed to Jesus, which suggest that marriage is not for all, and that some marriages are to be broken for his sake. It takes no notice of St Paul's insistence that the non-believing partner is free to renounce an existing marriage with a Christian and that, if he or she chooses to do so, the marriage will then cease to be binding on either party (1 Cor. 7.12–15). It fails to explain both a tendency in primitive Christianity to exalt the celibate life, even, perhaps to wholesale denigration of the married status (Heb. 13.4), and St Paul's remarkable ability to give sound and sensible rulings about marriage while wishing all Christians unmarried like himself.

That Jesus called men to follow him at great cost to themselves is continually affirmed in the synoptic Gospels. In Mark it is the subject of a brief speech to the multitudes, 'with his disciples', immediately after the first prediction of the passion and resurrection. Jesus calls upon all who would come after him to deny themselves, take up their cross, and follow him. 'For whosoever would save his life shall lose it; and whosoever shall lose his life for my sake and the gospel's shall save it' (Mark 8.34—9.1). The cost is stated in more detail in the sayings about the Danger of Riches and the Rewards of Discipleship, which follow the incident of the man who asks what he should do to inherit eternal life. Peter protests that the disciples 'have left all' to follow Jesus; and Jesus, assuring them that such discipleship will be rewarded, makes it clear that the call 'for his sake and the gospel's' may involve not only aban-

[1] W. M. Foley, in Hastings, *ERE.*, Vol. 8, p. 433b.

donment of property but the breaking of the natural bonds between brothers and sisters, parents and children (Mark 10.23–31). Again, in the so-called Apocalyptic Discourse, when Jesus foretells the persecution which the disciples will incur 'for his sake', he paints a terrible picture of brother delivering brother to death, the father his child, the children their parents (Mark 13.9–13). Jesus and his gospel provide both an overriding motive for self-denial and abandonment of possessions and human relationships, and an almost inevitable occasion of persecution. In effect, the relation with himself to which Jesus invites his hearers, the relation involved in following him, is to take precedence over all previous human ties and bonds. This is no ideal condition, no priority in a purely mental hierarchy of values, but something that has actually happened in the 'flesh and blood' experience of the disciples.

In this connection Mark makes no specific mention of marriage, neither including it among the ties that may have to be broken, nor excluding it from them. The author of the third Gospel, perhaps because of explicit references in his sources, perhaps because of his insight into the logic of Christ's demand, or perhaps simply because he knew what in fact had happened and was still happening among those who professed Christ, makes it clear that Christ's call may separate even husband from wife. In his version of the Rewards of Discipleship, based for the rest upon Mark, he includes those who leave *their wife* 'for the kingdom of God's sake' (Luke 14.26; cf. Mark 10.29). To a Matthaean saying which lays down the necessity of loving Jesus more than father and mother, son and daughter (Matt. 10.37), he has this rough parallel: 'If any man cometh after me, and hateth not his own father, and mother, *and wife*, and children, and brethren, yea, and his own life also, he cannot be my disciple' (Luke 14.26). Again, in the Lucan account of the Great Supper, the crowning excuse for not attending, given without any semblance of courteous apology, is: 'I have married a wife, and therefore I cannot come' (Luke 14.20)—a significant illustration of the priority attached to the call which the invitation to the feast illustrates, since it is clearly expected to override the Mosaic law allowing a newly-wed man to stay at home and cheer his wife (Deut. 24.5). In the Lucan idiom, the Kingdom of God takes precedence over every human bond, and even supersedes the Law.

Once more, this is not merely a statement of theological principle. It has been abundantly exemplified in the call of Christ and in the life of the apostolic Church.

The Gospel according to Matthew agrees explicitly with Luke at none of these points, but contains a saying that threatens the married state from quite a different angle. After retailing the Marcan account of the Question about Divorce, with some slight modification and change of order, Matthew goes on:

> The disciples say unto him, If the case of the man is so with his wife, it is not expedient to marry. But he said unto them, All men cannot receive this saying (that is, the saying that follows), but they to whom it is given. For there are eunuchs, which were so born from their mother's womb: and there are eunuchs, which were made eunuchs by men; and there are eunuchs, which make themselves eunuchs for the kingdom of heaven's sake. He that is able to receive it, let him receive it. (Matt. 19.10–12)

What is beyond the power of some men at least—what requires, as we might say, a special vocation and the grace to fulfil it—is the celibate life. That it is hard to keep the marriage bond as interpreted by Jesus (this appears to be the argument as it is now presented to us in this Gospel) is no justification for contracting out of marriage. Nevertheless, celibacy has a positive place in God's purpose, provided that it is embraced in obedience to his will.

Few and elusive[1] as these synoptic references to marriage are, there is in them an appearance of contradiction which is strikingly consistent. On the one hand, the evangelists present marriage as a unity demanding exclusive and permanent mutual commitment on the part of husband and wife, believing that they do so in obedience to the teaching of Jesus. On the other hand, well aware of the cost of discipleship, and well aware that it may demand the severance of any human tie or relationship, they do not exclude the marriage bond from the possibility of disruption for the sake (as they variously express it) of the Kingdom of God, of the gospel, of Jesus himself—and this also they attribute to him. All three record

[1] It is interesting to compare the difficulty experienced in trying to determine whether or not the sectaries whom we know of from the Dead Sea Scrolls were married or celibate: cf. G. Vermes, *The Dead Sea Scrolls*, p. 30.

his answer to the Sadducees' test question about the resurrection.[1] To them it seems not at all incongruous that Jesus should have combined a firm insistence upon the divine purpose of marriage in this world with an equally firm insistence that it has no counterpart in the world to come; or that men called to follow Jesus 'now in this time' may be required to anticipate the conditions of the Kingdom of Heaven.

Nor does St Paul appear to perceive any contradiction between his realistic appreciation of marriage as ordained by God—and indeed of the differing parts to be played in marriage by husband and wife—and his statement to the Galatian Christians that 'there can be no male and female—for you are all one in Christ Jesus' (Gal. 3.28). His thinking about marriage may have been influenced by the expectation of the imminent end of the present order, an expectation which he seems to have shared with other Christians and perhaps modified during the course of his ministry. But he candidly prefers other Christians to remain unmarried, like himself, because of their calling (1 Cor. 7.32), while protesting that he has as much right to have a wife, and take her about with him, as the brethren of the Lord, or Cephas (1 Cor. 9.5). For him, we might say, the Christian calling *must* have priority, and *may* therefore necessitate celibacy. Indeed, he seems to regard this as normal. Yet he goes out of his way to repudiate the doctrine that there is something essentially inferior, or sinful, in the physical intimacy of marriage, perhaps even before it had been mooted in the Church.[2]

---

[1] (Mark 12.18–27; Matt. 22.23–33; Luke 20.27–40): 'Is it not for this cause that ye err, that ye know not the scriptures, nor the power of God? For when they shall rise from the dead, they neither marry, nor are given in marriage; but are as the angels in heaven.' So Mark, from whom Luke differs only by introducing a reference to 'the sons of this world' who 'marry, and are given in marriage', and whom he contrasts with those who 'are accounted worthy to attain to that world and the resurrection from the dead . . . and are sons of God, being sons of the resurrection.' Matthew follows Mark without material change.

[2] This doctrine appears to have troubled the Church at least from the time for which 1 Timothy was written (cf. 1 Tim. 4.3): and it would be idle to deny that virginity was at times or in some quarters highly prized as a literal imitation of the Lord (Rev. 14.4–5). Its effect upon Christian thought and practice has been as devastating as an opposite doctrine (repudiated in Heb. 3.4) now threatens to become – the doctrine that sexual promiscuity is morally unexceptionable because it does not matter what you do with your body.

This sense of a contradiction unperceived may perhaps haunt us when we consider the problem presented by Jesus himself as a human being. It is not simply that, according to the New Testament, he remained unmarried but is not to be described as an 'ascetic'—at any rate as that word is now loosely understood (cf. Matt. 11.19; Luke 7.34); and not simply that he is presented as the supremely poor and lonely figure who none the less offers men and women alike a relation with himself far more exacting—and fruitful—than marriage, because, unlike marriage, it requires the surrender of the soul and its claim extends beyond death. Jesus calls men and women (whether they obey him or not) to follow him (Mark 1.17; 10.21), and to be with him so that he may satisfy their ultimate need (Matt. 11.28). He confidently declares that his 'lifting up'[1] will draw all men to himself (John 12.32). His prayer for those who believe in him is that they may be eternally one with the Father and himself (John 17.22–3). It does not seem to disturb the New Testament writers that only when his rejection, alike by his followers and his Father, appears to be complete is his purpose understood to have been realized. We are anxious to see the contradiction neatly resolved within our own experience in history: to see our relations with other human beings completely reconciled with our relationship with Jesus, so that there may be no conflict of loyalties, no tension, no occasion for faith illuminated only by his crucifixion and resurrection. But the apprehension that Jesus is 'the bridegroom'[2] makes a claim upon his followers that is immediate as well as ultimate, that sets their whole, *present,* behaviour under the shadow of the cross just because it presents him in the context of resurrection. Moreover, although this identification assumes that the Old Testament hope of Israel purified and united with God, as his bride, has been fulfilled in the relation established between Jesus and his Church, it is not introduced in order to show what

---

[1] See pp. 146f above.

[2] Jesus is referred to as 'the bridegroom', directly or by implication, in several of the New Testament writings. In the Gospel according to Mark, followed by Matthew, the identification is attributed to Jesus himself; in the fourth Gospel, to John Baptist (John 3.28–9). More than one synoptic parable is set in the context of a marriage feast (Matt. 22.1–14; 25.1–13; Luke 14.7–11). St Paul (2 Cor. 11.2) and the author of the Revelation of St John the Divine (Rev. 10.7–9; 21. 2,9; 22.17.) refer almost casually, as though the identification were universally accepted, to Jesus as the husband to whom the Church is espoused. The implication of this relationship, as will be seen, is most fully worked out in Ephesians (Eph. 5.22–33).

Jesus *is*. He is not called 'the bridegroom' in order that we may understand his 'future' or 'eschatological' or 'existential' significance. In the New Testament, the relation between Jesus and his Church is taken for granted, as being fundamental and self-evident; and the Old Testament imagery of the bridegroom seems to be recalled only when it is necessary to remind Christians of certain implications of their calling. An analogy familiar in everyday experience, but also commonly used to express God's ideal relationship with his people, lay ready to their hand. But it is this relationship that is now unquestioned and definitive. For Christ's calling of his Church is apprehended as nothing less than God's ultimate uniting of his redeemed creation with himself.

The most fully elaborated reference to Jesus as the bridegroom occurs in the Epistle to the Ephesians. It forms an important part of the second half of the Epistle, in which the writer[1] beseeches his readers 'to walk worthy of their calling' (Eph. 4.1). There is nothing unusual in this. Several of the Epistles end with similar exhortation, at almost as great a length, and the relation of husbands and wives is mentioned in five of them. Nor is it unusual that the key to walking worthy of Christ's calling is declared to consist in unity, and in unity through *mutual subjection*. This is one of the phenomena suggesting that a common and widely-used pattern of catechetical teaching may have been well known not only to St Paul but also to the authors of the Epistle of James, the First Epistle of Peter, the Epistle to the Ephesians, and perhaps to others as well. So here, when we try to trace the argument of Ephesians, we shall not be surprised to find the theme of unity developed as involving not only a common mind and mutual love (which we should welcome if the subject were so treated to-day), but also (which will be repugnant to us, perhaps, if we belong to our own time) mutual submission in a common obedience: 'subjecting yourselves one to another in the fear of Christ' (Eph. 5.21). For these New Testament Christians such subjection was a ground of hope. They pictured the consummation of God's purpose (for which they lived) as to be accomplished when Christ, having established complete order by abolishing all other rule and authority and power,

---

[1] For the present purpose it is immaterial whether the writer was St Paul himself; or someone editing fragments, or notes made, of his teaching; or someone who had his writings almost by heart and was trying to continue his work.

delivered up the Kingdom to the Father. Indeed, their hope embraced the eventual 'subjection' of Christ himself : 'and when all things have been subjected unto him (Jesus), then shall the Son also himself be subjected to him that did subject all things unto him, that God may be all in all' (1 Cor. 15.24–8). The same hope finds expression by means of other metaphors no less strange to us today—for instance, that 'Christ is head of the body the Church' (Col. 1.18; Eph. 2.22) and that 'the head of Christ is God' (1 Cor. 11.3) and, in being so expressed, demands recognizable expression in their corporate behaviour.[1] So a precept from the Proverbs, 'God resisteth the proud, but giveth grace to the humble' (Prov. 3.34, following the Greek) can speak to our writers not merely of interior, 'spiritual' virtues, but of the necessary condition of life in the Church. The author of James, quoting it, continues, 'Be subject therefore unto God'—and goes on to warn his readers against defamatory speech and moral judgements about others! The author of 1 Peter, having exhorted the elders to be examples to their flock and the younger members to 'be subject' to the older ones, at once universalizes his injunction : 'Yea, all of you gird yourselves with humility, to serve one another', reinforcing his words with the same quotation (1 Peter 5.1–5). 'Subjecting yourselves one to another in the fear of Christ' appears to rest on this assumption, that universal mutual submission in the Church, *if duly related to Christ,* is the means of achieving the Christian goal of total subjection to God. The nature of this relation to Christ is, of course, what we are examining.

It is in this immediate context, of subjection to one another in the fear of Christ, that the writer enjoins wives to be subject to their husbands, children to their parents, slaves to their masters (Eph. 5.22; 6.1; 6.5). Here again, at any rate at first sight, the modern reader may perhaps be scandalized. Two centuries of enlightened progress have seen wives at least given something like equal rights with their husbands, children emancipated from the more notorious presumptions of parental tyranny, slavery abolished in name if not

[1] W. L. Knox, in *St Paul and the Church of the Gentiles*, p. 161, points out that 'the political developments of the Hellenistic age had changed the conception of the state from a body in which each member played its part into a body in which the head was the all-important matter' and quotes Philo to the effect that 'the good man or nation dominates the surroundings *for their own good,* as the head does the body' (our italics).

yet, in spite of multitudinous safeguards, wholly in fact. Are we not bound to stigmatize these apostolic injunctions as reactionary; as calculated to impede all that we should wish to claim for the Spirit of Jesus Christ? What we may forget is that in all these instances, 'subjection' is the alternative not to more liberal conceptions of the relations between husband and wife, parents and children, employers and employees but to wholesale repudiation of those relationships by men and women carried away by the demands of the gospel. These injunctions originated in a situation in which marriage bonds were being disregarded, families broken up, and social or economic obligations ignored, *in the belief that only so could Christ's calling be given the priority it deserved.* And for this anarchical reaction there was, as we have seen, some apparent justification even in the words attributed to Jesus himself. Therefore, to insist upon the 'obedience' or 'subjection' that characterize these relationships in normal human experience was to insist that, even under the exacting scrutiny of Jesus Christ, these relationships remain real, and must be respected; more than this, that they have an organic and positive part to perform in the wholly desirable 'subjection' of the Church to God. What we have here, as in the Epistle of St Paul to the Colossians (3.18) and the First Epistle General of St Peter (3.1), is the firm definition of marriage as a Christian state within the purpose of God. That is the implication of the words, 'Wives, be in subjection unto your own husbands, as unto the Lord' (Eph. 5.22).

St Paul and these other apostolic writers certainly did not anticipate the modern obsession for equality of definition. Yet they were fully aware of the equality of all human beings in the sight of God. What made it possible for them to insist upon the duties of slaves to their masters and of masters towards their slaves was the knowledge that masters and slaves alike have one Master in heaven. This is the ground of hope, which enables the slave to perform his human service 'fearing the Lord', and 'heartily, as unto the Lord' (Col. 3.22—4.1; cf. Eph. 6.5–9). In the same way, even when St Paul is so deeply concerned about the temper manifest in the Corinthian Church's disregard of the convention that women should be veiled at prayer that he ransacks the Old Testament to justify the distinction between the roles of the two sexes, he feels bound to insist upon the 'headship' of God, which puts the distinction between man and woman into its true perspective: 'The head of every man is Christ; and the head of the woman is the man; and the head of Christ is God.' The man may be 'the image and glory of God' and the woman 'the glory of the man', but 'neither is the woman without the man, nor the man without the woman, *in the Lord*. For as the woman is of the man, so is the man also by the woman; *but all things are of God*' (1 Cor. 11.2–16). The author of the Epistle to the Ephesians secures a similar perspective by using the 'headship' metaphor slightly differently: 'The husband is the head of the wife, as Christ also is the head of the Church, being the saviour of the body' (Eph. 5.23). Wives must be subject to their husbands; marriage is a Christian state within God's purpose. But the reality to which it points and by which it should be conditioned is the subjection of the Church to Christ—its espousal to one who, for his part, is Saviour. What this entails the next sentence makes clear: 'Husbands, love your wives, even as Christ also loved the church, and gave himself up for it . . .' (Eph. 5.24–7). The writer is not thinking merely of the coming of the heavenly bridegroom to claim and purify his bride. He is thinking of the death of Christ as the willing sacrifice by which he achieved his purpose. Earlier he had said, of Christians in general, 'Be ye therefore imitators of God, as beloved children; and walk in love, even as Christ also loved you, and gave himself up for us, an offering and a sacrifice to God for an odour of a sweet smell' (Eph. 5.2). Now he picks up the same argument again, to impress upon husbands that their love for their wives must be modelled upon the love with which the Saviour laid down his life. We sometimes fail to notice how much more this demands of the husband than the subjection (in the mere sense of outward obedience) demanded of the Jewish wife.

But there is a further, and culminating, point to be noticed. The writer is leading up to the words of Genesis (2.24) quoted by Jesus according to Mark (10.7–8) and Matthew (19.5): 'For this cause shall a man leave his father and mother, and shall cleave to his wife; and the twain shall become one flesh.' And he will go on: 'This mystery is great: but I speak in regard of Christ and of the Church.' What he wishes to make clear is that this is far more than a putative unity. Christians are members of Christ's own body. Therefore Christ's love of the Church for which he died may be described as love of himself. 'Even so ought husbands also to love their wives as their own bodies. He that loveth his own wife loveth himself' (Eph. 5.28–32).

The writer's final comment may seem to us a falling-off: 'Nevertheless do ye also severally love each one his own wife even as himself; and let the wife see that she fear her husband' (Eph. 5.33). But, for his purpose, enough has already been said. If marriage has a recognized place in the Christian calling, bringing woman and man alike into a special relation with Christ in his body the Church; if it involves not merely mutual interdependence and commitment but love, at any rate on the part of the husband, like that with which Christ loved his own unto the end; and if this voluntary identification holds the promise of more than merely physical identity—then both the 'obedience' and 'fear' which the human phenomenon of marriage seems to require of the woman and the 'love' which it seems to require of the man have been redefined in accordance with the example of Christ and the ultimate relation which both man and woman have with Christ in his Church.

In the perspective of the New Testament, the natural institution of marriage has to be taken very seriously, since it speaks of a unity based upon voluntary, mutual commitment. It speaks, in fact, of the call of Christ and the unity with himself which he offers in his Church. And because this is the reality, fulfilling the parable of marriage (as we might say) it takes precedence over the 'parable'. The obligation of a man or a woman to Christ may dissolve the obligation of each to the other as husband or wife. In a Church consciously anticipating, in its living of life, the new age of God's Kingdom, it was perhaps inevitable that many Christians should conclude that there was no place for marriage. St Paul came near to this reaction when he wrote: 'But this I say, brethren, the time is shortened, that henceforth both those that have wives may be as though they had none . . . for the fashion of this world passeth away . . .' (1 Cor. 7.29–31). But that is not the final word, either of St Paul or of the New Testament writers in general. It is, rather, that when marriage is seen to point to the union of Christ with his Church, when a man or a woman embraces it 'in the fear of the Lord', or 'as is fitting in the Lord', or after the example of Christ's love for his Church, then the possibility of *Christian* marriage opens up, as a status within the Church which can be the means by which men and women are drawn into the final union of Christ with his Church. Such a marriage, apprehended (by the light of Christ's death and resurrection from the dead) as a parable pointing beyond itself, can in a true sense be said to be what it signifies. Or, to put it more boldly but still in faithfulness to the New Testament understanding of Christ, marriage thus enterprised and apprehended becomes what all marriage is intended to be, and what, apart from Christ, it could never have been.

This line of interpretation might lead to the conclusion that there is no salvation apart from marriage. That would be a travesty of the New Testament, for it is to ignore the hard word to which we have already referred: 'there are eunuchs, which made themselves eunuchs for the kingdom of heaven's sake' (Matt. 19.12); and much else besides. The fact that a state like that of marriage can be shown to be not merely a secular one, but a divine calling within the purpose of God and a means of identification with his Church, does not for one moment justify the explaining away of the pressure, both of Jesus in the Gospels, and of St Paul and other apostolic writers, towards the 'literal' following or 'imitation' of Christ, as though they were speaking 'figuratively' or even 'mystically'. St Paul gloried in his humiliations as an apostle, in his infirmities, in his sufferings, because they assured him that 'the sufferings of Christ abound unto us, even as our comfort also aboundeth through Christ' (1 Cor. 2.5). He was content to be one of those called to bear about 'in the body the dying of Jesus, that the life also of Jesus may be manifested in our body' (1 Cor. 4.10). It is possible that when he wrote to the Galatian Christians 'before whose eyes Jesus Christ was openly set forth crucified' he referred not only to the gospel they had heard but also to the sufferings in Christ's name which they had witnessed. The death and resurrection of Jesus does not dignify the human state of marriage only; it dignifies as well the visible 'cross' which some feel impelled to take up at his call, the way of life that can perhaps only be followed if marriage is precluded. We shall not wholly misunderstand the positive hope of the Christian revelation, if we sum up like this. In marriage, embraced in Christ and lived in fear of him, a man or a woman may be confronted with, and even submit to, the 'wholly otherness' of God. But a 'monk' or a 'nun', whether catholic or protestant, whether habited or following some human vocation that none the less cuts across the ordinary pattern of life, may be called to demonstrate, quite literally, the positive poverty of Jesus himself. The literal 'poverty' of such a 'monk' or 'nun' must never be presented as the norm of ordinary Christian life—that demands a poverty far less discernible, far more profound. But the *observable* poverty of the 'monk' or 'nun' should equally put the ordinary Christian in mind of the essential poverty of all men in the sight of God. In the death and resurrection of Jesus Christ the New Testament writers have not seen any resolution of the tension between his confirmation of marriage and his call which cuts across marriage, but they have seen both marriage and celibacy established as Christian vocations in so far as they point to his salvation and can therefore be embraced in the faith and fear of Christ.

CHAPTER 11

Government—and the Obedience
of Jesus

Biblical theology is evoked by the essential pattern of human life. Its insight consists, first of all, in its definition of this pattern. It shows it to be made up of very much more than individual needs and personal relationships. It regards human beings not only as subject to distress or infirmity, and requiring, in their distress and infirmity, the assistance of their neighbours: not only as parents and children, endeavouring to reproduce themselves or themselves to reproduce their origin; not only as men and women moving towards unity in marriage. In the biblical analysis, for instance, this intimacy of personal relationship is crossed by, interwoven with, and inseparable from the recognition of the fact of human government. That is to say, the Bible sees men not merely as individuals related to other individuals, or even to the sum total of other individuals, but as under authority. The order which government has created is an essential part of the structure of human life. In the New Testament, this order is ignored as little as hunger, or poverty, or paternity, or marriage. It cannot be ignored, because it is as eloquent of man's need for God as are these other fundamental needs.

Yet in the First Epistle General of Peter, obedience to the 'higher powers' is enjoined and associated with the duty of slaves to their masters and the duty of wives to their husbands (1 Pet. 2.13–17, 18–25; 3.1–17). Religious fanaticism not seldom conceives itself outside the Law. Had their understanding—or misunderstanding—of the gospel of the Kingdom of God persuaded some Christians that they ought to be anarchists? If so, we may discern a superficial parallel with the pattern of these other themes. The ordered structure of a state under a monarch provides an analogy for the monarchy of God and the nature of his sovereignty. And just as Christ, thought of as the Bridegroom and as the Master, offers a relationship which is first apprehended by means of these analogies and then seems to fulfil them in such a way as to be the reality by which they are evaluated, so it is with Christ thought of as the messianic King. Here is the reality to which all human government is pointing: the reality which, once apprehended, reveals all human government to be—what shall we say? It is at this point that some New Testament Christians seem to have supplied the wrong predicates, just as others have perhaps done, down through the centuries and even in our own day. Let us for the moment withhold any predicate and search for the pattern. Christ represents the Master over against *all* his servants—yet he is apprehended, in the humiliation of his ministry and his death on the cross, as, in relation to his Father, the righteous Servant. As the Bridegroom, he is the head of the Church yet, none the less, in St Paul's words, 'the head of Christ is God' (1 Cor. 11.3). Similarly, we might say that it is in the utter obedience of the King of the Jews, whose title is set up only over the cross on which he died, that the Kingdom of God is fully realized in flesh and blood. The King is made known as the perfect Subject. If so, can we not complete the pattern, and say that the life in Christ, the life inspired by his example and controlled by his Spirit, necessarily includes all the virtues of true citizenship, so that obedience to the earthly 'monarch' (provided that it is carried out in the fear of Christ) can be reckoned part of the positive Christian vocation in general?

At first sight, this is all that appears to be assumed by the author of the First Epistle of Peter, by the author of the Epistle to Titus (Titus 3.1), and by St Paul himself. But these writers seem to make two assumptions. They seem to assume that if the monarch, or the 'powers that be', are faithful to their office they will necessarily be concerned for justice and will accordingly perform a ministerial function, under God, in praising the well-doer and punishing the evil-doer (Rom. 13.3–4; 1 Pet. 2.14). Yet they also seem to assume that there is one charge for which Christians must *expect* to be brought before kings and governors and convicted, that is, 'for the name of Christ' (1 Pet. 4.14–15). To us it might seem inconsistent that a government should both be supposed likely to persecute Christians and yet be credited with a ministerial function under God. That it did not so seem to these apostolic writers suggests that we should look back to the Christian treatment of this problem at its most acute: to the part played by the Roman governor in bringing about the classical example of suffering as a Christian, the passion of Jesus himself.

The narratives of the passion move around two charges brought against Jesus. On both he was pronounced guilty and was, for that reason, put to death; on both, the evangelists declare him innocent. The first charge is the charge of blasphemy, for which he was arraigned before the Jewish high priests. The second is sedition, for which he was brought before the Roman governor, Pilate, at the instigation of the Jews. According to the synoptic Gospels, Jesus defended himself against neither of these charges. When evidence had been given against him in the court of the high priest, 'he held his peace, and answered nothing', in spite of the high priest's repeated questions, until the high priest, by demanding bluntly whether he was 'the Christ, the Son of the Blessed', elicited the answer upon which he was convicted of blasphemy (Mark 14.57–63). In Pilate's court, except for the perhaps deliberately equivocal 'thou sayest', he equally remained silent (Mark 12.2–5).

None of the evangelists makes any attempt to disguise the fact that Jesus was sentenced to death because of the apparent conflict between his claims, or the claims attributed to him, and those of Caesar. All four record that he was put to death for sedition. Yet, partly no doubt because, as they understood it, the gospel was primarily concerned with the rejection of the Messiah by his own people, they appear to feel constrained to explain this sentence as though it might not—and should not—have been pronounced.

In the Gospel according to Mark (Mark 15.1–20) Pilate is represented as not wishing to take the charge of sedition at all seriously. In spite of the high priests' many, but unspecified, accusations, he tries to take advantage of what is stated to have been a recognized custom of clemency at the time of the Passover in order to release Jesus, referring to him, surely ironically, as the King of the Jews. When this expedient fails, Pilate asks, as though wilfully misunderstanding the high priests in order to show how little importance he attaches to the charge they have brought : 'What shall I do unto him whom ye call King of the Jews?' In the end, to placate the crowd, and for no other reason given, he pronounces judgement : Jesus is to be crucified—the usual penalty for crime against the Roman state—and the accusation 'the King of the Jews' will tell the official story from the top of the cross of execution. But, as Mark describes it, Pilate's personal attitude seems more faithfully represented by that of his soldiers, who deck Jesus up in imperial purple, crown him with a make-believe royal diadem, and mockingly salute him as king with fatuous acts of reverence. Order must be preserved (so the explanation of the verdict seems to go); Jesus must pay the penalty prescribed for insurrection; but Pilate is not taking sides in the real collision between Christ and Caesar, for he has shrugged away this pathetic pretence to royalty as contemptible and ridiculous.

The Gospel according to Matthew follows Mark with one important addition, that both Pilate and his wife explicitly bear witness that Jesus is 'righteous' (Matt. 27.11–31).

The author of Luke reacts to the problem by emphasizing the charge of sedition brought by the high priests—no doubt with his eye partly on his own age and the growing tension between the Empire and the Christian Church. In his Gospel, the accusations are specific. 'We found this man perverting our nation, and forbidding to give tribute to Caesar, and saying that he himself is Christ a King . . . He stirreth up the people, teaching throughout all Judaea, and beginning from Galilee even unto this place' (Luke 23.2–5). And in this Gospel Pilate acquits Jesus of these charges: 'Ye brought unto me this man, as one that perverteth the people: and behold, I, having examined him before you, find no fault in this man touching those things whereof ye accuse him: no, nor yet Herod: for he sent him back unto us; and behold, nothing worthy of death hath been done by him' (Luke 23.14–15). Wisely in the circumstances—or weakly?—he delivers Jesus up to 'the will of his accusers' (Luke 23.25). None the less, in this, as in the two previous Gospels, the issue by which Pilate's decision is covered is the claim of Jesus to be Christ the King.

The author of the fourth Gospel faces the same issue, but to judge from the answers given by Jesus to Pilate's repeated questions, perceives its implications to be far more profound.

'Art thou the King of the Jews?'—'Sayest thou this of thyself, or did others tell it thee concerning me?' (John 18.33–4).

The representative of Caesar must not take refuge in the convictions of the accusers, however prejudiced or blind; the issue involves Caesar as deeply as it involves the Jews.

'Am I a Jew? Thine own nation and the chief priests delivered thee unto me : what hast thou done?'—'My kingdom is not of this world : if my kingdom were of this world, then would my servants fight, that I should not be delivered to the Jews : but now is my kingdom not from thence' (John 18.35–6).

Pilate is not confronted with a national Messiah, thrown up upon a popular insurrection and drawing his authority from the unrest and aspirations of his followers. His authority derives from a wholly different source.

'Art thou a king then?'—'Thou sayest that I am a king. To this end have I been born, and to this end am I come into the world, that I should bear witness to the truth' (John 18.37).

The at first sight ambiguous, perhaps deliberately equivocal, 'Thou sayest' of the synoptic Gospels is picked up with the positive and penetrating intention characteristic of the fourth Gospel. Pilate, the representative of Caesar, is, by the very sentence he pronounces, about to bear witness to the kingship of Jesus (John 19.15–19, 21–2). But the kingship of Jesus is an essential element in his witness to 'the truth'—which means, as always in this Gospel, the truth of God. The readers of the Gospel should now be in no doubt about the authority which confronts Pilate and puts the authority of the Roman Empire on trial even though Pilate, in his scepticism, cannot recognize it. The mock-royal investiture of Jesus now becomes a means of exhibiting not so much Rome's contempt for Jesus as his mere manhood—although the evangelist no doubt expects his readers to perceive far more than that in the public introduction : 'Behold the man' (John 19.5). What causes Pilate to hesitate once more is the Jews' disclosure of their real motive for destroying Jesus—the charge of blasphemy, 'because he made himself the Son of God'.

'Whence art thou?'—'But Jesus gave him no answer' (John 19.9). 'Speakest thou not unto me? Knowest thou not that I have power to release thee, and have power to crucify thee?'—'Thou wouldest have no power against me, except it were given thee

261

from above: therefore he that delivered me unto thee hath the greater sin' (John 19.10–11).

Pilate is reminded that he wields the power of life and death only by delegation from the government to which he is answerable, and is denied the small luxury of the potentate who feels that whatever decision he may make will be his own. And he is also reminded (though this is no doubt beyond his comprehension) that an empire exists only by the grace, and within the purpose, of God. If individual responsibility is to be assessed, it lies less with the governor who has to implement imperial policy than with those who should have understood their responsibility to God. His impotence is now starkly exposed. When he tries to release Jesus, the Jews insist that to do so will be tantamount to condoning sedition. This is the moment of truth, and the protagonists assume their ultimate, we might almost say, their 'existentially significant', roles. Pilate introduces Jesus to the Jews again, this time very differently: 'Behold your King.' The Jews vociferously deny their calling, their theocratic history, their understanding of God, their whole purpose in the world: 'We have no king but Caesar'; while in silence Jesus proceeds to accomplish the Father's will. He is delivered to the Jews, 'to be crucified' (John 19.12–26).

The part played by Pilate, though interpreted differently by each of the four evangelists, may very well approximate to the historical fact. Certainly, to sentence Jesus to be crucified rings true as the probable reaction of a provincial governor, answerable to a government many miles away and dominated by the necessity to avoid popular insurrection. Nevertheless, for none of the evangelists is the meaning of the crucifixion limited to the action and interests of those whom they represent as its immediate cause. Again, we may detect certain motives in the particular treatment of the trial before Pilate by all the evangelists; and these motives seem to fit in with the historical situation of the Church in the Roman Empire at the time when they may be presumed to have been writing their Gospels —a situation in which it must have seemed both just and desirable to lay responsibility for the death of Jesus squarely upon the chief priests, or upon the whole Jewish people, and to describe the part played by its representative in such a way as to exculpate the Roman government. But such motives as these lie only on the periphery of the evangelists' intention. By treating the passion of Jesus Christ as the fulcrum upon which the Gospel turns, and in desiring to recount the course of events convincingly, as historical fact, and to indicate, so far as they may, the motives of those taking part in them, they show how vital they thought the actual manner of Christ's death to be for the understanding of the gospel and the living of the Christian life. For them, the collision between the Kingdom of God and the empire of Caesar did not pose an academic question. They belonged, as they knew, perhaps only too well, to two worlds. As men, they lived under a secular authority. Yet, at the same time, as Christians they lived under the authority of one they called Christ the King. What they tried so hard to elucidate as they recorded it had much—indeed, in their view had everything—to say to men in their own double position: that is, as they apprehended the truth, to all men.

This perception that the tension between two authorities involves all mankind is not confined to the New Testament. The whole Bible sees all human life to be trembling between two worlds, each with an authentic order of its own. Perhaps we may summarize this biblical view like this. Both of these orders, or orderings—man's as well as God's, are to be taken seriously, for they cannot be separated. Order in this world is a necessity, and is to be attained only through obedience to some form of human government. To this end, human government must exercise its power, even though, in the last resort, this means making use of prohibitions, constraint, the threat of death. Yet the government of this world inevitably finds itself concerned with objectives beyond its own power of achievement, even by compulsion. Consequently, the necessity of this-worldly government, and the realization of its limited scope, combine to demonstrate man's need for the order that lies beyond it. Nevertheless, the wielding of human authority, the discharging of this-worldly government, must not be reckoned 'secular' because of its limitations. Government exists by God's will. It can, and should, subserve God's purpose. It may be the willing instrument of theocracy. Therefore it ought to be the minister of the sovereignty of God, who is the true king not of Israel only but of the whole world as well. This should perhaps be most obvious in the form which government normally takes in the Bible, the form of human monarchy. But all 'monarchy' in the sense of a single, recognized, source of authority and order, whether expressed in the person of a single ruler, or in an oligarchy, or in a democracy exercised through elected representatives, or in any other form of competent and accepted government, bears witness to the one ultimate source of authority and order, to the sovereignty of God, and to the ultimate necessity of his Kingdom. For this reason, at the inception of the monarchy in Israel, the anointed king is seen as the place where the monarchy of God is made known, in spite of the 'sin' of Israel in rejecting direct theocracy and requesting a human king. And for this reason, perhaps, even the emperor Cyrus is hailed by the prophet as 'the anointed of the Lord' (Isa. 44.28; 45.1).

Yet—and to this sombre conclusion Israel seems to have been forced, not only by the behaviour of the foreign empire-builders who from time to time dominated it but also by the behaviour of its own kings—the monarchy may equally be the place where God's monarchy is obscured. This comes about when the secular government arrogates to itself authority over the whole of human life. In the insight of the biblical writers, this is not only tyranny but blasphemy. Hence the terrible descriptions of Assyria and Babylon, and the triumphant accounts of the deaths of Sennacherib (Isa. 37.21–38), of Antiochus Epiphanes (2 Macc. 9), and of Herod Agrippa I (Acts 12.21); but hence, also, the cautious, disillusioned provisions for the king 'whom the Lord thy God shall choose' given by the Deuteronomist (Deut. 17.14–20): 'that his heart be not lifted up above his brethren, and that he turn not aside from the commandment'. That God can use for his purposes even the ambitious selfseeking of human demagogues and potentates (1 Kings 11.31; 12.24; Isa. 10.5–7) does not acquit them from the charge of denying their essential function of bearing witness to his ultimate rule.

It is against this background that the collision between Jesus and Pilate is to be understood. The Bible knows of no purely 'secular' authority, *except at this one point,* the point at which Jesus submits to Pilate, the point at which the evangelists fumble for an explanation. In the passion of Jesus we see the Roman Empire reaching its limit: we might perhaps adopt a modern phrase and say, its point of discontinuity: the point at which not any claim made by Jesus, but the arrogance of the Roman Emperor as expressed by his representative, constitutes the blasphemy. At this point imperial policy becomes nonsense to its own executive officer. Pilate cannot set Jesus free; nor can he conscientiously condemn him. In spite of their careful records, the evangelists are not offering us an episode the significance of which is merely that it took place. The limit of human authority in the state is here reached, once and for all, revealing the authority that lies beyond and behind the Roman and all other empires; and because Pilate feels bound to press his authority beyond that limit, Jesus is crucified.

We are now approaching the heart of our problem. With this searching exposure of human empire at the very centre of their gospel, we might well have expected the apostles to have condoned anarchy; to have stood aside from the state, indifferent both to its success and to its failure, careful only for the ordering of the new Israel, the Church. In the crucifixion of Christ they had witnessed what must have thrown into question all the Jew's reverence for the state as the potential sphere of God's kingdom, all the Roman citizen's loyalty to the Empire as the realization of the human *kosmos*. But they will not stand aside. Rather, precisely at this point they unwittingly prepare for the conception of the Christian state to emerge—the state, that is, whose rulers discern its true, God-given function and attempt to exercise it. There is no need to say that the New Testament writers had no experience of such a state. Indeed, there is no evidence that they considered it a possibility. But they will not discard the structure of human government as though it is essentially secular and of no Christian significance. They will not limit the Christian recognition of the state to the mere avoidance of uncitizenly behaviour. The possibility of the blasphemy of tyranny remains as real to them as to any Old Testament prophet or historian, if we may judge from the Revelation of St John the Divine. Yet they will not exclude the alternative possibility, of the monarch who knows his limitations and does not attempt to transgress them, exercising his authority, within those limitations, in obedient if unconscious service of God. This indeed is the norm—the human institution pointing *by analogy* to the truth of God. In their positive understanding of the world it is 'the abomination of desolation standing where he ought not' that is exceptional, though *even he* witnesses *by contrast* to the truth of God in Christ.

Was it the spectacle of the King of the Jews nailed to the cross that caused these writers to react in this way? And, if so, what had they seen there?—not, it would seem, in the first place what they at once recognized as the perfect example of human citizenship, though later, perhaps, they saw that that was implied. What they had seen there was an obedience to the Father in flesh and blood that not only confronted them with God's Kingdom come, but showed them the type of all human authority and the means of all human order. Indeed, the very humiliation of the King lifted up on the cross supplied the key to the human state's recognition and positive use of its own limitations. Are we now reading more than we ought into the minds of St Paul and the authors of Titus and 1 Peter? Does not their firm and positive recognition of the state as the minister of God demanding the obedience of Christians help to fill out the impression that, for the apostles, the crucifixion and resurrection of Jesus had made sense, not only of individual needs and personal relationships but also of the wider, corporate categories of human experience; and had in so doing defined the purpose of these categories, and the conditions of Christian vocation within them?

CHAPTER 12

Eating and Drinking – and the Self-Oblation of Jesus

The experience of government as essential to ordered human life ought, no doubt, to bring home to every thinking man the fact that, *as an individual,* he stands wholly and responsibly under the law of God. Nevertheless, to interpret the phenomenon of government as though it did no more than demonstrate the ultimate sanction of individual obedience to God would be to misconstrue the biblical insight. A similar error is possible in the case of other categories of human experience.

Nothing reminds us more insistently of the blunt fact of human dependence than the experiences of hunger and of thirst. It is not surprising that these experiences—and, indeed, the broader themes of eating and drinking of which they are part—should be frequently used in the Bible to illustrate a relation to God which every one who gives it thought is bound to interpret in regard to himself. The Deuteronomist may use the theme of hunger to instil the lesson in God's past dealings with his people as a whole, but he sums it up in a precept of absolute moment for every individual capable of conscious reflexion:

> He the Lord thy God humbled thee, and suffered thee to hunger, and fed thee with manna, which thou knewest not, neither did thy fathers know; that he might make thee know that man doth not live by bread only, but by every thing that proceedeth out of the mouth of the Lord doth man live (Deut. 8.3).

When the Psalmist employs the theme of thirst to express the urgency of his hope for the future, he seems primarily concerned with the ultimate satisfaction of a personal need formulated for him through his own particular physical experience, even though the thought of a redeemed remnant of Israel may also have been in his mind:

> As the hart panteth after the water brooks,
> So panteth my soul after thee, O God.

My soul thirsteth for God, for the living God :
When shall I come and appear before God?
(Psalm 42.1–2)

So we are no doubt justified in keeping the individual bearing of these themes before us when they are used to concentrate the argument upon the death of Jesus : 'My flesh is meat indeed, and my blood drink indeed' (John 6.55),[1] and perhaps also in finding in the fourth evangelist's exegesis of the Bread of Life and of the True Vine grounds for the familiar modern evaluation of the Eucharist in terms of personal communion.[2] But should we be loyal to the whole evidence if, in obedience to modern individualistic conceptions of the relevance of religion, we were to limit the scope of these themes in this way?

In the New Testament the themes of eating and drinking find their classical exposition in the actions and words of Jesus in the Upper Room, 'on the night in which he was betrayed' (1 Cor. 11.23). It has been suggested that the Last Supper was not unique but was, rather, the last of a series of characteristic acts of Jesus, of which traces may perhaps be seen in the accounts of the Feeding of the Five Thousand and the Feeding of the Four Thousand, and which may perhaps have become crystallized in regular fellowship meals partaken of by Jesus and his disciples in accordance with contemporary custom. Such suggestions are of great value, and not only for reconstructing the common life of Jesus with his companions. They must not, however, divert us from recognizing the plain fact that the context of all that took place in the Upper Room was a meal, a meal that came to be perpetuated in the assembling together of the Christian Church for the Lord's Supper (1 Cor. 11.20), understood as an occasion of which the significance was obscured if the eating and drinking were not 'in common', or if the fellowship became exploited as affording an opportunity for individual indulgence, or if the assembly did not include all Christians in the locality, regardless of the traditional ritual separation of Jew from Gentile (1 Cor. 11.21; Gal. 2.12).

Of the meal in the Upper Room, Jesus is both instigator and host. It is true that according to Mark, followed by Matthew, the

---

[1] See above, pp. 166–9
[2] See above, p. 172

disciples appear to take the initiative (Mark 14.12; Matt. 26.17). But if Luke deliberately altered this detail (Luke 22.8), Mark's own narrative makes it clear that Jesus already had the matter in hand and that this was to be the Master's Passover, in his guest-chamber, with his disciples (Mark 14.13–14). And although Matthew and Luke both smooth out Mark's repetitive detail that the disciples were sent to 'make ready' in a room already 'furnished and ready' (Mark 14.15–16),[1] all three synoptic accounts suggest that Jesus had taken thought, as a true host should, for the preparation of a formal meal and, as the head of a Jewish household should, for the eating of the Passover meal.

When they assembled, then, it was to a meal consciously and deliberately 'made ready' or 'prepared'. According to Mark and Matthew (Mark 14.17; Matt. 26.20), this was simply at the normal time for the Passover meal: 'in the evening'. Luke's 'when the hour came' might indeed mean no more than that—though it might, on the other hand, indicate that it was by divine appointment that Jesus came to this meal, on the eve of his crucifixion, as the fourth evangelist suggests:

> Now before the feast of the Passover, Jesus knowing that his hour was come that he should depart out of the world unto the Father, having loved his own which were in the world, he loved them unto the end. And during supper ... (John 13.1–2).

A formal meal implies an appointed time, and therefore lends itself for use as a parable of the fulfilment of God's purpose. Whether this was in Luke's mind or not, his next words, which he attributes to Jesus, leave no doubt that he perceives the significance of this meal to lie in its relation to the last things of God:

> 'With desire have I desired to eat this passover with you before I suffer: for I say unto you, I will not eat it until it be fulfilled in the kingdom of God' (Luke 22.15–16).

A little farther on, reporting, in the context of the Last Supper, a saying variously parallel in Matthew (Matt. 25.24; cf. Matt. 19.28), Luke significantly adds 'that ye may eat and drink at my table in my kingdom' (Luke 22.28–30). But this deliberate setting of the meal

---

[1] A detail that may perhaps have influenced the fourth evangelist; see Hoskyns, *The Fourth Gospel*, p. 453, commenting on John 14.2–3.

in the Upper Room against the eschatological background of the messianic feast in the Kingdom of God is no innovation of Luke's. All three synoptists give a saying of Jesus regarding the fruit of the vine, of which the tenor is equally eschatological :

> 'I say unto you, I will not drink from henceforth of the fruit of the vine, until the Kingdom of God shall come' (Luke 22.18; cf. Mark 14.25[1]; Matt. 26.29).

The synoptic evangelists agree in setting the meal in the Upper Room in the context of eschatological expectation. They agree also in depicting the behaviour of Jesus the host as the perfect example of the humility required in the disciples who are his guests—representing, no doubt, those invited (or called) by God to his heavenly feast. Luke seems once again to be importing into the context of this meal the gist of incidents recorded elsewhere in Mark and Matthew (Mark 9.33–7; 10.42–5; Matt. 18.1–4; 20.25–8) when he leads up to the question :

> 'Whether is greater, he that sitteth at meat, or he that serveth? is not he that sitteth at meat? but I am in the midst of you as he that serveth' (Luke 22.27).

The fourth evangelist develops a similar paradox in his account of the meal, first describing how Jesus washed the disciples' feet, and then interpreting what he had just done :

> 'Ye call me, Master, and, Lord : and ye say well; for so I am. If I then, the Lord and the Master, have washed your feet, ye also ought to wash one another's feet. For I have given you an example, that ye also should do as I have done unto you' (John 13.2–15).

All four evangelists, indeed, record the humility of the host as the supreme example of the humility required of guests, both in relation to each other and in the presence of their host. The fourth evangelist, however, interweaves this theme with its counter-theme, also attaching to a meal—the ancient theme of the guest, or companion, or familiar friend, who seeks the life of the host whose bread he has eaten (John 13.18–30; cf. Ps. 41.9). This theme is also

---

[1] Mark's version is: 'until the day when I drink it new in the kingdom of God'.

consciously evoked in the synoptic Gospels (Mark 14.18–21; Matt. 26.21–4; Luke 22.21–33).

We are now, perhaps in a better position to consider the central words of the Last Supper : 'Take, eat : this is my body'—'This is my blood of the covenant, which is shed for many' (Mark 14.22–4; cf. Matt. 26.26–8; Luke 22.19–20; 1 Cor. 11.24–5). Whatever particular Jewish ritual should be assumed in the breaking of the bread and the sharing of the cup, and whatever echo of sacrificial language we ought to be aware of as we ponder the words with which they were performed, it is clear that what we have here supplies the whole meal in the Upper Room, and the themes around which it revolves, with their urgency, their actuality, their concrete relevance. Jesus is now defining the death which he is about to undergo. In the manner of his betrayal and the entirety of his self-oblation, the themes of rejection and of service are to find acute and final fulfilment. Their fulfilment involves death on the cross. But without it they would issue in empty frustration, and their setting in the context of the messianic feast in the Kingdom of God would be cynical nonsense. Thus fulfilled, however, they have encountered the judgement and the mercy of God—for the death of Jesus has been met by resurrection from the dead. In the light of this belief, eating and drinking can no longer be matters of temporary sustenance or even of symbolic identification. For here we are made aware of an eating and drinking of which the satisfaction is unfailing and ultimate—an eating and drinking whose positive significance the discourses in the sixth and fifteenth chapters of the Gospel according to John cannot exhaust, which substantiates the bold claim of the writer to the Ephesians that in Christ Jesus 'God . . . has made us to sit with him in the heavenly places' (Eph. 2.6), and which caused the apostolic Church to perpetuate the Last Supper as the Eucharist, the great thanksgiving, not now for an expectation but for a hope already ensured.

The preparations necessary for a meal to which guests are invited; the fixing of a time for assembling; the attention to his guests required in a good host; the courtesy suitable in guests; the shocking but not unknown experience of guests who refuse or betray the hospitality offered to them; the central actions of receiving sustenance by eating and drinking—actions necessary for the continuation of life yet incapable of continuing life indefinitely,

actions that may satiate and yet can never satisfy (cf. Isa. 55.2–3)—
all these commonplace details would seem to have been deliberately
picked up by the evangelists when trying to communicate the meaning of the Last Supper. It might therefore be agreed that the use of
these details in this way has great importance for understanding
the primitive Christian conception of the Eucharist, but yet asked
whether it does indeed illuminate the universal pattern of socially
ordered human life, or whether it bears only upon the origins of an
esoteric rite.

It may help us to answer this question if we turn to a section of
Luke's Gospel (Luke 14.1–24) in which the evangelist brings
together a number of episodes set in the context of, or containing
some allusion to, a meal or a feast. Jesus goes to the house of one
of the rulers of the pharisees 'to eat bread' on the sabbath day. The
situation is tense. He is being 'watched', in the hope that he may
give substance to the charge of sabbath-breaking (Luke 14.1; cf.
Mark 3.2). Twice before, Luke has recorded that Jesus accepted
invitations to dinner with Pharisees (Luke 7.36; 11.37). It is, however, at first sight the sabbath context that seems uppermost in
Luke's mind, for we are told how the healing of a dropsical man
once more forces the question 'Is it lawful to heal on the sabbath,
or not?' (cf. Luke 14.3; 13.14; Mark 3.4; Matt. 12.10), and that
again Jesus appeals to the certainty that no exception would be
taken to rescuing a domestic animal from danger or difficulties on
the sabbath (Luke 14.5; cf. 13.15; Matt. 12.11). But there is no
reason to suppose that Luke has introduced this incident casually,
or because of some chance contextual reference in his source. Luke
is concerned with the work of God's salvation, of which healing is
one of the chief parables. It is the seriousness, the depth, and the
universality of Jesus's intention that supply the real answer to the
Pharisees' determination to trap him. Whether deliberately or not,
this first incident points the issue in all that will be recorded in the
context of this first-century 'coffee hour', after synagogue.

There follows a parable about the deportment of a guest bidden
to a 'marriage feast'. Unlike the guests invited to meet Jesus, he is
not to jockey for a chief seat, but to take the lowest. If the host
comes and promotes him, the incident will be parabolic of the oft-
quoted reversal of the present order summed up in the saying that
follows: 'Every one that exalteth himself shall be humbled; and

he that humbleth himself shall be exalted.' Mark has a word of Christ which includes a warning against the scribes 'which desire . . . chief places at feasts' (Mark 12.38–40); so also, perhaps, had a source known to Matthew and Luke (Matt. 23.6; Luke 20.46; cf. Luke 11.43). It may be that Luke's fuller treatment of this aspect of scribal behaviour has been introduced here a little clumsily. That does not obscure his point, that any meal—whether a sabbath-gathering to eat bread or a full-dress marriage feast— assumes a certain humility on the part of the guests in the presence of their host, and can therefore be, in respect of that assumption, parabolic.

But if, according to Luke, Jesus has a word for the guests, he also has a word for the host. When the guests bidden are friends, or brethren, or kinsmen, or rich neighbours, the hospitality will be rewarded, for it will be returned. Therefore, says Jesus :

> 'Bid the poor, the maimed, the lame, the blind : and thou shalt be blessed; because they have not wherewith to recompense thee : for thou shalt be recompensed in the resurrection of the just' (Luke 14.12–14).

Here again, the sanction lies in God's final disposition. Just as the promotion of humble guests speaks of the ultimate exaltation of the lowly in the Kingdom of God, so is hospitality for no foreseen or calculated reward, hospitality *directed towards the poor and physically dependent,* thrown wide open to the unconvenanted bounty of God 'in the resurrection of the just'.

In all this Luke has been moving towards a parable of some proportions, to which Matthew has a parallel (Matt. 22.2–14). He completes his transition brilliantly :

> When one of them that sat at meat with him heard these things, he said unto him, 'Blessed is he that shall eat bread in the Kingdom of God' (Luke 14.15).

Nothing could mar the utter rightness of this statement, except the platitudinous complacency with which it appears to have been made. As told by Luke, however, the Parable of the Great Supper offers no balm for easy piety. It is the story of a dinner-party well-prepared, with guests invited in advance—the word translated 'bidden' or 'invited' could as well be rendered 'called'. At the 'hour' or 'time' fixed for the dinner, the host sends 'his slave' to those who have been invited, with the express message: 'Come, for all things are now ready'. In view of the circumstance with which Luke relates these words, unparalleled in Matthew, it is difficult not to hear in them the announcement of the completion of God's preparations for accomplishing his final purpose.[1] The invited guests, however, spurn their host, and the slave is sent elsewhere to find others to take their place: first to the streets and lanes of the city, then to the highways and hedges. Here again Luke specifies the objects of hospitality—'the poor and maimed and blind and lame'—a specification also unparalleled in Matthew. All this is to be done 'that my house may be filled'. But the parable does not end, as some others do, with the thought of miraculous plenty or bounty in God's kingdom come. It ends with the doom of those for whom came the hour of calling to the feast now prepared, and who refused it— 'None of those men which were bidden shall taste of my supper.'

As Luke recounts it, the whole of this section, occupied as it is with the theme of host and guests at a meal, is pressed towards the poor, enjoins humility in the presence of the host, and is crossed by the rejection of the host by the guests. And it is relevant—relevant to the ministry of Jesus which Luke is recounting as well as to those for whom he is writing his Gospel—because the call to such a meal speaks of the call of God and the eschatological tension to which that call inevitably subjects those to whom it is made.

All this seems to lie on the surface in this half-chapter of Luke, and we need not doubt that that is partly Luke's achievement. But it is not the result of some peculiarly Lucan interest or perception. Unlike Luke, who is characteristically concerned with the supercession of the original, unwilling, guests by the 'poor and maimed and blind and lame', Matthew seems to be concerned (no less characteristically)[2] about the presence of 'both bad and good' in the community called together at God's command. But Matthew, too, is well aware that the pattern of a feast can bring home the final issues involved in the call of God. When he records a further

---

[1] Cf. Mark 10.40; Matt. 25.34; Luke 2.37; Heb. 11.16; Rev. 12.6. Picking up the words of Isaiah (Isa. 64.4), which describe God as 'working for him that waiteth for him', St Paul (1 Cor. 2.9) speaks of the 'things which eye saw not, and ear heard not, and which entered not into the heart of man, whatsoever things God prepared for those that love him.'

[2] Cf. Matt. 13.24–30, 36–43, noting Mark 4.26–9.

phenomenon, commonplace on formal occasions and not ignored in rabbinical parables of the first and second centuries[1]—the guest who was brought in unsuitably dressed—it is to show that the eschatological tension by which the unworthiness of the original guests was exposed extends no less to those gathered in from the highways to take their place. So it is with other incidents set in the context of meals (Mark 2.15–17; 14.3–9; Luke 12.37–40; Matt. 25.1–12). Here again the same, or similar, themes are used to intimate one aspect or another of some eschatological tension. In fact, according to the Gospels, Jesus perceived in all meals an ultimate significance in relation to the call of God and to the eschatological tension which it brings to bear. These themes therefore cannot be said to have emerged as the accounts of the meal were worked up with some esoteric motive. The case appears to be, rather, that when the narratives take us to the Upper Room certain themes already contained in their material become clarified because they become isolated[2]. Here we have the meal from which all the trappings of ordinary meals have been removed, the meal in which the eschatology inherent in all meals is entirely unobscured. The meal is therefore the key to the understanding of all meals. This does not mean that all meals are types of the Eucharist—the relation of the Eucharist to ordinary meals is a different matter.[3] It does mean that all meals are to be thought of as related to the specifically Christian meal, the historical meal in the Upper Room where the theme of crucifixion is manifestly dominant and where nothing 'comes to rest' or 'makes sense' except in an eschatological context, that is to say, in the context of the resurrection. When this relation is seen, all meals may be seen to be significant in relation to the Kingdom

---

[1] The Parable of the Wedding Feast is treated fully by W. O. E. Oesterley, in his *Gospel Parables in the Light of their Jewish Background*, 1936, pp. 122–130. He there gives translations of two rabbinical parables in Bab. Talmud *Shabbath*, 153 *a* and Midrash *Koheleth Rabba* on ix.8, respectively.

[2] See above, p. 115.

[3] Following this line of thought, the Eucharist might be said to interpret all meals in so far as it relates them to the Upper Room and so demonstrates (1 Cor. 11.23, 26) their 'fulfilment'; but that it obscures their meaning if it comes between them and the Upper Room, as *itself* comprising the 'fulfilment' of all ordinary meals, or as *itself* constituting the only meal within the scope of such 'fulfilment'. It has, of course, often been suggested that the fourth evangelist includes no account of the Last Supper precisely because, when he wrote, the Eucharist tended to be regarded in some such way as this.

of God, to resurrection, and to the eschatological meal in the Kingdom of God. In the light of the Last Supper, they bear witness to a satisfaction which they themselves, however much they may satiate, can never bestow.

Here we have a further example of the way in which Jesus throws light upon the ordinary world with which we are surrounded, not merely by his teaching, or by his participation in the day-to-day activities of his fellow men, but by the whole purpose with which he lived his life, culminating in his death set deliberately in the hope of God's final salvation. And here again crucifixion—resurrection lies in the very heart of the observable world, if only we can perceive it. For those who do perceive it there—for instance, in this pattern of host and guests eating and drinking together—all hospitality must wear a new dignity. For this reason, no doubt, the themes of eating and drinking are crystallized for the Church not only in the sacrament of the Eucharist but in the apostolic insistence upon the duty of quite ordinary hospitality (1 Tim. 3.2; Heb. 13.2; 1 Peter 4.9).

But we must now turn to the question basic to this book: What significance did those whose minds we encounter in the New Testament perceive in the resurrection?

PART THREE
The Risen Life

CHAPTER 13

The Resurrection Narratives

So far the New Testament concept of 'resurrection' has been referred to only circumstantially. Is it now possible to examine it directly? In inseparable conjunction with the concept of 'crucifixion' it has appeared to control not only the whole extent of the New Testament but also the whole texture of the thought at least of those who wrote, dictated, or edited its major documents. Moreover—in similarly intimate conjunction with 'crucifixion', it has been found to play a dominant and definitive part in the working out of various themes central to the New Testament. The evidence so far reviewed suggests that the New Testament theologians perceived in the crucifixion of Jesus significances far wider than that he actually suffered and died on the cross, 'under Pontius Pilate'—although that fact always remained to them primary and fundamental. The significances they perceived were far wider, even, than that a number of men and women believed themselves to be sharing in some way in his crucifixion as they moved (as all human beings must move) towards death although (unlike most of their contemporaries) in would-be faithful imitation of him. In studying the crucifixion of Jesus and its reflection in the thinking and lives of these first Christians, it has more than once become necessary to take account of the effects of his 'resurrection' because, under close scrutiny, his 'crucifixion' has seemed to remain meaningless, aimlessly contradictory, and even wholly nonsensical, *apart from his resurrection*—as St Paul implies when he concedes that Christ crucified is a stumbling-block to Jews and foolishness to Gentiles (1 Cor. 1.23). The 'resurrection' of Christ, on the other hand, has appeared to have led them to apprehend final meaning, positive affirmation, all-embracing reason and sense illuminating, and far more than illuminating, not only the course of his life but the circumstances and events of theirs as well, and indeed, the universe in which, as God's creatures, they found themselves placed. What then (it must now be asked) did this concept, 'resurrection', mean to those whose thought may be discerned in the New Testament?

How did they themselves interpret their own confident declaration that Jesus is risen from the dead?

The most direct evidence for the origin of belief in the resurrection of Jesus consists in the summary of the gospel which St Paul reminded the Corinthian Christians he had received and delivered to them, in the accounts of the empty tomb and the appearances of Jesus preserved in the four Gospels and the Acts of the Apostles, and in one or two other passages that appear to be relevant. No trail of historical research has been more zealously trodden over than this, or with more disparate results; and it is not the intention of this book to add to the existing dossiers. The purpose of this book would not, indeed, be achieved, either by simply reaffirming the traditional conclusion that the tomb must have been empty and that Jesus, risen from the dead, did undoubtedly make a certain number of appearances, to specified persons, in a particular sequence and in certain identifiable places or districts; or, on the other hand, by simply recording the equally familiar verdict that the tomb cannot reasonably be held to have been empty, and that, even though certain persons were credited by those who knew them with experiences of the risen Christ (or of his spiritual presence) these experiences defy both historical analysis and scientific description. Due regard must of course be paid to the fact that there are, in our own time, both some learned scholars, versed in the historical method, who confidently insist that the resurrection of Jesus must stand or fall as an event in history, and others, no less learned or well-equipped, who insist with equal confidence that, immediately we speak of the resurrection of Jesus, we pass beyond what is capable of historical description and analysis to something which a man may perhaps believe to be true so long as he does not confuse it with historical fact. Our present task, however, is to press behind this 'either-or', not in any great confidence that we shall find a definition of resurrection that justifies both these dogmatisms, but in the hope that we may learn what it was—or is—that has created them.

This task must be approached without any illusion that the jigsaw puzzle presented by the various episodic accounts of the resurrection appearances can be solved by putting the awkwardly shaped pieces together in some new way. It is the remarkable fewness of these pieces, and the apparently irreconcilable shapes which some of them take, that first of all demand consideration.

The latest English synopsis of the first three Gospels[1] divides
their whole material into 268 sections, and includes *in 13 sections*
all that is said to have taken place after the death of Jesus. As four
of these are concerned with the deposition and burial, the posting
and reporting of the guard, and the empty tomb, this means that a
remarkably small proportion of each Gospel is devoted to the witness of the disciples to the resurrection of Jesus, in view of the
weight put upon the resurrection throughout the New Testament.
Moreover, a count of verses indicates that the proportion of the
four Gospels concerned with what happened after Jesus died varies
not very greatly but none the less significantly: 2.09% of Mark;
2.8% of Matthew; 5.07% of Luke; 6.41% of John. Granted that
Mark may lack an original ending which may have contained fuller
accounts of appearances than those contained in the spurious longer
ending, the consistent increase none the less suggests that the
authors of Luke and John were dissatisfied with such a small proportion. Luke completes his Gospel with a narrative that seems to
have been developed with his usual literary skill. John had apparently completed his narrative with accounts of appearances to Mary
Magdalene and the Eleven, when he thought it desirable to add an
account of a further appearance, to seven of the Twelve, almost as
long again. Without their evangelists' 'writing up', the sources
lying behind the Gospels of Luke and John may well have been as
terse and haphazard as Matthew's would seem to have been.

If we examine side by side with the appearances recorded in the
Gospels those mentioned in 1 Corinthians[2] and in the Acts of the
Apostles,[3] we have references to resurrection appearances that
might number in all as few as nine, or even eight (assuming the
greatest possible duplication), or as many as twenty, if the most be
made of circumstantial differences.[4] And this uncertainty regarding

[1] H. F. D. Sparks, *A Synopsis of the Gospels.*
[2] 1 Cor. 15.5-8, including, with Kirsopp Lake (*The Historical Evidence for the Resurrection of Jesus Christ*), the appearance to Paul himself.
[3] Acts 1.1–14 (including the ascension). Kirsopp Lake adds 7.55-9: to the dying
St Stephen, though from the formal point of view this seems to belong rather with
the baptism of Jesus, the transfiguration, and perhaps Luke 22.43. Acts. 9.3–9;
22.6–11; 26.12–18 are the three accounts of St Paul's 'heavenly vision'.
[4] Acts 1.3–5 refers to appearances 'by the space of forty days'. This is here taken to
justify raising the total by one, although many will think this over-generous. The
appearances recorded in the longer conclusion of Mark (Mark 16.9–20), although
generally regarded as spurious, are also included in this census.

the independence of these various records arises less from the perennial problem of the independence of the 'sources' or 'traditions' behind the final redaction of the Gospels (although that problem in a particularly acute form persists through their ultimate chapters), than from the abundance of apparently irreconcilable contradictions within this whole 'resurrection material', scanty though it is.

Many Christians are familiar with the traditional apology that differences in the accounts of eye-witnesses of the same incident are to be expected, especially when those eye-witnesses are recalling what they have experienced under great emotional strain or excitement. There is force in the reflection that the sources would command less confidence if they all fitted smoothly and neatly into each other. We are inclined, perhaps, to regard the story of the sealing of the tomb and the posting of a guard, and of the subsequent bribing of the soldiers by the chief priests (Matt. 27.62–6; 28.1–4, 11–15) as secondary, not chiefly because it bears the marks of having been constructed or developed under the pressure of controversy, but simply because it exudes a certain aroma of plausibility. But what about the stubborn contradictions implicit in the less smooth material which it is far more difficult to brush aside as secondary? If Mark (Mark 15.46; 16.3–5; cf. Matt. 27.60; Luke 24.2) clearly describes a tomb hewn in the *side* of the rock, how can John (John 20.1) use a word[1] which suggests that he visualized the tomb as hollowed out in the ground and covered by a stone? Was Mark's 'young man sitting on the right side, arrayed in white robes' (Mark 16.5) rightly taken by Matthew to be 'an angel of the Lord', who descended from heaven, whose face shone like lightning, and whose garments were whiter than snow (Matt. 28.2–4)? Was Mark repeating, though misunderstanding, an appearance of the risen Christ comparable with his appearance to Mary Magdalene (John 20.14–18)? And, if so, was the first appearance of the risen Christ to

---

[1] This contrast may not be intended. But it is curious, especially if the fourth evangelist knew the Gospel according to Mark, that, where Mark speaks of 'rolling the stone up against the door of the tomb' and 'rolling the stone away' from it, he uses a word meaning 'taken' or 'lifted' and describes the beloved disciple 'stooping and looking in'.

Mary Magdalene—or to Peter?[1] Do these suggestions bear out Matthew's story that Jesus appeared to the women as they ran from the empty tomb (Matt. 28.8–9)? If so, did they deliver the message to the disciples, and was that why the disciples went to Galilee and not, as John suggests (John 21.2–3), because they had given up and gone back to the work from which they had been called? Or were the women simply the bearers of a message they thought they had received from an angel, or angels, which the disciples disbelieved (Luke 24.8–9)? And were the two on the road to Emmaus equally disbelieved by the rest (Mark 16.13) or welcomed into a company already convinced of an appearance to Peter (Luke 24.35)? Both Luke (Luke 24.30–6, 51) and John (John 20.19–26) agree that Jesus appeared to his disciples suddenly, although they were within locked doors, so that (Luke 24.27) they 'supposed that they beheld a spirit'. But Luke then tells how he ate a piece of fish, to prove that he had flesh and blood, and John says that he bade Thomas 'reach hither his hand and put it into his side' (John 20.27). Were Luke and John unconsciously disregarding the suggestion in their sources of a purely spiritual presence, in their desire to emphasize the corporeal reality of the risen Christ in the face of the doubts or the docetism that seemed to them, at the time they wrote, to be threatening true faith? Or again, did Luke intend to distinguish between the appearances of the Lord before and after his ascension, as though the former were corporeal, the latter purely spiritual? Ought we to infer from the words 'I am not yet ascended unto the Father' (John 20.17) that John believed the ascension to have taken place before Jesus stood, on the first day of the week, in the midst of his disciples and said: 'As the Father hath sent me, even so send I you' (John 20.21)? If so, not the timing only but also the physical (or metaphysical) implications of ascension are altogether different in the Lucan and Johannine accounts.[2] So too is it with their records of the gift of the Holy Spirit, which is, according to John (John 20.23) the immediate gift of the risen Christ to his disciples, but

[1] The longer added ending of Mark (Mark 16.9-20) has an appearance to Mary Magdalene inspired, it is commonly supposed, by John 20.11–18. But it is curious that this thoroughly imitative summary retains, not in this instance only, contradictions implied in the earlier accounts, and even complicates them further.
[2] Perhaps the detail in the longer Marcan ending that, after appearing to Mary Magdalene, he appeared 'in another form' to the two walking into the country (Mark 16.12), is relevant here.

according to Luke (Luke 24.49; cf. Acts 1.5–8) something they must wait for, to be fulfilled, presumably, on the day of Pentecost (Acts 2.4). Finally, where did the resurrection appearances take place, above all those to the Eleven? Was it in Jerusalem, as Luke, and John in his penultimate chapter, would have us believe, or in Galilee, as we may suppose to have been recorded in the lost end of Mark, as Matthew affirms, and as the final chapter of John and even one or two hints in Luke strongly suggest? But even if we incline to believe that the appearances took place in Galilee, can we justifiably dismiss the tradition of Jerusalem appearances as issuing from some misunderstanding, or from some theological motive of Luke? Or should we rather conclude, that the evidence at this, as at almost every point in these narratives, is conflicting and ambiguous?

Yet, when as much weight as possible has been laid upon these contradictions, the resurrection material shows, under a different analysis, a remarkable consistency—a consistency which is reflected in relevant passages of the Acts of the Apostles and the Epistles of St Paul. This consistency strikes us forcibly when we ask what motive, in each case, may appear to lie behind the record.

The first, and overriding, motive seems to be to affirm that the disciples, or apostles, or brethren, singly or in varying numbers, saw the risen Lord. Seven of the separate accounts are bare records of such appearances (1 Cor. 15.5 (2); 1 Cor. 15.6; 1 Cor. 15.7 (2); 1 Cor. 15.8; Luke 24.34; Mark 16.12–13). In all these the only extraneous information given is that Jesus appeared 'in another form' (Mark 16.12), and that the appearance to Paul was 'as to one born out of due time' (1 Cor. 15.8). The detail that 'the most' of the 500 remained alive at the time 1 Corinthians was written appears designed to emphasize the validity of the evidence for this appearance. So does the statement that 'the rest did not believe' (Mark 16.13), like other references to an initial unbelief later to be overcome by the evidence.

In five other accounts an additional motive is recognizable—insistence upon the identity of Jesus. He is identified in breaking of the bread (Luke 24.31); in the showing of the hands and feet (Luke 24.40; John 21.27); in the sound of his voice as he says 'Mary' (John 20.16); or 'by many proofs' (Acts 1.3). Later, in the fourth Gospel, identification gives way to apostolic recognition: it is the beloved disciple—who had believed on seeing the empty tomb (John 20.8) —who identifies Jesus to Peter (John 21.7), suggesting that, ideally, external proofs should not be necessary since this recognition appertained to the apostolic insight; and this is confirmed in the case of the five other disciples who did not dare ask Jesus who he was, 'knowing that it was the Lord' (John 21.12).

Almost all the other 'motives' discernible in these accounts seem to have to do with the origins and sanctions of the apostolic witness. In Matthew, Jesus declares that all authority has been given unto him in heaven and earth, and then commissions the Eleven to go and make disciples of all the nations (Matt. 28.18–20), promising them his presence until the end of the world. In John the risen Jesus states his commission, derived now from his glorification, before giving his disciples theirs 'as the Father hath sent me, even so send I you'—and immediately gives them the Holy Spirit and authority to remit sins (John 20.21–2). In Luke and Acts, although the gift of the Holy Spirit is delayed, the sequence is the same— indeed, the delay serves to heighten the expectation and circumstance of the gift. Repentance and remission of sins are to be preached in Christ's Name 'unto all the nations', and the disciples are to be witnesses of these things (Luke 24.47–8). But they are to wait in Jerusalem until he sends them the Father's promise and they are clothed with power from on high (Luke 24.49; cf. Acts 1.4–5). In the account of the ascension, the promise of power after the Holy Spirit has come upon them is repeated, and they are told that they will be witnesses to Jesus both in Jerusalem, the whole of Judaea, Samaria, and unto the uttermost part of the earth (Acts 1.8). The day of Pentecost, of course, sees the fulfilment of this promise and the first apostolic witness duly and successfully begun in Jerusalem. Even the longer Marcan ending has the same sequence of themes in the same order, though here the promise of the Lord's presence with them until the end of the world, or of the Holy Spirit clothing them with power, becomes 'the Lord working with them, and confirming the word by the signs that followed' (Mark 16.20). In the appearance to Thomas, besides the motive of underlining the basis of faith by showing unbelief overcome—and even rebuking it (cf. Mark 16.19)—it seems to be this apostolic mission that is in mind: 'Blessed are they that have not seen, and yet have believed' (John 20.29). This mission is the consistent motive of the last chapter of the fourth gospel, holding together the vivid accounts of the miraculous draft of fishes and Christ's repeated pastoral charge to Peter.

So far no mention has been made of the appearances to the women together, and to Mary Magdalene alone. At first sight these might seem to have no connection with the apostolic witnessing to the risen Jesus from which the mission of the Church derived, and to call for separate treatment. But to relate them to the apostolic witness seems necessary. The women are given, or deliver, the news that the tomb is empty (Matt. 28.6; Mark 16.6; Luke 24.6). Mary Magdalene does the same (John 20.2). It is not they but only the 'beloved disciple' who, as has already been noted, sees the significance of the empty tomb—and this, of course, only in the fourth Gospel. In the same way, in every instance—whether the women are said to have seen Jesus or to have had some vision of angels, and even in the case of the classical appearance to Mary Magdalene recorded in the fourth Gospel—the motive for recording the incident appears to be that a message should be carried to the disciples. It is not the present purpose to discuss what actual historical events lay behind these narratives, or to speculate whether, although such care is taken to represent them as contributing towards the convincing of the disciples, the appearance to the women may earlier have played an independent, and more central, part in the disciples' recollections of the first Easter Day. What has to be noted is that, even when they report that they have seen the Lord, the women are introduced, not as witnesses or interpreters in their own right, but as messengers bearing instructions or news that will help to create the apostolic witness and its interpretation.

This analysis of the 'resurrection material' is now complete, save for one motive discernible only[1] in the appearances recorded in Luke and Acts: the firm setting of the crucifixion, the resurrection, the gift of the Holy Spirit, and the witness of the apostles, in the context of the Scriptures, as providing the key to their understanding (Luke 24.25–7, 32, 44–8). To this the author of Acts seems to

[1] It must however be remembered that the accounts summarized in 1 Cor. 15.5–8 follow immediately upon the statement that Christ 'died for our sins according to the scriptures' and that 'he hath been raised on the third day according to the scriptures' (1 Cor. 15.3,4).

be referring when he describes the risen Christ as 'speaking of the things pertaining to the Kingdom of God' (Acts 1.3), though he has been taken to mean 'the things pertaining to the Church'.[1] What he certainly does not mean is what other ancient accounts of visions of those who have penetrated into Hades or Heaven would have prepared us for, accounts of unearthly, infernal, or celestial experiences. That 'motive' is conspicuously absent from the Gospels, as from the New Testament as a whole.[2]

If the appearance of Jesus to Stephen, when he 'saw the glory of God, and Jesus standing on the right hand of God' (Acts 7.55–6), is rightly reckoned a 'resurrection appearance', it is so exceptional that little is to be gained by comparing it with the Gospel accounts. If it must be included, let it simply prove the rule. Not so the appearance to St Paul, which reveals the same motives as have been discerned in the Gospel appearances. In each of the three accounts of this appearance, Jesus identifies himself (Acts 9.5; 22.8; 26.15). And although in the first two, it is Ananias who is told, or who tells Paul, that he has been chosen to see 'that Just One, and to hear the voice of his mouth' in order that he may be a witness to all men of what he has heard, in the third account it is Jesus himself who tells Paul that he has appeared to him for the express purpose of making him a minister and a witness 'both of the things which thou hast seen, and of those things in which I will appear unto thee', in order that the eyes of the Gentiles may be opened and they be turned from darkness to light, receiving forgiveness of sins and inheritance among those that are sanctified by faith in Jesus (Acts 26.16–18). Moreover, immediately after the appearance, Paul receives the Holy Spirit (Acts 9.17). Writing to the Galatians, Paul tells them that the revelation of Jesus Christ 'in him' had as its purpose his preaching of Jesus Christ among the Gentiles (Gal. 1.16). Elsewhere he says that it was from this 'grace' that his apostleship derived (Rom. 15.16). The most elaborate of the greetings with which he customarily began his letters appears to derive from the

[1] Cf. Foakes-Jackson and Kirsopp Lake, *The Beginnings of Christianity*, vol. IV, p. 4, ad loc.

[2] E. G. Selwyn, in his 'Essay on 1 Peter 3.18ff. and 4.6' (*The First Epistle of St Peter*, pp. 313–62) showed how completely different is the motive of the New Testament allusions to Christ's *Descensus ad inferos*. St Paul's remarkable diffidence and restraint in describing how he was 'caught up to the third heaven' is as remarkably surpassed by the complete reticence ascribed to his risen Lord.

memory of his vision of Jesus. If so, it is highly significant that it includes nearly all the characterstic motives of the resurrection narratives:

> Paul, a servant of Jesus Christ, called to be an apostle, separated unto the gospel of God, (which he had promised afore by his prophets in the holy scriptures,) concerning his Son, who was born of the seed of David according to the flesh, who was declared to be the Son of God with power, according to the spirit of holiness, by the resurrection of the dead; even Jesus Christ our Lord, through whom we received grace and apostleship, unto obedience of faith among all the nations, for his name's sake . . . (Rom. 1.1–5).

The accounts of the appearances of the risen Jesus are meagre; quite insufficient to the purpose of making a consecutive narrative or a consistent description; in certain respects irreconcilable, even contradictory, among themselves. They give the impression that the person of the risen Jesus, as apprehended by these witnesses on these various occasions, was not in itself a subject of interest to those who handed on the tradition or wrote the Gospels in their present form. What seems to have been to them all-important was the fact that he was risen, and that this fact had been forced upon the apostles and the brethren as a result of historical experiences. This fact was the essential basis of their faith. From it issued the commissioning of the Church, the definition of its objective and authority, the gift of its power. But although it seems certain that, but for the conviction of resurrection appearances, there would be no gospel, the substance of the gospel of the risen Christ lies elsewhere—in the accounts of the ministry of Jesus, his passion, and his death, and in the life of the Church.

Paradoxical though this may seem, there is a further paradox. When we turn back to the ministry according to the synoptic Gospels we find, with one exception, what we have termed the 'motives' of the resurrection narratives, nowhere all together, but in various, unrelated sayings ascribed to Jesus. The one exception (for obvious reasons) is the affirmation of the bare fact of the appearances of Jesus risen from the dead, although several 'prophecies' of his rising again are recorded (Mark 8.31; 9.9; 9.31; 10.34; 14.28, and parallels). There is, for instance, the identification of Jesus as the Christ, first enunciated by Peter (Mark 8.29) after much misunderstanding, on the part of his fellow-townsmen, the scribes and Pharisees, the crowds, even his own disciples. Closely associated with this is the disbelief which, for the reader of the Gospels, leads on by contrast to underline the emergence of belief. Then there is the revelation of the authority of Jesus, implicit in the astonishment of his hearers at the authority with which he taught (Mark 1.22, 27, etc.) and in the demand of the chief priests, scribes, and elders that he should state his authority (Mark 11.28), and explicitly set forth in the Thanksgiving of Jesus (Matt. 11.25–30; cf. Luke 10.21–2): 'All things have been delivered unto me of my Father: and no one knoweth the Son, save the Father; neither doth any know the Father, save the Son, and he to whomsoever the Son willeth to reveal him.' The Mission of the Twelve, in all three synoptic Gospels, and the Mission of the Seventy, in Luke, appear to be confined to the towns and villages of Galilee and Judaea. But in the Great Apocalyptic Discourse in Mark Jesus is said to have looked forward to the preaching of the gospel 'unto all the nations' (Mark 13.10), which bears out hints in all three synoptic Gospels that the scope of the gospel is world-wide (Matt. 8.11; Luke 13.29; Mark 14.9; cf. Matt. 26.13). The fourth Gospel's explicit authorization to forgive sins (John 20.23) is anticipated in the two Matthaean sayings about binding and loosing, the one to Peter (Matt. 16.19), the other to the disciples (Matt. 18.19). The commissioning of the disciples in the fourth Gospel—'as the Father hath sent me, even so send I you'—is paralleled not only in sayings in discourses in the same Gospel (John 12.44–8; 13.20) but also in the Mission Charge common to Matthew and to Luke (Matt. 10.40; Luke 10.16) and known also to Mark (Mark 9.37; Matt. 18.5; Luke 9.48). The setting of the passion and resurrection of Jesus in the context of the Scriptures, conspicuously developed in Luke's resurrection narratives, is anticipated, not only in the body of his Gospel, but in the three statements of the *dei pathein*[1] in all three synoptic Gospels, a necessity of suffering explicitly defined in Mark (9.12) and Luke (18.31–3) as grounded in the Scriptures. It is only upon Jesus that the Holy Spirit descends, in the body of the synoptic Gospels, at his baptism (Mark 1.10; Matt. 3.16; Luke 3.22); but all three record

---

[1] See above, pp. 160, 161, 165. The full references are: Mark 8.31; 9.31; 10.33, 34; Matt. 16.21; 17.22–3; 20.17–19; Luke 9.22; 44; 18.31–3.

John Baptist's prophecy that he that would come after him would baptize with the Holy Spirit (Mark 1.8; Matt. 3.14; Luke 3.16). Although the promise of the continuing presence of Jesus with his disciples appears explicitly only in Matthew (18.20), it is to be inferred from other synoptic sayings (Mark 9.37 and parallels). Even the prophecy, in the longer end of Mark, of the signs 'that shall follow those that believe' (Mark 16.17–18) is anticipated in the joyful Return of the Seventy (Luke 10.17–18), though with verbal similarities that warn us that this may have been the spurious writer's source. Finally, some have seen a dependence in the reverse direction in the curious resemblance between the Lucan account of the Call of Peter (Luke 5.1–11) and the Johannine account of the Miraculous Draft of Fishes (John 21.1–11); and have supposed that Luke, wittingly or unwittingly, set back, to the beginning of the ministry, what was originally an account of the appearance of the risen Jesus to St Peter.

It is by no means material to the present purpose to discuss the literary relations between the resurrection narratives and the parallels, in the body of the Gospels, to the 'motives' with which they seem to have been recorded. What *is* material, and what must be stated succinctly, is that, in spite of these parallels, scattered at many points in the records of the ministry of Jesus, the mission of the Church is universally stated to have sprung from the resurrection, having as its instigator and director Jesus apprehended by the disciples (or apostles, or brethren) as risen from the dead, empowered with the full authority of the Father, and sending them to all nations to remit sins and to baptize, with the assurance of his abiding presence and the gift of the Holy Spirit. It is here, where the crucifixion of Jesus is revealed and apprehended as having issued in his resurrection, that, by common consent, the mission of the Church is defined, authorized, and actually begun.[1]

Yet, once this has been stated, it must be stated equally emphatically that, when it is asked what the *material* of primitive Christian

---

[1] Apollos, with his knowledge of John's baptism, instruction in 'the way of the Lord', and ability to teach the things concerning Jesus, perhaps illustrates the possibility of a mission springing from acquaintance with the ministry of Jesus but not with the understanding of his crucifixion derived from faith in the resurrection and consequent involvement in the mission of the Church. It is 'the way of God' that he has to have expounded to him more exactly (Acts. 18.24–8). But there are, of course, very different explanations of this obscure contrast.

preaching and teaching was, there are two certain answers only: the synoptic tradition of the ministry of Jesus, and the problems and needs of particular Christian churches. Dr Dodd has recovered a consistent pattern of apostolic preaching from six Christian speeches recorded in Acts, which tally with certain passages of Galatians and 1 Thessalonians, 1 Corinthians, and Romans.[1] No doubt the author of Acts had heard, and perhaps made, many missionary sermons under the heads comprised in this pattern. Very probably St Paul had a similar array of essential points in mind whenever he raised his hand for silence and spoke to audiences with a grounding in the Jewish religion. Perhaps behind them both lay deliberate and conscious systematizing of the proclamation of the gospel. And perhaps this process of systematizing had been accompanied by an exhaustive searching of the Scriptures in order that the theological apprehension of Jesus Christ might be fully documented.[2] It is possible that there is reflected in Luke's resurrection narratives a period of intensive formulation on the part of the apostles; possible, too, that this bore eventual fruit in collections of 'testimonia' or lists of Old Testament passages bearing upon the gospel and of 'sayings' of Jesus grouped roughly under subjects by key-words. There are traces and hints of all these aids to evangelization, and unless something of this kind took place first of all in Jerusalem it is difficult to explain either the importance in the foundation of Christianity ascribed to the apostles, or the consistency with which it was proclaimed and illustrated. But all this can be speculation only, however well informed and scientifically pursued. On the other hand, in contrast with these speculations, we actually possess a corpus of letters in which, as their apostolic writers discharged their care for churches involved in particular historical situations, they exemplified and elaborated their faith in Jesus crucified and risen, and their understanding of his gospel; and four Gospels in which, whether we try to press back towards 'origins' by means of source and form criticism, or evaluate the final, complete documents as set down by their last redactors, we are nowhere allowed to escape either from history or from interpretation—the interpretation issuing from faith in Jesus crucified

[1] C. H. Dodd, *The Apostolic Preaching and its Development*, 1936.
[2] C. H. Dodd, *According to the Scriptures*, 1952; cf. Barnabas Lindars, *New Testament Apologetic*.

and risen, and the history of episodes in the life, and ministry, and suffering of Jesus recounted again and again as directly relevant to Christian faith, and vocation, and life. Both in the concentration upon the history of Jesus up to the moment of his death, and in the concentration upon the illumination and edification of particular Christians as they try to follow him in life, we find what seemed to be missing in the narratives of the resurrection : preoccupation with Jesus himself, whether accomplishing the will of his Father upon earth or exalted to his Father's right hand as Saviour, Redeemer, and Lord. Neither the Gospels nor the Epistles would ever have been written had it not come about that the disciples of Jesus were convinced he had risen from the dead—no fact of New Testament history can be more confidently affirmed than this. There must have been, historically, a point or moment of insight. But what his resurrection meant to them, how they interpreted it, and what they were compelled to think and say and do as a result of the revelation of truth which they believed they had been given—to learn this we are driven, either back *behind* the crucifixion, or *forward,* on to the life of the Church. The point of insight remains, as it were, invisible. But even though this is so, it is certain that, if we can analyse the insight that characterizes the synoptic tradition, if we can estimate, from their Epistles, the essential apprehension of the writer to the Hebrews, of St Paul, and perhaps of others who wrote Epistles, if we can determine what constitutes the fundamental grasp of the fourth evangelist, we shall be in a better position to understand what the resurrection meant to them. From time to time in the course of this book we have spoken of the 'eloquence' of St Paul, or St John, or the New Testament writers. It is because we have reason to suppose that the origin of their eloquence is to be found, not only in the crucifixion but also and above all in the resurrection of Jesus, that we must now proceed to consider the eloquence of the resurrection.

POSTSCRIPT
The Resurrection Faith[1]

Wherefore God has highly exalted him and
given him a name which is above every name
(Phil. 2.9)

(Therefore my beloved—do all things without
murmurings and shine ye as lights in the world)
(Phil. 2.9)

WHEREFORE God – highly exalted him
By this 'wherefore' Easter Day is linked to the scene of the crucifixion—is linked to passion and death. The two must never be
separated, for resurrection is the gospel which is proclaimed over
death, over the broken fragments of human thought and actions,
over this world as we see and know and live it; over you and me as
we pass not to maturity but to death, whither we do most assuredly
pass, for this is the one quite certain visible fact about us all.

The word resurrection can then be spoken only at one place, at
the place of death, but there it must be spoken, and there it has been
spoken.

Wherefore GOD – highly exalted him
But who has spoken the word? who has exalted Christ? who is to
bring in the new world? who is to create it, and call it out of
nothingness? Resurrection is not *an idea of the Church*. It is not a
logical or illogical deduction which clever or stupid men have made
out of the facts of their experience or of the experience of others.
Resurrection is not a doctrine of immortality, of the immortality of
the soul, a doctrine built up upon the pride of those who suppose
their souls to be so good and holy, so refined and cultured, that they
must be indestructible, whatever may happen to their bodies.

This would be a doctrine, a human idea ministering to the pride

---

[1] This was preached by Sir Edwyn Hoskyns in Wigan Parish Church on Easter Day,
probably in 1933. F. N. Davey repeated it, without substantial change, at St Benet's,
Cambridge, in 1972. See p. xv.

of pure souls. It would be no gospel over the grave, over the grave of those who may not regard themselves of so great value after all.
Resurrection is not a doctrine at all.

Nor is resurrection a drug administered by the Church to those who are unwilling to die.

Indeed, the exhortation of the Church is that men must die far more fundamentally than is involved in mere physical death, for they must be prepared to lose all, to find they have no security either of thought or emotion or action. To make men face up to this loss, this emptiness, this sacrifice—which is, indeed, the meaning of death—is the terrible responsibility of the Church.

(You have been baptized into the death of Christ.

You are riveted to that same death in the sacrament of the Lord's Body and Blood.

The Church is not romantic, or idealistic. It is far more realistic than any modern novel, for it alone dares to see human life as it actually is.

It sees that men are really poor, that they are really weak, and that this is a universal truth from which no hero, however famous, can escape.)

Resurrection then is neither a human doctrine which we proclaim, nor a drug which we administer, nor is it indeed another world of which *we* have intimations.

God EXALTED him

Notice the subject of the verb 'exalted', God exalted him. (Nor can the Church ever alter that subject. It does not say the man Jesus raised himself from the dead, or that we shall exalt ourselves.)

Resurrection is that which we wait for, hope for, and we must use these words, waiting and hoping, for resurrection is the new world which God creates, it is our emptiness filled by him with his fulness, it is the new creation, by God. It is the new heaven and the new earth.

It is the fulfilment of all things. It is eternity, it is eternal life, but we are mortal, living in time. Resurrection is therefore infinitely more than ever we can conceive of.

And so we must remember on this Easter Day that we are singing and praising the glory of God, not our own glory. And we believe that in singing his glory we do make sense of death and sorrow and sin and distress, because it is these things which make room for the glory of God, more than do our harping upon *our* success or *our* wealth or *our* righteousness.

And so, in proclaiming that God raised Jesus from the dead, we praise God and believe his glory will overcome our weakness and the weakness of all men.

And therefore, over the grave, we burst into song. Alleluia, alleluia, alleluia.

Wherefore God exalted HIM

When once we have made God the subject of the verb exalted, and have really made room for him to speak and act, then we can come back to Jerusalem, to Jesus the man, for there at that visible point on the edge of this world God's power stands almost visible.

> At that point time touches eternity;
> what is finite touches what is infinite,
> what is human touches what is divine,
> and so *we* dare to say : God exalted Him,
> Jesus Christ our Lord.

And having sung Christ is risen, we cry : God is King over all distress and poverty and death, for death is swallowed up in victory.

Therefore, my beloved—do all things without murmuring—and shine ye as lights in the world.

> Shine ye, because ye sing,
> Christ is risen, is risen,
> Christ is risen.

CHAPTER 14
The Problem of History

Those who wrote the New Testament were vitally concerned with the *living of life* in this world. The author of 1 Peter, beseeching his readers to abstain from fleshly lusts and to have their behaviour 'seemly among the Gentiles', declares that they are called to this way of life because the purpose of Christ's suffering and death was 'that we, having died unto sin, might live with righteousness'. For instance, St Paul urges his readers, who have been baptized unto Christ's death, to 'walk in newness of life' (Rom. 6.4; cf. 2 Cor. 5.10) and declares, on another occasion, that 'through the law' he had 'died unto the law', that he might 'live unto God'. He goes on 'I have been crucified with Christ; yet I live; and yet no longer I, but Christ liveth in me: and the life which I now live in the flesh I live in faith, the faith which is in the Son of God, who loved me, and gave himself up for me' (Gal. 2.19–20). According to the fourth Gospel, Jesus said, 'I came that they (the sheep) may have life, and have it more abundantly. I am the Good Shepherd: the Good Shepherd layeth down his life for the sheep' (John 10.10–11). These passages, chosen almost at random, bewilder the modern reader with a number of unintelligible qualifications—dying unto sin, living unto righteousness, newness of life, have life more abundantly, faith in the Son of God—qualifications which he is inclined to dismiss as theological jargon—and they manifest the still more awkward conviction that 'life' bridges the worlds separated by physical death 'for God appointed us not unto wrath, but unto the obtaining of salvation through our Lord Jesus Christ, who died for us, that, whether we wake or sleep, we should live together with him.' (1 Thess. 5.10). But yet, if these complications are for the moment set on one side, the fundamental fact remains that, as a result of the death of Christ, the Christians, to whom and for whom St Paul writes, believe that they have been offered and have been given life in this world: such life as can be adequately described in our idiom only by epithets like 'true', 'real', and 'full'.

It is in this wide context, life in this world, that the problem of history seems to have forced itself upon the apostles and those they taught. They did not share our obsession with the problem of 'historicity'—the question whether events recorded in their sacred books, or events such as they believed to have taken place, happened exactly as they were recorded or as described; nor did they stop to argue whether these events took place at all. They were indeed more intent upon declaring that Christ had come in the flesh (as we should say, had come in history); that he 'went about doing good, and teaching all that were oppressed of the devil'. The apostles believed that they were witnesses 'of all things which he did both in the country of the Jews and in Jerusalem, whom also they slew, hanging on a tree . . . God raised up the third day, and gave him to be made manifest, not to all the people, but unto witnesses that were chosen before God, even unto us' (Acts 10.38–41). And all this, they declared again and again was 'according to the scriptures' (1 Cor. 15.3–4). The question raised for them by these events was not 'did they happen just like that, or did they happen at all?', but rather, for they themselves were in no doubt, 'How are we to bring men and women to see what these events mean to us and should mean to them?'

Let us be quite clear of this from the outset: they could not detach themselves, or their hearers, from the history with which they were concerned: and therefore they could not try to contemplate that history, as we try to contemplate history, as something with no repercussions for themselves, as something in which they were not in some sense directly involved.

If 'historicity' had no counterpart in their thinking, neither did the word 'history', at any rate as we commonly use it. They did not make delicate distinctions (as we have been used to do, at any rate in times past) between political history, economic history, religious history: nor did they differentiate sharply between the history of their nation, the biography of individuals, the records of the inner experience of godly men and women. Rather they had been nourished on Scriptures written by men who saw a common pattern running through all history, corporate and personal, external and internal. They were familiar in their Scriptures with passages in which Israel's experience was described as that of an individual,

297

God's servant, as well as with passages in which the joys and griefs attributed to the whole nation in fact expressed the hopes and fears of a particular few. For them, the scope of history was the whole of life : its raw material the whole gamut of human experience.

They were of course familiar, even from passages in their Scriptures, with what we should call 'interpretations' or 'theories' of history, some of them as naive or as cynical as some with which we are familiar today. They were aware of people who said that 'there is no God,' though they called them fools; yet they accepted as wise men those who, while professing to believe in God, saw nothing but vanity in the course of human affairs and the experiences of human beings. They were used to the rough and ready conclusion that 'the fathers had eaten sour grapes, and the children's teeth are set on edge'; and the confident counter-assertion made, with as little absolute confirmation in actual experience, that 'every man that eateth sour grapes, his teeth shall be set on edge.' But they none the less inherited a common view of life—a view shared in the main by those who, with prophetic insight, wrote and rewrote the history of Israel; by the great unknown author of the book of Job; and by the men whose prayers and tears, whose short-lived joys and suffering long-endured, had created the volumes we call the Psalms.

According to this view, all life is related to God; all life stands under his command and has his promise set upon it, as his law and his covenant bear witness : but unlike the material and brute creation, which is and does what it was created to be and to do, man, men, the nation, mankind, are in an always unresolved tension; craving for the fullness for which they feel destined, for the dignity and permanence for which they were made; but incapable by nature of the obedience, the righteousness, the holiness, the faith, the humility they know to be the prerequisite of their bliss. God seems to offer so much in life, only to snatch it away. Here and there they find satiety, but nowhere the satisfaction for which they yearn; now and then they liberate themselves from external bonds, but they can never free their souls from sin; nor is it possible for them to attribute their sufferings wholly to the wickedness of the nations that dominate them, or to the tyranny of the kings whom they have wantonly set up, or to the rapacity of the rich and worldly classes to whom they are sold : even the poor godly men find enthroned in their hearts and minds that which runs counter to God's will, and as they cry out to him for consolation confess that their guilt delays the realization of his Kingdom. It is this word, or rather, the hope contained in this word, 'Kingdom', that perhaps best sums up this Old Testament view of history. God must have conceived and made the whole of life for his purpose: that purpose must be perfect. They can but think of God as King, yet all their experience denies his kingship: why then does the King not establish his Kingdom? Is it not because man is only then seeking to establish his own righteousness, in a kingdom of his own making, to attach to himself a glory that usurps the glory of God? Is it not because God for his part is, through the sweet-bitter, cup-snatching, God-denying experience of life as it is, unperfected in his Kingdom, leading man to repentance? and to faith? This is the burden of Jeremiah's oft-repeated commission: 'The Lord said unto me, Behold I have put my words in thy mouth: I have this day set thee over the nations and over the kingdoms, to pluck up and to break down, and to destroy, and to overthrow, to build and to plant' (Jer. 1.9–10; cf. 18.7; 31.28; 45.4). It is the burden laid upon St Paul—'For though we walk in the flesh, we do not war according to the flesh (for the weapons of our warfare are not of the flesh, but mighty before God to the casting down of strongholds); casting down imaginations, and every high thing that is exalted against the knowledge of God, and bringing every thought into captivity to the obedience of Christ; and being in readiness to avenge all disobedience, when your obedience shall be fulfilled.' (2 Cor. 10.3–6).

If this summary be at all just, the stark differences between the Old Testament view of history and that of the humanism of the Greek and Roman world will be evident. The Jews saw man and creation as one, wholly (as we should say) within history, and, in spite of the exemplary obedience of the natural order, held back from the attainment of its God-given purpose and fulness by the reckless, self-centred, disobedience of man. The Greeks differentiated between the historical stream of events and the actual reality of the world. The primary object of their study and speculation (wisdom) was the world, which they sought to grasp in its unalterable stability, and so to wrest from it ultimate and universal truths. Along this road, for their philosophers, lay, if anywhere, the knowledge of God.[1] The historical stream of events, on the other hand, was for them the arena in which man struggled to overcome fate and to achieve apotheosis. At the height of the Roman Empire, the triumph of man in the flux of history must have seemed supreme, justifying 'imaginations' that made highly topical St Paul's definition of what is opposed to the knowledge of God.

It is arguable that the modern conception of the universe, as being wholly within the flux of history, approximated rather to the Jewish than to the Greek view: none the less—and in spite of the disillusionment of the last decades—humanistic interpretations of history are still dominant: adherents of evolution, progress, dialectical materialism abound. If history is regarded as bunk, it is only to enhance the powers and prestige of man. If there are no fixed perspectives in history, it is only because the eye of man, the only observer, must be free to interpret, and to speculate from any standpoint into which he likes to project himself or his imagination. Any suggestion that history is bunk because God alone can make sense of it and that its true perspective is revealed only when it is seen through his eyes is as foreign to the modern world as it was to that of the Athenians who jeered when Paul preached resurrection.

Involved in the pattern which the Old Testament prophets and writers perceived in history was the belief that God's will must prevail and his purpose be achieved in the future as in the past. For this reason they secularized history not at all; but saw, or thought they saw, or tried to believe that they saw or ought to be able to see, all things, all events, in relation to him, and that in so doing they were looking for fulfilment of his promises. God was for them as truly the protagonist of the history of Israel as he was of the Book of Job and of the Psalms. Moreover they found this conception entirely compatible with the belief that God is transcendent—exalted in his being above the universe and wholly distinct from it. Yet, precisely because they found room for his will everywhere in

---

[1] Fr Gogarten *Demythologizing and History* (SCM Press 1955), p. 21. Nevertheless, according to Professor Lattimore, *The Poetry of Greek Tragedy* (OUP 1959), Euripides' *Bacchae* is rightly rendered: 'I have no quarrel with wisdom. I am happy to track it down, yet there is something else. Something big, something manifest, that directs life through good.' (1005–8). If this translation is correct, here is one of not a few examples of 'intimations' in classical Greek writing of the biblical view of life.

history, they pictured God's intervention in fulfilment of his pro-mises as lying within history. The reign of God must come on earth. Whatever form his Kingdom may take, whether it be expounded in the interests of nationalism or of universalism, it will manifest itself materially in a new order and a new age. The Messiah who will usher in this 'good time' may be thought of as an earthly king of David's line or as the heavenly man coming upon the clouds of heaven. In either case his rule will be—as we should say—in time and space. This will be the final empire, the culmina-tion—albeit by the direct intervention of God—of the successive empires of this world. It is important to notice this concentration. The fulfilment of history is itself within history. To visualize the historical flux as finding consummation beyond itself, as being taken up by some miracle or sublimation into the order of eternity, would have been as foreign to the prophetic mind as the Greek conceptions of communion with the Godhead by means of mystical contemplation or ecstasy. Yet—and perhaps this is even more important—even though these Old Testament prophets and writers made pictures of historical righteousness, historical vindica-tion, historical beatitude and bliss, God himself remained always the all-sufficient centre of their hope. And the more necessary this hope became to them, to vindicate the God in whom they believed, the more profoundly aware did they show themselves of the essen-tial distinction between God and man, between the creator and his creation. Although God's law—God's nature, indeed—imposed an absolute demand upon his people, they never debased the coming of God's Kingdom into a human achievement. Human sin might delay the day of the Lord: but human obedience and holiness would not force it to dawn. So the longing and hope of the prophets is not based upon forces within history, but presupposes in the last resort a revelation cutting across the continuity of history.

The Psalter holds closely together, sometimes in the compass of a single psalm (e.g. 22, 89, 94), the cry of extreme despair, of dereliction by God—out of the deep—and the firm assurance of his mercies, not merely in aspiration for the future, but as a present fact, whether experienced or not: 'thou dost . . .'; 'thou hast . . .'.

In the book of Job the problem of suffering is examined, and the conventional solutions of it are shown to be inadequate, but the problem is never solved. Job abases himself in dust and ashes leaving the problem to God, not only in the sense that it is left to his inscrutable wisdom, but also in the sense that having been confronted with God Job has no further thought for himself.

Confronted with the suffering of Israel, the servant of God (Isa. 52.13–15), the nations shall see what they had not been told; and understand what they had not heard. This vicarious suffering marked him out to men as smitten of God, as afflicted—that was its visible appearance: but its meaning—the justification of many, and the bearing of their iniquities—gives the lie to all *visible appearance,* and is the fact of revelation. The hope—that God shall 'divide him a portion with the great, and that he shall divide the spoil with the strong' still appears to be material *vindication in history,* but its fulfilment (of this the prophet has no doubt) lies with God alone.

Similarly, towards the end of Old Testament times Hebrew literature begins to contain fleeting anticipations of the resurrection of the dead (e.g. Daniel 12.1–4). The hope is set in history, but it is not an evolutionary hope, to be realized through some gradual process or achievement within time and space, just by human obedience or endurance: the initiative remains with God: 'At that time thy people shall be delivered'.

And yet the widespread conviction that the Kingdom of God would come within history inevitably provoked the expectation that its coming would be historically recognizable. This was the situation when what we call New Testament times began. Those who, like Simeon, 'looked for the consolation of Israel' had no doubt that they would discern the signs of the Messiah. All this is assumed in the various reactions to the ministry of Jesus, which find their culmination in Peter's confession at Caesarea Philippi: 'Thou art the Christ' (Mark 8.29). The logical sequel to this recognition is given us in the fourth Gospel: 'When therefore the people saw the sign which he did, they said, This is of a truth the prophet that cometh into the world. Jesus therefore perceiving that they were about to come and take him by force, to make him King, withdrew into the mountain himself alone.' (John 6.14–15). His Kingdom, as the fourth evangelist was to record, is not of this world. Nevertheless, according to St Mark, Jesus entered Jerusalem to cries of 'Hosanna, Blessed is he that cometh in the name of the Lord. Blessed is the kingdom that cometh, the kingdom of our father

David: Hosanna in the highest.' (Mark 11.9–10). A number of evidences of this reaction to his ministry—to his words and deeds —are preserved in the Gospels: some of them, at least, apparently deliberately evoked by Jesus himself: all of them—as we shall presently see—deliberately recorded by the evangelists. Yet, in the sense which they seemed to require, the history of Jesus did not lead to the coming of the Kingdom of God in history. The Messiah did not inaugurate the visible rule of God in time and space. We might almost feel ourselves driven to Schweitzer's famous picture of Jesus expecting the Kingdom to come and then, since it did not come, throwing himself upon the wheel, believing that through his death it might revolve and the Kingdom of God be set up: believing in an intervention of God in history evoked *by* the historical career of the Son of man; believing—and (so I understand Dr Schweitzer) receiving no answer from his Father.

But that is not the origin of the faith of the apostles and evangelists. Whatever the hopes had been of those who companied with Jesus, their faith, their Christian faith, when at last it was kindled, was based upon an understanding of history that precluded such an expectation in time and space: the focal point of this understanding was the death of Jesus on the cross. There it was, according to the fourth evangelist, that Jesus said 'It is finished.' Where? Where it was clearly and unmistakably made manifest to the apostles that, in the rough and tumble of life, there was that in Jesus which was capable of no evolution. To this almost all the words from the cross—preserved as they were by different evangelists—bear witness: 'My God, my God, why hast thou forsaken me?'—'I thirst.'—'Father, into thy hands I commend my spirit.' What they saw there was no more than the fulfilment of the will of God in human flesh and blood. All human expectation of a life in history, leading up to and achieving a new order in history, is thereby ruled out.

I have used the expressions 'clearly and unmistakably made manifest to the apostles and evangelists'; 'what they saw there'. In doing so I am anticipating two experiences absolutely fundamental to their faith: the conviction that the risen Christ had appeared to them; the illumination which they believed they owed to the gift of the Holy Spirit. Now they saw the historical fact of crucifixion —the historical fact of history laid bare and revealed as without historical effect, as completely empty—and they beheld there, in it, through it, *resurrection*: the power of the living God meeting the perfect obedience of Man.

It will help us to understand this apostolic insight into the crucifixion of Jesus if we note the following facts.

1. Although the resurrection appearances of Jesus were essential to their faith (essential in the sense that they, partly at least, occasioned it), there is no sign whatever that they thought of the appearances themselves as though they in some sense constituted a final chapter in the earthly existence of Jesus Christ. In the fourth Gospel, the raising of Lazarus is important because it demonstrates the power of the living God in Jesus Christ to reverse the progress of death and corruption, and so was a great sign of his resurrection from the dead. Lazarus's restored existence is of no interest otherwise: it is in no sense a higher form of life on earth. Nor was it so with our Lord's own appearances risen from the dead. The well-known fact that the stories of these appearances fit awkwardly together, are not easily reconciled into a continuous narrative, seem sometimes to contradict each other in detail, and evidence at certain points different interpretations of his risen state of life, brings it home to us that these experiences in history were remembered and valued simply because of what they *meant,* although what they *meant*—resurrection from the dead, exaltation to the right hand of the Father, glorification with the glory which the Son had had from the beginning with the Father—was palpably beyond history, and in a sense indescribable in history.

2. Secondly, it was where crucifixion laid the meaning of the history of Jesus utterly bare that his resurrection could be apprehended; but immediately it had been apprehended there, the minds of the apostles were turned back to the previous history of Jesus Christ.

3. There they now saw what we can perhaps best describe as two things:

First, they saw the obedience of the Son of man—absolutely empty of self, entirely centred upon the Father, altogether looking to his will—as characterizing all that Jesus had said and done and been. The wholly significant truth about him; and by the light of this truth, all the partial truths of which they, as his disciples, and the people to whom he had ministered, had had glimpses during his ministry; must now be supplemented and corrected.

And secondly, just as they now saw crucifixion everywhere: history nowhere significant in itself in the sequence of time, but significant simply in its relation to the will of God beyond time, so they now saw resurrection everywhere: the power of the living God revealed, not in visible achievement, but to the eye of their faith, revealed and fulfilled in all that Jesus said and did and was. This is what the fourth evangelist seems to mean when he sums up the apostolic witness in the words 'we beheld his glory (the glory of the only begotten of the Father, full of grace and truth)' (John 1.14).

This twofold perception of crucifixion–resurrection remains in the synoptic Gospels to some extent episodic: we are shown the crucifixion laid bare, for instance, in the temptation stories, or in the scene in Gethsemane, in such parables as the Parable of the wicked Husbandman, or in sayings like 'the Son of man hath not where to lay his head'. And on the other hand, the theme of resurrection, the glory of the Son of man, comes to the surface in the accounts of the baptism and the transfiguration, in the great so-called nature miracles, in certain reactions of the crowds, in such sayings as 'if I by the finger of God cast out devils, then is the Kingdom of God come upon you.' But in fact even in the synoptic Gospels, the two themes are, to the evangelists, always inseparable: the grim predictions that the Son of man must suffer and be rejected cannot be uttered without the sequel 'and in three days rise again'. And in the fourth Gospel episodic, double, apprehension has almost entirely disappeared. The hour of the Son of man is the hour of his passion *and* of his glorification. The only conscious distinction is between the former partial understanding of the disciples as the events took place—which was in truth misunderstanding—and the fullness of understanding which they would receive only through his resurrection, by the light of his Spirit, in the light of which the gospel must be recounted for Christians, because it is the truth of God.

This is not an academic digression, to help us make an apology for the Gospels. It is all very much to the point; for it shows us that for Christians the history had to be recorded in the light of the power of the living God which is manifest in resurrection, and could not be truly recorded simply as crucifixion, that is, simply as having its meaning in achievement in time and space. Indeed, in time and space, to Christians, it achieved nothing whatever.

The apostles, as a result of their persuasion that they had seen Christ risen, and by the illumination which they believed to have come from the Holy Spirit of God, saw the truth of God in the crucifixion of Jesus, and then in his whole life and ministry. But with the same insight they were convinced that all this was of the utmost significance for their own history, and for the history of all mankind. If they had seen the life of Jesus Christ and his death to be meaningless in history as history, apart from the revelation of the power of the living God, so they had seen their own lives in the world, and all life, to be meaningless apart from that power. And as they had seen, by the light of the resurrection, the life and death of Jesus to be of infinite and ultimate and all-embracing significance (they called it glory), so they had seen their own lives as his disciples, and, potentially, the lives of all men in this world, to have this same hope, through his crucifixion and resurrection, written over them; even in their smallest and, from the point of view of this world, apparently most insignificant details; even, nay, above all, where their weaknesses and infirmities, and sufferings, were most in evidence.

The problem of history was forced upon the first Christians by their observation of life in the world starkly illuminated, de-romanticized, by the crucifixion of their Lord. In his case, no mere description of what eye-witnesses saw and of what he seemed to have experienced could solve the problem of the dereliction of the sinless, obedient, Son of God. This seen, no mere description of history in terms of history could satisfy any who, as they had done, had tried to accept history as something given by God for his recognizable good purpose here on earth. But the crucifixion met by resurrection, the obedience of the sinless Son of God unto death, achieving nothing as men reckon achievement—there they apprehended the glory and fulfilment of God. And now the whole of life became luminous by their faith and hope in Christ; everywhere crucifixion–resurrection offered them the mercy and glory of God.

Perhaps one might over-simplify the issue like this.

The Greeks tended to debase the historical as secondary, transitory, shadowy, and to try to find escape from it into the realm of eternal verity. Christians cannot describe resurrection like that.

The modern man tends to limit all reality to what is historical, and to be agnostic about all that cannot be achieved and observed in history. Resurrection cannot be described like this.

The Jews, with a clearer insight, perhaps, saw all history as waiting upon the intervention of God—but expected his intervention to achieve observable fruits in time and space, a tangible new order. That is not resurrection.

The Christians believe that the Kingdom of God is of God, by God's intervention and in the dimension of God's eternal order. But they believe it is wrought by the living power of God out of the flux of history, wherever that flux becomes identified with the crucifixion of Christ, lived and offered in faith in him, for God alone; and this truth, which has been revealed in the crucifixion and resurrection of our Lord; and which has been actually achieved once and for all then and there; means ultimately that every part and moment of human life on earth presents an opportunity of eternal glory through the creative power of God; not when used as a means of escape from history, but when used realistically, in obedience to God's will through faith in Christ.

CHAPTER 15

The Problem of Time

The tendency of people living in time and space, that is, in history, is to think that the problems raised by their experience here and now, can, and will, be solved within history. Ancient man thought that the righteous must eventually be justified by events, and the ungodly punished. Modern man tends to look forward to a good time assured by the advance of human science and knowledge. The Jews in Old Testament times, however, came, through their bitter experience, to believe that the problems they recognized could be solved by the intervention of God; but they tended, none the less, to suppose that the results of his intervention, the coming of his Kingdom, would be evident in time and space. In fact, they looked forward to a new world order still within history, bringing plenty, and prosperity, peace, and bliss.

For the disciples of Christ, the problem was rendered absolutely acute. For whereas the Jew could say : '*My* sin, *our* sin, is causing Almighty God to delay his intervention', the disciples, expecting the Kingdom of God to come with power, saw instead one they believed to be entirely without sin suffer a criminal's death, rejected by men, and apparently forsaken by God. They could not lay the blame on man. They could not hold sin responsible for the fact that the fate of Jesus in this world did not seem to make sense. The goodness of God himself must have seemed to be thrown into question. Could there be a God at all? Was the fool, after all, not justified in his scepticism?

That to argue like this is not to read modern reasoning back into the New Testament is shown by St Paul, who was clearly familiar with such thoughts. 'Now', he says, 'if Christ is preached that he hath been raised from the dead, how say some among you that there is no resurrection of the dead? But if there is no resurrection of the dead, neither hath Christ been raised; and if Christ hath not been raised, then is our preaching vain, your faith also is vain.' By 'preaching', I have no doubt that St Paul means the whole Christian gospel, and by 'faith', the whole Christian life in response to God.

He goes on, 'Yea, and we are found false witnesses of God; because we witnessed of God that he raised up Christ: whom he raised not up, if so be that the dead are not raised. For if the dead are not raised, neither hath Christ been raised: and if Christ hath not been raised, your faith is vain; ye are yet in your sins' (1 Cor. 15.12–17).

At every other point in history you can evade the crucial issue of history. You can say: 'Wait and see, the righteous will have their reward; or you can say, 'Yes, but that man is a sinner, it is just that he should perish miserably'; or you can say: 'It doesn't make sense to me, but you must take the rough with the smooth, and no doubt God in the long run will even things up.' But at this point, the crucifixion of Jesus Christ, you cannot run away like that. You cannot find an explanation within history that will enable you to rest satisfied with this history and nothing more. *The observable history demands what is beyond history to make sense of history.*

At this point, in the preceding chapter, we tried to show that when the Christians were assured that God had raised his Son from the dead, and as they began to understand what this meant, by the light which they believed to be his Holy Spirit, they came to recognize that the obedience which was displayed absolutely on the cross was characteristic of his whole life on earth. They were persuaded that the Kingdom of God had been realized in the flesh and blood of the Son of man; that Jesus Christ, truly the Messiah, the anointed King, had reigned on the cross; and, moreover, that his whole life had been, in God's sight, not failure but triumph, so that, looking back on it with the eye of the Spirit of God, they must rightly confess: 'There, there, in all that Jesus said, and did, and was, and suffered, *we beheld his glory*' (John 1.14). That is how all Christians, all men, must see him. Not, 'after the flesh'—that is, as he appeared in history to the outward eye of the unenlightened historical observer, but 'after the spirit'. So St Paul writes: 'Even though we have known Christ after the flesh, yet now we know him so no more' (2 Cor. 5.16).

This new, God-given, insight into the history of Jesus made sense, to the apostles and evangelists, of the whole of history: of the lives they were called to live in the world, of the very world itself. It also affected their understanding of time.

In some religions, time is regarded as an illusion. The only reality is what is conceived to be outside time, exempt from the continual movement from future to present, and from present to past.

In the prophetic religion of the Old Testament, however, time is taken very seriously indeed; for time seems to offer those who experience it something to use, in one way or another.

In those days, when there was as yet little concept of an after-life, the hope of a man was that he would be given long years in which to obey God; he wanted to have something to show for his life on earth. Man, according to the Old Testament, stands under the law of God. Duties are laid upon him—this he should do, that he must not do; and the nation, Israel, is bound as a people to God by a covenant. God will preserve his people, and bless their existence on earth, on condition that they keep his law in faithfulness and truth.

Perhaps there were ages when Israel could live in the present. But during the disillusioning days of the divided Kingdom, and later, after the fall of Jerusalem, when years and years of servitude and oppression set in, the natural reaction was that God must intervene to vindicate himself and to fulfil his part of the covenant. The Jews, therefore, began to look forward to a time or 'day' of the Lord, in the first place as the occasion of a display of his mercy upon his people, and of his vengeance of those who oppressed them.

But the prophets, aware of God's nature—that he is righteous, loving, holy, faithful, declared that the covenant between him and Israel demanded of Israel, and ultimately of every member of the nation, the qualities of the God to whom they believed themselves bound. Israel must be righteous as God is righteous,

> merciful as he is merciful,
> holy as he is holy,
> faithful as he is faithful.

As the nation is rotten with iniquity, as the rich oppress their poor brethren without mercy, as idolatry is rife, as the leaders of the nation put their faith in alliances with other nations rather than in God, the day of the Lord will be darkness and not light.

From such beginnings there grew up a developed expectation of the end of the present world order; of what would happen when present time reached its term—or, rather, was terminated by God. This expectation we call by the hard and hideous word 'eschatology', which means, the last things of God, that will be manifest when he intervenes finally in the present order.

The Day of the Lord—so the prophets taught—would be the Day of Judgement, when God would be fully revealed as he is, when his Kingdom would be inaugurated, when his authority would be vindicated in the sight of all nations, and his Spirit poured out upon all flesh.

The great prophets of Israel dwelt much upon this hope of God's final intervention, and many of their writings describe, or were in later times taken to describe, the events that would lead up to it, and how it would take place. Much of these writings was poetry, and inevitably employed pictorial imagery and symbolism, for they were attempting to describe events that baffled description. In the last centuries of Old Testament times a whole library of such books came into existence developing this imagery still further, and using it often in a dark, mysterious way, that makes it hard for us—and, indeed, made it hard for their own readers—to catch the complicated allusions. And more and more, since the Jews had little hope for the present, attention became focused upon the longed-for, though sometimes equally dreaded, future action of God, often visualized as beginning with a time of tribulation and woe, when the Messiah would come, and usher in the Day of the Lord.

It was against the background of such expectations, often conflicting in detail, that Christ's ministry took place, as we can see, for instance, from John the Baptist's 'Repent ye, for the Kingdom of Heaven is at hand'; or from the question he later conveyed to our Lord: 'Art thou he that cometh, or do we look for another?' And our Lord's answer to this question is a firm assertion that the expectation of the prophets was being fulfilled:

Tell John the things which ye do hear and see:
> The blind receive their sight,
>> and the lame walk,
> the lepers are cleansed,
>> and the deaf hear,
>> and the dead are raised up,
>>> and the poor have good tidings preached to them

And blessed is he whosoever shall find no occasion of stumbling in me.   (Matt. 11.4–6).

To anyone knowing the prophecies of Isaiah, associated as they were with the expectation of the coming of the Messiah and of the Kingdom of God, such an answer could mean only this, that our Lord saw in his own coming, and in what he was saying and doing, evidence that the last times were upon Israel, and that he was ushering in the longed-for time of God.

The disciples, following Peter's lead, seem to have recognized Jesus as the Christ, quite rightly, but to have persisted, right to his death, in interpreting his Messiahship in terms of popular expectation. They expected God to restore the Kingdom to Israel, under his authority as a supremely glorious leader and king. They rightly apprehended that the times were crucial; they rightly saw that the times seemed ripe for the end of the ages, the last things of God (although Jesus was careful to warn them that 'of that day or that hour knoweth no one, not even the angels in heaven, neither the Son, but the Father' (Mark 13.32).) But the last things of God for which they were looking were still that old bugbear, men's human ideas of how God would intervene, and what he ought to do.

But when they knew Jesus risen from the dead, their insight was very different. They realized then that the last things of God were upon men indeed, but these last things did not consist in the fulfilment of prophetic imagery in detail, but in the actualization of what that imagery had been trying to convey. Once more, this perception was no doubt forced upon them by the spectacle of Christ's crucifixion seen through his resurrection by the light of what they believed to be his Spirit. There, in that death on the cross, men had judged the sinless Son of God, rejecting him. That was the outward appearance, indeed, the outward fact. But they knew this to be God judging his people, and rejecting them. And as they were driven back by their new insight to reconsider all the events of Christ's life on earth, they saw that in all he said and did and was, God's final, ultimate judgement had confronted men, at every moment of his ministry.

It is worth looking through the theme of judgement in the fourth Gospel. You will find apparent contradictions, for that is the method of this Gospel. You will find, for instance, that Jesus contrasts the this-worldly judgement of men, their judgement within history, with his own judgement, like this :

'Ye judge after the flesh; (they fail to see him in relation to God)
  I judge no man.
Yea, and if I judge, my judgement is true; for I am not alone, but
  I and the Father that sent me' (John 8.15).

(He makes no human, no historical judgements, if he judges, it is
with the final judgement of God.)
  Earlier he has said:

'Neither doth the Father judge any man,
      but he hath given all judgement unto the Son;
  that all may honour the Son, even as they honour the Father.
He that honoureth not the Son, honoureth not the Father that
  sent him' (John 5.22–3).

Later, this becomes far more explicit. Jesus says to the man born
blind, when, his sight restored, he worships him,

'For judgement came I into this world,
      that they which see not may see;
      and that they which see may become blind.'

(Here he judges the Pharisees, who have no excuse because they
think they see.)
  The Word, which Jesus utters in his ministry, therefore brings
men and women, and the whole nation, under judgement; his
judgement, yes, but the ultimate judgement of God, because he is
the Word of God.
  Similarly, his ministry, culminating on the cross, bestows life,
the life which God alone can give; and his mercy bestows forgiveness, the forgiveness which is God's alone. In the fourth Gospel,
every discourse of Jesus ends in the tension between forgiveness and
judgement, for every discourse brings those who hear it the opportunity of accepting the Word of God which is Jesus Christ, or
rejecting him.
  Here we are veritably dealing with the last things of God:
Mercy, Judgement, Death, Life, offered to men, not only in the one
all-important moment of the crucifixion where resurrection is made
known and apprehended, but in every moment of Christ's direct
dealings with men in time. The whole weight of all that God wills
at the end of time comes to bear upon each moment. And now we

see that the right insight of the prophets, that our use of time is vitally important, and that God, at the last day, will reveal the secrets of men, and reward them for their use of the present opportunity, is justified, but far more urgently than they knew. For the last things of God do not intervene simply at the end of the time sequence; time itself is revealed, by the light of Christ, as demanding mercy and judgement, death and life, at every point at which his Word comes to bear. At every point it is not a question of referring man's actions to the law and hoping that, taking the rough with the smooth, the results will add up on the credit side at the future judgement; at every point it is a question of being found in Christ through faith in him, in the choice that every moment brings, or of rejecting him and the love and life he offers.

Now we see what this tension means to a Christian with the insight of St Paul. 'I know', he writes to the Romans, 'that in me, that is, in my flesh, dwelleth no good thing: for to will is present with me, but to do that which is good is not. For the good which I would I do not: but the evil which I would not, that I practise. But if what I would not, that I do, it is no more I that do it, but sin which dwelleth in me. I find then the law, that to me who would do good, evil is present. For I delight in the law of God after the inward man: but I see a different law in my members, warring against the law of sin which is in my members. O wretched man that I am! Who shall deliver me out of the body of this death?' (Rom. 7.18–24).

Here is St Paul frankly facing the fact, the condition, of man's life in the flesh, in history, in time. There is a world of difference between his situation and that of Christ on the cross, for at every point it is *his sin* which is brought home to him by his knowledge of the law of God. But it is precisely this situation of his in the flesh, in history, in time, that has been—so to say—invaded by Christ. You remember how he goes on: 'I thank God through Jesus Christ our Lord! So then I myself with the mind serve the law of God; but with the flesh the law of sin. There is therefore now no condemnation to them that are in Christ Jesus. For the law of the Spirit of life in Christ Jesus made me free from the law of sin and death' (Rom. 7.25—8.2).

Compare with this an equally famous passage in the Epistle to the Philippians. St Paul is warning his readers against 'evil workers', men who are drawing Christians back from faith in Christ to the old Judaism of law. We, he says, are the 'true circumcision, who worship by the Spirit of God, and glory in Christ Jesus, and have no confidence in the flesh'. Then he catalogues the reasons why he himself might have confidence in the flesh, more than anyone. He has been circumcised the eighth day. He is of the stock of Israel, of the tribe of Benjamin, a 'Hebrew of the Hebrews'—so far, 'flesh' might mean simply physical origin, race, privilege, but he goes on 'as touching the law, a Pharisee; as touching zeal, persecuting the Church, as touching the righteousness which is in the law, found blameless'. Here 'flesh' clearly means the use that man makes of his life, *his way of life,* his supposed religious activities. 'Howbeit, what things were gain to me, these have I counted loss for Christ. Yea verily, and I count all things to be loss for the excellency of the knowledge of Christ Jesus my Lord : for whom I suffered the loss of all things, and do count them but dung, that I may gain Christ, and be found in him, not having a righteousness of mine own, even that which is of the law, but that which is through faith in Christ, the righteousness which is of God by faith : that I may know him, and the power of his resurrection, and the fellowship of his sufferings, becoming conformed unto his death if by any means I may attain unto the resurrection of the dead' (Phil. 3.3–11).

Not only has Christ invaded St Paul's situation, and liberated him from the death which he sees reigning in his life, but St Paul's ambition is now to conform his whole life to the death of Christ. The horror of returning to Judaism and life by the law, of living by privilege of birth and by performance of behaviour, is that it is once more looking for results and values and achievements and rewards *within history.* His mind, and the mind of every Christian, must be identified with the mind of Christ, who saw the *meaninglessness* of history lived for itself, and lived entirely in obedience to God outside and beyond history. The truth about that human life of Christ, as St Paul and all the apostles had seen, is that it is met by the power of the living God, that it is therefore not the pitiable spectacle it appears to be, but glorious. St Paul therefore looks also for this glory : 'If by any means I may attain unto the resurrection from the dead.'

But here two words of warning must be uttered.

First, not for a moment does St Paul suggest that God will bestow glory upon him automatically. Glory comes only from Christ, whose strength, whose perfect obedience, can fill up all that is lacking in those for whom he suffered and died.

Secondly, although he is looking and living for what is beyond history, for resurrection, St Paul insists that the resurrection is not yet come. 'Not that I have already attained', he writes, 'or am already made perfect : but I press on, if so be that I may apprehend that for which I was apprehended by Christ Jesus.' St Paul is still in history : but he must try to live his life in conformity with that unique and all-important history of Jesus Christ, which he knows to have been met by the power of the living God raising him from the dead; and which he believes conveys the same power of the living God to those who live in history in faith in Jesus Christ, even though, except by the eye of faith, they cannot yet see the hope that this conveys.

Nevertheless, such is St Paul's understanding of the resurrection of Jesus Christ, that the world he lives in, while still in history, is the world he hopes that God is making, through the power of the resurrection, beyond history. In the Epistle to the Ephesians, the Ephesian Christians are told that 'God, being rich in mercy, for his great love wherewith he loved us, even when we were dead through our trespasses, quickened us (made us alive) together with Christ (by grace ye have been saved) and raised us up with him, and made us to sit with him in the heavenly places, in Christ Jesus' (Eph. 2.5–6). This hope of the Christians is so firmly rooted in the resurrection of Christ that Christians are to treat it as already the fact. This may be illustrated from three passages in St Paul's Epistles to the Corinthians. Their rhythmic, almost metrical, structure is notable.

In the great fifteenth chapter of the first Epistle to the Corinthians, which every mature Christian will wish read at his funeral, St Paul writes :

So also is the resurrection of the dead.
It is sown in corruption; it is raised in incorruption :
It is sown in dishonour; it is raised in glory :
It is sown in weakness; it is raised in power :
It is sown a natural body; it is raised a spiritual body.

(1 Cor. 15.42–4)

That might simply be a splendid affirmation of faith in resurrection to life from physical death—as indeed it is. But when we pass to the Second Epistle to the Corinthians, we find the same almost poetical pattern employed in an attempt to convey the whole experience of Christian apostles *now*.

'But we have this treasure in earthern vessels', writes St Paul, 'that the exceeding greatness of the power may be of God and not from ourselves.

We are pressed on every side,	yet not straitened;
perplexed,	yet not unto despair;
pursued,	yet not forsaken;
smitten down,	yet not destroyed;

always bearing about in the body the dying of Jesus, that the life also of Jesus may be manifested in our body.'

He virtually repeats this last sentence, to rub it in. 'For we which live are always delivered unto death for Jesus' sake, that the life also of Jesus may be manifested in our mortal flesh' (2 Cor. 4.7–11; cf. 1 Cor. 4.11–12).

A little further on in this Second Epistle to the Corinthians St Paul returns to the same theme, though here its pattern is much more complicated.

With the utmost gravity he is intreating the Corinthian Christians 'that they receive not the grace of God in vain', and he quotes Isaiah to show the urgency of the times:

'At an acceptable time I hearkened unto thee,
And in a day of salvation did I succour thee'—that is Isaiah.

Now St Paul:

Behold, now is the acceptable time;
Behold, now is the day of salvation.

Then he speaks of the ministry of the apostles, which cannot be understood except in this urgently pressing situation.

'In everything' he says 'commending ourselves as ministers of God,

in much patience,
in afflictions,

in necessities,
in distresses,
in stripes,
in imprisonments,
in tumults,
in labours,
in watchings,
in fastings.'

So far this is a list of hardships endured, some of them of external necessity, others through inward compulsion. He goes on

'in pureness,
in knowledge,
in long-suffering,
in kindness,
in the Holy Ghost,
in love unfeigned . . .'

More and more his thoughts are turning to what the power of the living God is making positively, though invisibly, out of these hardships :

'in the word of truth,
in the power of God,
in the armour of righteousness on the right hand and on the left,
by glory, and dishonour . . .'

The word glory seems to have pulled him up, and recalled to his mind that the outward appearance of this glory is the very opposite, dishonour; and this seems to make him hark back to his habitual pattern, and he goes on :

'by evil report   and good report;
   (i.e. evil report to the world, good report to God and to
      Christian insight)
as deceivers (that is what Christians are said to be)
                and yet true (as God knows)
as dying,   and behold we live
   (here is the hope of resurrection)

as chastened,	and not killed;
as sorrowful,	yet always rejoicing;
as poor,	yet making many rich;
as having nothing,	and yet possessing all things.'

(2 Cor. 6.1–10)

All these last eight verses are affirmations of resurrection apprehended by hope *now*. They do not mean that, however severely they are treated, the apostles can never be put to death—one of them already had been; nor that however sorry a time he had St Paul always smiled. They mean that although they were living on the very edge of death, in the most patently critical condition, they believed that the power of the living God was making out of their 'crucifixion' the perfection, the fullness, of all they seem to lack. Notice, for instance, that sentence:

as poor, yet making many rich.

That is not a casual piece of rhetoric: later in his Epistle St Paul is going to return to the metaphor in one of his finest interpretations of the crucifixion and resurrection of Jesus Christ. 'For ye know the grace of our Lord Jesus Christ, that, though he was rich, yet for your sakes he became poor, that ye, through his poverty, might become rich' (2 Cor. 8.9).

The poverty which the apostles experience *is*, by the power of the living God, the poverty deliberately embraced by Jesus Christ; and through their poverty, the riches which Christ's poverty bestows upon men is bestowed upon those to whom the apostles are sent.

St Paul and the other apostles were living on the frontiers of time; where at every moment he experiences he believes himself immediately and directly confronted by the end of time, by the last things of God, by the power of the living God.

Of course St Paul knows himself to be still in history. But his hope as a Christian is that our history in time and space may be by God's power conformed to the history of Jesus and raised up in the resurrection.

Of course St Paul knows himself to be still in time. In common with all the New Testament writers he looks forward to a future, and contrasts his present state with it:

> For now we see in a mirror darkly; but then face to face.
> Now I know in part; but then I shall know, even as I have been known.   (1 Cor. 13.9–12)

or again, using another metaphor,

> The night is far spent, and the day is at hand.   (Rom. 13.12)

Similarly, St Paul appeals to the past:

> While we were yet sinners, Christ died for us.   (Rom. 5.8)

> O foolish Galatians, who did bewitch you, before whose eyes Jesus Christ was openly set forth crucified?   (Gal. 3.1)

Yet the road from the present to the future is not one of gradual development. And the past cannot be left behind, as we leave it behind, but has crucial importance for the present.

St Paul's hope in Christ is not that he may become a better man, but to be clothed upon with the Holy Spirit, and raised up, with all Christians, in perfection. 'Seeing that ye have put off the old man with his doings, and have put on the new man, which is renewed unto knowledge after the image of him that created him' (Col. 3.10). 'Christ in you, the hope of glory: whom we proclaim, admonishing every man and teaching every man in all wisdom, that we may present every man perfect in Christ Jesus' (Col. 1.27–8).

It is this hope that makes the moral imperative so urgent. It is not that we shall be found of God if we obey his law—that is the old Judaism. It is that we must have the mind of Christ in us, we must be conformed to his death, we must live our lives sacrificially, as he did, looking only to the Father, in order that we may, as it were, leave room for the power of the living God; in order that we enable his mercy, his glory, to work upon us now, unto eternal life, rather than his judgement, his rejection. Therefore the death of Christ, although indeed a definite event in history, cannot drop back into the past. Where Christ is preached, his death confronts men directly now, at this very moment as your eyes scan this page; and with it the hope of resurrection, through humble faith in him.

To return for a moment to that hard word 'eschatology'. The presence of eschatological language, particularly in the Gospels, has made scholars and students of several generations very uncomfortable. Some have been tempted to say that it is not a really essential part of the gospel. Others have said that it is a relic of first-century thought. Others have thought of it as a half-way house, necessary for a time for the propagation of the gospel, but now to be translated into other language and quietly dropped. But the eschatology, the conviction that the last things of God are upon men, cannot be dismissed like this. No doubt, the imagery in which expectation had been set forth can be said to date. But something far bigger is being said, by means of this imagery. It is this : that in time, every point is confronted by God, and therefore all that that involves hangs upon every point and moment of time.

That is a grave and serious matter, for it means that our use of this given moment of time is subject to God's final judgement. But, although the first Christians were serious enough, they were never oppressed, weighed down, discouraged by this. Rather, because of the crucifixion–resurrection of their Lord, their situation was one of hope, joy, thanksgiving, peace. The Christians knew themselves, as it were, at the ends of time, exposed to the power of the living God. And their faith was such that they became aware only of his love, from which no peril, bodily, or spiritual, not even physical death itself, could separate them.

CHAPTER 16

The Problem of Knowledge

The early Christians seem to have believed that their own lives, in history, were being given meaning and content by the power of the living God in the resurrection of the dead, provided that, through their faith and through his Holy Spirit, their lives—their history— were identified with the death of Jesus Christ in history. And they seem to have believed that they were living at the extreme end of time, confronted at every point, every moment, with the final alternative of God's judgement or mercy. Moreover, such was their understanding of the crucifixion and resurrection, such their resultant faith in Jesus Christ, that they lived their lives *in hope,* believing their situation, however grave, however over-clouded with suffering and constant proximity to physical death, to be one of joy, thanksgiving, peace. Indeed, what was virtually a new word had entered their vocabulary, and came to dominate more and more their thought about God and what they believed to be their experience of God: a word that before the last books of the New Testament had been written was to be used by itself to describe God: the word 'love'. In the most famous of all his purple passages St Paul saw in the relationship which this word 'love' describes a relationship that bridges the gulf of physical death. His whole outlook derives from the certainty of this present and at the same time eternal relationship. The winding-up of the present age, the remaining years of our life on earth, the shadow of death itself— all these are almost a matter of indifference to him in comparison with the present knowledge of God's love. God's last things confront us now, as immediately as they ever will; and the man who sets his hope only upon history, within time; who says, 'This will I do, and that, and perhaps other things before the end', is dethroning God from his situation over against us here and now, and forcing his own 'ego' into the position which—if we are to learn from the crucifixion and resurrection of Jesus—God alone can occupy. Compare with this St Paul's unegotistic desire that 'with all boldness, as always, so now also, Christ shall be magnified in my body, whether by life or by death. For me to live is Christ, and to die is gain. But if to live in the flesh—if this is the fruit of my work, then what I shall choose I wot not. But I am in a strait betwixt the two, having the desire to depart, and be with Christ; for it is very far better; yet to abide in the flesh is more needful for your sake' (Phil. 1.20–4). Compare this again with the ordinary Christian's attitude to the possibility of death, in our day, and you will begin to see how Christian hope had completely uprooted St Paul from all that makes us cling on to survival here on earth. He would far rather be with Christ, yet he believes that he will be kept in the flesh for a time at least, for the sake of those committed to his care —'for their progress and joy in the faith' (Phil. 1.25). He is not even calculating the desirability of his survival by this-worldly criteria, but only in accordance with what he supposes to be the exigencies of the gospel. His attitude is based, of course, upon his knowledge of God. And so this brings us easily to the subject of this chapter. For if we have seen that there is a problem of the meaning of history which is not solved by the mere description of what is seen and experienced; and that there is a problem of man's use of time which is not solved by simply distinguishing between what is good and bad; we are now reminded that there is a problem of knowledge that is not solved by the manner in which men observe and see and know.

St Paul and other apostolic thinkers had probably considered the problem of knowledge more explicitly than the other problems with which we are concerned. It was impossible to live side by side with men of the Greek world without being conscious of the great, organized pursuit of human wisdom and knowledge that had by that time been in progress for centuries. On the other hand, the Jews also had a tradition of wisdom based upon the knowledge of God. And even if there ran through much of the Old Testament the refrain 'the fear of the Lord is the beginning of wisdom', the Law of Israel, implemented by the tradition of the elders, was in fact in normal Jewish thought the mediator between man and God, and wisdom was to be found in keeping the commandments of God.

It was indeed largely because of these two different, almost dia-metrically-opposed, conceptions of knowledge or wisdom, that St Paul had been driven to write some of his earlier Epistles. On the one hand, the Epistle to the Galatians seems to have been written because certain men were leading the Christians back to a religion based upon 'Law'. On the other hand, in the Epistles to the Corinthians, St Paul seems to have been confronted with a wave of arrogant 'knowledge', which smacked rather of the speculation of the Greek schools.

At the end of his life, these problems were still being forced upon him, for the pursuit of wisdom, in one form or another, was the obsession of the age; and such a fundamentally un-Greek religion as Judaism was inclined to try to commend itself for those so obsessed by presenting itself as a system of wisdom or knowledge. It was in this situation that the problem of knowledge formulated itself for St Paul and the other Christian apostles, and it was in meeting this situation that they appear to have discerned the Christian solution of this problem.

At the beginning of the Epistle to the Romans, which St Paul may perhaps have regarded as a systematic statement of Christian theology, he makes two radical statements about human knowledge of God.

First, he maintains that the truth of God ought to be accessible to men from the creation. 'For the invisible things of (God) since the creation of the world are clearly seen, being perceived through the things that are made, even his everlasting power and divinity' (Rom. 1.20).

Secondly, St Paul says that men 'knowing God, glorified him not as God, neither gave thanks; but became vain in their reasonings and their senseless heart was darkened. Professing themselves to be wise, they became fools, and changed the glory of the incorruptible God for the likeness of an image of corruptible man, and of birds, and of four-footed beasts, and creeping things' (Rom. 1.21–3).

Again, St Paul writes to the Corinthians 'the world through its wisdom knew not God' (1 Cor. 1.21).

Earlier, we quoted St Paul's description of the Christian war in which, though we walk in the flesh, we do not war according to the flesh (for the weapons of our warfare are not of the flesh, but mighty before God to the casting down of strongholds); casting down imaginations, and every high thing that is exalted against the knowledge of God (2 Cor. 10.3–5).

So far as the wisdom of the Greco-Roman world is concerned,

St Paul sees it as vitiated because it is man-centred, based upon human observation, human reasoning, and human arrogance. The Greeks, as he calls them, are therefore incapable of true knowledge of God—not because the created world does not bear witness to God, but because they have a conception of man and of man's place in the world that makes it impossible for them to perceive this witness. Knowledge of this kind assumes that man, as an undisturbed observer, can investigate the truth of things in detachment from them, assessing them simply by their function and properties in time and space, by their interrelation with each other, and by their usefulness for man's present purposes. It assumes, further, that man can observe similarly the facts of life in this world, evaluating it for what it is worth here and now, without reference to what St Paul calls 'the invisible things of God, his everlasting power and divinity'; and above all without any recognition that the very existence of the man who observes, in time and space, implies a relation between himself and God, and throws all detached observation—above all when it becomes speculation about God—entirely into question.

Accordingly, St Paul is most sensitive to any re-emergence in the Christian Church of what he would have called 'knowledge after the flesh'; or 'knowledge as of this world', particularly, as had happened in Corinth, when this supposed knowledge seemed to exalt the man who possesses it, to enable him to judge others as ignorant of the truth of God, and to give him something to stand upon in his own sight and right before God.

How then does he deal with this knowledge? He is concerned with the particular problem of forward-thinking Corinthian Christians who are saying that as idols are nothing it is right for Christians to eat meat sacrificed to idols, and who are thereby scandalizing their less forward-thinking brethren, who cannot believe that a Christian should sit at meat in a pagan temple. 'Now concerning things sacrificed to idols', he writes, 'we know that we all have knowledge'—St Paul is always conciliatory—and besides, as we shall see later, there *is* a Christian knowledge. He goes on 'knowledge puffeth up, but love edifieth. If any man thinketh he knoweth anything, he knoweth not yet as he ought to know; but if any man love God, the same *is known of him*' (1 Cor. 8.1–3). There is no road to the truth through arrogant human knowledge, only

325

through love—and now what St Paul says, most significantly, is not 'if any man love God, *the same knows him*' but 'if any man love God, the same is known of him.' This reminds us of the phrase 'Then shall I know, even as I have been known' (1 Cor. 13.12).

It is, as we have said, not the Greeks only who are disturbing the Church with a wrong kind of knowledge, but also those who attach importance to exact human behaviour and performance. In the Epistle to the Galatians, who had been greatly disturbed by such people, perhaps active Judaizers with a gloze of Christian doctrine, St Paul writes: 'Howbeit at that time, not knowing God, ye were in bondage to them which by nature are no gods; but now, after ye have come to know God, *or rather to be known of God,* how turn ye back again to the weak and beggarly rudiments, whereunto ye desire to be in bondage over again? Ye observe days, and months, and seasons, and years' (Gal. 4.8–10). Here again, a Christian knowledge of God is assumed to be possible—ye have come to know God—but St Paul immediately restates it: 'or rather to be known of God'. Clearly, whatever sub-Christian view of knowledge he is combating, he is ill at ease with any theory of knowledge of which man is the agent, upon which man thinks to stand. In the Christian view, man stands *under* God's knowledge of him, he is known by God. The most perhaps that we can say is that man begins to know God when he acknowledges that he is known by God; for that recognition dethrones man from the exalted, central, position of the observer, and defines him simply in relation to God.

Why does St Paul tend to handle the idea of knowledge like this? The key is no doubt in his single-minded grasp of the gospel of Christ crucified and risen. Christ had sent him, not to baptize but to preach the gospel; not in wisdom of words, 'lest the cross of Christ should be made void'. He goes on 'the word of the cross is to them that are perishing foolishness; but unto us which are being saved it is the power of God. For it is written, I will destroy the wisdom of the wise, and the prudence of the prudent will I reject' . . . 'The Jews', he says, 'ask for signs, and the Greeks seek after wisdom: but we preach Christ crucified, unto Jews a stumbling-block and unto Gentiles foolishness; but unto them that are called, both Jews and Greeks, Christ the power of God, and the wisdom of God.' Therefore, when he came to Corinth, St Paul determined, as he says, 'not to know anything among you save Jesus

Christ, and him crucified.' Their faith should not stand in the wisdom of men, but in the power of God.

Even St Paul supposes that there *is* a Christian knowledge, and our purpose for the rest of this chapter is to try to see what this involves.

First of all, it is clear that knowledge springs directly from the spectacle, or the preaching, of the crucifixion of Christ, viewed, or heard, with understanding. The Galatians who had 'come to know God' had had Jesus Christ crucified openly placarded before their eyes—that was the horror to St Paul of their relapse, for they had evidently responded rightly to the cross of Christ, receiving the Spirit by the hearing of faith—and were now seeking perfection in the flesh—in the vanity of human religious performances when thought of as themselves the basis of salvation. Christian knowledge implies identification with Christ crucified, through reception of the gospel. The 'ego' of the person who observes and knows has to be crucified as effectively in men and women confronted by the cross, as our Lord showed all human self-centred observation to be excluded by his own obedience to the Father even unto death.

Secondly, Christian knowledge proceeds from the recognition that we are known by God; from the insight, that is to say, given by the resurrection of Jesus Christ crucified. One day we shall know what this means—but that does not matter now. The triumphant news, the truth and the grace that makes all the difference, the glory that spells perfection for us, is that we are already known by God. For they mean that we are exposed to the power of the living God; and if only we have faith in Jesus Christ, we know that this means for us not judgement but forgiveness and love.

Thirdly, the recognition that we are known by God means that we must believe that the Holy Spirit is at work upon us. To modern Christians, the working of the Holy Spirit denotes, I suppose, first of all, illumination, guidance; the witness in our conscience as a result of which we know what choice to make. We pray frequently that the Holy Spirit may guide statesmen in conference, or the proceedings of a committee or even of a Church Council. And we do well. This undoubtedly follows from the understanding of the Holy Spirit. But, as we observed in the previous chapter, the outpouring by God of his Holy Spirit was part of the expectation connected, at any rate in New Testament times, with the advent of

327

the last things of God; and Christian understanding of the Holy Spirit did not limit his activity to illumination or guidance. Rather, the Holy Spirit meant, as it were, the power of the living God in action; and the Holy Spirit illuminated men, through the crucifixion and resurrection of Jesus Christ, by convincing them of this action, in their hearts, in their lives, in the Christian community, in the world at large.

It is important to notice that in the New Testament the work of the Holy Spirit is always directly related to the revelation of Jesus Christ. Nowadays we tend to be tritheists—to think of three Gods working within a unity of purpose but more or less independently. Such a conception is entirely foreign to the New Testament.

In the eighth chapter of his Epistle to the Romans St Paul continually alternates between mention of Christ and mention of the Spirit. He starts from the tremendous affirmation that 'The law of the Spirit of life in Christ Jesus made me free from the law of sin and death' (Rom. 8.2).

How has this come about?

'God, sending his own Son in the likeness of sinful flesh, and as an offering for sin, condemned sin in the flesh'—here is the crucifixion–resurrection of Christ—'that the ordinance of the law might be fulfilled in us, who walk not after the flesh but after the Spirit'—that is, not according to this world we know, in which we always seem to have another chance, not by present experience centred on ourselves, not in our own human perception and strength; but in recognition that God confronts us finally, therefore by hope in him, therefore in the power of God (Rom. 8.2–3).

For three or four verses St Paul continues to differentiate between those who mind the things of the flesh and those who mind the things of the Spirit—the one mind is death, the other mind life and peace, for to mind the flesh is to war against God—but St Paul's readers are not in the flesh but in the spirit, '*if so be that the Spirit of God dwelleth in you*' (Rom. 8.4–9). The great dividing line can now be drawn. St Paul goes on 'If any man hath not the Spirit of Christ, he is none of his. And if Christ is in you, the body is dead because of sin; but the Spirit is life because of righteousness. But if the Spirit of him that raised up Jesus from the dead dwelleth in you, he that raised up Christ Jesus from the dead shall quicken also your mortal bodies through his Spirit that dwelleth in you' (Rom.

328

8.9–11). St Paul is not here concerned to state the basis of Christian belief in the Holy Trinity; although all that he says is very pertinent for this belief. But the effect of this passage seems to be this:

The Spirit which dwells in the Christians is the Spirit of God, the Spirit of him which raised up Jesus from the dead. Yet—and St Paul seems simply to be saying the same thing another way—Christians have the Spirit of Christ. Indeed, Christ himself should be in them. And this presence of the Spirit of God, of Christ, is the assurance that, just as God raised up Jesus from the dead, so, through his indwelling Spirit, he will 'quicken', that is, make alive, the Christians' mortal bodies.

If this is the Christian position, living after the spirit in the spirit because the Spirit dwells in them; exposed, therefore, to the same power of the living God of which they have witnessed, or heard about, the effects, in the crucifixion–resurrection of their Lord, it follows that they must *mortify,* that is, put to death, *by the spirit,* the deeds of the body—unlike those who live after the flesh and therefore die with it. This mortification no doubt describes exactly the mind of Christ, which made his whole life and death an act in which human egotism was dethroned and his Father's will entirely obeyed. It is absolutely essential that Christ's mind should dominate the lives of the Christians; absolutely essential that they should *assent to and themselves will* God's work of crucifixion–resurrection in them (Rom. 8.12–13). Now it is possible to speak of the guidance of the Spirit. 'For as many as are led by the Spirit of God, these are the Sons of God.' The guidance of the Spirit means assenting to his final work in us, perhaps through us (Rom. 8.14).

With the statement that men thus guided are the sons of God, St Paul recalls the baptism of those to whom he writes. What happened to them then? They were removed from a situation of bondage and fear—bondage to the flesh, fear of the judgement of God upon those who live after the flesh. They were adopted as sons. They rightly addressed God as Jesus was accustomed to address him, by the most intimate term that a Jewish child could use for his father, Abba (Rom. 8.15). To men in this situation St Paul can state the resurrection hope—and note that as he does so he returns to his constant theme that where Christians suffer in this world, there they may be all the more certain of glory already by God's act theirs albeit not yet experienced: 'The Spirit himself beareth witness with our Spirit, that we are children of God; and if children, then heirs; heirs of God, and joint-heirs with Christ; if so be that we suffer with him, that we may be also glorified with him' (Rom. 8.16–17). This is another passage which we know too well to give full weight to.

The rest of the chapter is all very much to our subject. St Paul goes on to elaborate the Christian hope: 'the sufferings of this present time are not worthy to be compared with the glory which shall be revealed to us-ward'—remember, those to whom he was writing *were* suffering, not living luxuriously and undisturbed in ideal conditions. The whole creation, in St Paul's view, hangs also in earnest expectation upon the revelation of the sons of God—the final realization of glory—participating in the hope revealed to the Church. The Christians therefore groan within themselves, waiting for their adoption as sons, to wit, the redemption of their body. 'For by hope were we saved: but hope that is seen is not hope: for who hopeth for that which he seeth? But if we hope for that which we see not, then do we with patience wait for it' (Rom. 8.18–25). Hope is the ground of the Christian life. Hope, indeed, is the characteristic of all life in this present flesh, history, experience, that is lived towards God, as opposed to life lived in the flesh after the flesh. St Paul carries this hope out right into creation, because it is to him the truth about all created things, seen in relation to the power of the living God: all are capable of the perfection God revealed and effected in Christ, all therefore are subjects for hope.

In this situation, everything is on the side of the Christians. They are helped by the intercession of the Spirit. 'He that searcheth the hearts knoweth what is the mind of the Spirit, because he maketh intercession for the saints according to the will of God' (Rom. 8.27). Then follows this great statement—a firm statement of Christian knowledge: 'We know that to those that love God all things work together for good, even to them that are called according to his promise. For whom he foreknew, he also foreordained to be conformed to the image of his Son, that he might be the first-born among many brethren: and whom he foreordained, them he also called: and whom he called; them he also justified: and whom he justified, them he also glorified' (Rom. 8.28–30). At every point knowledge is knowledge of what we cannot observe but what we are to believe is finally true, that God is doing everything for us,

everything for the perfecting of his creation. This is what the Spirit
revealed to us—and it is the Spirit that is achieving it and interceding so that he may achieve it in us; but all this is placarded
before our eyes in Christ crucified and risen, and it is the Spirit of
Christ which constrains us to be conformed to his death, that we
may be raised in him. So St Paul passes to another of his purple
passages. And once again the word 'love' comes irresistibly into
what he is saying. In tribulation, distress, persecution, famine,
nakedness, peril, sword—all the patently evil experiences which he
and his fellow Christians were well acquainted with—they are more
than conquerors through him that loved them (Rom. 8.35–7)—a
cry of triumph as significant in the context of Christian experience
as was the cry attributed, in the fourth Gospel, to Christ on the
Cross, 'It is finished!' (John 19.30). Paul ends, 'I am persuaded,
that neither death, nor life, nor angels, nor principalities, nor things
present, nor things to come, nor powers, nor height, nor depth, nor
any other creature, shall be able to separate us from the love of God
which is in Christ Jesus our Lord' (Rom. 8.38–9).

In the fourth Gospel, where there is a more developed doctrine
of the Holy Spirit than anywhere else, we find a similar intimate
relation between the Holy Spirit and the Christ. To begin with, it
is made clear during the Gospel that after the crucifixion, when the
Spirit is breathed into the Christians by the risen Christ, the disciples will understand the meaning of all that Jesus said and did,
as well as of his death. In those great discourses in the Upper Room
the same function is attributed to the Spirit. 'I will pray the Father,
and he shall give you another comforter, that he may be with you
for ever, even the Spirit of truth; whom the world cannot receive;
for it beholdeth him not, neither knoweth him; but ye know him;
for he abideth with you, and shall be in you. 'When the Comforter
is come, whom I will send unto you from the Father, even the
Spirit of truth, which proceedeth from the Father, he shall bear
witness of me : and ye also bear witness, because ye have been with
me from the beginning'—notice, that the joint witness of Spirit and
spotless is directed back upon the life of Christ.

'When he, the Spirit of truth is come, he shall guide you into all
the truth : for he shall not speak from himself; but what things
soever he shall hear, these shall he speak : and he shall declare
unto you the things that are to come.' (This could perhaps be better

translated 'he shall make known to you the meaning of things that happen'). 'He shall glorify me, for he shall take of mine, and shall declare it unto you. . . .'

'The Comforter, even the Holy Spirit, whom the Father will send in my name, he shall teach you all things, and bring to your remembrance all that I said unto you.'

The essential point for our present purpose is that the function of the Spirit is not to reveal to the Christians, as time goes by, all kinds of new truths revealed by Jesus Christ. Rather, as time goes by, he will reveal more fully, to Christians, or according to their present needs, or in relation to their present experiences, the meaning of the one truth revealed in the life and death and resurrection of Jesus Christ. There is no understanding of crucifixion–resurrection of Jesus Christ except through the Holy Spirit; there is no revelation by the Holy Spirit that does not illuminate the crucifixion–resurrection of Jesus Christ.

Consequently, those apostolic Christians knew themselves confronted by God in two different events, which their faith held close together, so that each interpreted the other; indeed, so that these two events became inseparable and as it were one event in their experience. On the one hand, the life and death of Jesus Christ, understood in the light of his resurrection, interpreted therefore by his Holy Spirit; on the other hand, the present time through which they were passing, their whole contemporary situation, which they accepted equally as from God, and as equally exposed to the power and promise of his Holy Spirit. What happened in Corinth, as we have seen, gave St Paul deeper insight into the mind of Christ as disclosed in his ministry; what happened in Ephesus enabled St John to understand certain episodes in the Gospels. Both St Paul and St John could interpret the working of God's love for the Christians committed to their charge, in situations developing twenty, sixty, years after the crucifixion, because of their concentration upon the love of God in the life and death of their Lord. Those are practical examples of growth in Christian knowledge.

There are two other characteristics of Christian knowledge in the New Testament which are illuminating. First, we must notice that Christian knowledge thrives equally upon experiences that men would call good and bad; if anything, more confidently upon bad experiences, since there is a danger in what makes us too comfortable, too undisturbed in the flesh. Both by contrast and analogy the experiences of this life point us to the power of the living God: the good because they show us by analogy what God is making out of our experience here, out of the things with which we have to do; they point towards God's perfection of them; the bad, because they assure us again, by contrast, that God's will is perfect. In Christ's use of parable we find that the same thing is happening; all is grist to his mill; anything in human experience, good or bad, may be seen to point towards the Kingdom of Heaven, by contrast, or by analogy. Following Christ's example, the apostles find equally in the rough and in the smooth of Christian life in the world, means by which Christians should bear fruit unto God; but, when we say 'bear fruit unto God', what we are really speaking of is the fruit of the Spirit, which God brings out of the smooth and the rough; love (of God); joy, in his promises; peace, with him; long-suffering, because the present tribulation passes; kindness, because we have received mercy; goodness, because our hope is perfection; faithfulness, because we must cleave to him; meekness, because our hope is crucifixion; temperance, because we must not be rooted to this life.

The second point is this; good works. Good works, according to St Paul, are done by those who, 'by patience, in well-doing, seek for glory, and honour, and incorruption (Rom. 2.7); who look, that is, for fruits beyond this life; the fruits that only God can give, resurrection; who assent therefore to God's purpose for everything and identify themselves with the invisible working of the Holy Spirit, the unseen power of the living God, as made known to us in the crucifixion–resurrection of Christ.

To sum up, briefly—Christian knowledge is knowledge directed wholly towards God, and wholly towards God's action. Because we are still in the flesh, we can only see darkly and know in part; therefore, it is a knowledge demanding at every point *faith*—the absolute opposite of the knowledge of the modern world, of modern science, which refuses to know unless it can verify in experience, *check*. Christian knowledge is not so much an insight into the inscrutable nature of God, as the firm apprehension of what God is doing, of the tremendous, irresistible, all-embracing power of the living God. The key to the working of this power, the only key by which we can know, is the crucifixion of Jesus Christ, interpreted to those confronted by the assurance of his resurrection through the Holy Spirit. But the scope of the knowledge that ensues is all embracing. Everything is to be seen in relation to the power of the living God. We do not understand the flesh—whether it be our own mortal lives or the context in which we are set here on earth, other people, or the things we use—unless we can see them calling out for, and so pointing towards, the perfection that God alone can give them. When we thus see them pointing beyond their present being, beyond themselves, then we begin to know them for what God means them to be, because we see them 'in hope', making room for the power of the living God. It follows that, when we begin to see what a thing, or an experience, is meant to signify in relation to God, pointing beyond itself, then in a sense, reading God's promise over it, we can say that it *is* what it signifies. That is true Christian Knowledge of it. And that is very hard language indeed. But there is a translation in the words of St Paul : 'To them that love God all things work together for good.' Those that love God know that the power of the living God is working upon all things for good, and therefore see all things in the light of the promise of his perfection.

There is another passage in which St Paul defines his knowledge. 'Yea, verily, and I count all things to be loss for the excellency of the knowledge of Christ Jesus my Lord : for whom I suffered the loss of all things, and do count them but dung, that I may gain Christ, and be found in him, not having a righteousness of mine own, even that which is of the law, but that which is through faith in Christ, the righteousness which is of God by faith : that I may know him, and the power of his resurrection, and the fellowship of his sufferings, becoming conformed unto his death; if by any means I may attain unto the resurrection from the dead.'

CHAPTER 17

The Problem of Personality

In the last chapter we quoted much from St Paul, and he is bound to be heard again. But let us open up this subject, by asking how the fourth Gospel presents the personality of Jesus Christ. The author of the fourth Gospel is well aware that there are two ways of looking at the history of Jesus Christ. On the one hand, his history is the record of humiliation, of apparent failure, of the Son of man exposing the inadequacy of the positive but historical interpretations put upon his person by the Jews, and even by his own disciples. His works of compassion evoke faith, as they are meant to do. But it is not that faith in God which is the purpose of the gospel, and Jesus distrusts it. He is the Christ, the Messiah—yes—but he escapes in case the people should take him and try to make him a king as this world knows kings. At the end of his long discourses to his disciples on the eve of his crucifixion, they say: 'Lo, now speakest thou plainly, and speakest no proverb. Now know we that thou knowest all things, and needest not that any man should ask thee.' He *had* spoken plainly, and what he had just said was a tremendous pointer towards the truth; but he answers: 'Do you now believe? Behold, the hour cometh, yea is come, that ye shall be scattered every man to his own, and shall leave me alone' (John 16.29–32). It is possible, as St Paul puts it, to know Jesus Christ 'after the flesh', to attach to him a significance within history with exclusively historical effects, based upon historical achievement. Yet, on the other hand, as we have seen, when the crucifixion has shown that any such interpretation is meaningless, when the Holy Spirit has opened the eyes of the disciples and they apprehend Christ—to use Pauline language again—'after the spirit', then the whole of his human life becomes full of meaning beyond itself, and at every point, as the fourth evangelist records it, the reader with apostolic insight 'beholds his glory, glory as of the only begotten of the Father, full of grace and truth' (John 1.14).

If this latter way of looking at the history of the Son of man is

335

the right one, the truth about him defies us until we behold his 'glory'. What is his glory?

Some Johannine paradoxes

The fourth Gospel puts this in paradoxes. For example:

1. 'No man hath seen God at any time' (John 1.18).
   'He that hath seen me hath seen the Father' (John 14.9).

It is impossible to see God with the eyes of the flesh, for God is Spirit. Yet, those who behold Jesus with the eyes of the Spirit see the Father.

2. 'Why do ye not understand my speech? Even because ye cannot hear my word' (John 8.43).
   'I spake not from myself; but the Father which sent me, he hath given me a commandment, what I should say, and what I should speak' (John 12.49).

What Jesus says is unintelligible except as the Word of God; yet it is none the less his Word, delivered in human words.

3. 'I can of myself do nothing' (John 5.30).
   'My meat is to do the will of him that sent me, and to accomplish his work' (John 4.34).
   'My father worketh even till now, and I work' (John 5.17).
   'If I do not the works of the Father, believe me not' (John 10.37).

All that Jesus does is entirely ineffective, except as the final work of God himself which, on the cross, at the point of utter visible impotence, he declares completed: 'It is finished' (John 19.30).

We could add further paradoxes of this sort—Christ judges no man, yet 'his judgement is true' (John 8.15). Christ says, 'If I bear witness of myself, my witness is not true' (John 5.31). But he also says: 'I am he that beareth witness of myself, and the Father that sent me beareth witness of me' (John 8.18).

The theme is always the same. Nothing that Jesus says or does has any significance as a human opinion or act *in itself* (note those words *in itself*—they must be added). Seen as the truth or act of

336

God they are seen to have absolute significance *as human words or acts in history.* What Jesus said and did, apprehended as the speech and action of an individual man, in history, has no consequence beyond its event, historically speaking, completely ineffective. This is made terribly clear by his isolated passion and death on the cross. What Jesus said and did, apprehended as the Word and Work of the Father, is of supreme consequence for every moment of history and time.

The use of the verb 'send' in relation to Christ and the Church

How then are we to understand the personality of Jesus? It may be helpful to examine the use in the fourth Gospel of a phrase which has already been quoted twice above. The Church for which the fourth Gospel was written treasured, above all and quite rightly, the memory of the apostles—all of them perhaps dead by the time it was written, if we take the view that the fourth Gospel was written after the death of the last surviving apostle, John, to perpetuate his teaching. Yet, the word apostle, which means someone 'sent', appears in the fourth Gospel only once, in the significant phrase 'A servant is not greater than his Lord; neither an apostle greater than he that sent him.' This is a shrewd reminder that the revered pillars of the Church were important only *because Jesus had sent them.* There is other evidence of the same intention (John 4.38), and it is interesting to note that in this Gospel our Lord describes John the Baptist also as having been sent (John 3.28). But in this very Gospel, not once but often (to be exact, seventeen times—3.17; 3.34; 5.36; 5.38; 6.29; 6.57; 7.29; 8.42; 10.36; 11.42; 17.3; 17.8; 17.18; 17.21; 17.23; 17.25; 20.21) Jesus describes himself as he whom the Father has sent.

The intention seems to be twofold.

First, to show that Jesus has no significance *in himself by himself,* but entire significance as the apostle, the emissary, we might almost say, the plenipotentiary, of the Father.

Secondly, to show that it is vitally important that the faith focused upon Jesus should, as it were, pass through Jesus and come to rest upon the Father.

337

The Jews misunderstand the personality of Jesus

Consequently, the significance of Jesus is completely misunderstood by the Jews when they try to understand him simply by reference to his supposed human origin. Such questions as 'Can any good thing come out of Nazareth?' (John 1.46), and 'What, doth the Christ come out of Galilee?' (John 7.41) reflect their fatal obsession. Referring to his human origin, some of the Jews say: 'We know this man whence he is: but when the Christ cometh, no one knoweth whence he is' (John 7.27). As usual in this Gospel, they are wrong and yet right. They insinuate, perhaps, as was commonly said among the Jews, that he was born of fornication (John 8.41); or say that he is a Samaritan and possesssed with a devil (John 8.48), so determined are they to repudiate the truth of his statements by reference to their worldly estimation of his origin, and the origin of his powers.

Christ's counter-affirmation: his origin and destiny

Those who take this line, who try to dismiss the words and works of Jesus as coming from one whose origin is merely human, think that they themselves can stand upon their own descent from Abraham—indeed, they go further, and say 'We have one Father, even God.' Our Lord's answer is: 'If God were your Father, ye would love me: for I came forth and am come from God; for neither have I came of myself, but he sent me' (John 8.41–2). Moreover, using the very name by which the Jews in the Old Testament knew God, Jesus goes on to say, 'Before Abraham, I am' (John 8.58). Although he is truly man, the Son of man, born of a woman, flesh and blood, there is a whole world of difference between him and the unbelieving Jews, as is shown infallibly by his obedience to the Father, and their rejection of him: 'Ye are from beneath'; he says 'I am from above: ye are of this world; I am not of this world. I said therefore unto you, that ye shall die in your sins; for except ye believe that I am he, ye shall die in your sins'

338

(John 8.23–4). The personality of Jesus can be understood only by reference to his origin and to his destiny. Whereas all that is flesh originates in history and, apart from God's intervention, ends in history, in death, Jesus can say—*indeed* speaking quite plainly : 'I came out from the Father, and am come into the world : again, I leave the world, and go unto the Father.' Any interpretation of him which does not hold fast to this falls short of belief. Only so understood can we understand not only in what sense he is the Christ, in what sense the Son of man; but even what it means that he is Son of God. But—and this is the point—by the light of the Holy Spirit, all that Jesus says and does and *is* in this world, kindles this same, solely-sufficient, belief. His obedience in the flesh, as Son of God, above all, in the hour of his passion and death, reveals his glory.

The difference between believers and unbelievers— new birth from above

Let us now return to those unbelieving Jews, revealed by their rejection of Jesus to be from below : to be sons of the devil. Their works also declare their origin—and, alas, their end. Is this the truth about all men other than the Son of man? What are we to say about those who 'loved Jesus and believed that he came forth from the Father' (John 16.27)? And of those 'who believe through their Word' (John 17.20)?

Let us look for a moment at an episode which forms a good starting-point for understanding the fourth Gospel, in the third chapter : the story of Nicodemus who came to Jesus by night.

Nicodemus has come to talk about the things of God, in which he is interested; and he begins : 'We know that thou art a teacher come from God : for no man can do these signs that thou doest, except God be with him.' Jesus answers : 'Except a man be born anew, he cannot see the Kingdom of God.' Nicodemus is being warned that seeing God's kingdom is not a matter of physical sight; to behold our Lord's miracles is not necessarily to behold the Kingdom of God. What is required if a man is to perceive that the Kingdom of God is a change so radical as to be represented by the

339

completely revolutionary idea of being born—how? The word that qualifies this birth has two meanings, 'anew' and 'from above'. Probably we are to keep both meanings in mind.

Nicodemus cannot understand this at all. He can think only of physical birth, and he asks how this can possibly happen twice to the same person. Jesus answers: 'Except a man be born of water and the Spirit, he cannot enter into the Kingdom of God.' What Jesus is speaking of is a birth involving repentance—a complete change of heart, and mind, and life, symbolized by water—and the action of God's Holy Spirit. Then Jesus goes on: 'That which is born of the flesh is flesh: and that which is born of the Spirit is Spirit.' There is no evolution upwards to the Kingdom of God. Man as man cannot elevate himself to the Kingdom of God by any means whatever. Entry into the Kingdom of God is the result of God's action, met, of course, by man's emptying himself by faith in Christ so that God's action may take hold of him (that, very roughly, is what is meant by 'water'). Jesus continues: 'Marvel not that I said unto thee, Ye must be born again, from above. The wind bloweth where it listeth, and thou hearest the voice thereof, but knowest not whence it cometh or whither it goeth: so is every one that is born of the Spirit.' 'The man who is thus born is like a gust of wind. Uncontrolled by our will, or desires, or capacity, we neither set the wind in motion nor guide it to its goal. And yet, how undeniable a thing wind is! We do not doubt either its power or its reality. So it is with the man who has been born of the Spirit. The man of the world, even though he be a Rabbi like Nicodemus, can locate *neither the origin nor the destiny of those* whom God has made his own by a creative act initiated by himself. Beginning and ending belong to God, and men are what they are in *relation to their origin and their destiny.*'[1]

On the one hand, we have the men of this world, whose origin and destiny are known, for they originate within history and are moving surely to death. And their world, their motives, their intentions, their achievements, their total understanding, begin and end within history, within time. On the other hand we have those who are born of the Spirit, whose origin is God, whose destiny is God. The first class can never elevate themselves into the second by their own effort. But God can elevate them—unless they reject him by

[1]Hoskyns, *The Fourth Gospel* (2nd edn, 1947), p. 204.

rejecting Jesus Christ—because his Spirit from above brings to new birth those who being in the flesh are confronted with Christ—and believe on him who gives living water, water which becomes in those to whom it is given a well of water springing up unto eternal life (John 4.10–14). This has already been rehearsed in the Prologue to this Gospel: 'He was in the world, and the world was made by him, and the world knew him not. He came unto his own, and his own received him not. But as many as received him, to them gave he power to become children of God, even to them that believe on his name, which were born, not of blood, nor of the will of the flesh, nor of the will of man, but of God' (John 1.10–13).

God the beginning and the end— what between?

In this Gospel, the Christians are Christ's own, whom he loved unto the end (John 13.1). They are those that the Father has given *him*. His prayer is that they, and all who believe through their word (that is, Christians in all ages) may all be one. He has given them the glory which the Father has given him. He is in them, as the Father is in him, that they may be perfected into one: in order that the world may know that the Father has sent the Son and has loved them even as he has loved the Son. These phrases are taken from the seventeenth chapter of the fourth Gospel—the great Consecration Prayer in which Christ dedicates himself to death and his disciples to their mission. It is not enough that Christians have their origin in God and their end in God. This origin and this end must determine the whole character of their whole lives, in the same way that the glory of Christ's origin and destiny is visible to the believing eye at every point in his life. This is the glory of Christians; that their whole life should bear witness; *can,* by God's grace, *bear witness,* to the fact of God's love for them. And not to that only, but, far more important still, to the fact that contradicts the observable history of Jesus Christ, namely to his glory, to his heavenly destiny, to the love of the Father displayed in his incarnation and submission to physical death. But to speak like this is possible only if we speak of the Father abiding in the Son, and of the Son abiding in his Church. You can define men in the flesh, men

341

of this world, as individuals. The children of God can be defined only in relation to Christ, and, in him, to the Father. But this takes us back to St Paul.

St Paul on Christian personality

When he learned of the sectarianism at Corinth St Paul was horrified—'how each one of you' he says 'saith "I am of Paul; and I of Apollos; and I of Cephas; and I of Christ".' Here you have an egotism smacking of the world. Significance is estimated from below, and is based upon individual opinion, or performance, or talent. In this egotism Christ himself is made a single, separable 'ego' (which is precisely what the Jews had made him, and his disciples in their unbelief, when the latter left him alone in the garden, and the former nailed him to the cross). The personality of Christ is not such as can be ranged over against other authoritative Christian figures in competition. Nor can the personality of Christians be so treated.

1. The key passage for our purposes seems to be this, from the Epistle to the Galatians: 'I have been crucified with Christ; yet I live; and yet no longer I, but Christ liveth in me; and that life which I now live in the flesh, I live in faith, the faith which is in the Son of God, who loved me and gave himself up for me. I do not make void the grace of God' (Gal. 2.20–1).

The 'ego' of St Paul's 'old man' has been crucified, put to death without heroism. But Paul lives; lives through the power of the living God which raised Christ from the dead. Yet now there is no 'ego' of St Paul's; it is Christ that lives in him. And Paul's life here on earth is to be lived entirely in faith in Jesus Christ; in faith in what God is making out of it. St Paul knows by faith that all this has been accomplished by the love of Christ in history, the love that can be measured only by Christ's voluntary death. St Paul's ego must therefore be entirely dethroned to make full room for the effective grace of God, the power of the living God, in his person and his life.

2. Nowhere else is St Paul quite so explicit, but various passages taken together will fill this conception out.

He reminds the Romans that they and he were baptized into

Christ's death. 'We were therefore buried with him into death: that like as Christ was raised from the dead through the glory of the Father so we also might walk in newness of life. For if we have become united with him by the likeness of death, we shall be also by the likeness of his resurrection; knowing this, that our old man was crucified with him, that the body of sin might be done away, that so we should no longer be in bondage to sin' (Rom. 6.4–6).

Paul's readers are therefore to reckon themselves dead unto sin, but alive unto God in Christ Jesus (Rom. 6.11).

3. St Paul tells the Corinthian Christians that: 'if any man is in Christ, he is a new creature: the old things are passed away; behold, they are becoming new' (2 Cor. 5.17).

4. The Galatians, distracted by the Judaizing demand for outward observance, are told: 'Far be it from me (Paul) to glory, save in the cross of our Lord Jesus Christ, through which the world hath been crucified unto me, and I unto the world. For neither is circumcision anything, nor uncircumcision, but a new creature' (Gal. 6.14–15).

5. This new creature, or new man, is Christ. To the Colossians St Paul writes: 'Seeing ye have put off the old man with his doings, and have put on the new man, which is being renewed unto knowledge after the image of him that created him: where there cannot be Greek and Jew, circumcision and uncircumcision, barbarian, Scythian, bondman, freeman: but Christ is all and in all' (Col. 3.9–11).

6. We may compare this fragment to the Romans: 'For whom he foreknew, he also foreordained to be conformed to the image of his son, that he might be the firstborn among many brethren' (Rom. 8.29).

7. This building up of the new creation, the new man, after the image of Christ, is the work of the Spirit. 'We all,' says St Paul, 'with unveiled face, reflecting as a mirror the glory of the Lord, are transformed into the same image, from glory to glory, even as from the Lord the Spirit' (2 Cor. 3.18). We notice that new Christian knowledge, received from God, is a vital factor in their transformation.

8. Do not think that all this is an easy demonstration of God's mercy, as though transformation were a mere matter of removing names from one side of a ledger to the other. It calls for all the

343

creative power of the living God; for crucifixion–resurrection. But because of this, St Paul is quite certain that 'this corruption must put on incorruption; and this mortal put on immortality' (1 Cor. 15.53). That is God's whole purpose revealed and achieved in Christ. To the Corinthians Paul therefore makes with absolute assurance this great statement of the Christian hope : 'We know that if the earthly house of our tabernacle be dissolved' (that is, if our earthly body die) 'we have a building from God, a house not made with hands, eternal, in the heavens. For verily in this (that is, in this present fleshly body) we groan, longing to be clothed upon with an habitation which is from heaven : if so be that being clothed we shall not be found naked (the fear of those who die unrenewed, unregenerated by the Spirit). For indeed we that are in this tabernacle do groan, being burdened; not for that we would be unclothed, but that we would be clothed upon, that what is mortal may be swallowed up of life. Now he that wrought us for this very same thing is God, who gave unto us the earnest of the Spirit' (2 Cor. 5.1–5).

9. St Paul says much more that would be relevant to our subject—indeed, our subject is the theme of all his writings. But let his last word be that splendid definition of the gospel manifested to the saints (that is, to the believers in Christ) 'to whom God was pleased to make known what is the riches of this mystery among the Gentiles, which is *Christ in you, the hope of glory*' (Col. 1.27).

The Christian conception of personality

What shall we say then about the problem of personality? The Jews thought of Jesus as an ordinary, though perhaps extraordinarily gifted, 'ego', of this world, significant in himself, in time and space, here and now, for reasons that made a few of them welcome him, and more repudiate him. Thus they displayed him on the cross—and there we see the whole conception of the human ego, of man achieving perfection in himself, as the highest product of evolution, shown up; entirely thrown into question as a convincing, attractive, successful, entity. And now those to whom he appears risen from the dead, or to whom he is preached risen from the dead, behold in him, or apprehend in him nothing less than the glory of the invisible God; and discover this glory, and the will to reveal this glory through his own perfect obedience to the Father's will, to be the meaning of all that he said and did and was, from Bethlehem to Calvary.

The Christian hope written across personality is, in a word, not I, but Christ in me. The old ego crucified with him, the new man raised up in me newly created after his image, Christ himself possessing my mind, my heart, my limbs, my very being. Christ my Lord and my God.

The hope of the Church

But here there is a significant blurring of the Christian hope. Christ in St Paul is St Paul's hope for himself—if, indeed, except as a member of Christ, except as an apostle sent by him, he thinks of himself at all. Yet, equally, or rather, much more, Christ in all the Christian churches, Christ in the whole Church, Christ in all things, is St Paul's hope for the world. In the Epistle to the Ephesians we are told that Christ's purpose is that 'we may all attain unto the unity of the faith, and of the knowledge of the Son of God, unto a fullgrown man, unto the measure of the stature of the fullness of Christ'. Christ is the hope set over the whole Church as well as over every former individual in it—(those old 'egos' jostling each other must be utterly crucified). Moreover, Christ is the hope written over every human relationship in which God sets men to work out their salvation.

All this is the ground of our hope as Christians, the promise of which the resurrection of Jesus Christ assures us, which we are to apprehend as the object of the Holy Spirit's violent work among us and all around us, which we are to regard (even while we still groan in the flesh waiting for the future revelation of its meaning and results) as already the real truth about us, because it is God's promise, and what the living God has promised he will certainly perform.

Christ, then, is *our origin and our destiny,* the alpha and the omega, the first and the last, the beginning and the ending. But from this it follows, as always when Christ is preached, that we are offered here and now, in between our origin and our destiny, the

345

perpetual choice of God's judgement or God's mercy; and that therefore, as Christians, we must offer our whole lives in history with our whole will, that they may be conformed to Christ's life in history, conformed, therefore, to his sacrificial death.

The difference between a psychological and Christian analysis of personality

Our problem is to define the 'ego' of the man who observes, and experiences, and thinks, and does good actions. If, in the manner of the psychologist, we define such a man's observation, and experiences, and thoughts, and actions, we shall no doubt find origins and motives for them within history; we shall be able to account for such a man's personality by reference to his present and past environments, and no doubt also by reference to what happened to him soon after, and perhaps even before, his birth; perhaps even, to his forebears. No one this side of death, not even the greatest Christian saint, can move outside the legitimate scope of such analysis. Yet the Christian hope is that the man who accepts Christ crucified and risen in faith, who is crucified with Christ and raised up with him, *observes,* not according to the flesh, but according to the spirit, with the eyes of Christ, knowing himself to be confronted at every moment by the last things of God. The Christian hope is that such a man *interprets* what he experiences, not by reference to his present brief past, present, and future, but by reference to Christ, whose history in the flesh alone makes sense of all history. The Christian hope is that such a man thinks, not with the mind of the flesh, concentrated upon himself, but with the mind of Christ, opened up in one direction to the love of the Father, and opened out in the other direction in love for all mankind. The Christian hope is that such a man tries to do actions that are good not as men reckon human actions to be good, redounding to present honour, reward, comfort, and survival, but good because they are directed towards God, done *emptily* for him to make fruitful if he wish, as the unprofitable confession of one who seeks only glory and honour and incorruption, having therefore, as their ultimate motive, nothing short of the eternal life which no man can earn by his actions, and which only God can give.

And finally, although all this we know to be the real Christian hope written, by Christ's crucifixion and resurrection, over this 'me'; although we must be quite sure that nothing of value to God will ever be lost, and that our individual experience and personality here *are* through Christ, part of the material of his heavenly riches; that he has, that is, a destiny for the persons whom he has initiated in leading each of us to accept his Son in faith and regenerating us; yet the eyes of our expectation must be fixed on the fullness of Christ himself, whose risen body is the whole Church, whose final purpose it is to hand all creation to the Father, perfected, that God may be all in all. On the cross we have seen the awful spectacle of human personality isolated in *apparent* dereliction by God, in *apparent* separation from all his fellow men. God forbid that *we* should die in *real* isolation, with no claim upon God's mercy, with no part in the fellowship of those who have been found by God's love. Therefore let our hope for ourselves as individuals always be contained within our hope for all men. And to this end let our eyes seek always the vision of Christ risen and glorified, recalling frequently this most humble description of our destiny : 'Behold what manner of love the Father hath bestowed upon us, that we should be called children of God, and such we are. For this cause the world knoweth us not, because it knew him not. Beloved, now are we children of God, and it is not yet manifest what we shall be. We know that, if he shall be manifested, we shall be like him; for we shall see him even as he is. And every one that hath this hope set on him purifieth himself, even as he is pure' (1 John 3.1–3).

Here we must live entirely by faith. By sight, this side of physical death, we can never see the Kingdom of God. And therefore only by faith can we behold the glory bestowed upon us, and know ourselves as God knows us. But it is this glory that really matters. And although in this life we see all around us terrible evidences, even in Christ's Church, of human sin, and although we know ourselves to be the very chief of sinners, we must have faith that, viewed with the eyes of God, the history of the Christian Church is radiant with the glory of his Son. That is the hope set over human personality. Not—I—I—I—millions of sinful egos—but the one Christ *in us*, the hope of certain glory.

Editorial Epilogue

Bibliography   *Indexes*

Editorial Epilogue

A work so large and so incomplete cannot be 'concluded' by anyone apart from those who conceived it. But pursuing our early analogy of a cathedral two-thirds built, it is possible to sketch a plan and elevation, drawing in the unfinished parts in dotted lines and indicating what materials might have been used for the task at a later period.

What follows is bound to reflect the limitations of my own theological knowledge and point of view. It will be indebted to those who have helped to shape my own beliefs, some of whom I have now doubtless forgotten. How often is a piece of supposedly original thought derived from what was heard or read years ago, which may have sunk below the level of the conscious mind; while so many of one's ideas are breathed in from the theological atmosphere in which one lives, and precise references cannot be supplied.

There are, however, two theologians whose work has interested me greatly in the past decade or more, and who *mutatis mutandis* seem to me to have carried on Hoskyns's work. One is Donald MacKinnon; the other Christopher Evans. If you want to see how Hoskyns's theology might have developed had he lived to Bultmann's age (he was born in the same year), there are glimpses in their writings. Christopher Evans often refers to the one who first fired him, as he did so many more, with zeal for the New Testament, and his Corpus sermon of 1974 on 'The Faith of an Exegete'[1] seems to me to be a republication of Hoskyns's own beliefs. MacKinnon often echoes ideas which are found in Hoskyns—not least in some of the unpublished fragments and *obiter dicta*. He makes much for instance of the movement in Christ's ministry from Galilee to Jerusalem and everything he writes about the fourth Gospel seems an extension of Hoskyns's approach. MacKinnon, however, has shown deep appreciation of the work of Charles Raven, is politically of a different persuasion from Hoskyns and the

---

[1] 'The Faith of an Exegete' is published in *Theology*, LXXVII, June 1974, pp. 287ff. Evans has however advanced beyond 'Biblical Theology'.

Corpus of Spens and Pickthorn, and is primarily a philosophic theologian.

The death of Jesus dominates the New Testament. It occupies a great proportion of the gospel narrative, is presupposed by all the writers as the key event, and is the 'scandal' with which they have to grapple both in their own religious experience and theology, and in commending the Christian message to the world.

It was not a hero's death, even if medieval romanticism tried to make it so. There was no glamour or dignity about it like the last stand of a beleaguered general, or even Charles I at his execution; while Jesus with the terror of death on him in Gethsemane and crying out forsaken on the cross is very different from Socrates drinking the hemlock with philosophic courage and calm. There is a strong tradition that he kept impassively silent for much of his trial, and two of the Gospels record words of serene faith and compassion from the cross itself. But these could well be the insertions of early expositors attempting, in the light of what they believed about Jesus and his acceptance of his destiny, to remove some of the ignominy from what was otherwise all shame and defeat.

There is also the fact that from some points of view the death of Jesus was unnecessary. In spite of the ambiguity of some of his words and deeds, he was not so dangerous as to have merited such a death, had he not forced the issue and persisted in his challenge to the religious system of his people; whereas he might have retreated as disaster loomed; and sought alliance with reforming parties. The Christian who wrestles with the records and tries to reconstruct events, must sometimes ask: 'Was not this death suicide?'

But St Paul and indeed all the leading contributors to the New Testament say that it was 'according to the Scriptures', all compatible with the ways of God to men which are declared in the Old Testament. 'Behoved it not the Christ to suffer these things and to enter into his glory?' (Luke 24.26). This is what we should have expected to happen when love is at issue with sin, or—in case that over-simplifies the matter—when God's own agent proclaims and acts out his Kingdom amid the confusions and compromises of the world, the appalling complications of human behaviour and its motives. The good is rejected, the innocent suffers.

From one aspect, the death of Jesus is the great sign of the futility of everything. 'The whole creation is subject to vanity.' It is not only that human weakness and sin have the last word; the holiest intentions and acts are unavailing, indeed may be exploited and perverted by evil. Nothing endures, or is capable of saving Christ from the cross.

But this is not the whole story. 'Behoved it not the Christ to suffer these things and to enter into his glory?' Not all is disaster. Even in the midst of the horror, there is a certain splendour. A bandit is converted, a centurion moved to testify to the victim's goodness. The words from the cross, fact or not, symbolize the dedication of the Jesus of history to his task of preaching God's rule, seeking the lost, disclosing a divine mercy to those who are cast out by men, and of reversing the values by which the world lives. The death of Jesus was the result of his life, of his refusal to draw back, or compromise, or forsake those to whom he had offered the forgiveness and healing of God. And therefore the New Testament interprets this grisly event as the act of God himself, the revelation of the goodness which made the world and which bears the consequences of his own creation, as well as the complete self-sacrifice of a human life for love of God and men. It is not only the sign of the creation's bondage—all is vanity and evil—but of God's unceasing purposes of love and of his power to rectify what is wrong and vindicate his justice. It changes the balance of spiritual forces in the whole universe. It is at once complete—God's final word—and yet continuing, in that it reveals God's eternal nature, his unceasing activity and the pattern of human behaviour for all time. Henceforth the way to deliverance for mankind is for Christ's sacrifice to be re-presented—even 'mimed'—in the lives of his people and the corporate life of the Church.

But the New Testament writers are able to say this—are made 'eloquent', to use the word of which Hoskyns and Davey were so fond—because the Christ who suffered has entered into the divine glory, and therefore the credal summary of Scripture was able to add to those words at which the authors of *The Riddle of the New Testament* stopped—'*et sepultus est*', the triumphant '*et resurrexit*'.

In this very phrase we pass from brute historical realities to metaphor and symbolism. What does it mean to assert that 'God raised him up'? It is the claim that he who was dead is alive for evermore, and that he, defeated on earth, has been declared cosmic victor. It is a claim which demands the concept of ascension as well as resurrection—'Behoved it not the Christ to suffer these things and to enter into his glory?'. The two concepts 'jostle one another' in many parts of the New Testament.[1] Had Hoskyns and Davey devoted a chapter to the examination of the letter to Hebrews, which they talked about but did not decide on, they would have had to reckon with a treatise which deals entirely with Christ's exaltation, and does not—apart from the final benediction in 13.20— refer to the resurrection as such at all.

But 'resurrection' is the term which most adequately conveys the fullness of the gospel. It presupposes that Jesus really died. He was not simply 'assumed' into heaven like Moses and Elijah in Jewish legend or Mary in Roman Catholic dogma. He passed through 'the grave and gate of death'. And he was not raised out of this life, but with it.

> As reversal and resuscitation it is the recovery intact from death of this particular man, and of what made him the particular man he was. Like Janus, it looks both ways, and in opening into what is new brings with it that which is old and otherwise past. The historical past is not discarded as a snake sloughs off its skin, but is recovered. The showing by the Lord of his hands and side (feet) has been taken as symbolic expression of this truth, and led to the comment of Scott Holland that at the resurrection it was not only Jesus who rose, but his whole life with him.[2]

The early Christians seem to have become convinced of Christ's resurrection because they 'saw' him, though transiently and in a form which made them uncertain and inconsistent about the corporal nature of his risen life. There was also a strong tradition that the tomb in which he had been laid was found empty; and apparently no corpse was ever discovered. But the affirmation 'God raised him up', though it is historical in the sense that it presupposes a before and after, and also that it relates to an experience of Christ's

[1] Evans, C. F., *Resurrection in the New Testament* (SCM Press 1970), p. 136.
[2] Ibid. p. 142.

followers which redirected the course of their lives, takes us into the realm of myth. This does not mean that it is either false or unscientific, since scientists live by myths or 'models', such as light waves, which are entirely analogical.

But since Hoskyns's time, the controversy has sharpened between those theologians who would regard the resurrection as something which took place primarily in the disciples' minds and those who feel that somehow it must be grounded in the physical world. The most celebrated protagonists are Bultmann and Pannenberg. For the former the resurrection is faith in the efficacy of the cross established by the word of preaching, through which Christ is alive and active in the Church. The latter takes the gospel stories with a degree of literalness which gives them consequences not simply in the experience of the Church, but throughout the universe, though no more than any others of a moderately conservative position does he solve the historical problem satisfactorily.

In 1966, the Cambridge theologians G. W. H. Lampe and Donald MacKinnon debated the resurrection. Lampe doubted the reality of the empty tomb, which in any case cannot be decisive. It is as likely to inspire speculations about a corpse revived as belief in a decisive act of God. For Lampe, God has indeed acted in the resurrection of Jesus, acted objectively and finally, though not in discontinuity with his previous revelation as God of Love. Mackinnon requires the empty tomb, because he does not look simply for a spiritual event which transforms the disciples and creates the Church, but for 'a publicly observable state of affairs in the spatial and temporal world, not disclosing, not containing, but still pointing towards (in a way that I agree remains entirely ambivalent) that which is, in my view, necessarily *unique* and creative'.[1]

The debate will continue because there is no final solution in this world. But Hoskyns would have been hostile to any view that seemed to lay primary stress on the subjective and the experiential, ambiguous as these terms are. Had he lived he would have found himself increasingly unsympathetic to Bultmann.

The resurrection was an act of God. It was a decisive intervention of the power of his eternal love and judgement to vindicate Christ's life and death of sacrifice, and not simply something which the

[1] *The Resurrection: A Dialogue between two Cambridge Professors in a Secular Age.* (Mowbrays 1966): p. 112.

disciples felt had happened. Whether this means that the tomb in which Jesus was buried was found empty, we shall never know with the certainty of science.

What is of the utmost importance is that the New Testament was written, not from beneath the cross, or looking into the empty tomb, or gazing after Jesus into heaven, but from a conviction that crucifixion–resurrection is unitive.

One of Hoskyns's earliest published pieces was a contribution to the *Journal of Theological Studies* in April 1920, little more than a year after he was demobilized. It is about 'Genesis 1—3 and St John's Gospel' and it is not incorporated in the later Commentary; but he makes much of the peculiar Johannine reference to the site of the crucifixion. 'In the place where he was crucified there was a garden' (John 19.41). There could be here an allusion to Eden and the story of man's disobedience and expulsion from paradise. And it is in this garden that Jesus rises from the dead and appears to Mary Magdalene. Crucifixion–resurrection are in the same place, juxtaposed, there is one location both for tragedy and its transcendence.

And crucifixion and resurrection are read back into the story of Jesus, which is told by all the evangelists in a manner conditioned by this reality. The acts and sayings of Jesus are reported in terms of it.

This does not mean that the records are any less human. As Hoskyns writes in one of his preparatory notes for this volume, 'Death–resurrection lies at the very heart of the observable world if only we can learn to perceive it'. And what Hoskyns calls the 'eloquence' of the New Testament writers is their ability, under the influence of what happened to Jesus of Nazareth, to discern and articulate the fact that the visible forms and structures of human life bear witness to the invisible truth of God. The difference between them and pagan writers is that because of the crucifixion–resurrection of the Lord, they are able to observe more closely, speak more plainly, and make ever more urgent demands.

This is why miracles and parables are important to the synoptic writers and the signs and 'I am' sayings to the fourth evangelist. They are both concerned with human life; parables with its scenes, characters, activities, its work, its leisure, its natural surroundings; miracles with its accidents, diseases, and mortality. Hoskyns was much exercised by what he called in jargon less hackneyed then than now, the vertical and horizontal references of the parables. They lead directly to an understanding of the Kingdom of God, but also they refer to Jesus himself, the Son of man, and to his mission and destiny. This is why their exegesis demands all the tools and techniques of historical criticism.

Although one of Hoskyns's notes declares that 'Parable is presence—parousia', the parables are a problem. They are incomplete in the treatment of human life and relations, and lack the detailed profundity of Shakespeare's plays, since they are a different art-form. Perhaps they are like a Rembrandt portrait in which the whole may be darkened to show a medallion on a soldier's helmet. But even the Prodigal Son begs some questions, as Donald MacKinnon has pointed out in passages which may be paralleled in the Hoskyns/Davey notebooks: 'As a piece of human life the tale is saturated with ambiguities.' Suppose the prodigal turns out to be a Goneril or a Regan, the elder brother a Cordelia?[1]

Parables are also puzzingly enigmatic. In the very difficult saying which links the parable of the Sower to its explanation in St Mark's Gospel, Jesus seems to suggest that the purpose of parables is not to illumine but to darken further the minds of those who live already in the twilight of the uncommitted:

> Unto you is given to know the mystery of the Kingdom of God: but unto them that are without, all things are done in parables. That seeing they may see and not perceive; and hearing they may hear and not understand; lest haply they should turn again, and it should be forgiven them (Mark 4.11–12).

For Hoskyns this is the heart of the matter—'even if it be a manipulated logion, it is rightly manipulated not wrongly'. He sees the deep, bitter, sorrowful irony in it, carried over from Isaiah 6.9–10. 'The point is, I think, that no understanding is really possible from outside however plausible such religion may seem to be, so plausible that in the prophet's irony, echoed by Jesus, even God himself might well be deceived into pardoning his people, who are not *his* people'.

But parables should be translucent to those within, to the dis-

---

[1] MacKinnon, D. M. *The Problem of Metaphysics.* (Cambridge 1974), p. 137. Cf. *The Resurrection*, p. 79.

ciples of Jesus, not because they are with him in the body, nor because they have some mystical immediacy of esoteric knowledge like the neophytes of the mystery religions, but because they have stood at the place where Christ was crucified and rose again. They are able to read the reality of the creator's rule from nature and from human life refracted from the cross and tomb; in other words, they see what Jesus saw.

The fourth evangelist would seem to suggest this:

> These things have I spoken to you in parables (*paroimia* not *parabole,* but the word means the same): the hour cometh when I shall no more speak to you in parables but I shall tell you plainly of the Father. . . . I came out from the Father and am come into the world: again, I leave the world and go unto the Father.
> His disciples said, Lo, now speakest thou plainly and speakest no parable (John 16.25, 28–9).

Miracles and parables belong together and point to the same truth of crucifixion–resurrection. Hoskyns goes so far as to say, in a letter to Davey dated 25 November, 1933, that the 'whole tumultuous collection of miraculous narratives' in Mark finds its meaning in the Old Testament quotation with which the parable of the Wicked Husbandman ends:

> The stone which the builders rejected
> The same was made the head of the corner:
> This was from the Lord,
> And it is marvellous in our eyes.
> (Mark 12.10–11 from Ps. 118.22–3)

Apart from this, he says, the miracle stories in Mark are nonsense.

But does not this imply that to the one who sees from the perspective of crucifixion–resurrection the age of miracles is over? In the stilling of the storm in Mark 4, the Lord seems to suggest that the miracle was a concession to the disciples' lack of faith. If they had really believed, they would not have disturbed him or themselves by their frightened clamour for deliverance. They would have known that they were as near to heaven by sea as by land because of him who slumbered in the stern of the ship, and would indeed slumber in the depths of the grave. In the fourth Gospel, the signs, from the changing of the water into wine to the raising of Lazarus, all point beyond themselves to the great and decisive sign of crucifixion–resurrection, and, apart from this, though described with the greatest realism, and in no fairy-tale language, they are but solemn play-acting. In his Gifford lectures, Donald MacKinnon writes of the raising of Lazarus that the evangelist asks his readers to find in the narrative 'a manifestation of omnipotence *in concreto.* The manifestation is dramatically decisive in that here the very frontiers of human life are revealed as subdued to the feat of the central figure of the story.' Yet immediately there is a question-mark. 'It is almost as if the writer (who is a supreme ironist), is ironically reminding his readers that very soon they will realize, if they follow the story to the end, that this is not "the real thing". Rather it is an episode that must take place in order that the substance not the shadow of divine omnipotence may be shown'.[1]

The resurrection is the supreme miracle; the sign to end all signs:

> An evil and adulterous generation seeketh after a sign and there shall no sign be given it but the sign of Jonah the prophet: For as Jonah was three days and three nights in the belly of the whale; so shall the Son of man be three days and three nights in the heart of the earth. (Matt. 12.39)

This is not the view of the Acts of the Apostles or of the longer ending of Mark's Gospel. There would be many more signs as the work of the Church went on in the power of the Holy Spirit, and even John talks of 'greater works' to be performed by the disciples because Jesus goes to the Father, though these are not necessarily supernatural wonders and marvels.

Charismatics and 'enthusiasts' will always look for miracles. Others will feel, as Hoskyns seem to have done, that the resurrection is enough. If we are given other glimpses of the 'powers of the age to come', they may well be as enigmatic as the parables and miracles of Jesus, and their truth will be discerned only by those who live by the faith of Jesus Crucified and Risen.

Resurrection is, of course, an eschatological concept. It implies something that has happened, a new relationship to Christ which

---

[1] *The Problem of Metaphysics*, pp. 119–120.

takes its character not from our circumstances but from his in glory, but also something which is yet to be, of which it is, as Paul says, an 'earnest'. Therefore, although 'at the point at Jerusalem where the Lord was crucified, the whole world—please notice the *whole world*—comes back to us',[1] we are not yet in the perfect Kingdom of God. And although there is a new exhilaration and enjoyment about our life on earth, and everything is sacramental of our final salvation, we cannot live as though we were not still mortal with life still unredeemed and ourselves in process of being saved and the old Adam an unconscionable time a-dying and coexisting with the new Christ.

This helps us to understand the ethics of the New Testament. Eating and drinking for instance is not only a human necessity and pleasure, it is an activity of our fellowship in Christ. And wine makes glad the heart of man and is the symbol of the intoxication of the Spirit—the Christian is *Gottbetrunkener*—as well as of the conviviality and joy and abundance of the Kingdom of God. It is the cup of the new covenant, and yet this was not sealed without the shedding of blood and the Lord's draught of the bitter cup of wrath and suffering. Therefore there must be some restraint, not only because drunkenness is loathsome and destructive, but because even while we think of the banquet which celebrates the resurrection we cannot do so without showing forth the Lord's death and having part with him in his sacrifice.

New Testament teaching about marriage is difficult for us because it presupposes a culture in which woman is clearly subordinate: 'Wives be in subjection unto your husbands as unto the Lord' (Eph. 5.22; cf. 1 Peter 3.1ff): though Paul's assertion that in Christ all distinctions are void and that 'there is neither male nor female' (Gal. 3.28) is a charter for woman's equal rights; though perhaps it denies to sexuality the importance that both Genesis and our natural instincts, to say nothing of our culture and its commerce, would give it.

The writer to the Ephesians has a high doctrine of marriage that could derive only from the resurrection, when he declares that it signifies 'the mystical union that is between Christ and his Church' (Eph. 5.25ff). Hoskyns himself once said that it was from marriage

---

[1] *Cambridge Sermons*, p. 93. See above pp. 85ff.

that one could learn about the 'wholly otherness' of God—a pregnant remark, which probably meant both that the sacred union and mystery of marriage may teach us more of God than any other relation or experience of life, and also that if marriage is to be sustained all the resources and the power of the transcendent are needed and it is not a sentimental view of God which suffices to keep us faithful, but the sense of his holiness, his remoteness from our animal passions, 'the infinite qualitative distance' which makes our sensual desires appear so limited, our romantic love so self-indulgent and so mean. Yet Hoskyns would see the lover—and doubtless the lunatic and the poet too—as a parable of the ways of God.

No consideration of marriage in the New Testament is complete without some reference to the saying in Mark 12.25: 'When they shall rise from the dead, they neither marry nor are given in marriage, but are as angels in heaven'; and also to what Paul writes in 1 Corinthians 7.

Paul insists on monogamy and fidelity within the marriage bond, together with a full sexual life. He demands mutual respect, and is more concerned to assert that husband and wife belong to one another than to establish male dominance. But he wishes that all men were like himself, presumably celibate, and seems to regard marriage more as a remedy for incontinence than as an end in itself: 'It is better to marry than to burn'. And then, later, comes the curious and inconsistent injunction that because of contemporary distresses and the shortness of the time, those who are married should be as those who are not. Marriage is a distraction as in the parable of the Great Feast, where one of the invited guests reneged on his acceptance because he had just acquired obligations of wedlock which were regarded as having prior claims above all others. Nine times out of ten he would have been justified, but not as an apology for absence from this supper.

Is this the resurrection life? It should be noted that the supposed distractions of marriage may not be those of sex, but of the worldly commitments which marriage and family involve—the need to make money and have property. But Paul in 1 Corinthians seems less conscious of the values of marriage than the author of Ephesians. Yet I think that we can piece together certain positive principles:

1. The resurrection-life in its heavenly consummation is free from those bodily appetites which are necessary for the propagation of the species, but which may be all-consuming.

2. Yet these appetites are not altogether carnal. They are means for the expression of love and care, as well as the fount of creative inspiration. But they must be controlled, by monogamy and mutual respect within marriage and by a partnership of mind and spirit. Then they may be sacramental and teach us more of the love of God in Christ than any other relationship in life.

3. Control, however, is possible only if a higher loyalty is recognized, if allegiance to Christ is paramount and we learn to love one another in him. Sublimation and sacrifice are necessary conditions of life on earth.

And so, while 'the whole world' is given back to us in the place where Christ was crucified, we subsist here in a state of 'having and not having'. There is—the cliché cannot be avoided—perpetual tension. As Hoskyns put in once to the Corpus congregation: 'You are not to dream through life; you are not to wander about with no roots anywhere; you are not cosmopolitan gentlemen floating about; you are grounded in the earth, men of the world.' The man or woman who receives life from Christ's death may have to be in military service, or professional sport, or entertainment, or politics, or a multi-national company, or research into nuclear weapons. The decision whether or not to participate in the various industries and pleasures of a deluded civilization, which may nevertheless achieve some temporal good and not be wholly instruments of wrath and folly, is one which Christians have always found hard, indeed agonizing, to take, and on which the New Testament is not of direct help, written as it is from a position of weakness in a social order which it was believed had not long to run. Hoskyns went on to say this:

> But Christian hope, based upon belief in God and upon the return of Jesus to the Father, declares that the tension will be resolved, not by death but in life eternal. 'In my Father's house are many mansions; if it were not so I would have told you.' But more important words for us here and now run thus: 'I pray not that thou shouldest take them out of the world, but that thou

shouldest keep them from the evil. . . . Sanctify them through thy truth'.[1]

'Christian hope': that is the virtue which has its root in Christ's tomb, but which springs up and follows him to the Father.

> And now we watch and struggle,
> And now we live in hope.

Hope is not secular optimism based upon the calculations of the economists, or the prognostications of social science, though we are not wrong to share in that if we can, and these may be useful in the short term. Hope is entirely to do with crucifixion–resurrection. It is not the euphoria of enthusiasts, who may claim that they have the Spirit. They are not to be despised. 'Christ's little ones', they may recall us to the simplicity of the gospel and save us from the cynicism to which the good are sometimes prone and from apocalyptic gloom. But hope is always realistic and never wishful. It cannot brace itself with the robust Rabbi ben Ezra and cry 'The best is yet to be'. The words of the dying John Wesley are nearer the truth 'The best of all is, God is with us'. Christ has come, Christ has lived, Christ has died and risen again and nothing can separate us from God's love in him. Such hope is possible only as we abandon ourselves to God and are prepared for our selfishness to be crucified with Christ. Then we shall fear nothing but sin and our life in the world will be like that of the apostles:

> As unknown and yet well known; as dying and behold we live; as chastened and not killed;
> As sorrowful, yet always rejoicing; as poor yet making many rich; as having nothing and yet possessing all things.
>
> (2 Cor. 6.9–10)

Christian theology and ethics may have one of three starting points. They may begin with the incarnation and regard the Christian life as 'an extension' of it. Hoskyns was an Anglo-Catholic and incarnationalism was much in the air in his earlier years. It was his father's theology. Every now and then there are traces of it in his own utterances, in his insistence on the earthiness of the gospel, in

---

[1] *We are the Pharisees*, p. 100.

his partiality at times for a carnal interpretation of the Eucharist. 'We do not worship a disembodied spirit. We worship the Christ. We eat his body and drink his blood (crude though the language may seem, the truth of the gospel is here).'[1] But, as has become notorious through recent reinterpretations and controversies, a full incarnationalism takes us beyond the New Testament and demands the thought-forms of Hellenistic philosophy, even though its origins may be clearly seen in the earliest writings. And it may lead us to the Chalcedonian Christology of 'two-natures', which the young Hoskyns in Egypt was questioning. New Testament Christology is more of 'event' than of 'being'. Before speculations about the eternal nature of Jesus of Nazareth comes the certainty that in this man and his total self-offering God acted to reconcile the world to himself. And before talk of our deification, to which incarnational language leads, change of our 'substance', comes the ethic of our response to what God has done for us in Christ.[2] Incarnational theology cannot, of course, ever be dismissed. It will always engage the minds of Christian philosophers because it represents Christianity's search for a metaphysic.

Christian theology and ethics may instead be charismatic.[3] Pentecost will be seen as the climactic event of the gospel from which all blessings flow. The danger here is that Calvary is almost forgotten, that Christianity becomes a religion of power, not of strength made perfect in weakness, and we fail to reckon with the inescapable cross. In a Church Congress paper of 1926, Hoskyns spoke almost prophetically on this theme:

> *Till He come.* The effectual working of the Spirit of God and of Christ in the Christian Ecclesia remains still, as St Paul says, but *an earnest of the Spirit which is to be.* This is the tragedy of the Christian religion. The hope remains still a hope. Each Eucharist is still an exhortation to take up the cross, to pray that we may be delivered from the power of evil, to believe in God. We still see him only through a glass darkly, and we still know but in part. The work of the Spirit must still be tested by charity and

---

[1] Ibid.

[2] For an attack on 'Deification' see the essay by Ben Drewery in Brooks, Peter, ed., *Christian Spirituality*, Essays in Honour of Gordon Rupp. (SCM Press 1975), pp. 35ff,

[3] See Mühlen, Heribert, *A Charismatic Theology.* Burns and Oates 1978.

by righteousness, not by knowledge nor by the vision of God. The Church remains in the world, though not of it. The work of the Spirit is still incomplete.[1]

There remains crucifixion–resurrection. This is a theme which unites all the writers of the New Testament. It is a concept which faces the realities of human suffering and sin and of a world which, two thousand years after Christ, is still in travail, its problems ever more complex, its perfection still delayed, its earth still soaked in blood. Yet it also looks to salvation through the bearing of pain and the acceptance of death, a salvation which recognizes not only that there is sacrifice at the heart of things, the Lamb slain before the foundation of the world, but that God's creation is good, and shall be restored. Every day the truth of this gospel may be proved in life.

> The trivial round, the common task
> Would furnish all we ought to ask;
> Room to deny ourselves, a road
> To bring us daily nearer God.

Yet it affirms that we are saved not by our own efforts and struggles, our regimes of piety, our disciplines and prayers, but by God-in-Christ, who accepts us as we are, is with us in our frustration and our sin, and will lead us through death to life eternal, to the new heaven and the new earth, where Christ reigns and sin is all destroyed and we share in the inheritance of the saints in light.

At this point we have fallen into very traditional New Testament English, the language of the pulpit rather than the study. And although crucifixion–resurrection is so much concerned with the concrete—to use another of Hoskyns's favourite terms—the life of earth, the elements of nature, human experience, that which we touch and see and feel—the hope it inspires does demand faith in realities other than those with which we deal in our habitual doings. It is possible to spend most of our time without needing to refer in any way to ultimate questions, even though these are posed by much

---

[1] J. B. Lancelot (ed.) *The Spirit in Life and Thought* (Hodder and Stoughton 1927), p. 98.

of what is around us if we had eyes to see. And the fact that now we are so often removed from nature by technology means that faith which uses the things 'that lie about the world'[1] has less to work on. The internal combustion engine, shopping precincts, and computers are from a different order from that of the Sunday sermon, and our spiritual powers could become atrophied by their mastery of our lives, though if they make possible more leisure, there may be more chance for the exercise of the faculties of faith. Be that as it may the realm of the gospel is different from that of most of our interests and attitudes. There is a 'scandal' here, which demands an intellectual and spiritual revolution as well as the risk of faith. Dare we commit ourselves to follow a crucified carpenter and believe that what happened to him gives the clue to the meaning of the worlds, and the hope of unlimited life, here and now, and, beyond death, eternal joy?

It is interesting, and ironic for the student of Hoskyns, the Tory baronet, that Hugo Assmann, something of an extremist, has advocated in *Practical Theology of Liberation*[2] a dialectic of cross and resurrection to overcome the oppressive images of the sorrowful and triumphant Christ which have been an incubus upon the traditional Catholic piety of South America. In that unhappy continent, which has had more than its share of tyranny and holocaust, those Christian thinkers who are anxious to help to free peoples from cruel and corrupt governments, have found a relevant Christian theology in a combination of the Bible and Karl Marx. There is much in this which we must criticize. It over-estimates the scientific nature of Marxism, it finds too simplistic a parallel between the biblical history, particularly the Exodus, and the world today, it does not escape the charge of being Utopian. But it does show that biblical theology and ethics still provide paradigms for action in the last quarter of the twentieth century. And though there is much that we must repudiate, if not condemn, especially in the justification of violence, it may shed further light on crucifixion—resurrection as the central truth of history and renew our faith in the

---

[1] A pregnant phrase of E. M. Forster's at a critical moment of *Where Angels Fear to Tread*.

[2] An English translation is published by the Search Press. I owe this allusion to the Revd Stuart Jordan.

Christ, who is not dolorous victim, nor triumphalist conqueror, but the one who has laid down his life and taken it again as the revelation in effective deed both of God's love for the world and of the way for all to tread.

Bibliography

E. C. HOSKYNS

1920

'Genesis 1–11 and St John's Gospel', *Journal of Theological Studies*, XXI, pp. 210–18.

'Adversaria Exegetica: St John III: 1–21' *Theology*, I, pp. 83–9.

'Adversaria Exegetica: The Old and the New Worship of God: John II: 13–22', *Theology*, pp. 143–8.

1921

'Adversaria Exegetica: The Good Shepherd, John X: 1–18' *Theology*, II, pp. 202–7.

Reviews of Shears, H., *The Gospel according to Paul*; McNeile, A. H., *St Paul*; Nairne, A., *The Faith of the New Testament*; Nairne, A., *The Epistle to the Hebrews, Journal of Theological Studies*, XXII, pp. 184–9.

1922

'Catholicism in Germany', *Theology*, V, pp. 257–62.

Review of *The Beginnings of Christianity*, ed. Foakes-Jackson, F. J., and Lake, K., Part I, *Theology*, IV, pp. 298–304.

1923

'Christ and Catholicism', Anglo-Catholic Congress Books (SS Peter and Paul Press), pp. 1–20.

'Adversaria Exegetica: But after I am risen I will go before you into Galilee' (Mark XIV: 28), *Theology*, VII, pp. 147–55.

1925

Review of Guy, D. S., *Was Holy Communion instituted by Jesus? Journal of Theological Studies*, XXVI, pp. 203f.

1926

'The Christ of the Synoptic Gospels', in *Essays Catholic and Critical*, ed. Edward Gordon Selwyn (SPCK), pp. 151–78.

1927

'The Eternal Spirit' (b) In the Epistles of St Paul and in the Writings of St John', in *The Spirit in Life and Thought*, Papers Read and Addresses Delivered at the Southport Church Congress, October 1926. Liverpool Diocesan Publishing Co. and Hodder and Stoughton.

'The Other-Worldly Kingdom of God in the New Testament', contribution to the Canterbury Anglo-German Conference, *Theology*, XIV, pp. 249–55.

'Some New Testament Teachings about the Holy Spirit: I The Holy Spirit in St Luke's Gospel', *The Sign*, July 1927.

'Some New Testament Teachings about the Holy Spirit: II The Holy Spirit in the Epistle to the Ephesians', *The Sign*, August 1927.

Review of Bultmann, R., *Jesus*, *Journal of Theological Studies*, XXVIII, pp. 106–9.

1928

Review of Haitjema, T. L., *Karl Barth's 'Kritische Theologie'*, *Journal of Theological Studies*, XXIX, pp. 201–4.

Review of Bacon, B. W., *The Story of Jesus and the Beginnings of the Church*, *Theology*, XVII, pp. 173–5.

'Jesus Christ Son of God Saviour' contribution to the Wartburg Anglo-German Conference, *Theology*, XVII, pp. 215–7.

'The Johannine Epistles' in *A New Commentary on Holy Scripture* ed., Gore, C., Goudge, H. L., Guillaume, A. (SPCK), pp. 658–73.

Review of McNeile, A. H., *An Introduction to the Study of the New Testament*, *Church Quarterly Review*, CV, pp. 367–70.

1929

Review of Quick, O. C., *The Christian Sacraments;* Wotherspoon, H. J., *Religious Values in the Sacraments*; Smith, C. R., *The Sacramental Society*; *Journal of Theological Studies*, XXX, pp. 86–9.

Review of Lilley, A. L., *Sacraments: A Study in Some Moments in the attempt to define their meaning for Christian Worship*; Hodgson, L., *And Was Made Man*; Foston, H. M., *The Evening of the Last Supper; Journal of Theological Studies*, XXX, pp. 418–24.

1930

'Jesus the Messiah' in *Mysterium Christi*, ed. Bell, G. K. A. and Deissman, Adolf (Longmans), pp. 69–89.

'The Apostolicity of the Church', Anglo-Catholic Congress Report, pp. 85–90.

Reviews of Anderson Scott, C. A., *New Testament Ethics—An Introduction; The Call for Christian Unity:—The Challenge of a World Situation;* a volume of essays contributed at the request of the Anglican Evangelical Group Movement; Pribilla, M., sj., *Um Kirchliche Einheit—Stockholm, Lausanne, Rome; Journal of Theological Studies*, XXXI, pp. 411–15.

1931

The Riddle of the New Testament, with Francis Noel Davey. Faber and Faber.

Reviews of *Commentaries on St Luke's Gospel* by Balmforth, H., Manson, W., and Creed, J. M., *Theology*, XXII, pp. 349–54.

'The Incarnate Christ', *The Sign*, August 1931.

1932

Review of Hoyle, R. B., *The Teaching of Karl Barth, Journal of Theological Studies*, XXXIII, pp. 204–6.

1933

The Epistle to the Romans, Karl Barth, tr. Hoskyns, E. C., Oxford University Press.

'A Theological Lexicon to the New Testament', Review article on *Theologisches Wörterbuch zum Neuen Testament*, ed. Kittel, G. *Theology*, XXVI, pp. 82–7.

1936

'The Rediscovery of Abraham', Review of Sir Leonard Woolley, Litt.D., *Abraham—Recent Discoveries and Hebrew Origins*, Faber and Faber, *The London Mercury*, April, pp. 636ff.

1938

Cambridge Sermons, with an appreciation by Charles Smyth. SPCK.

1940

The Fourth Gospel, ed. Davey, F. N., Faber and Faber.

1960

We are the Pharisees, a Course of Sermons originally entitled 'Contemporary Judaism', to which is added a Course on Studying the Bible. SPCK.

F. N. DAVEY

1931

Review of *The Historic Jesus* by James MacKinnon, D.D., *Theology,* XXII, June 1931, no. 132, pp. 347–9.

Review of *The Meaning of the Revelation* by Philip Carrington, *Theology,* XXIII, December 1931, no. 138, pp. 344–6.

The Riddle of the New Testament, with Hoskyns, E. C., Faber and Faber.

Biblical Criticism. Catholic Literature Association.

1933

Review of *The Gospel in the Early Church* by James Mackinnon, D.D., *Theology,* XXVII, September 1933, no. 159, pp. 171–4.

1938

'The Early Church and Messianic Teaching' in *An Outline of Church History from the Acts of the Apostles to the Reformation* edited by Caroline Duncan-Jones (Allen and Unwin), pp. 34–45.

1939

'Biblical Theology', *Theology,* XXXVIII, March 1939, no. 225, pp. 166–76.

1940

The Fourth Gospel by Hoskyns, E. C., ed. Davey F. N., Faber and Faber.

1941

Review of *The Messianic Consciousness of Jesus* by Hatch, H. G., *Journal of Theological Studies*, Vol. 42, 1941, p. 81.

1945

'The Hope of Christendom Authentic' in *Prospect for Christendom*, ed. Maurice B. Reckitt. Faber and Faber 1945.

1946

'How to Make Nonsense of the Bible', *Church Teaching Review*, January 1946, p. 3; May 1946, p. 3; October 1946, p. 16.

1947

The Good Shepherd and His Flock. National Society and SPCK.
'Drama—The Theatre and Propaganda', *Church Teaching Review*, June 1947, pp. 4–5.

1951

The Word of Testimony (Gore Lecture). SPCK.

1952

Review of *A Study in St Mark* by Farrer, A., *Journal of Theological Studies*, III, October 1952, pp. 239–42.

1953

Review of *The Interpretation of the Fourth Gospel* by Dodd, C. H., *Journal of Theological Studies*, IV, October 1953, pp. 234–46.

1957

'Sin, Righteousness and Judgement' in *Good Friday at St Margaret's*, ed. Charles Smyth. Mowbrays.

Review of *St John's Gospel* by Lightfoot, R. H., *Journal of Theological Studies*, VIII, October 1957, pp. 308–10.

1960

Preface to *We are the Pharisees*, Hoskyns, E. C., SPCK.

1961

'The Gospel according to St John and the Christian Mission' in *The*

Bibliography

Theology of the Christian Mission, ed. with an Introduction by Gerald H. Anderson (McGraw-Hill), pp. 85–95.

Review of *Sakramentssymbolik im Johannesevangelium* by Paul Niewalda, *Journal of Theological Studies,* XII, April 1961, p. 78.

Review of *Agapé dans le Nouveau Testament* by Spicq, C., ibid., pp. 79–80.

1964

'Healing in the New Testament', Theological Collections 3. SPCK.

1967

'The Three Hours Devotion' in *A Manual for Holy Week,* ed. Jones, C. P. M. (SPCK), pp. 122–43.

1969

'William Kemp Lowther Clarke, D.D.', *Theology,* LXXII, February 1969, no. 584, pp. 55–65.

1973

Rural Ministry: A Study. Diocese of St Edmundsbury & Ipswich.

Index of Biblical References

Genesis
1.—3.— 356
1.27 243
2.24 243, 253
5.2 243

Exodus
3.14 165n
4.22–3 234
24.15 242

Leviticus
19.18 104, 188

Deuteronomy
6.5 104, 188
8.3 267
13.1–5 140n
13.1–3 146
14.29 213
17.14–20 264
18.15–22 140n
24.5 246
28.36–7 219
31.16 242

1 Samuel
1.8 241

1 Kings
11.31 264
12.24 264
17.18–19 181

2 Kings
4.33 181

Job
29.12–16 213
31.16–22 213
42.3–6 219

Psalms
22.— 301
22.1 220
32.1–2 184
32.7 218
41.9 270
42.1–2 268

Psalms (cont'd)
68.18 190
69.— 137n
69.9 137n
73.27 242
78.24 168
82.4 213
89.— 301
91.13 181
91.14–15 181
94.— 301
103.15 171
110.1 180
113.3–4 171
118.22–3 358

Proverbs
3.34 251
31.10–31 241

Isaiah
6.9–10 357
7.3 226
8.3 226
8.18 226
10.5–7 264
14.12 146
14.13–15 180
26.20 181
34.4 146
37.21–38 264
42.1 157
44.6 16
44.28 264
45.1 264
46.10 16
50.1–3 242
52.13–15 302
52.13 142
54.1–8 242
54.5 242
55.1–5 213
55.2–3 272
55.3 218
55.5 218

Isaiah (cont'd)
59.19 171
64.4 274n

Jeremiah
1.9–10 299
3.1–5 242
3.14–15 242
18.7 299
31.28 299
31.30–4 243
35.6–7 233
35.18–19 233
45.4 299

Ezekiel
16.30–4 242
16.60–3 242

Daniel
7.13–14 146
12.1–4 302

Hosea
1.2 242
3.1 242
11.1 234
14.1–8 242

Malachi
1.11 171
3.2–4 137
4.6 91, 235

Ecclesiasticus
48.10 91, 235

2 Maccabees
9.— 264

Matthew
3.9 231
3.14 290
3.16 289
4.23 102
4.24 214
5.2–9 103
5.3 ff 215

375

379

Index of Subjects